Robert Kershaw who until recently held a senior position within NATO, joined the Parachute Regiment in 1973 and has served actively in Northern Ireland, Bosnia and the first Gulf War, for which he was awarded the US Bronze Star. He has written seven book of military history, featured in numerous TV documentaries and has contributed to the *Daily Mail*, the *Daily Telegraph*, the *Sunday Telegraph*, the *Sunday Times* and *The Times*.

Also by Robert Kershaw:

Never Surrender
Tank Men
It Never Snows in September
D-Day: Piercing the Atlantic Wall
War Without Garlands
Red Sabbath

Robert Kershaw

SKY MEN

THE REAL STORY OF THE PARAS

HODDER

First published in Great Britain in 2010 by Hodder & Stoughton
An Hachette UK company

First published in paperback in 2011

1

Copyright © Robert Kershaw 2010

A CIP catalogue record for this title is available from the British Library.

ISBN 978 0 340 96252 7

Typeset in Bembo by Hewer Text UK Ltd, Edinburgh

Printed and bound in the UK by CPI Mackays, Chatham ME5 8TD

Hodder & Stoughton policy is to use papers that are natural, renewable
and recyclable products and made from wood grown in sustainable
forests. The logging and manufacturing processes are expected to
conform to the environmental regulations of the country of origin.

Hodder & Stoughton Ltd
338 Euston Road
London NW1 3BH

www.hodder.co.uk

This book is dedicated to those members of British Airborne Forces, friends and comrades, who have been killed, wounded or injured in war and training since their inception in June 1940.

CONTENTS

PROLOGUE

SKY MEN

I was fresh from university, Sandhurst, selection and the parachute course. My red beret was still a trophy as I stood waiting for my transport in the foyer at Belfast airport in the late spring of 1973. A 'Pig' armoured vehicle pulled up and an enormously thickset Parachute Regiment colour sergeant dismounted and motioned me across. His flak-jacket appeared to double his massive physique and at his hip hung a .45 pistol, not service issue, more like war contraband. The colour sergeant and escort looked me up and down with unabashed curiosity; the new sprog commanding officer had arrived for his first tour in Northern Ireland. 'Hello, sir,' he said in a barely intelligible Glaswegian accent. 'Ye'd better get yirsel' inside – ah heer ye're pretty deadly wiv a pen!'

The issue watch I was offered was still smeared with gristle and bloodstains from the sergeant major who had been blown up the week before I arrived. I declined, pointing out that it did not work, frozen in time at the instant he had died.

Before the afternoon was over I had been caught, shielded by a vehicle, in the blast of a massive car bomb. I quickly discovered the loneliness of command when asking one of my corporals the best way to set up a bomb cordon. 'You're the boss,' he responded, '*you* tell *me*.' Yet when I directed my soldiers to their tasks I found they appeared to be executing the commands before I had even got the words out of my mouth. The colour sergeant took me under his wing and proceeded to patiently teach me all the things they never taught you at Sandhurst, and has remained forever in my memory.

Acceptance by my men was automatic. It was understood as a result of passing Pre-Parachute Selection Company – P Company

1

– and jumping on the parachute course that, as an officer, I had to be better, fitter, wiser and the equal of them all. In any other department. And they were Sky Men, the finest soldiers in the world.

Nobody liked parachuting but everybody had to do it. Nearly all of it was from low-level, mass parachute descents and mostly by night. Soldiers controlled their air-sickness vomiting just before the jump, wiped their faces clean, attached huge parachute packs to their harnesses, hooked up and jumped out. The experience created an intangible bond, an airborne spirit that transcended all ranks.

Shortly after my first operational tour in Northern Ireland I was sent to Germany alone to conduct an exchange German parachute course with the Bundeswehr. Despite the language difference, communication was never a problem: being a paratrooper translated to immediate acceptance. This ease of contact overcame many difficulties when working as a staff officer later in my career and on active service with foreign armies in the first Gulf War and Bosnia. Foreign airborne officers would readily approach, offer help, and wish to share experiences and then, without further ado, invite a total stranger into their homes.

I had a complete 'Roman candle' parachute failure, sometimes called a 'bundle of washing', jumping with the German Fallschirmjäger, and was saved in the nick of time by operating my reserve parachute. My host's response was to offer to mount the emergency handle I had pulled on a commemorative plinth. I declined but sentimentally kept the handle. In the course of my career I was to meet parachutists from all nations, from Europe and America to the Middle East and Africa. Everywhere I served the airborne brotherhood was a uniting bond.

SIERRA LEONE, 10 SEPTEMBER 2000

Condemned men tend to sleep fitfully. This was the case for Major Alan Marshall and five other hostages from the Royal Irish Regiment, enduring their seventeenth day of captivity in a stand-off hostage crisis in Sierra Leone. Curled up on the earthen floor of a dilapidated concrete building, Marshall ached from beatings. There had been mock-executions. The paranoid character of his so-called West Side

Boys captors suggested the next play-acting might well be their last. Above the nocturnal jungle insect sounds he could just detect the thump, thump, thump of distant helicopter blades. If there was ever to be a rescue it would be now, at dawn. The hostages were being held together in a single room in the same building. Instinctively Marshall knew the moment they both savoured and dreaded had arrived and scrambled about on his hands and knees urgently waking the others.

The Occra Hills where they were being held appeared a tropical paradise. They were surrounded by lush green thickets, palm trees and deciduous trees near a deserted palm oil plantation in the small hamlet of Gberi Bana on the banks of the Rokel Creek. This flowed westward, swollen by the wet season, joining the muddy Sierra Leone River before Freetown. It was humid but still relatively cool in the pre-light of dawn. Marshall suspected their survival prospects were slim. There were about 150 West Side Boys militia in their encampment and another 100 in the small settlement of Magbenny, further west on the other side of the 250 yard wide fast-running river. He had noticed the four-ton Bedford lorry with its twin 14.5mm heavy Russian AA guns mounted on the back and 'technicals', four-wheel drive pick-up trucks with heavy machine guns. Marshall ruefully recalled they had given up a .50 Browning mounted on one of their two captured Land Rovers.

The camps were mutually supporting and boxed in on three sides by thick jungle, too dense for a ground advance in large numbers. Submerged sand-banks precluded a river approach, so their rescuers would have to arrive by air. They would have to penetrate scores of fighters before they could even attempt a rescue. Only a swift blow directed concurrently against both camps could hope to succeed. This was asking a lot. Special Forces would be required for a mission of this type and Marshall appreciated the numbers needed to match these odds were unlikely to be in theatre or even arrive without his captors finding out. Nevertheless, the approaching throb gave some indication of hope. He did not know that Special Air Service (SAS) four-man observation teams were already creeping into position 50 metres from his building.

Four months before, rebel forces had nearly captured Freetown and UN forces were in disarray. The unexpected arrival of British

3

paratroopers had restored the situation but only 250 trainers and 70 advisors remained behind. Militias like the West Side Boys were encroaching on a potential power vacuum which their easy seizure of British soldiers appeared to demonstrate. The 24-year-old self-styled 'Brigadier' Foday Kallay had taken 11 British soldiers and deigned to release only five. He miscalculated that hostage dramas, with their insinuation of political and military failure, were one of the few crises that guarantee responses from traditionally docile liberal western democracies. Kallay's actions could not be ignored.

One hostage was separated from the rest and this was Marshall's Sierra Leone Army guide, Corporal Musa Bangura. Having served with some of the West Side Boys before the last army mutiny, he alone appreciated how vulnerable Marshall's patrol had become when they turned off the main road to enter the Occra Hills. 'As we drove further and further the tension started building up in me and I said, this area is infested with the West Side Boys,' he recalled. 'They will not take it lightly if they happen to see us.' They did not and Bangura had been severely beaten, humiliated and tortured for 17 days. Recognition brought singularly vicious treatment. He spent the best part of his day in a five-metre square stinking cess-pit enclosed by a lattice trap-door. As he lay injured within his tormentors took extraordinary delight in ceremoniously urinating over him and flinging the contents of night-time chamber pots inside.

Bangura lived with his demons amid the stench, anticipating limb amputation and death as simply a matter of time. 'They thought if they carry out amputation, civilians will support them,' he later explained. 'They will fear them, and if they fear them, then they definitely have to support them.' Bangura was currently outside the pit, bound alongside Kallay's hut, near the British hostages, on probably his last night. He too heard the throb of approaching helicopters. Hope was tinged with fear as he pondered his survival prospects.

The West Side Boys were formed from a bunch of mutinous soldiers in 1997 and joined by criminals, women and pressed boy soldiers. Sporting garishly coloured clothes, they were well armed with British SLRs, AK-47s, mortars and heavy machine guns. They were dangerous and unpredictable, emotionally fuelled by heroin, cocaine and alcohol. Bizarre titles and exotic names like 'Savage', 'Bomb-blast' and 'Turkish' carried considerable weight in the surreal conditions that reigned within failed African states, where murder, rape, torture and mutilation were common. 'When I had drunk alcohol I got extra courage to do anything the commanders told me to do,' admitted 23-year-old Turkish, a West Side Boy. 'Some of the men smoked heroin, but me, I just smoked marijuana, because it was wartime.' Brigadier Kallay had recently executed 27 disenchanted followers. The ease with which the British had been kidnapped and the control he had exercised over subsequent meetings led Kallay to regard the British with the same contempt previously reserved for ineffective UN soldiers.

Normal routine was to party the afternoon away on drink and drugs to the accompaniment of loud gangster rap. Some wore articles of female clothing, including wigs. Cross-dressing was designed to intimidate their foes because an aggressive man wearing a summer frock or pastel-coloured housecoat over military fatigues is a grotesque sight. Regional superstition held that soldiers can 'confuse the enemy's bullets' by assuming two simultaneous identities. Musa Bangura knew he had not long to live and was scared. The roar of helicopters soared above the nocturnal jungle activity and set birds to flight. 'The sound of the helicopter motors kept coming,' Bangura recalled, 'kept coming.'

The two Lynx AH-7 helicopters and three CH-47 Chinooks combined at the mouth of Rokel Creek and powered along the fast-flowing river line to the east. Inside two of the Chinooks was the equivalent of a squadron of SAS troopers divided into six-man fire teams and a hostage rescue group. The third Chinook carried two platoons from A Company, the Parachute Regiment. The force numbered about 120 men in all with likely a further 60 for a second wave. One SAS participant likened the approaching two-pronged air assault to that of a special forces 'stiletto' and a paratrooper 'sledgehammer'. The first was to administer the precise insertion required to rescue the hostages at Geberry Bana, while the second would defeat the opposition's heavy fire power with an air-mobile assault at Magbenny. It was an unequal conflict with initial odds of just under three to one against the rescuers. The force multiplier for the British would be Lynx helicopter fire suppression and the speed, aggression and shock of the attack.

Captain Danny Matthews, a parachute officer with the third Chinook, was not complacent. 'We were dealing with intelligence updates which were quite an eye-bleed in terms of the numbers we were dealing with, potentially, and the types of kit and equipment they had,' he recalled. 'You knew it was the real thing from the off and were very worried,' confirmed Private Julian Sheard in the same helicopter. 'You are worried for your own safety of course, but you are more worried about letting the team down.' The average age of the paratroopers was about 19 to 20, not dissimilar to that of the boy soldiers high on drugs they were about to attack.

Sitting opposite each other in the subdued red light within the low-flying Chinooks, the paratroopers reflected on the coming action. 'I did not expect something like this quite so early on,' recalled 19-year-old Julian Sheard, who had barely arrived in the battalion as a newly trained recruit. 'I had not really settled in, I hadn't even got my kit for the jumps course fully sorted out.' There was no special selection for this mission. A Company was simply chosen for the task. They were elite soldiers and regarded themselves as such and it did not matter how recently they had arrived. 'If you're good enough to join the battalion you're good enough to go on ops,' declared one paratrooper veteran. Sheard, like a number of the others was not aware he was going on an operation until their mobile phones were taken away at their South Cernay departure point ten days before. Major Matthew Lowe, the Company Commander, had lined them up and announced they were not going on exercise but on an operational deployment.

They had taken off at 0615 in the dark. 'You are excited, the adrenalin kicks in, you are going to battle,' remembered Captain Danny Matthews. Common to all soldiers at this stage is the thought that if I am to be killed, make it quick, but please let me not be crippled or let my mates down. Captain Liam Cradden, another paratrooper, admitted, 'I can safely say that I have never been as frightened.' This was a risky operation with an uncertain outcome. Cradden 'was very frightened the night before, during deployment, and again when you see the casualties and injuries'. The twin 14.5mm guns at Magbenny represented a serious threat. 'You feel quite vulnerable as an infantry soldier, you want to get off the helicopter onto the ground,' remembered Matthews. 'You don't want the helicopter to be taken out.'

The helicopters flew the line of Rokel Creek at treetop level to deaden the sound of their approach. At 0635 the paratrooper Chinook swerved off to the right to swoop down just to the south-east of Magbenny village. The two lead Chinooks swept into Gberi Bana. One hovered over a clearing next to the hostage house while the other came down over the football pitch 200 metres further north. The first bursts of machine gun fire and rocket blasts from the Lynx shattered the pre-dawn jungle stillness.

Gberi Bana was a dispersed hamlet of 27 ramshackle buildings most of which were 50 to 100 metres from the river bank. The essence of the stiletto SAS assault was speed, precision and violence. Drug and alcohol-befuddled fighters had one minute to distinguish the helicopter beat was real and a further minute to get moving before the machines were upon them. The first shocking realisation for many was when helicopter down-draughts snatched the rusty corrugated roofing from shacks and sent it clattering and tumbling on top of the dazed occupants. Musa Bangura was immediately buried under the debris of the collapsed roof from Kallay's bungalow.

Mayhem reigned as fighters came running up clutching RPGs. Lynx helicopters were rocketing and strafing identified heavy weapon locations. 'Corporal Blood' later admitted, 'We never experienced anything like this.' They saw shadowy shapes dropping beneath the helicopters. Mohamed Kamara, another West Side Boy, thought they were bombs until he realised they were fast-roping soldiers. Ropes dangling down had as many as three men on each, slipping down with only leather gloves to arrest their fall. When they landed they immediately began to shoot down the fighters milling around. Turkish 'felt bad', precisely the aim sought by the attackers, and was convinced 'I would die during this operation'. Saving their own lives was more important than finishing off the hostages and many bolted for the security of the surrounding jungle.

'We saw the soldiers coming down to the ground,' Corporal Blood described. 'I fired my RPG two times, but both times the helicopter balanced and I missed.' A combination of flustered reactions by the opposition and expert jinxing by the pilot avoided catastrophe.

Self-styled Brigadier Kallay knew the game was up: 'I was scared because I knew the British must have come with heavy weapons and back-up to destroy me.' He ordered the hostages to be killed and then hid under his bed.

Within two minutes the stiletto attack had been slid into the vitals of Kallay's encampment. Six-man SAS fire teams fanned out to deliver the mortal twist as the hostage rescue team sprinted to the hut. Stop-watch rehearsals had identified the crucial importance of charting the precise time lapses of each action required to achieve the objective. The West Side Boys had about 60 seconds to react and the SAS had calculated a 20-second sprint to reach the target. Ahead of them the executioners ran to complete their mission.

The hostage house had been precisely identified and even now was covered by the four-man close observation teams, who had yet to break cover. They had infiltrated the jungle surround five days before. Each fighter who appeared anywhere near the house was put down with a double-tap of gunfire, one round to the head and chest. The six-man fire teams rapidly cleared their allotted zones, engaging the enemy firing from houses by shooting through the walls with armour-piercing rounds. They quickly consolidated, settling down to a pre-planned synchronisation of interlocking arcs of fire to await developments as the West Side Boys began to reorganise in the jungle.

The Lynx helicopters meanwhile were pounding the suspected heavy weapons locations at Magbenny, a line of 29 dilapidated buildings resembling an abandoned training village on the opposite bank of the Rokel Creek. 'The helicopters were almost on the water,' observed an amazed Mohammed Kamara. 'They fired again and again until there was no more shooting.' In all airborne operations, there is a fine dividing line between success and failure. Always expect the unexpected is the airborne soldier's maxim. When the Chinook hovered over its identified site to the south-east of the village the first paratroopers stepping off the rear ramp disappeared up to their shoulders in swamp water. 'It was almost chaos when we first got off, people were under water and it wasn't what was expected on the ground,' remembered a perplexed Captain Danny Matthews. 'I was amazed at the time that no one drowned.' The paratroopers had to wade some 450 yards up to their necks and shoulders in water to reach the village even as enemy fire was cracking and whining all around. 'It looked like grass,' recalled Julian Sheard. 'You jumped out, expecting ground to be there and then we were in very deep water. We had to slog through the water as fast as we could in order to get into the battle.'

Matthew Lowe, the company commander, was required to coordinate a two-wave insertion, relying on another Chinook to reinforce his first landing. Each of the houses had been denoted by a letter from the phonetic alphabet and he intended to roll up its linear configuration from west to east. His oversight was a key factor to ensure success but Lowe was among the first to go down, demonstrating how few plans survive the crossing of the start line.

'There was a massive explosion, then you obviously hear the cries and screams,' Matthews recalled. 'I saw the OC go down and he called my name.' Lowe was severely injured by shrapnel in his lower leg and ordered Matthews to take command, find the lead platoon commander and get him to push on. 'Two paces later I discovered that he was lying to the right of the OC and was also injured.' Coping with the unexpected formed an integral part of their training. Matthews reached the lead platoon sergeant, who asked, 'Where's my boss?' 'I told him he was the boss. He said: 'Where's the OC?' and I said, 'I'm the OC, let's push on.'

The young Sheard lost his section corporal and another man from his six-man group soon after landing but 'had to leave the casualties there'. They had to push on. 'We had to get our job done.' Matthews explained, 'I had to ensure we were not going to lose momentum', but the corporal section commanders were already fighting the advance forward. 'That was where the young NCOs were fantastic and that is where they really started gripping people,' recalled a company soldier. 'As we eventually broke into the village, there was a massive amount of fire,' declared Matthews, 'a lot of it very inaccurate, to be honest.' This enabled Matthews to begin directing the swing of the sledgehammer.

The West Side Boys fought back fiercely on both sides of the river, much of it psychologically fuelled by voodoo. 'I know men who went through a ceremony for protection,' explained Turkish. 'Even I had that ceremony, they washed me with native medicine.'

They were convinced the ritual would enable bullets to run off like rainwater. 'From then on, bullets will never touch me,' Turkish believed. Moreover, as Jason Burke, a veteran *Observer* newspaper reporter, asserted: 'These kids have grown up fighting and killing and committing atrocities. They also don't understand the rules. No one has ever told them that war is not like a *Rambo* video, about how soldiers should behave, when to be scared, so they just stand there and blast away.'

Surrender was not an easy concept for militias in Sierra Leone. Prisoners were inevitably killed but not before humiliation and torture was applied. The West Side Boys counter-attacked.

'We took a lot of the front elements by surprise,' recalled Mathews, clearing Magbenny village. 'They were bewildered by the sheer speed, the aggression and the numbers that overwhelmed them so early on and so quickly.' The militias were unused to an equally merciless but highly mobile and proficient foe. Smoke lingered among the trees and undergrowth as the methodical clearance continued. 'When I heard the screams of the injured people and the explosion, the screams went right through you,' recalled Julian Sheard, 'but you just had to ignore it and get on with it.' Progress was marked by smoke, cries, the dull thud of grenades and then a crescendo of automatic fire as each resistance point was overcome, leaving bullet-scarred cornices and walls. It was difficult to see inside the dark mildew-stained windowless houses. 'This is the first fire fight I have been in where rounds were coming my way,' recalled Corporal Dawes. 'It was scary.'

Within 30 minutes of the attacks a Chinook had taken off from Geberry Bana with the traumatised hostages, including the badly beaten Musa Bangura, found beneath Kallay's roof. Kallay was discovered still cowering under his bed. The sledgehammer in Magbenny needed another three hours of swinging before it was all over. Groups of West Side Boy prisoners were laid face down in lines, amid piles of captured weapons, their hands plasti-cuffed behind their backs. 'Many corpses and wounded people were lying on the ground moaning,' remembered one West Side Boy. 'One commander was standing and his friend was trying to remove a fragment from his shoulder.' By 1100 the helicopters had disappeared and the deserted compounds resumed their sauna-like humidity.

Ten per cent of the Sky Men were wounded and one killed and 27 West Side Boys counted dead. Some two dozen corpses were seen floating down the Rokel Creek days after the attack. They had been stunned by the violence and speed of the assault and some 300 emerged from the jungle in succeeding days to surrender to the UN. Stories about the fighting prowess of the British, who took no nonsense and shot back, began to circulate among the militias. One West Side NCO who changed sides and reported for training with the Sierra Leone Army was asked by his British trainer, 'How did you find the SAS?' Perplexed, he replied, 'The SAS found us.'

Operation Barras was the first air-mobile assault conducted by the British Army in the new millennium. It demonstrated two capabilities that were identified for Sky Men from their very inception in the early 1930s: lethal precision and the sledgehammer blow.

There is a plethora of coffee-table books on the airborne, filled with stories of derring-do, but little about the men themselves. Very few histories have attempted to distil this human perspective from an international viewpoint and tell the story of the soldiers who go to war on the ground but arrive from the air. Trying to encapsulate who these men are is the purpose of this book.

1

THE LOCUST WARRIORS

FROM GUARDIAN ANGEL TO INSTRUMENT OF WAR

Part of the human psychological condition is a fear of falling. People jerk awake plunging through space in falling dreams just before hitting the ground. Early primates living in trees perished if they fell from their protective branch cradles among predators below. Sudden drops in altitude on modern airliners induce a stomach-churning chill. Man has longed to soar free as a bird, fascinated by the mystery of flight, closer to the gods he worshipped, but fearful of a fall. Icarus in the Greek myth abandoned caution and, despite warnings from Daedelus his father, flew too near the sun. Wax holding his wings together melted and he plunged into the sea below.

In 1483 Leonardo da Vinci sketched a human figure hanging on by his arms beneath a cone-shaped construction. Alongside the drawing a note read: 'If a man is provided with a length of gummed linen cloth with a length of 12 yards on each side and 12 yards high, he can jump from any great height whatsoever, without injury.' There appeared little attraction in doing this apart from the thrill of controlled fall because man did not fly. The contraption of wooden poles, ropes and canvas needed for such a device with fifteenth-century materials would have weighed 187lbs, hardly portable by a single man.

Five hundred years later on 17 July 2000 a 38-year-old skydiver from London tested Leonardo's aerodynamic design by jumping it from a hot air balloon at 7,000 feet. 'All the experts agreed it wouldn't work,' claimed Adrian Nicholas. 'It would tip over or fall apart or spin around and make you sick – but Leonardo was right all along.' Overflown by helicopters and accompanied by two traditional parachutists, Adrian Nicholas was hoisted 10,000 feet over Mpumalanga, South Africa, on a beautifully clear winter's day. The balloon dipped briefly to fill the parachute with air before the contraption floated free. The 70 square foot prototype made such a smooth and slow descent that the two accompanying parachutists had to brake to stay level. None of the dips or oscillation associated with modern parachutes were apparent. The photographer Heathcliff O'Malley covered the drop from a helicopter: 'It was amazing, really beautiful. But none of us knew if it would fold up and Adrian would plummet to earth . . . It works, and everyone thought it wouldn't.'

'The whole experience was incredibly moving, like one of those great English *Boy's Own* adventures,' explained Adrian Nicholas. He experienced the same emotions that characterise early parachute pioneer accounts. 'I had a feeling of gentle elation and celebration,' he recalled. This was the supreme thrill, floating like a balloon. 'I was able to stare out at the river below, with the wind rattling through my ears. As I landed, I thanked Leonardo for a wonderful ride.'

He cut away from the contraption and deployed his own free-fall parachute for the landing. The da Vinci 'chute floated down and sustained only minor damage on impact. 'It took one of the greatest minds who ever lived to design it,' commented Nicholas after the event, 'but it took 500 years to find a man with a brain small enough to actually go and fly it.'

Despite technical refinements, the unexpected can still occur with modern parachutes. Icarus paid a penalty for flying too near the sun; Adrian Nicholas was tragically killed in a skydiving accident five years later.

Leonardo da Vinci's concept could never be trialled before the maiden flight of the first hot air balloon, which occurred over Paris on 21 November 1783. American scholar-scientist Benjamin Franklin, who witnessed the event, visualised some military potential. 'Five thousand balloons, capable of raising two men each, could not cost more than five ships of the line,' he calculated, declaring two months later: 'Where is the Prince who can so afford to cover his country with troops for its defence, as that 10,000 men descending from the clouds might not in many places do an infinite deal of mischief before a force could be brought together to repel them?'

This remained fantasy until in October 1797 André-Jacques Garnerin made the first recorded human parachute descent from a balloon. Not until the advent of controlled flight at the beginning of the twentieth century was a silk parachute developed that could be stowed in a small bag fastened to a balloon or aircraft and pulled out by the bodyweight of a jumper. Garnerin combined two words to describe his contraption: *parer*, to avoid or ward off and *chute*, a fall. Descending devices were initially called 'fall-breakers' and later 'parachutes'.

In 1914 the American Charles Broadwick jumped the first static-line parachute. This so-called 'parachute coat' had the parachute packed inside a canvas backpack, sewn onto a sleeveless coat-like garment worn by the jumper. A line fixed to an aircraft strongpoint pulled the parachute out of the bag, should the pilot have to exit the aircraft in extremis. On the eve of the First World War the parachute was seen as a life-saver and for some time that was viewed as its sole utility, rather than as an instrument that might be used in war. Although Broadwick had demonstrated his device to a military audience, there was no interest whatsoever.

All along the Western Front at the end of 1915 the silent sinister shapes of tethered observation balloons could be seen directing artillery fire onto opposing trenches. Warfare accelerated technological development. As more durable and faster aircraft began to fly, they started to shoot at each other, at first with pistols and shot guns before gravitating to swivel-mounted machine guns. Anthony Fokker fitted an interrupter gear in 1915, enabling him to fire a machine gun through his propeller blades. Technological superiority swung like a pendulum between both sides. By 'Bloody April' in 1917 the average life expectancy of a British Royal Flying Corps pilot on the Western Front was eight days. They had no parachutes. Fitting a 'Guardian Angel' parachute to a British DH-4 bi-plane reduced its speed by 3 mph and its rate of climb by 50 feet per second, an unacceptable impediment.

German balloon crews, by contrast, stowed parachutes in canvas pouches above their heads beyond the edge of the wicker basket. 'Balloon-busting' pilots were always prepared to risk intense machine gun fire and flak to get at their tethered victims. One German observer recalled: 'One must never allow oneself to be disturbed by the thought that, if his balloon were set on fire above him, he would only have a few seconds in which to make his leap for safety with his parachute.' They could not see enough to make a judgment, relying on the ground officer to make the call to jump. Too long a delay could result in the parachutist being engulfed by the falling mass of blazing balloons set on fire by tracer. 'When the order came through the telephone,' remarked the observer, 'he had to jump from his basket into the depths below without a second's hesitation.'

Leutnant Ernst Struck, directing artillery fire from his tied balloon on the eastern Galician front, recalled 'a sudden crackling and howling, and then a wild shriek beneath as an aircraft shot at us – and how he fired!' A second aeroplane flashed past as Struck frantically called through the telephone to be wound down: 'Good grief – again! The chap was coming directly against the balloon. "*Get us down!*" I shrieked into the phone.' With a jerk the cable started to wind down, but it was too late. He saw the pilot holding fire so as not to hit his own propeller and then the swivel machine gun began winking at him once he was past. 'Tracer flashed by under the basket.' They were at 950 meters. '*Over the side,*' he called to his NCO observer as he closed his eyes and baled out. 'At first everything was dark, then the glimpses of green and blue sky before the eyes. There was a rush and fluttering and then – bump – a halt! The parachute opened cleanly! I had a feeling I was simply hanging without falling. I glanced quickly about and then looked under. Swinging below was a white thing, yes, that was my NCO. Thank goodness his parachute had also developed.'

One British balloon officer, Stephen Wilkinson, recalled that a jump 'required no small amount of nerve to make the effort', even under attack. 'When the actual moment arrived and the jumper looked down to earth about 2,000 feet below there were many cases of wind-up.' This was usually resolved by an urgent shove from the remaining fearful occupant, sent reeling by the after effect, a 'rather alarming' shift of balance in the small basket. 'Even then his troubles were not over,' recalled a German balloon observer: 'The attacking aeroplane would direct a furious fire against the defenceless man hanging from the parachute and blazing tracer bullets would leap at him. Only extraordinary will-power, self control, strong nerves, and a stout heart enabled him to stand the strain; and to go up again after his descent!'

An estimated 800 to 900 balloon observers saved their lives parachuting from burning or disabled balloons during the First World War. The Guardian Angel was aptly named, but this man-carried system, like the Mears Parachute and an AEF America-designed model, were not available to flyers until the end of the war. German pilots flew with the Heinecke parachute from May 1918.

'I was agreeably surprised to see my first burst had set fire to the Hun's fuel tank and that the machine was doomed,' recalled US Captain Eddie Rickenbacker in the final months of the war. He was surprised and 'almost equally gratified the next second to see the German pilot level off his blazing machine and with a sudden leap overboard into space let the Fokker slide safely away without him. Attached to his back and sides was a rope which immediately pulled a dainty parachute from the bottom of his seat. The umbrella opened within a fifty foot drop and lowered him gradually to earth within his own lines.'

Rickenbacker considered, 'I truly wished him all the luck in the world. It is not a pleasure to see a burning aeroplane descending to earth bearing with it a human being.' But he was still frustrated. 'Why the Huns had all these human contrivances and why our own country could not at least copy them to save American lives,' was anathema to him.

In mid-1918 an old Savoia-Pomlio SP4 bi-plane piloted by two British fliers, Lieutenant Colonel W. Barker and Captain William Wedgwood Benn, flew over the Piave River in darkness. Fixed searchlight beams guided them toward the approaching Austrian lines. Nervously sitting in the back with a brave face was Italian agent Alessandro Tandura, attached to a black-canopy Guardian Angel parachute fixed to an iron frame beneath the undercarriage. To drop accurately on targets in total darkness, Wedgwood Benn explained: 'We arranged that the agent should sit in a cockpit on a trap-door hinged at the sides and opening in the middle. This floor was held in place by bolts controlled by a rope connected with the observer's seat. The result was that it was the observer who decided when the bolt was to be drawn and the agent, waiting presumably with some qualms, at the right moment found himself suddenly with nothing under him and thus launched into the future.'

Several attempts with dummies had taken place and the uneasy Tandura was instructed to fold his arms on nearing the objective. His predicament was closely akin to the hangman's drop. Wedgwood Benn dryly added: 'with little required of the agent other than exceptional fortitude, it was not thought necessary to train him in the art of parachuting.' Two hand-dropped bombs were lobbed out to aid deception. Barker, piloting the aircraft, gave the signal and slowed to stalling speed, while Wedgwood Benn jerked the trap-door handle: 'I pull, and wait. No jerk, no apparent result. The bolts have stuck! I pull again. The wire slacks with a rush, the machine shivers and resumes its course. For good or ill, Tandura is gone.'

Tandura survived the experience and successfully completed his mission. Two other agents, Nicolso and Barnaba, were also dropped behind Austrian lines with a consignment of carrier pigeons on the same sector of the Italian Piavre front. Other nations independently followed suit. French officer Lieutenant Evrard jumped with two others over the German-occupied Ardennes forest region with explosives and radio equipment that same summer. They were back behind their own lines within a week after blowing up a road. German air-landed agents were dropped off in 1916 when Leutnant Kossel flew across Russian lines near Rowno with Oberfeldwebel (senior sergeant) Windisch. They successfully sabotaged a Russian railway line 50 miles behind the front and then their aircraft returned to pick them up.

The parachute had only a limited military utility in 1918, either as a life-preserver or for delivering agents behind lines for clandestine operations. Colonel Billy Mitchell, the 39-year-old head of America's Air Service in Europe, offered a totally new perspective on 17 October 1918 when he briefed the American Supreme Commander General John Pershing on an imaginative vertical envelopment by parachutists to capture Metz. He argued the 1st (US) Division could be deployed in the following way: 'We should arm the men with a great number of machine guns and train them to go over the front in our large aeroplanes, which can carry 10 or 15 of these soldiers. We could equip each man with a parachute, so that when we desired to make a rear attack on the enemy, we could carry these men over the lines and drop them off in parachutes behind the enemy position.'

After forming a strongpoint in the rear and blocking approach routes they would be supplied by air and protected by close combat air support. Once the enemy was disorganised a general offensive would be mounted on the front. He proposed the operation should be launched in the spring of 1919. Mitchell had already employed mass 200-bomber air raids. Converted Handley Page bombers would be used, but 2,000 would be needed for this and some would have to air-land. Nobody, however, was yet parachute-trained and neither did an organisation exist to launch such a specialised airborne force.

His staff assistant Major Lewis Brereton was ordered to produce a workable plan. There was no headquarters capable of assembling and flying such an air transport fleet. How would ammunition and rations be re-supplied to the assaulting troops? The experience needed to direct the complex assembly and tactical handling of so many aircraft and dispersed troop landings was unavailable. There were not even enough army radios to control it. The idea was not so far removed from Benjamin Franklin's fantastic idea of launching 10,000 troops from 5,000 hot air balloons.

Pershing not surprisingly rejected the idea, and 25 days later the war ended.

FROM STUNT MEN TO LOCUST WARRIORS

Jumping from a stricken aircraft in an emergency requires the parachute jumper to be well clear. Circus performers had devised stratagems to achieve this. Leslie Irvin, an American parachute designer and circus high diver since the age of 16, introduced a totally new concept to parachuting. His 'free-fall' type parachute was not automatic, but was opened by the parachutist pulling a rip-cord at a time of his own choosing. In early 1919 he demonstrated the device at McCook Field in Ohio as part of a US Air Service scheme designed to pick a standard pilot parachute.

Ignorance often acted as a brake on early parachute innovations. It was thought the wind force during a long fall would pin a jumper's arms to his body and prevent him pulling the rip-cord. Others felt that psychic paralysis might set in through fear of falling alone and the jumper would be incapable of rational action. 'Sky High' Irvin's circus experience suggested otherwise.

On 28 April 1919, Floyd Smith flew his DH-9 aircraft at 1,500 feet above McCook Field airfield and remembered Irvin 'climbed over the cockpit and sat on the edge with his legs hanging down and tried to leap-frog off – instead he tumbled over and over'. First World War veteran fighter pilot Major E.L. Hoffman, coordinating the trial, watched open-mouthed below with his board members. 'For God's sake, why doesn't he open his parachute!' he appealed. A small drogue 'chute popped out and dragged out the main canopy. Floyd Smith watching from above saw: 'The 'chute opened almost immediately, in 1.4 seconds to be exact. His descent was steady, there was practically no oscillation. The demonstration of the 'chute was almost tame.' Irvin broke his ankle on landing but secured the US Air Service contract. It was generally acknowledged throughout the aviation world that this model, which was to remain in service for the next 50 years, represented the ultimate in parachute design.

British resistance to providing its wartime flyers with parachutes had been based on the cynical premise that they would encourage pilots to bale out at the first sign of trouble. Official prevarication was relaxed in August 1918 and the order given to fit aeroplanes with parachutes, but the signing of the Armistice stopped the process. Irvin's American parachute was adopted for use by the Royal Air Force after 1919, but few knew how to use it.

John Corlett recalled the early parachute courses conducted at RAF Henlow in the mid-1920s. RAF parachute packers were 'invited' to test their newly acquired skills by jumping the very 'chutes they had packed. 'Nah don't fergit, it's all quite volunt'ry,' he recalled his flight sergeant instructor explaining. 'Anyone 'oo's too windy to 'ave a go 'as only gotter come an' see me an' 'is name'll be took off the list an' no questions asked.'Harry Ward joined the RAF in 1921 as a mechanic and was soon a member of the RAF's travelling parachute demonstration team, having received the 'griff' on the Irvin parachute. They were tasked to demonstrate parachutes to squadron aircrews before they were issued. Few aircrew volunteered to have a go. 'The majority of the pilots were a bit wary of jumping,' he recalled, 'they thought they were inviting disaster just wearing a parachute, never mind jumping out with one.'

Harry Ward had to learn himself before passing on the experience to others. There was 'no training whatsoever! It was a case of trial and error,' he admitted. 'On the first one I did, the ground just came up and hit me. I landed stiff-legged and was rolled over onto my back. But with time, we learned how to take heavy falls by adopting the stage-tumbler's attitude where they did a roll onto their buttocks and shoulders.'

There were only two ways to practise and these were virtual show stunts in themselves. One was the 'drop-off' from a short ladder affixed to the fuselage of a Fairy Fawn bi-plane. Hanging onto the ladder in flight, John Corlett explained when he received the thumbs up from the pilot in the cockpit, his right hand grip transferred to the rip-cord handle. 'As soon as this was seen to be safely secured a "wave away" signal – crossed hands waved in front of the face – meant let go, count three and pull the rip-cord.' As Corlett's instructor pointed out to the uneasy students: 'Nothing to it.'

Harry Ward described the alternative which was jumping from the wing of a Vickers Vimy bi-plane bomber. Parachutists perched on platforms on the outer wings, 'facing aft, so that the slipstream pressed him onto the wing strut'. They had to hang on to the strut through take-off to jump. The jumper had to edge around the strut, battling the slipstream in flight, and hold on with one hand while he pulled the rip-cord. The blossoming parachute canopy snatched him off the wing, 'whipped off', as Ward explained. 'You usually saw the plane shoot away . . . between your legs.'

'Make sure you've got them crutch-straps good 'an tight,' John Corlett's flight sergeant advised, 'don't want ter ruin yer matrimonial prospects.' As he took off standing on the outer wing platform of a Vimy bomber, he hugged the wing strut 'as closely as a pair of lovers embracing in a shop doorway', bumping and taxiing over the uneven ground. 'Hang on tight – wouldn't half look a Joe Soap to fall off now,' he thought. At about 1,500 to 2,000 feet he edged his way around the strut, through the howling slipstream:

Can I keep myself on with one hand? Gradually ease the grip off
the right hand and see if the left can hold me. Yes, OK. Feel for
the rip-cord handle; ease it gently out of the pocket. Now he's
waving his arms frantically [looking at the pilot] – thinks I'm not
going to pull it.

Hasn't it gone quiet all of a sudden. God!! Where's me 'chute?
Should be up there, no sign of it – I'm falling . . . why do I keep
getting glimpses of earth and then sky? Take a chance and look
down. Lord! Nearly level with the tops of the trees . . . Fair
knocked the puff out of me – good job there's no wind.

'Drop-offs' were kinder than 'yank-offs' because, as John Corlett
explained, one 'swung past the vertical to the near horizontal again
and continued in a series of gradually diminishing oscillations' which
meant there was 'barely time to gather their wits before the ground
came up and hit them'. Quite often the pupils were sick.

Gleb Kotelnikov, a junior artillery officer in the Tsarist Russian
Army, developed an emergency parachute for pilots between 1910–
11. It was designated the RK-1 and Russian aviators were using it
by the end of the First World War. In 1929 he produced a second
version with an envelope-type opening parachute pack and later an
'aviation postman' cargo parachute.

In much the same way as cricket and football were thought to
contribute to manly qualities in English life, parachuting was adopted
as a Russian national sport which stirred the blood, manifesting
just the sort of challenge the state sought to promote in a society
emerging from generations of serfdom and autocratic feudalism.
Competition jumping started from maximum heights and progressed
to other exciting variations like who could drop the lowest before
he opened his parachute. On 16 July 1934 Evdokimov claimed this
world record, jumping at 25,000 feet and delaying his parachute
opening until he was 650 feet above the ground.

The Leninist Komsomol or Young Communist League established parachuting as the new Soviet mass sport. Using the slogan '*Do
as I do!*' thousands of youngsters became involved in aviation sport
activities. There were demonstration jumps by parachute organisations, airfield excursion days and special holidays announced via press

and radio propaganda to fire the youthful imagination. Parachute towers were erected in parks and sports fields and were copiously used in many towns and cities. A.M. Lukin, a retired parachute sport instructor, recalled: 'anyone desiring to do so could acquaint himself with the feeling which one has in making a parachute jump.' Young and old leaped at the opportunities. One observer remembered an old woman of 80 jumping alongside a small boy of six; the old lady made it while the boy was badly injured.

Jumping was a state-sponsored rather than spontaneous evolution. Parachuting offered martial skills to a newly established Soviet state acutely suspicious of the west. The Leningrad Military District conducted psychological research on 41 parachutists in the early 1930s, and found there were no negative physical effects; rather 'it fosters and strengthens resoluteness, self-possession and other volitional qualities'. The report advocated parachuting should be encouraged among young people and included within the physical training systems of higher education and in societies and schools. 'Jumps from an aeroplane develops courage, decision, resourcefulness, trains will power and the ability not to lose one's head in an emergency and to make quick decisions in case of complications,' declared a People's Commissariat of Public Health pamphlet in the late 1930s. As Ilya Lisov, a Soviet airborne commentator, explained, encouraging these areas within the sporting medium 'permitted them to be trained not only as first-rate aviation sportsmen, but as skilful defenders of the Homeland, unconditionally devoted to the Communist Party'. In short, future defence potential.

Russia became the first nation to bring substance to Colonel Billy Mitchell's earlier discredited concept of vertical envelopment conducted by parachute soldiers. In 1928 M.N. Tukhachevsky, the Soviet commander of the Leningrad Military District, prepared a study entitled *Operations of an Air Assault Force in an Offensive Operation*. Aircraft, he advocated, could provide fire-power and open a new dimension of offensive manoeuvre, vertical envelopment from the air. 'Winged infantry' could support penetrations by mechanised forces, which Tukhachevsky saw guaranteeing success in the 'Deep Battle'. Russia's long borders had never been easily defensible. Parachuted and air-landed forces could create unexpected fronts against the flanks of enemy attackers or breach defences at key points and operate deep in the enemy's rear. The first successful military parachute insertion was accomplished on 2 August 1930 when six parachutists dropped at Voronezh in the Russian heartland and were re-supplied by cargo parachutes. Reinforced by six more parachute jumpers, they rallied and prepared for further action. An experimental Parachute Assault Unit was established and expanded to a brigade by 1933 in the Leningrad Military District and joined by two others in the Kiev and Byelorussian Military Districts between 1934–6. Six hundred paratroopers landed in a mass exercise drop behind 'enemy' lines near Minsk in September 1934. Mitchell's concept was proven.

'As was always the case before a jump, my heart was pounding,' remembered Captain Ilya Grigoryevich Starinov during a 1932 exercise jump. 'It seemed to be expanding, trying to burst out of my chest.' Medical research convinced the Soviets that the intense emotions engendered by parachuting required beginners to be immensely fit. They found normal pulse rates of 77 recorded before jumps rose to 117 in the aircraft and climaxed at 155 on landing. Starinov found typical landing hazards to be 'pulled muscles, dislocations and other injuries impeding parachutists collapsing 'chutes on landing'.

Even an organisation as harsh as the Red Army recognised some overly creative technical schemes were simply unsustainable in human terms. Bi-planes flying at head height across steppe grassland tried dropping 'air buses' or heavy-duty aerodynamic trolleys. They bounced and careered through a welter of dust before skidding to a halt. The dazed airborne soldiers within were rarely fit for combat. Tests were discontinued after the trolleys were dropped over lakes where they broke up and sank on impact. Another idea was to drop parachutists blind, inside sealed cradles attached to aircraft bomb racks. These opened automatically and tipped them out over the drop zone with an automatic opening canopy. It soon became apparent this method too was not delivering combat-effective soldiers and it was stopped. Fatigue rather than fear was cited; but for men to fly in darkness and then be pitched out of a roaring aircraft without warning was unsustainable. Two air-land gliders, a light 17-man version and a heavy 50-man monstrosity, were also abandoned as hopeless experiments in the early 1930s. The need to parachute or air-land heavy equipments alongside the fledgling parachute units was recognised from the outset but met with intermittent success.

On 14 September 1935 foreign observers and military attachés at Brovary airfield north-east of Kiev looked up at the drone of approaching aircraft shortly after dawn. Fifty Tupolev TB-3 bombers lumbered into sight in clusters of four, gently rising and falling amid a fighter escort. These massive four-engine corrugated metal-skinned aircraft had a wing span of nearly 133 feet. They slowed to between 80–100 mph as they approached the drop zones. 'The roar of the transport plane's motors was deafening,' recalled Captain Ilya Starinov. 'The 83 foot fuselage shook and vibrated.' An average load was 35 to 40 parachutists but up to 50 men was possible depending on fuel. The airborne regiment used on this exercise numbered 1,188 men and had flown in from 175 miles away.

At the order 'Get Ready!' the men began to clamber out onto the aircraft fuselage and wings, emerging from open machine gun compartments and a small door at the base of the wing. Some remained poised inside the aircraft to jump through the door and bomb bays. The aim of jumping the doors, wing, bomb bays and hatches together was to lessen ground dispersal. Negotiating tight hatches encumbered by a 70lb main parachute and reserves and struggling against 85–100 mph slipstreams was not easy. Film of the drop was taken from accompanying aircraft and shows figures clustering like ants around the base of the wings. They became known as the Locust Warriors. Hardy self-control was required to jump. 'Nothing is more dangerous than giving in to self-serving rationalisations,' claimed Starinov. 'I'd already trained myself not to surrender to such weakness.' The troops were mesmerised awaiting the number one at the bomb bay opening. 'The pilot raised his hand and turned around, giving the signal that it was time to jump.' The jump controller in the forward machine gun turret raised his signal flag and they commenced jumping.

Parachutists clinging onto the corrugated grooves and handles on the wing released their grip and began to slip and slide down. It often took a final backsliding wriggle to clear the backpack parachute from the wing edge to fall free. 'Wild acceleration' followed, recalled Starinov: 'I pulled the rip-cord. It seemed as though the 'chute would never open. This was just my senses deceiving me; in jumping, fractions of seconds stretch into seconds, and seconds into minutes. I felt a jolt – the 'chute had finally opened! Everything was going well . . . I wanted to sing.'

Such personal impressions were completely lost on the spectators looking up below. They saw waves of aircraft roaring overhead in 'V' formation, followed by a trail of parachute clusters popping open like flak bursts below the fuselage, a panoply of blossoming canopies.

The foreign observers were stunned. This was the first time the Soviet Union, indeed any nation, had demonstrated it had a parachute capability. Brovary airfield was secured by the parachute assault and then an impressive air-land followed. Waves of Tupelov bombers deposited 1,700 troops, six light trucks, ten artillery pieces and even a T-37 light tank. After one hour and fifty minutes 2,500 troops had jumped or been air-landed with heavy equipments. General Loiseau, the Deputy Chief of the French General staff, was visibly impressed: 'Western Europe is lagging behind!' he declared. Italian General Monti admitted he was 'literally amazed by the employment of such airborne landing forces'. The British military attaché Major General Archibald Wavell was more circumspect, commenting 'a most spectacular performance' but 'its tactical value may be doubtful'. The force had been inserted within a benign air environment, that is with no enemy fighter or flak opposition. Visiting Oberst (Colonel) Kurt Student, representing the newly created German Wehrmacht, was enormously attentive. Recognising the same limitations identified by Wavell, forthcoming German experimentation would not be stymied, like the parsimonious British, by its defence budget.

The French immediately sought Russian advice on the creation of their own airborne contingent. Colonel Dastikh with the Czech military mission made a press comment that 'the airborne landing is a new combat arm created by the Bolsheviks'. Primitive though the start may be, Russia was clearly leading the way and the whole point of the spectacular display had been to demonstrate just that. 'There is no country in the world which can say that in this field it can even nearly be equal to the Soviet Union,' announced Comrade Voroshilov, Marshal of the Soviet Union. In his view no country was in a position to catch up, never mind overtake. The complexities were too great. 'I must tell you, comrades,' he announced in a speech after the Kiev exercise, 'that this parachute business, one of the most complicated and delicate technical arts, is perfected by the Red Army' and had become 'an important branch of our fighting strength.'

General Archie Wavell returned to England and reported his impressions. Infantry Lieutenant John Frost recalled a lecture given to the officers of Aldershot Command about the Kiev exercise. It projected a view that Frost, later a distinguished parachute commander, claimed would bedevil Britain's own airborne development. 'I advise you when you go home to forget all about it,' Wavell told his audience. 'The endemic trouble with British Airborne Forces was that the Army never really believed in them,' Frost later claimed.

The German Wehrmacht thought otherwise.

2

NEW SKY MEN: FALLSCHIRMJÄGER

SPECIAL MEN FOR A SPECIAL TASK

In November 1935 the newly formed General Göring Regiment, some 1,500 strong, assembled at Jüterbog airfield south of Berlin to witness their first parachute demonstration. The gathering was bizarre. These ex-Berlin–Brandenburg policemen had been dressed months before in the distinctive green uniforms of the Landespolizeigruppe Berlin; now they paraded in Luftwaffe blue. 'We were told that our old duties were over, for by then the Nazis had taken power and were reorganising everything, including the police,' remembered Karl Baumer. Confusing perhaps, but the police were used to unequivocally obeying orders. What might come next, they wondered? 'Our leaders told us that the Luftwaffe was forming a parachute troop unit and that we would be the first regiment.' Knowing nothing about soldiering, 'we were thunderstruck', Baumer commented, but infantry training had started.

Today was to be the moment of truth. They could either opt to volunteer for a new elite Fallschirmjäger (paratrooper) unit or simply carry on military training. Parachuting was really for circus stuntmen, they felt. Hardly any of the assembled ex-policemen had ever flown in an aeroplane. They focused on the solitary Junkers W-34 aircraft silhouette hanging in the sky with intense proprietary interest. As the engine note changed pitch to a virtual stall Baumer saw: 'At last a tiny figure appeared from it and soon a parachute opened. It was quite exciting to watch and all very new to us. The figure came down in a few moments but there was a slight wind and a gust must have caught the 'chute unexpectedly as the man fell backwards at the last moment and hurt his back on landing. An ambulance quickly took him away.'

It was only the second time the gefreiter (corporal) demonstrating had jumped. There was an uncomfortable silence. 'Not a good thing to happen in front of would-be volunteers!' mused Baumer. A mixture of nervousness, banter and bravado broke out. 'I had no great desire to become a paratrooper,' Baumer admitted but he was swayed by dare-devil friends, the promise of more pay and the kudos of being part of a glamorous elite unit. 'You boys will have all the girls in Berlin after you in no time,' a recruiting lieutenant assured them. 'So come on, become a parachutist and you'll never regret it!'

In October 1935 the German press had reported soberly on the Kiev mass parachute descents. One newspaper warned; 'the efforts made by Soviet Russia to train large numbers of parachute jumpers and the propaganda carried on in order to introduce parachute jumping as a popular sport, deserves serious attention.' The détente that had secretly existed between the Soviet Union and the German military since the Treaty of Rapello in 1922 had evaporated with Hitler's election in 1933, and was replaced by ideological enmity. However, training youth to prepare for war was encouraged equally by the Soviet Komsomol Communist Youth League and the Hitlerjugend (Hitler Youth) of the new Third Reich. The newspaper observed that: 'Soviet Russia intends to land not only troops but also spies and first of all political propagandists in hostile rear areas' with the aim of undermining powers of resistance.

General Hermann Göring was Hitler's right-hand man, an ex-World War One flying ace and now head of the Luftwaffe. On 1 November 1935 he transformed the crack Prussian paramilitary Wecke police force into a Wehrmacht Luftwaffe formation and then a parachute unit. It was originally designed for counter-terrorist and internal security operations. A parachute school was set up at the Stendal-Borstel airbase 60 miles west of Berlin. Eight hundred of Karl Baumer's regiment freely volunteered. From the outset it was realised exceptional physical fitness would be required for the rough and tumble of parachute training. Volunteers had to weigh less than 85kg, be physically well developed and pass the equivalent of a flyer's medical. The course would last eight weeks with four weeks of parachute ground training and tactical weapons instruction, followed by four weeks' parachute jumping. Six descents would be made independently, including one in a row or 'stick' order and one by night. This initial training would provide the basis for future experiments. The Germans developed an automatic opening parachute that could deploy within 150 feet. This was the RZ-1 (Rückenpackung Zwangauslösung Model 1), followed later by the RZ-16 and 36. 'We relied on that little piece of rope and hook at one end and connected to the 'chute at the other,' Karl Baumer pointed out. 'If anything went wrong we were dead.'

Granting Luftwaffe primacy for training made sense because the army was doubtful about paratroopers from the start and the air force controlled the key functional training assets. Army scepticism of the Soviet experience was based on their appreciation that paratroopers would not fare well in the face of the heavy anti-aircraft capabilities possessed by most modern European armies. Moreover, highly developed western road networks would result in countermeasures being brought to bear far more rapidly than in the trackless expanses of Russia.

Recruitment came in waves: gently pressed pioneers at first and then volunteer conscripts to expand the newly created Luftwaffe Fallschirmjäger arm. Economics and social status played a role. With six million unemployed in Germany in the early 1930s and the cost of raising a family of five estimated at about 100 Reichmarks a month, a labourer earned 40 marks and a foreman perhaps 250. Unemployment benefit was five marks but an army captain earned 350 marks. Offering a policeman future security in Göring's Luftwaffe was therefore no mean attraction. Karl Baumer went back home to Berlin dressed in Luftwaffe blue and 'created a good deal of fuss in my different outfit . . . my parents and lady friend were amazed' and doubtless relieved that the uncertain times might be over.

This early group of volunteers was steeped in the autocratic social conditions that characterised the previous Kaiser's Germany. Wearing uniform conferred status in a nation acutely conscious of its hierarchical divisions and martial values. One respected the upper classes. It was entirely acceptable for Göring to *order* an entire regiment to make a choice 'for or against' remaining with the unit. Karl Lothar Schulz, a huge Prussian ex-policeman, lined up his 15th Company on decision day and announced: 'Men, are you willing to do everything I decide for you?' '*Jawohl*, Herr Oberleutnant!' was the shouted response. 'Good! As of this day, you are all Fallschirmjäger!' he bellowed. Many were nationalists.

Jäger Felix Merreys claimed: 'I am German, I feel German and I am proud to be a German! I love my family, I love my hometown, and I love my country.' There were idealists: 'I heard about the paratroops,' recalled Karel Weise, a German-Czech, 'and as I had always had some interest in aerial matters I decided to try to transfer to the Luftwaffe and the paratroops.' Ideological conviction impelled him to join up because 'my heart, I'm afraid, embraced the "New Order", as did most I knew, for we only knew what our leaders wanted us to know.'

'Fallschirmjäger! That enabled courage to be shown – to demonstrate that one was a complete man!' recalled later company commander Alkmar von Hove. A mystical attraction coupled with adventurous bravado motivated these men, just as it had the early parachute pioneers. 'If I'm standing on a mountain side, I always have the feeling I would like to leap just once into the valley,' confided Karl D., a 22-year-old from Kärnten. 'Now I will experience such missions from an aeroplane and show what a Kärnter villager is made of.' Many of the small elite group of 800 that transferred from the Berlin police went on to make distinguished careers for themselves. Seventeen were to be awarded the Knight's Cross later in the war, four became generals, six colonels and four majors. Seven of these former policemen were commanding divisions by the end of the war.

Berliner Konrad Seibert spotted a poster for the paratroops in the Hitler Youth and Labour Service Training Office and it 'at once struck me as something different' and he resolved to give it a go. 'I had no idea if I could find the courage to jump from an aeroplane, but I thought that if the worst came to the worst I could opt out.' Conscription had been introduced in 1935. His parents, who were wealthy restaurant owners, were aghast at his decision.

Setting off for the Wehrmacht, like the first day at school, was celebrated as a family event. Suitcases were packed with basic clothing and food by mothers amid sage advice from fathers and grandfathers who had already experienced First World War service. Small gifts were presented by grandparents, brothers and sisters and the whole family would wave from the railway platform as trains took their menfolk away. Martin Pöppel joined the paratroopers believing he might achieve a scam of serving only two years instead of four. When he arrived at Stendal for his parachute course the local band welcomed them with an excruciating version of the song 'All the little birds are here'. Not necessarily out of place, he recalled, 'We were soon to become eagles after all.' They were met and marched through the town in civilian clothes, immediately aware they were part of a large plan and that they were joining an elite unit.

Virtually none of the officers who joined the Falschirmjäger in the early years had been in the Hitler Youth because they were too old. By the late 1930s this had changed; in 1938 there were 7.7 million boys and girls in the Hitlerjugend movements, membership of which soon became compulsory. German history and sports became the two most important subjects at school, with boxing being introduced at primary school. At age 16 nearly all German boys could handle a rifle, were superbly fit, and could march for hours with map and compass. 'In the Hitler Youth they taught us how to to be tough,' recalled Johannes Köppen. 'What did Hitler say a German boy must be? Swift as a greyhound, tough as leather and hard as Krupp Steel.' 'Nobody wanted to be a Mummy's boy,' echoed Günther Damaske, 'so we cut the apron strings.' The Hitler Youth was followed by a six to twelve-month period with the Reichsarbeitdienst (RAD). Fallschirmjäger Felix Gaerte hated RAD service which, apart from helping German farmers and building roads, provided pseudo-military training before conscription. 'We were harassed and bullied from 0500 in the morning to 1900 hours in the evening with barracking and drills in the exercise yard – often also during the nights,' he complained. He likened it to the mindless training methods employed during the Imperial Kaiser Army's recruit training, 'which often drove youngsters to despair and suicide'.

Despite this conditioning, two out of every three volunteers failed paratrooper training, which combined rigorous physical training with basic infantry instruction. *Harte und Ausdauer* (toughness and endurance) was interspersed with gymnastic routines for parachute landing preparation. Relentless long marches were followed by night exercises and dummy alerts, designed to break up a night's rest by requiring recruits to form up ready to move, dressed in full kit and carrying weapons and equipment. Martin Pöppel labelled this highly intense phase 'unbelievably hard but basically fair', commenting: 'We were drilled so hard from morning til night that we never got a

moment to think.' Forty-kilometre marches across soft and undulating terrain provided the climax for this first eight-week period.
Anticipated rest on return to barracks was rudely shattered by the
order to carry on for a further two hours. At the 50-kilometre point,
with men barely able to stand with blisters and aching muscles, two
more hours were ordered to achieve 60 kilometres. Any man dropping out was dismissed. The very obstinacy and aggression sought by
the process was what kept them going. 'This inhuman hardness had
the purpose of testing the limit of our ability,' recalled Jäger Felix
Merreys at his physical and mental end-point. 'An incredible fury
welded our comradeship together,' he remembered, pulling them
through, 'which was probably also the purpose of this drudgery.'
'Sweat saves blood, that was a truism that was often confirmed later,'
reflected Pöppel years later. 'We didn't know it yet though, so we
cursed and swore at everything and everyone, at every stripe and
every star.' Such training produced the intended results.

Parachute training began with gymnastic landing routines carried
out on mats across aircraft hangar floors. 'First came the ground
exercises,' recalled Karl Heinz Pollmann, 'ground rolls forward and
backwards, jumping into soft sand from an aircraft and finally being
dragged along the rugged surface of the exercise yard by a parachute
driven by the propeller blast of two powerful engines', the so-called
'wind-donkeys' or wingless aircraft. Lectures on parachute packing
were given around long trestle tables. Students focused on the maze
of parachute silk and lines they would jump the next day. What first
took half a day to pack was reduced with practice to less than an
hour. Practical training took students through the whole sequence of
a parachute jump. It began with jumping through mock-up aircraft
doors and hanging from harnesses practising crucifix position flight
drills to ground landing rolls on mats and quickly disentangling the
parachute harness. Three-metre high platforms were used for an hour
each day for students to practise landing on mats with full equipment.

Six training jumps were made from Junkers Ju-52 transport aircraft.
These started with single jumps and graduated to groups. 'My early
training was very interesting, until we reached the actual jumping part
from the Jus!' recalled Konrad Seibert at Stendal parachute school. 'I
had never been up in a plane, so when we climbed aboard that Ju we

were all very thrilled as I doubt if any of the others had flown either.'
Martin Pöppel recalled his first jump in glorious sunshine after being
delayed a week by persistent rain. 'Why is it so quiet all of a sudden?'
he mused, contrasting the atmosphere with the animated barrack-room
chatter of the night before. 'The jokes and platitudes tail away,' he
remembered, 'and somehow everybody becomes thoughtful.' Aviation
fuel and aircraft smells was sufficient to set the stomach juices racing,
quickened more by the sound of the engine starting up. Karl Pickert
recalled the noise of the engines ticking over on climbing aboard and
sitting down. 'We were very nervous but put on our best smiles.'
Training flights were never long, to maximise the student throughput. 'We did not go very far, just to a few hundred feet in a big circle,'
remembered Konrad Seibert. 'The ground seemed very far below and
the wind whistled past the open door.'

Twelve soldiers sat facing each other in the narrow confines of
the Ju-52 fuselage with knees touching. 'NCOs looked at us and
grinned,' recalled Karl Pickert. 'We could not sit well, nor could
we look out of the windows.' At the command '*Fertig Machen!*' (Get
ready!) the soldiers stood up and hooked their static line to the bar
above and turned and faced the exit, the small door on the port side
at the rear of the aircraft. 'We lined up, our stomachs churning,'
recalled Konrad Seibert, third in line. They were deafened by the
wind-slapping slipstream and propeller draught.

'*Fertig zum Spring!*' (Ready to jump!), was the next command
which meant they all moved up as the first man shuffled to the door.
He bent at the low opening, knees inward, holding onto the hand
rail at either side, face quivering as the slipstream pulled at his skin. At
the open door Pöppel remembered, 'strangely, my anxiety suddenly
disappears.' He was ready to dive through the door with his arms
outstretched and feet together as if from a pool-side high board. The
aim of this seemingly death-defying leap was to completely clear the
aircraft without snagging the long static line.

'*Blaaaaa . . . ah!*' blared the klaxon horn, the signal for the number
1 to launch himself out head first. Ex-policeman Karl Baumer jumped
number 2 first time and 'wished clearly that I was last . . . But I gritted
my teeth and saw the first lad go out of the door. I was petrified, but
the Feldwebel [sergeant] slapped my back and shouted *Los!* [Go!]

And I dived out in a complete faint – or very nearly! I shut my eyes as the wind hit me, and then felt the great tug as the 'chute came out and pulled me into an upright position. I dared to open my eyes . . .'

Konrad Seibert jumped third. The first went out without hesitation, followed closely by the second, 'and I recalled his face – he looked terrified!' Siebert was in a mechanical trance, receiving a slap from the NCO jumpmaster and 'diving head first into the wind that took my breath away'. Abruptly the aircraft roar receded into the distance. 'I was hurled about for a second or two, but the 'chute opened quickly and then I was in Heaven! The relief was tremendous.' Jäger Karl Heinz Pollmann described the frantic rough-and-tumble of a typical exit: 'Go! Ten men, one behind the other, rushed out through the door. One more deep breath and the show was on! The world tumbled about. Then a sharp jolt as the parachute deployed. I felt at the top of the world. During the next 45 seconds, we were dangling from our harness as the ground rushed up to meet us.'

The rough jolt was a particular feature of the low-opening RZ-1 parachute, the static line jerking open the pack after a fall of about 50 metres. Initial training descents were from 250 metres, progressively lowered to 120 metres. Jäger Feri Fink described the 'shock of opening as being cruelly hard', the jolt on the upper body flinging the legs into the air. Muscle strain often resulted, something that could only be overcome by a hefty tightening of the parachute harness. The descent then proceeded at about 4.5 to 5.5 metres per second. 'Strong wind and a hefty oscillation made it dangerous,' Fink declared. 'Only sporty, well-developed gymnastic jumpers were able to sustain rough and tumble landings without damage.'

The problem with the RZ-1 parachute was the single lift web which suspended the parachutist from a single point above his shoulder blades. This left the jumper hanging face forward with no control over direction except by violently flinging his limbs about. The spread-eagling this involved could be dangerous as feet and knees needed to be together on striking the ground. Elbow and knee pads were provided to compensate for knocks and bangs as a parachutist attempted to 'judo roll' in the direction he landed. Back landings and an unnatural stance on landing were to cause many future injuries. Fallschirmjäger company commander Arnold von Roon likened typical landings to jumping off a low roof. There were invariably wind and oscillation problems, but the 100,000 jumps completed by the Fallschirmjäger by 1939 resulted in only a 2–3 per cent injury rate. Another officer, Alkmar von Hove, believes it was 'safer than driving today', pointing out that as each paratrooper packed his own 'chute, 'who would make a mistake?'

Common to all parachute descents is the sense of relief and ecstatic satisfaction that comes on landing. 'Wonderful – I'm out,' recalled Martin Pöppel, and when he gathered his parachute together on the ground, 'I have a fantastic, indescribable feeling of pleasure, mixed with pride.' Konrad Seibert felt 'terribly thrilled and on top of the world', Karl Pickert 'felt a tremendous relief to be alive'. It was a cocktail of emotions that included well-being and the surge of energy that came as a reaction to the adrenalin rush. In short they felt invincible, a sensation easily translatable to aggressive action and a seemingly tireless initial capacity for dynamic physical effort. This was the genesis of considerable individual fighting power, as yet unappreciated.

The first jump was a thrill but one of many. The primal fear of falling should the parachute not open was always there. 'Enthusiasm faded with the next jumps, even though none of us was prepared to admit it,' admitted Jäger Rudolf Nass. 'We wanted to be heroes.' In the final resort, as Felix Merreys pointed out, 'it was completely up to each man whether he wanted to jump or not.' Everyone was given two chances: 'The ones that did not jump out of the machine the second time, could pack his bags. And so the first jump followed the old Fallschirmjäger adage: "Throw your heart out of the hatch and jump after it."' Six of Merreys' comrades failed to complete the parachute course.

These were indisputably special men, but their full defence potential could not be realised without further experimentation. Early Fallschirmjäger jumped only with pistol and grenades. They had then to find and fight their way to a weapons container, dropped like a bomb from beneath a Junkers 52 in the midst of the stick. Conventional battles would not be won with such lightly armed soldiers, so the army remained unimpressed with the Luftwaffe's progress. It remained a show stunt. There was no tactical concept dealing with practical deployment of parachute troops. A total veil of secrecy had cloaked Russian developments since Hitler came to power and it had been these that had set experiments running. Ironically it was to be the political and diplomatic events of 1936 that were to provide the necessary stimulus to advance airborne developments.

VERTICAL ENVELOPMENT OR CIRCUS STUNTING?

Lufthansa commercial airline pilot Flugkapitän Henke was diverted to Las Palmas airport and on to Tetuan airport in North Africa. On 26 July 1936 he flew a Spanish delegation of officers sent by General Francisco Franco to Berlin to ask Hitler to transport elements of the Army of Africa stationed in Morocco to Spain. An army rebellion had begun in Morocco and civil war had broken out in mainland Spain. The Nationalists had achieved limited success in central Spain and the north. A coup in the southern city of Seville by General Queipo de Llano had created a potential assembly area for Franco's Moroccan divisions to form a base for future offensive operations. The Communist Comintern, an international organisation sponsored by the Soviet Union, agreed to seek volunteers and funds to support the Republican cause. Hitler decided to support Franco's Nationalist request, promising to despatch 20 Junkers Ju-52 transport aircraft.

Flugkapitän Henke flew back to Tetuan, joining nine other machines that were secretly flown in, commanded by Oberleutnant Rudolf Freiherr von Moreau. Moreau's contingent had flown out from Tempelhof airport, Berlin on 31 July with 186 Luftwaffe volunteers in civilian clothing. They were despatched by Air Ministry State Secretary Erhard Milch, whose parting advice was, 'I am sure you will manage this thing.' Political and diplomatic rather than operational considerations were to provide the spur for future German Luftlande (airborne) development time and again during the late 1930s. There were few historical precedents able to provide lessons. Britain had flown imperial troops from Egypt in 1932 to dampen unrest in Baghdad and in 1935 the Russians had transported a division by stages from Moscow to Vladivostok by air.

Oberleutnant Moreau had to improvise as he began to fly General

Milan Astray's Spanish Foreign Legion out of Tetuan. There were no navigational aids. 'Maps don't exist,' he announced to his crews. 'I have made a few calculations on a piece of paper about routes and flight times to Tetuan; apart from that, follow me and land where I land!' HISMA, an acronym for the civilian airline Hispano-Marokkonische Transport AG, began operating between Tetuan and Seville. Its mix of Lufthansa and Luftwaffe employees flew in civilian garb. The rugged tubular steel and corrugated aluminium-skinned Ju-52 former airliners powered by three 660 hp engines proved exceptionally reliable, and one of the few airframes capable of under-taking such a mission at that time. Up to five one-hour flights were achieved each day. The aircraft had an 800-mile range.

It was a unique operation. Many of the Moroccan troops had never even seen an aeroplane. Cabin room for 12 to 14 civilian passengers was expanded by stripping out the seats and packing them with up to 42 soldiers, crammed knee to knee with rifles between their feet. Ammunition and equipment was stowed in the freight space. Flights were short but aircraft had to be hosed through with water after each sortie because the Legion proved to be fragile travellers.

Crews soon reported that every warship in the Republican Navy appeared to be lurking beneath as they flew the Straits of Gibraltar and flak opposition began to intensify. The battle cruiser *Jaime I*, fitted with anti-aircraft batteries and 31.5cm guns able to menace Tetuan airport, proved particularly troublesome and had to be confronted. Vertical bomb magazines were improvised on two of the Junkers transports and these, flown by Moreau and Henke, attacked the ship on 13 August. Ironically the Luftwaffe's Oberleutnant Moreau missed, while airliner pilot Henke managed two hits with SC250 bombs flying through vicious flak at 500 metres. Badly damaged, the *Jaime I* suffered heavy loss of life and had to be towed into Cartagena.

By 15 September the first strategic air-land operation in history was over. Over 12,500 soldiers, 35 field howitzers, 100 heavy machine guns and 134 tons of ammunition were flown into Seville. The Army of Africa was to break out of this assembly area and begin to advance on the capital Madrid from the south. The air-land concept had transitioned from landing single agents behind enemy lines to trans-porting army elements at the operational level.

Technology in the evolution of battle can often remain one step ahead of ideas. The German Army finally acknowledged an interest in airborne operations when it formed its first parachute infantry battalion in April 1937. During the traditional autumn manoeuvres on Mecklenberg Training Area an infantry company jumped to practise blocking a defile before being relieved by ground troops. The Luftwaffe General Göring Regiment dropped 14 squads of sabotage troops. 'In those days it was not clear how parachute operations should be planned,' recalled Oberleutnant J. Paul. They trained for sabotage missions as small unit raiders. 'So we learnt how to drive trams and locomotive engines, planning both in practice and during theoretical exercises how to destroy important communications and logistic installations.' During the Anschluss Wehrmacht occupation of Austria in March 1938 the IV Company of the General Göring Regiment air-landed at Graz airport. Both the Luftwaffe and Heer (army) expanded their contingents while following different tactical concepts in parallel. On 1 April 1938 the 1st Battalion of Fallschirmjäger Regiment 1 was established under one of its pioneers Oberstleutnant (Lieutenant Colonel) Bruno Brauer, while two months later the Heer Company was expanded to battalion size under Major Heidrich. Both battalions joined in July within a single Luftwaffe regiment to form the core of an envisaged airborne division to be commanded by Generalmajor Kurt Student. This rationalisation meant a single Luftlande or airborne concept would now emerge under the Luftwaffe.

Hauptman (Captain) Heinz Trettner was the operations officer (Ia) of the newly forming division. 'Vertical envelopment', he claimed, stemmed from the example of mass Russian parachute drops in the 1930s and the German air-land experience at the start of the Spanish Civil War. Three tactical options had to be reconciled. Were the new troops to be employed as raiders behind enemy lines, as advance units ahead of ground troops to secure key objectives and then link-up, or should they conduct independent 'operational level air landings'? Student, the new division commander, favoured the latter option: 'operations carried out by larger self-sufficient units behind the enemy front out of direct contact with ground forces'. This would require a division of three regiments, one of paratroopers and two of airborne or air-land infantry. From the start it was appreciated that for such a force to succeed alone they would have to be unusually self-sufficient, adaptable and aggressive soldiers capable of considerable initiative. Sky Men would need to be specially selected.

Another imperative driving organisational development was the rapidly deteriorating political situation caused by German designs on the Czech-Sudetenland. Hitler's desire to incorporate its ethnic Germans within the Reich climaxed in the Munich Crisis of September 1938, threatening a general European war. Hitler had briefly viewed para-troopers during the 1937 autumn manoeuvres at Mecklenburg and, seeing the potential, had encouraged further systematic development. General Student, tasked with this, was summoned to Berlin on 4 July. Oberstleutnant Bassenge, overseeing the expansion of the parachute school at Stendal, recalled the background to the summons: 'For the planned "liberation" of the Sudetenland it was necessary to break open the frontier fortifications as quickly as possible. The intention was to land strong airborne forces behind the line of fortifications in order to take them from the rear . . . It was a difficult task for a beginning, particularly since the new division had to be set up in a few weeks.'

The trained manpower was not in place; there were about 1,200 qualified paratroopers within the only Fallschirmjäger regiment but no air-land infantry. The army handed Infantry Regiment 16 to Student for tactical and air training but there needed to be a third. Heinz Trettner, Student's operations officer, recalled, 'we were helped by an unusual idea.' Göring took the Sturm Abteilung (SA) ceremonial regiment, the Feldherrnhalle, and transferred them without further ado into the Luftwaffe. Bassenge, tasked with sorting this out, dryly observed the newly pressed Feldherrnhalle soldiers 'were much more interested in the question of their future status than in their purely military obligations'. These were the Brown Shirts who carried the mass Nazi regalia and flags at Nuremburg party rallies. Göring was their honorary commander. They 'strove for a double position' in the Luftwaffe, Bassenge recalled. 'They should be an active unit in the German Air Force with fixed pay, right of pension, insignia and so on' and remain a party political formation. They sought both their cake and to eat it while operational urgencies beckoned.

The necessary flying units were attached to the new division and after an accelerated training programme Student declared it ready for action on 1 September 1938. Labelled the 7th Flieger (Air) Division for deception, the unit was an ad hoc creation to complete the specific task in hand and would be disbanded thereafter. Student appreciated his future, ironically, depended upon hostilities breaking out with Czechoslovakia. The mission was to vertically envelop the rear of the Czech defences near the Goldoppa stream, to create a gap so that Wehrmacht ground units could break into the Bohemian-Moravian basin. Army and Luftwaffe critics viewed the daring plan with scepticism; only a successful deployment would win them over.

Martin Pöppel saw the force take off with some frustration because he was still under training. 'Some hundred Jus, or Junkers aircraft, were due to set off and take our 1st Parachute Regiment for immediate service in Czechoslovakia,' he recalled, having noticed a perceptible thinning of the regular soldiers around barracks. 'The fact that we "boys" aren't allowed to go is the biggest load of shit this century, there's only a month to go before we finish training and then we'd have been there – shit and damnation!' he moaned. Despondently they watched the aircraft go 'with genuine anger and tears as the machines took off and flew in formation'.

Fifth column assistance was employed in support. Photographs passed to Ju–52 pilots due to air-land revealed rows of poplar trees and ditches hindering Landing Sites I and II near Freuden in the Sudetenland. Oberleutnant von Roon, who later accompanied Student around these landing sites, remembered that trees were felled and ditches filled in 'through sympathetic farmers of German origin, including one of the landowners, organised by German intelligence'. British Prime Minister Chamberlain's diplomatic appeasement policy resolved the crisis peacefully, but Student, with all his resources in place, was allowed to land the first wave as a trial.

Swarms of Ju–52 air transport aircraft bobbed and wheeled like huge gulls with outstretched wings as they descended on the rough landing strips, fields and hillsides around the Freuden valley. Göring witnessed part of the massive fly-in when 250 aircraft landed 3,000 men on 7 October 1938. Visibly impressed and excited, he watched planeloads of troops being disgorged and quickly move off the landing sites, many towing trolleys loaded with heavy equipments or wheeling bicycles. One after the other the huge aircraft swooped in, feathering their engines, seeking landing points as they descended. They came down occasionally in pairs, leaving engines running for the unload before accelerating and lifting away again with a surge of power.

The operation, conducted with no local airfields, was unprecedented. Twelve aircraft were so badly battered on landing they had to be dismantled and carried out by lorry. Bassenge, well used to witnessing such activity, laconically remarked, 'this completely insignificant demonstration won over the C-in-C spontaneously to such a degree that in emphasising the importance of this "new method" he told Student that he was going to form an airborne corps immediately and make him commander of it.' Little of substance followed the effusive praise, but at least the future of Student's division was now assured. A second Fallschirmjäger Regiment 2 was formed; an anti-tank company attached to the 1st Regiment and further division support service units created. Command of all parachute and airborne troops was vested in the Luftwaffe at the end of 1938 while the army continued air transport experimentation with Infantry Regiment 16 and the 22nd Infantry Division. When six months later the rest of Czechoslovakia was occupied on 15 March 1939, Fallschirmjäger were air-landed at Prague airport.

By 1939 the secretly formed and trained 7th Flieger Division numbered 3,200 qualified parachutists in two regiments. Stendal parachute school expanded to 12 training companies with 180 parachute instructors able to throughput 4,000 paratroopers each year. Hitler unveiled them to the German public for the first time at his 20 April birthday parade in Berlin. Fallschirmjäger Regiment 1 marched past wearing their distinctively shaped helmets and parachute harnesses. The crowd roared its appreciation as an impressive phalanx of troopers with slung rifles and fixed bayonets goose-stepped past. They were the talk of Berlin that night. Military attachés observing the parade took note, as did the ladies of Berlin. 'I had no girlfriend,' explained Jäger Karl Pickert, 'but I can tell you that once you had some of the right sort of badges and insignia, one became popular with them.'

These developments provided a stark contrast to the development of other airborne forces in Europe. British sceptics felt the concept would never fly, apart from a few raids if faced with determined air opposition. Major General Wavell, who watched the Kiev drop, remarked it had taken the Soviets more than one and half hours to assemble. It hardly appeared worth the effort. One isolated article did appear in the *Journal of the Royal United Services Institute* in the summer of 1935. 'Winged Armies', written by the British military attaché in Warsaw, Major J.T. Godfrey RE, saw some relevance for the Russian model within the Middle East, as a possible British imperial strategic reserve. He had witnessed small scale Polish developments. Posters appeared all over Poland in 1936 calling *Youth to the Parachutes!* as in Russia earlier. Seventeen parachute towers were erected by 1939 and an experimental airborne platoon set up in 1938. Parachute courses were initiated for officers and NCOs primarily as a character-forming activity. Nations began to realise that parachuting could instil precisely the sort of martial kudos they sought for their own elite units.

Parachuting was still regarded in many circles as a show stunt with some military relevance as a life-saver for pilots in extremis. British Royal Air Force understated humour held that no sane man would wish to exit from a perfectly serviceable aircraft. Parachute instructor Harry Ward, tiring of the poor financial rewards offered by the RAF, retired in 1929 but still sought the thrill that came with demonstration jumping. While driving London buses he 'made his number known to do the odd exhibition jump', for which he earned £10. 'I was really in the money in those days!' he claimed. Driving solid tyre London buses 'skidding sideways down Cheapside' on wet roads sticky with manure from horse-drawn traffic was scarier than the easy money he made from demonstration jumping. By 1937 he had made 2,000 drops, mainly with the Russell Lobe parachute, which he considered superior to the oscillation-prone Irvin type.

Ward remembered an incident jumping for British hospitals air pageants from a typically low military altitude. 'I left the kite at 1,000 feet,' he recalled, 'because the public liked to see you get out.' What followed was commonplace to many a military parachutist:

I left at 1,000 feet, ripped [pulled the rip-cord] at about 700, and the thing turned inside out. I was coming down at a rate of knots – spiralling down – and I thought, well, if I land feet first, I'm going to kill myself. So, watching the ground racing up towards me, I took a grip of the lift web, and just as I thought I would touch down, I swung my whole body sideways, and took the heavy fall on my right buttock and shoulder. At the shock of landing I passed out for a minute or two but I certainly saved my life by doing that. If I had landed feet first I would have broken my back.

The popular British *Picture Post* magazine mocked the German parachute arm in a February 1939 article. 'The latest gambit of the Nazi Air Ministry is the organization of parachute regiments,' it read. 'This presumably is to impress its own people with the sterling courage of the members.' The magazine personified the prevailing official British view, that 'it impresses no strategist, no tactician'. Nigel Tangye, its correspondent, observed the mission of such regiments was to drop behind enemy lines to harass from the rear: 'The trouble for the parachutists will start when they come floating down an easy prey to the rifles of those beneath. Assume there are no rifles: they will find it extremely difficult to form up on strange ground. And then, suppose they do manage to form up, their activities are confined to the limits of ammunition they will have brought with them. When these are exhausted they have no recourse but to surrender.' Such media savvy was of course appealing to a Europe clearly edging toward war. 'The British Air Ministry is not wasting time on such play activity,' *Picture Post* readers were assured.

The French established their parachute training school at Avignon in October 1935, following Russian instruction. An experimental two-company force of Infanterie de l'Air, the 601st and 602nd, were set up in April 1937. The Italians, who had jumped a platoon in 1927 – before the Russians – opened a jump school at Tripoli in Libya, and another at Tarquinia in Italy the following year. Parachute training at Castel Benito in 1939 cost 15 dead and 72 seriously injured before leading to the disbandment of the thoroughly shaken 2nd Libyan Parachute Battalion, which was entirely replaced with Italian volunteers.

The Fallschirmjäger march-past at Hitler's 1939 birthday parade prompted a spate of military attaché reporting. General George C. Marshall, the US Chief of Staff, responded by directing his Chief of Infantry to make a study of 'Air Infantry' ten days later on 1 May 1939. The conundrum was to decide whether they should be raiders or pre-advance dropped units capturing key objectives ahead of advancing ground forces. It was accepted such units would likely be small and lightly equipped and would require 'a considerable amount of athletic drill, utilisation of parachutes, demolitions and exercises'. Despite detailed study, shortages of transport aircraft and the low priority the project attracted meant there was no action for seven months.

Vertical envelopment beyond raids was in effect fantasy until technology could deliver the heavy equipments needed to support parachutists. German Army scepticism was well founded. Experiments were tried to suspend 75mm light artillery mountain guns beneath a cluster of five parachutes, but once on the ground they remained frustratingly immobile. Dogs and small horses were harnessed to them to no practical effect. Fallschirmjäger officer Arnold von Roon remembered that 'trying to calm a wild pony within the narrow confines of the freight compartment of a Ju-52 required some nerve, and the horse handlers were not to be envied'. By 1937 serious consideration turned to gliders.

German gliding sport had developed in the early 1920s within an atmosphere of national frustration over aviation limitations imposed by the post-World War One Treaty of Versailles. The great expansion of sail-plane clubs came about in part through a secret Reichwehr-Luftwaffe instigation, before the Nazis took over in 1933 and began to organise clubs on military lines. 'First, we will teach gliding as a sport to all our young men,' Göring had confided, 'then we will build up commercial aviation. Finally, we will create the skeleton of a military air force.' He added, 'When the time comes, we will put all three together – and the German Empire will be reborn.' The former Allies began to discern this sinister intent following remilitarisation after 1933. By 1936 Göring was addressing 1,000 young Luftwaffe lieutenants in Berlin with the words: 'You will one day be my corps of vengeance.'

New aviation technology was as attractive to the young in the 1930s as digital technology is today. The National Socialist regime kept perceptively in step. 'Strongly impressed by the Nazis' propaganda and spurred on by a strong desire to become a pilot, I started to collect and read all the aviation articles I could find,' remembered future Fallschirmjäger K. Räbel. Encouraged by the Flieger-Hitlerjugend, the flying arm of the Hitler Youth, he made 20 glider flights. 'My enthusiasm had soared to undreamed-of heights,' he reflected, the 'next best thing to Heaven!' Räbel's desire to become a pilot, despite passing all the exams, was unfulfilled. Like many disappointed would-be Luftwaffe pilots, he was encouraged to join the paratroops. 'They had no trouble convincing me,' he claimed, 'without hesitating I agreed to serving with this fighting unit.' Many therefore joined with glider flying experience.

Glider training, like all Hitler Youth activities, was about 'comradely cooperation' as pointed out by *Der Adler* (The Eagle), one of the popular aviation magazines that Räbel read. Groups of learner glider pilots pushed and shoved their machines onto the launch overhangs of the popular Rhön Valley or Wasserkuppe mountains south-east of Fulda. 'I was interested in gliding,' declared paratrooper Robert Frettlohr, 'and there was no better opportunity than to learn to glide with the Hitler Youth.' He compared it to the air force cadets in England today. This pseudo-military aviation training developed self-confidence and after a dozen or so launches physical stamina, because 'by evening', as one *Der Adler* article described it, 'they know what they have done!' Glider launches required maximum team strength and effort to launch flyers who, once aloft, had to apply courage, coordination and dexterity to successfully complete their flights. 'It makes something of you,' declared Frettlohr. 'You were not just running around like some of the youth today. You had an aim to do something. You had your friends and you went around *doing* things.'

'Germany seeks to rule the air as Britannia rules the waves,' trumpeted the magazine. German glider flying associations boasted 50,000 members by 1932, with schools established at Rossiten in East Prussia, Dörnberg near Kassel and Syat in Westerland. The Hitler Youth was providing a future reservoir of sky soldiers, varying from aircrew and assault glider pilots to Fallschirmjäger.

Civilian gliders or sail planes were designed to soar and seek thrills within a fragile frame, not carry cargo. Yet the capability appeared logically transferable. The British *Daily Mail* newspaper offered a £1,000 prize in 1931 for the first glider to fly the English Channel both ways. Although a German won the competition, there was huge interest in the flight of the *Barbara Cartland*, named after the novelist and pilot, which was towed aloft by a powered aircraft for the first time. Releasing at height enabled long distances to be traversed across the ground. 'This seemed to me to be an excellent and cheap proposition for commercial flying,' recalled Barbara Cartland. Her stunt was to deliver air mail from Manston aerodrome to Reading. 'We rose slowly,' she remembered, on a perfectly calm and sunny day. Her tow pilot Flying Officer Wanliss was 'extremely anxious' as it had been suggested that weight at the back of the glider might cause it to turn turtle, but it did not. Instead: 'We sailed smoothly across the green face of England. A cricket match was stopped to wave to us as we passed, golfers stared at us from the fairways of famous courses, the world was very beautiful and we were excited at what we were achieving.'

The stunt was successful and air mail delivered over 100 miles by glider. The *Barbara Cartland* also won a race, outstripping a railway steam express, carrying a passenger from London to Blackpool. 'I think a new epoch in air travel has begun,' remarked German commentator Herr Kronfield. The British Air Ministry did not think so. On the contrary, tow-gliding was condemned as too dangerous and stopped, but the gem of a strategic idea had been sown in the Reich.

In 1933 the Rhön-Rossiten Gesellschaft Research Institute opted to design and build an enlarged glider capable of carrying a meteorological laboratory manned by scientists and technicians. They produced an ugly duck variant with short stubby wings more akin to a transport aircraft without a propeller, rather than a sleek sports glider. The 'flying observatory', as it was called, was committed due to its loaded weight and design to descend over distance rather than soar for height. Luftwaffe General Ernst Udet spotted it on an inspection visit and recognised its potential military application. It could be a re-supply vehicle or 'Trojan Horse', he thought, able to land soldiers unnoticed behind enemy lines.

Three gliders released above the annual Nuremberg Nazi party rally festivities in 1936 drew awed attention and spontaneous applause from the stands. Skimming the tops of the audience, they dramatically dived into the demonstration bowl before gracefully coming to rest in formation before the greatly surprised Hitler's viewing box. Shortly after Hitler met Professor Georgie, the Head of the German Research Institute for Gliding, who was told to task his flight construction manager Hans Jacobs to see whether gliders might be deployed in a military role. 'This question naturally came as a great surprise to me,' confessed Jacobs later.

'Up until then we had only developed various types of civilian gliders so it was difficult for me to answer the question.' He set to work applying the prevailing technology and after much thought concluded: 'A glider towed at a height of 2,000 to 3,000 metres can, with a gliding angle of 1 in 18, fly silently for 10 kilometres inside enemy territory; all this in morning twilight so that the plane cannot be seen. With this the basic idea for developing such an aeroplane was born.'

The DFS ten-seater glider came from trials in 1937. The interminable dilemma – how to deliver heavy equipments alongside the Fallschirmjäger – seemed potentially solved. The 'flying observatory' transitioned to the so-called 'sticking-plaster bomber'. Not only could loads in excess of one ton be flown, but ten soldiers could land together. Indeed the production price of the DFS glider was based on the premise that each aircraft should not exceed the cost of ten parachutes.

The potential of the glider capability was kept secret; none were ever flown on army manoeuvres. But as is often the case with technological innovation, progress could be stymied by bureaucratic inertia. General Hans Jeschonnek, the Luftwaffe Chief of Operations Staff, was supportive, and explained to a surprised Student shortly before he took over the 7th Flieger Division that 'nobody gives a damn for the new glider'. Student did not even know a secret glider programme was in progress. 'The best thing that could happen is if you would take it under your personal wing,' Jeschonnek confided, 'otherwise the whole damn thing will lie dormant.' As far as Student was concerned this was manna from Heaven: gliders opened up the possibility of independent airborne operations for the first time in history. He gladly took on the sticking-plast bomber which transitioned to the DFS-230 attack glider. Concern over inertia was, however, unfounded, because the attack glider idea unveiled at Nuremberg was indelibly etched on Hitler's memory.

'It happened very quickly,' recalled Jäger Martin Pöppel, now with the signals platoon of the 1st Battalion Fallschirmjäger Regiment 1. 'On 1 September the alarm came: pack rucksacks, arm weapons containers, deal with your private affairs, be ready.' Europe was going to war again. After a succession of crises the Wehrmacht invaded Poland. Hitler's bluff was called by the western Allies and Britain and France declared war on 3 September 1939. Pöppel, standing by at an operational airfield at Liegnitz, recalled, 'the more we heard about the advances by our soldiers the more restless we got'. German *Blitzkrieg*, or Lightning War, conducted at panzer tempo meant Pöppel and his comrades might not even get into the war before it was over. 'That would be unbearable,' he reflected. They were warned off for a parachute assault the next morning. 'We all beamed and hugged each other,' he recalled, but when morning came, 'we learned that the operation had been postponed because our armoured units, our panzers, were already breaking through to Warsaw and we weren't needed.' The objective had been Posen. Aircraft were disarmed and radio transmitters taken off. 'It was enough to drive you crazy,' he complained.

The next alert came with no warning at 2300 hours a few days later. 'Everything was packed again,' recalled Pöppel, 'and the barracks and sick-bays cleaned.' A bridge at Pulawy, south-east of Warsaw, had to be captured to cut off the retreating Poles. Leutnant Arnold von Roon recalled 'a Fallschirmjäger battalion was already sitting in its aeroplanes ready to take off for this mission', which was aborted; as also another mission to reinforce an army bridgehead across the San River at Jaroslaw. Pöppel's unit instead left by lorry and was re-employed to remove military booty before the Russians who had entered Poland from the east took over their zone. Only two minor ground actions were fought by the paratroopers. 'The truth was,' declared Pöppel, 'we never got the chance to be heroes in Poland,' it was 'back to barracks and room 9'. Total frustration and glum resignation reigned. 'We were the ace of trumps of the German Wehrmacht,' recalled the disappointed Pöppel, 'but we hadn't been allowed to prove ourselves in battle.'

In London Major J.C.F. Holland, heading Military Intelligence Research (MIR), suggested to the War Office that an experimental parachute establishment should perhaps be set up, so that if paratroopers were needed later 'we should know a little about the technical difficulties of dropping men and arms'. Holland was at the time researching irregular warfare. As he recalled: 'it went all the way up to C.I.9.S General Ironside, and came back minuted with his own handwriting, which read: *I'm not going to ask Englishmen to do that.*' There was no follow-up by the dubious War Office. Nevertheless, within six months Holland would have all the convincing information he needed.

3

THEORY INTO PRACTICE:
THE LOW COUNTRIES, MAY 1940

SCANDINAVIAN PRELUDE, 9 APRIL 1940

On 7 April 1940 Fallschirmjäger Hauptmann Walther Gericke, languishing in his modest officer's garrison flat in Stendal, Berlin, was summoned to Hamburg at no notice. *Sitzkrieg* or 'Phoney War' had characterised operations in western Europe since the invasion of Poland the previous September. This was about to change on the northern flank. Gericke flew in and was transported to a hotel and immediately engaged in discussion. 'They wanted to know if I believe I can take the bridge connecting Falster and Sealand [in Denmark] intact with one parachute company; and hold it until relieved by German infantry, which would be disembarking at Gedser.' Gericke, appreciating this was likely the first chance for action in this war, predictably said yes, at which point 'one could hear a load fall off the chests of the assembled generals'.

The first parachute raid of the war was directed against the Storström four-kilometre long railway bridge in Denmark. All Gericke had for intelligence was a civilian road map and a picture postcard with scribbled information noting it was 26 metres above the water and that each of the 51 bridge supports were 140 metres apart. It was decided to attack it from two small platoon drop zones nominated at either end; Gericke's third platoon would capture Aalborg airport nearby.

Twelve Ju-52 transport planes flew low-level, hugging the sea, toward their objective on 9 April 1940. 'Then suddenly a light appears,' Gericke recalled, 'it is the Danish coastline . . . Flares go off. The island is on the left. The sun rises as a red ball of fire, and its beams are reflected on the wings of the grey planes. Now the sea also shines. The first fishing boats can already be seen. A giant railway bridge, which connects two islands, shows that our objective is not far away.'

There was little room for error when the platoons jumped. Strong winds carried most of the weapons containers too far away. The men sprinted toward the bridge from both sides armed with just pistols and grenades. Inside the fort on the central island, which had batteries of 120mm and 37mm guns manned by 225 marines during the First World War, there was only a civilian janitor and two conscript marines. They confronted the paratroopers, mouths agape, armed with two ancient Remingtons but no ammunition. Gericke recalled they came out 'knees trembling, surprise and fear mirrored in their faces'. Bicycles were immediately commandeered from a nearby farmhouse and the bridge rapidly traversed. By the time the Danish conscripts had gathered together to mount a counter-attack from the garrison town of Vordingborgon on the north bank, the Danish government had surrendered. Operation Weserübung, the occupation of Denmark and Norway, was under way.

Theo Krupp with the 3rd Company of Fallschirmjäger Regiment 1 (FJR 1), flying toward Sola airport off Stavanger in Norway, had, like Gericke, taken off from Uetersen airport at Hamburg. 'We have already been sitting in the coffin for three hours,' he recalled. 'It is awfully cold. The fog won't go away, and we get into a shower of rain.' There were fears that accompanying aircraft had already gone missing in the poor visibility. Peering out the window he saw: 'The pilots descend even more. We get out of the fog. On the horizon small dots appear. Is that supposed to be the coast? Yes – Norway! The peaks of the mountains are covered in snow. The lakes are in fact still frozen.'

In total contrast to the weather they had left behind in Germany, spring had yet to break in Norway. As they descended toward Sola airport people waved to the aircraft, while others threw themselves to the ground. 'Are we going to meet so light opposition?' he thought. Klaxon horns sounded as they began parachuting from their aircraft at 1000 hours. Within 35 minutes the airport was in German hands following a short fire fight.

Escorted by Messerschmitt 110 fighter aircraft, Junkers 52 transports carrying Hauptmann Erich Walther's battalion staff and 2nd Company were groping their way through a thick fog 600 metres high to Fornebu airport outside Oslo. A row broke out between the Luftwaffe commander Oberstleutnant Drewes and Walther, still smarting from missing the Polish campaign, when they were told to 'return due to bad weather'. Oberleutnant Schmidt, one of the company commanders, was also incensed. 'The weather was killing us!' he complained. With the Norwegian mountains tantalisingly in sight poking through the fog, all but three Ju-52s turned back to the newly captured Aaborg airport in Denmark. 'An ice-cold silence set in,' recalled Schmidt. 'Disappointment was spreading to all faces. What was the point of it? Everybody wanted to shout *It can't be true!*'

Air-launched operations were proving as unpredictable as the weather they were required to overcome. Hauptmann Richard Wagner approached Fornebu with a follow-on stream of Ju-52 transports carrying the second wave, with the 2nd Battalion of Infantry Regiment 324, scheduled to air-land. He ignored the return order because he thought the weather was clearing slightly. Returning Ju-52s were also tipping their wings at him as if to signal all was OK. His 53 planes continued on, overflying the newly sunken German heavy cruiser *Blücher* capsized in the Oslo Fiord. Soon their 60 aircraft were circling the sky over the small airfield. Thirty minutes before, solitary Ju-52s had dropped Oberleutnant Wilhelm Götte with nine NCOs and six men. They knocked out a Norwegian searchlight platoon and two machine guns. Wagner's congested stream circling above was in an untenable situation. They had to land and Wagner came in first. On the approach the corrugated sides of his fuselage were violently punched open by 40mm gunfire. Wagner was killed alongside four soldiers and, with the aircraft still banging and thumping under the colossal impacts, it took off again. The second plane landed under fire and its occupants baled out near the cliffs at the western side of the airfield fortuitously secured by Götte.

In one of those bizarre circumstances of war the escorting Me 110 Zerstörer fighter aircraft had to land, having run out of fuel. They taxied around in a wagon-circle for protection, shooting out at ground targets with cannon and rear cockpit-mounted swivel machine guns. As more and more Ju-52s made emergency landings Norwegian defenders were forced to thin out under increasingly heavy aircraft and paratrooper fire. There were surprisingly few Norwegian troops in Oslo.

Walther returned with the 2nd Company and by 1700 they were driving into Oslo in a column of requisitioned civilian buses, trucks and cars. Link-ups were achieved with the sea-landed forces. Presently a military brass band was put together and marched into the city at the head of a suspiciously thin column of German troops. Bluff, surprise and subterfuge, matched with ruthless aggression if opposed, won the day. The 2nd Company quickly disarmed Norwegian units taken by surprise en route. One Norwegian officer offering resistance was promptly shot dead.

Five days later Oberleutnant Schmidt's 1st Company FJR 1 was dropped in the Gudbrandsalen Valley at Dombas 95 miles north of Oslo with 65 men to prevent a link-up of British and Norwegian troops. They were, however, heavily outnumbered and were fought virtually to extinction by 14 April in the frozen snow-covered valley. Thirty-four survivors surrendered when they ran out of ammunition. The following month more paratroopers were dropped at Narvik to reinforce soldiers cut off from the 3rd Gebirgsjäger (Mountain) Division. Jäger Karl Pickert, whose aircraft had initially been turned back by fog, summed up the general opinion of the operation, declaring it was all 'very experimental'. Lessons were emerging. 'First of all, the weather was always a very big factor and secondly, the enemy had to be taken by surprise, otherwise disaster could occur.'

Committing limited airborne forces to the occupation of Scandinavia had not been to General Student's taste. Dropping isolated companies of paratroopers to unlock airfields for a second wave of air-land troops was successful, but in Student's view gave too much warning of his capabilities to potential adversaries in western Europe. Hitler simply overruled him. The Dutch in particular began to fortify their airfields and mobilise vehicles to drive onto and block runways in anticipation of similar tactics in the future.

Student need not have worried. Allied complacency over their much-vaunted static Maginot defence line meant there were more than enough anti-air defences and quick reaction forces to deal with parachute raids. Nobody could conceive of anything greater than the coup de main limited assaults that had been seen in Norway and Denmark. Ironically, allied senior commanders were as sceptical as their Wehrmacht counterparts. Generaloberst von Brauchitsch, the German Chief of Staff, had witnessed a disappointing air-land performance by the 22nd Air Land Division during manoeuvres in June 1937. He shared his uncharitable viewpoint with Student, tasked to build up airborne capability, insisting he had witnessed a 'drip-landing', not an operational flow, and in his view airborne operations remained a 'Kindergarten' aspiration, unsuited to supporting ground operations at the operational level. Student remonstrated but was dismissed out of hand as a 'huge optimist'. Nevertheless, Fallschirmjäger 'dummy-dolls' dropped in the rear areas of ground formations during the next large exercise in July created mayhem, enabling real paratroopers to capture a senior headquarters.

Allied commanders viewing the German airborne capability demonstrated in Scandinavia anticipated what they thought they had viewed during Hitler's birthday parade in 1939, namely company level operations, little beyond battalion level. Apart from judiciously reinforcing airfields, they had no comprehension of the division-size force that could materialise from thin air. Operation Gelb (Yellow), the assault in the west, was not a traditional military stroke. It was more akin to the bluffing and bewildering diplomatic approach that Hitler had conducted against irresolute opponents, beginning with the re-occupation of the Rhineland in 1936 up to the invasion of Czechoslovakia in 1938–9. Everything turned on calculating the likely enemy reaction. The assault on the Low Countries through Luxembourg, Belgium and Holland was to be unlocked from inside by the 7th Flieger Division. Student was to launch 4,500 highly trained paratroopers to secure landing sites and bridges, reinforced by 12,000 air-transported infantry from Generalleutnant Graf Sponeck's 22nd Air-land Division. The essence of the attack would be speed, surprise and disruption: occupy key defences with German paratroopers before the enemy can get there.

The Dutch defence was based on their previous 1918 concept of defending on the border until retiring into the heartland of 'Fortress Holland', protected by innumerable canals and water courses. The demolition of some half-dozen key bridges provided the modern equivalent of pulling up the drawbridge of a medieval castle. The German plan was to seize these bridges spanning the great waterways of the Rhine delta. They were the great road and rail bridges at

Moerdijk across the River Maas, Dordrecht across the Old Maas and the third great waterway spanning the New Maas in the built-up area on the southern edge of Rotterdam. This 'airborne carpet' would be laid by the Fallschirmjäger regiments of the 7th Flieger Division broadly east-west and then north-west.

The political task of capturing the Queen of the Netherlands and her government at The Hague was given to General Sponeck. Two parachute battalions were to capture the airfields that formed a triangle around The Hague at Valkenburg, Ypenburg and Ockenburg, giving control of the three motorways that led into the city. Two regiments of air-land infantry would land on these airfields. Waalhaven airfield to the south of Rotterdam formed part of a bridgehead to push units north into Rotterdam, relieve initial coup de main attacks and support the airborne corridor covering the bridges coming up via Moerdijk and Dordrecht from Antwerp. The initial jumping-off point for the ground force spearheaded by 61st Division was the Albert Canal. Three bridges at Veldwezelt, Vroenhoven and Canne had to be captured, all protected by the massive Belgian fortress at Fort Eben Emael.

The scale of this combined airborne operation with battalions of parachute, glider and air-land infantry regiments was unprecedented. For the first time airborne theory was to be put into practice at the operational level. Divisions were to fly in from the air to independently fight ground operations until relieved by advancing forces.

AERIAL BREAK-IN: THE LOW COUNTRIES, 10 MAY 1940

Mounting an airborne operation is a highly complex and technically demanding task calling for precise staff work. Civilian travellers are aware of the enormous effort required to despatch waves of passengers from international airports during public holidays. They are aided by a digital computerised technology unavailable in 1940. The 4,500 paratroopers and 12,000 air-land infantry from the 7th Flieger and 22nd Air-land Divisions had to be gathered and organised from mounting airfields in Westphalia around Paderborn, Munster and Cologne. Accommodation was so crowded that paratroopers camped on hangar stone floors while the laborious process of allocating groups of ten Fallschirmjäger or 15 air-land infantry to respective aircraft was worked out. Parachutes had to be drawn and aircraft loaded and fitted for task. Final orders and practical rehearsals were conducted on the grass surrounds around hangars while the Luftwaffe laboriously calculated routes, distances and fuel, and men and equipment ratios against take-off loads. The flight plan had to mirror the tactical needs of the ground action plan. The requirement to load, prepare and check orders with the uncertainty of pending combat took its toll on physical and mental reserves. Troops would be exhausted before they even landed.

Gefreiter Wilhelm Alefs with the seventh glider squad about to assault Eben Emael, code-name Granit, was constantly on edge. He was listening out for the hangar bell or whistle that would call them forward for action. 'If it was possible for tension to increase daily, then it did,' he remarked. He could not tell if his comrades were 'numbed by tenseness, were imperturbable, or just completely relaxed, content with what fate promised'. Leutnant Rudolf Witzig, his commander, recalled, 'the mood of our soldiers was serious and composed, we weren't noisy, everyone was aware of what he was facing now.' Alefs slept fitfully and, dreaming incessantly, 'woke in terror, but I would not tell my comrades, since they seemed unafraid'. Their glider assault mission was top secret. Two soldiers who had carelessly compromised the task were under sentence of death. Witzig, like all the other commanders, was completely immersed in the detail of getting everything ready for the operation. 'We were told when we would have supper, breakfast, when we would be woken, insofar as everybody was not already awake. When we would be sent out to the aeroplanes, when the transport gliders would be loaded, which had meanwhile already been brought onto the runways at the beginning of the night by the aerodrome staff.'

Their gliders had been delivered in civilian removal vans and assembled in hangars behind barbed wire. Gliders had not been used on any exercises involving other troops. Glider pilot Heiner Lange recalled on reporting to the new unit the previous November: 'that was the first time I saw a Ju-52 on the ground with a DFS-230, a ten-seater glider – I knew nothing of their existence before.'

Hauptmann Karl Lothar Schulz commanding the III Battalion

FJR 1 remembered visiting his sleeping soldiers during the period of enforced rest in the hangars before take-off. Many were too excited to sleep. At 0300 hours whistles blew to rouse the men and the aircraft hangars began to hum with subdued chatter, rising gradually as weapons containers were packed amid shouted directions, ribald jokes and banter-fuelled bravado. Jäger Willi Kammann with FJR 2 remembered paratroopers clambering into the aircraft and sitting opposite each other with 'pockets stuffed full'. Their distinctive so-called 'bone-bag' parachute smocks were designed to cover the equipment and items jammed into their pockets to prevent them falling out during the jump. 'Everything must somehow be taken, from a small bar of soap to rations for several days, pencil to toothbrush. Then came all the military essentials: tarpaulin, ration bag, cooking-set, map cases, binoculars, first-aid pack, water bottle, a few hand grenades in the trousers in the event of an emergency, ammunition in the pockets, knife, compass, steel helmet – they looked like astronauts.'

This 20lb load was tightened in place beneath the parachute harness, which accounted for another 17lb in weight. They were uncomfortably squashed inside narrow Ju-52 fuselages, practically unable to move with a two to three hour flight ahead. Whatever the reception, the jump would be a physical relief.

Wilhelm Alefs recalled things started to happen for the glider squads at about 2030, before the rest of the Fallschirmjäger were awakened. The usual 'guards tramping around the barbed wire were spirited off', they had been under tight security for some time, and this made them feel 'sort of bare'. Feldwebel Heinemann, their squad leader, called them over and said, 'Put on your gear and your insignia and post your last letters. Keep within hearing distance.' Many aeroplanes began to roar overhead, distinguishable from their blue-flashing exhaust signatures against the night sky. Ju-52s were taxiing out of the darkness when at 2130 Witzig gave the order, 'Load-up!' This was almost immediately followed by, 'All out – Return to billets.' Tension and disappointment was mingled with a momentary 'not yet' relaxation interrupted once again by another order to re-assemble at the gliders at 2310. Witzig announced: 'Force Granit will go by glider to land and take a fort in the Belgian's defence system. Ostheim zero hour is 0325. You have your assignment! That is all.'

That left about four and a half hours to kill. Alefs noticed 'something powerful radiated from each man's face'. This was it. 'How some of these men could sleep puzzled me,' he wondered later. 'I had no desire for it in me.'

'Every pilot was allotted to his group of paratroopers,' recalled glider pilot Kurt Pfitzner, due to land alongside one of the Albert Canal bridges. 'They loaded the machine with weapons, ammunition and explosives etc under the watchful eye of the pilot, so that the machine remained air-worthy on account of the weight.' In addition to rifles and machine pistols and other small arms each of the gliders bound for Eben Emael carried an average of five of the new hollow charge prepared explosive sets. There were 28 110lb and a similar number of 25lb charges making up a combined Granit force total of 5 tons of explosives; equating to 110lb for each man in the assault.

The larger charges came in two parts with carrying handles, which could be hastily assembled and then blown in situ. These rudimentary shaped charges were being employed for the first time. The destructive energy of the explosion was designed to be canalised through a molten jet that could penetrate 25cm of steel. The huge shock wave that accompanied the blast could break off metal scabs inside armoured cupolas and produce the sort of damage previously only achievable by heavy siege artillery. So secret was the concept that the assault engineers had only been allowed to practise blowing charges on flat earth. There was no comprehension of the latent power of the devices they carried. General Student had been asked by Hitler whether it was feasible to land gliders on top of Fort Eben Emael because the site resembled a small meadow. He was at first sceptical, but saw the potential if a precision raid could be supported by such lethal explosive technology. Hitler assured him, 'If they can be delivered to the enemy positions, then nothing, nothing can withstand it.'

Shortly after 0300 Wilhelm Alefs woke up with all the commotion around him, someone pushed him and said, 'Get ready!' The glider squads moved out to the dimly illuminated lamps that were set up on stands under the wing of each glider. The airfield started to come to life. 'I could hear a single engine splutter, then another from elsewhere in the gloom,' recalled Alefs and then, 'more and more engines caught and the noise grew in crescendo, towards an ear-splitting thunder.' The soldiers climbed into the dark interiors of the gliders, sitting on the central benches. 'I patted the pockets of my jacket to feel the grenades, then the ones above to see if my machine-pistol ammunition was there, unconscious but reassuring gestures,' recalled Alefs. Everyone did the same as the gliders began to rock, buffeted by the engine back blast, but muffled inside. Engine notes rose and fell amid the scent of high octane exhaust as the Ju-52 tugs taxied ahead in line, powered up, and sped down the runway. 'Suddenly a jerk on the glider forced me backwards,' remembered Alefs. 'There was a jockeying and sloshing motion as the tow rope tightened and swung the glider in behind the straining plane ahead.'

Some 70 Heinkel III bombers belonging to Kampfgeschwader 4 began taking off from the Westphalian airfields of Delmenhorst, Fassberg and Gütersloh. They were due to strike the airfields at Rotterdam and The Hague. Runway lights were only briefly switched on, to illuminate their path. 'One by one, we follow, making blind take-offs into the black night,' recalled Oberleutnant Werner Baumbach, 'assembling in loose formation, guided by the exhaust flames from the aircraft ahead.' They were headed for the dark expanse of the North Sea. 'Formation after formation emerges from the mist which hides the moors of the Ems Estuary.' The intention was to fly parallel with the coast of Holland until opposite The Hague and Rotterdam, then turn inland from the direction of England, to deliver the initial surprise blow before the air landings.

'As we picked up speed, the roller-coaster noise of the wheels, the slapping of the propeller winds against the canvas fuselage' drowned out all other sounds, recalled Alefs. Presently the squeaky-wobbling wheel noises stopped, replaced by 'only the drumming of the wind and a low whistle'. Forty-two DFS gliders towed by Ju-52s rose up from the airfields of Butzweilerhof and Ostheim north-west and east of Cologne and steadily climbed to an altitude of 2,600 metres, heading toward the bridges across the Albert Canal and Fort Eben Emael. They were five minutes ahead of the launch of the ground operation and 35 minutes ahead of the parachute assaults. Ahead lay a steady climb of 45 miles to the envisaged release point just north-west of Aachen, near the Dutch border.

Feldwebel Helmut Wenzel, in charge of the fourth glider squad, recalled all went well until 'a tow plane suddenly flew over us and we ducked involuntarily'. The roar of the passing aircraft caused 'a few doubts about how well the start had gone successfully across the board'. Gefreiter Pilz, steering Leutnant Witzig's glider, lost his tow in the mishap and Witzig and his men turned the air purple as they involuntarily descended, striving to land if possible near Cologne.

The remaining Ju-52s pulling the gliders carried on, blissfully unaware they had lost two gliders en route. Attention was focused on keeping station with the tug ahead illuminated only by its flashing exhaust trail and eight small lights set in a 'V' facing to the rear and cloaked from the ground. A huge bonfire burning at the crossroads near Effern was the first navigational beacon and three miles further west a searchlight beam could be seen piercing the blackness. 'We flew according to a flare path,' recalled Feldwebel Wenzel, 'every 20 kilometres a searchlight had been set up' and the soldiers behind sang out the numbers in rhythm as each beacon was passed. 'At Aachen there were three searchlights,' Wenzel explained, 'and when we were over these three, my trainee pilot Unteroffizier Brautigen broke away.' Glider release was delayed for ten minutes because the Ju-52 stream commander decided they were 1,500 feet too low, which meant another ten minutes climbing beyond the Dutch border. The whole point of release over Germany was to ensure a stealthy glide approach into enemy territory. This was compromised when Dutch tracer spat up and anti-aircraft fire began to boom around Maastricht. Force Granit earmarked to attack Eben Emael had shrunk to 70 men or 80 per cent of the force thought required. At 0415 the gliders, only distinguishable by a low wind-emitting howl, began to descend to their targets.

There were eight small square-shaped apertures on either side of the DFS 230 glider, giving only restricted downward vision. Casting off was the point of no return. Five men and the pilot sat face forward on the central bench and these, with the pilot, would exit through the cockpit window. The four men sitting looking aft where the heavy kit was lashed down would have to get out of the small port door in front of the tail wing. Hermetically sealed within the narrow fuselages, no one relished the prospect of bouncing along the ground on landing with hundreds of pounds of TNT liable to break loose and fly around. Jäger Engelmann, flying with Wenzel, recalled releasing at 2,600 metres: 'It was dawn, and very cold in our glider and its thin fabric skin offered us no protection from the cold.'

On arrival at the release point the Ju-52 glider-towing stream was stretched out at over 40 miles. There was a lurch as the tow rope parted and the separated gliders began to diverge in four directions. Peering through the early morning murk, pilots tried to distinguish the three bridges north and south-west of Maastricht on the Albert Canal and the massive outline of Fort Eben Emael. 'We could see the lights of Maastricht,' to their right, Engelmann recalled, as they made their descent and 'the first tracer bullets appeared in the distance'. The bridges were difficult to pin-point. As the light of day began to play on the luminous waters of the Albert Canal, the easily distinguishable junction of the Meuse, Liege and Albert Canals pointed to the shadowy fort outline. The nine men steeling themselves in the back felt little more than a light cushion of air as they glided the final 20 minutes across 25 kilometres of enemy territory, arriving 800 metres above the fort. Minutes remained before the shock of impact.

Hitler had been visibly impressed by the skill and accuracy of the glider landings he had seen at Nuremberg in 1936, but doing it under fire was not the same. Skilful flying by these champion pilots using low and dead angles of approach neutralised much of the low-level flak directed at them by the stunned Belgian defenders. Hans Distelmeier arrived first and 300 metres too high over the fort. 'There were still none of the other transport gliders to be seen,' he recalled, descending into a stomach-churning full turn at seven metres per second. He lined up on his objective, carrying squad eight from the south. With tracer spitting out at him, 'I rolled the glider from side to side on the approach, so that I was not a steady target.' He had to decelerate from 190 kmph free flight to 90 kmph in order to land, which he did by stalling and dropping into giddying spiral turns to arrest the descent. There were no air brakes, but Distelmeier was lucky and landed unscathed, declaring, 'I wasn't hit and my glider remained whole and spotless, and nobody was injured either.'

'A few observation posts and a flak emplacement suddenly saw the great grey birds just before they landed,' recalled Belgian conscript, Henri Lecluse. 'What could these queer-looking birds be?' One battery deduced they may be German gliders with paratroopers inside because they were unmarked except for small swastikas on the tail wings. 'We still hadn't heard any declaration of war,' Lecluse indignantly remembered, 'it was all so queer.' Figures began jumping out as soon as the gliders were down, but they were so few. 'That couldn't possibly be a German attack,' Lecluse mused.

As they came in the airborne assault pioneers jettisoned the roof hatch and side door and were out 'at the fastest possible speed', recalled Distelmeier. They assaulted Cupola 31. Two engineers scrambled forward carrying 25kg charges which were assembled on the dome and detonated. The resulting explosion was so violent, 'I was actually thrown up in the air' from the lying position, Distelmeier remembered. They were astonished at the 'incredible strength' of the combined charge. 'The whole of the ground around shook.'

Heiner Langer flew in with squad five to attack the casemate and cupola alongside. He too rolled the glider from side to side to dodge hissing and crackling tracer. 'It was somewhat strange,' he recalled, 'when things were coming straight at you, and then at the last moment they veered off to the left or right.' The signature of incoming fire spelt out the direction to the objective. 'I knew exactly where I had to go,' Langer described later, '*there*, where the things were coming from, that was where I had to go.' He came in so low his wing jerked a Belgian machine gun from its socket, which spun the glider violently around right next to the trench. 'They were sitting there,' he recalled, 'and there stood the glider – an absolute egg of a landing!' He pulled back the cockpit, released his straps and dropped inside the trench with two startled enemies, pistol in one hand and knife in the other. 'I may have made a sort of fearful impression,' he blandly commented. Feldwebel Haug, his commander, dropped a grenade in amongst them at the same time, unaware Lange had jumped in. It exploded but neither the paratrooper nor the Belgians were injured and to this day Lange has been unforgiving, condemning Haug's 'stupid act!'

After Feldwebel Helmut Wenzel from the Stürmgruppe Granit had blown an entry into Casemate 19 he carefully felt his way through the smoking inky blackness, finding two dead Belgians in the dark. Suddenly a telephone jangled urgently behind him. 'I have to say,' the German Fallschirmjäger later admitted, 'that was the first time I was really shaken on Eben Emael.' He used his torch to find the telephone tucked into a wall niche. At the other end a terribly agitated voice was gabbling in French. He could not understand but once he detected a pause he responded in halting English, stating calmly and emphatically that 'Hier are the Germans!' '*Oh mon Dieu!*' was the response. 'That I understood,' Wenzel recalled, 'Oh my God!'

At 0450 hours on 10 May 1940, 20 minutes after the last glider had landed on the seemingly impregnable Belgian fortress at Eben Emael, the whole nature of warfare had changed. Although the fort took a further 30 hours to die, it had already fallen. Witzig resourcefully managed to muster a fresh glider tow and flew in two hours later to reassert command. Nine occupied and defended installations were successfully attacked in the first ten minutes after the landings. Seven armoured domes were blown, and nine 75mm guns and four 120mm guns were put out of action. This carnage was wreaked by 77 boldly led men from ten gliders carrying 56 new hollow-charge explosives. The other glider raids captured the Veldwezelt and Vroenhoven bridges but the Canne bridge nearest to Eben Emael was blown in their faces. Panzer spearheads crossed the remaining bridges and began to flow into Belgium and Holland.

THE ENVELOPMENT OF FORTRESS HOLLAND

As Witzig's men fought their furious battle to retain their hold on the surface casemates of Fort Eben Emael, the first waves of over 430 Ju-52 aircraft passed over. Two air transport Geschwader (wings) crossed the Dutch frontier north of the Rhine and Lek rivers, droning westward toward Rotterdam and The Hague. Eight waves of transports were due to land 4,350 Fallschirmjäger and air-land infantry on the first day. Paratroopers had just 30 minutes to capture their airfields before being joined by the first air-land troops. They were about to fulfil US Colonel Billy Mitchell's aspiration of 22 years before.

Hauptmann Karl Lothar Schulz recalled 'roaring along' with his II Staffel (squadron) of 50 Ju-52s from Kampfgeschwader z.b.V.1 heading towards Waalhaven airfield, just one of the immense streams of aircraft flying west. 'Never before has any of us seen such a sight,' he recalled. 'Wherever one looks, around or above, there are transport planes carrying our parachutists.' Martin Pöppel, due to jump on the north bank of the Moerdijk bridge south of Dordrecht with the 1st Battalion FJR 1, saw 'aircraft filling the sky like flocks of birds gathering in the autumn'. It was developing into a beautiful cloudless day.

Morale inside the lumbering transports crossing into Holland was exuberantly high. Lined up in darkened hangars prior to departure, they had been pepped up with inspirational short speeches proclaiming 'the hour of decision has come', before marching out to the assembled aircraft as emerging light began to illuminate the clouds above. Engine start-up was as stirring as a Wagnerian opera to the idealists facing battle for the first time. Everything about this vast aerial armada exuded power. Take-off was in groups of three to form streams quickly and save time and fuel. Schulz recalled the slower transports were overtaken by faster Heinkel III bombers on their way to deliver surprise aerial bombardments. 'We had thought the sky was full of planes when we could only see our own transports, but now it is many times more crowded.' He described excited soldiers peering out of windows, pointing out the Messerschmitt fighters and Zerstörers flashing by. 'If Hermann [Göring] puts everything up, the birds will have to walk,' remarked one of Shulz's men, 'there won't be room for them in the air!'

Few landmarks made it obvious they were crossing the Dutch border. Soldiers peering down saw strips of sunlight illuminating dykes and larger waterways, indicating they were getting near the objective. Little puffs of smoke haphazardly appeared among the aircraft and would suddenly whip past. 'My men looked puzzled,' recalled Shulz, 'then one of them shouts: "Dutch flak!"' It was ineffective. 'The little bursting puffs of smoke, when they do appear, are too far away to hurt us, and the boys are laughing.' Flying onward they noticed bridges disappearing in flashes obscured by rolling grey-black clouds of smoke. 'This display was repeated at nearly every bridge we pass,' Schulz observed. 'Down there, they seem at last to be aware that the war has begun.' The lumbering stream descended to drop height for the final run-in to target. Aircraft shadows were clearly silhouetted on the sunlit landscape flashing past below.

At low level it is difficult to fix navigational landmarks that suddenly loom up. Transport pilots generally flew from airfield to airfield using towns, river estuaries and woodland shapes as markers. They thought in multiples of kilometres rather than in the metres more familiar to the paratrooper infantry sitting behind. Navigation on approaching urban conurbations like Rotterdam was reduced to assessing minutes of flying time because urban sprawl cloaks the precise outline of cities. They were unable to fly at the heights that enabled them to spot the airfields clearly. The Junkers air transport formations flew low-level, popping up to clear factory smoke-stacks, water towers and tall buildings, before descending into urban obscurity again. Engines would suddenly power up followed by a queasy drop on the far side. Paratroopers sought to fix their location as hamlets, roads and canals whizzed by. Doors were open in readiness for the jump and engine and slipstream noise made only shouted conversations possible. Orientation was difficult. Arrival was going to be sudden and a surprise to both sides.

Not only were the crews unfamiliar with low-level navigation, they had to concentrate hard to keep in formation and avoid collisions. Normally they flew alone or in dispersed groups. 'Despite the noise of the engines, we can now clearly hear the explosions of shells beginning to burst uncomfortably close,' recalled Schulz. Multiple smoke puffs were literally filling cockpit screens, unsettling anxious pilots trying to determine their locations. Aircrew called, *'Fertig machen!* Get ready!' to the paratroopers crowded in the rear, who stood up and began to hook up. The lead stream aircraft flew a fluttering pennant through the cockpit machine gun hatch to alert those behind. *'Fertig zum spring'* was the signal for number ones to stand in the door as the rest of the stick closed up. Schulz could feel the 'little cracks and clacks inside our machine, and the lads look at each other, more than a little surprised'. The flak was intensifying to a level never seen before: 'They aren't laughing any more. This seems to be in earnest. The plane is being turned into a sieve and the order to jump will be the relief to this tension.' The cohesion of some of the streams began to fragment amid this heavy flak.

'Air raid alarm red! The sirens howled in city and harbour,' recalled a Dutch officer stationed at Waalhaven airport, Rotterdam. 'Through the misty dawn came the deep droning of many aircraft.' About 175 bombers, He IIIs, Ju-87 Stukas and Ju-88 dive bombers hit targets in and around the designated landing zones. Twenty-eight Heinkels of the II Gruppe of KG 4 descended on Waalhaven airport. Oberleutnant Baumbach, approaching through the haze, remembered: 'then we came through into the clear, the leading squadrons turning away already for the attack.' The Dutch Queen's Grenadiers had been crouched in trenches and dugouts manning weapons since 0300 and were 'tired and shivering', the Dutch officer recalled. The station commander had considerately allowed his reserve to sleep on in the aircraft hangars, because it was after all peace time. Baumbach saw 'bombs exploding on the southern perimeter of the aerodrome as I make up my mind to come in low from the north, where the mist is still pretty thick . . . I want to surprise them.' Hangars filled with sleeping troops were straddled by a stick of bombs and began to blaze furiously. The Dutch reserve ceased to exist.

Even as the screaming dives of the aircraft receded, replaced by the crackling reports of exploding aircraft and ammunition and anguished cries, a deep drone began to permeate the air. Swarms of Ju-52 transport aircraft approached, buffeted by intense flak and straightening up to home in on the smoke pall boiling up from the shattered hangars. They throttled back and began to decelerate. The Dutch officer watched appalled: 'As if by magic white dots suddenly appeared over the airfield like puffs of cotton wool. First there were twenty, then fifty, then over a hundred of them! And still they came popping out of the planes and began their slow, oscillating descent . . . A hoarse command, then every machine gun opened up . . . at the parachutes, at the planes. With so many targets, the men just did not know where to aim.' They watched in awe the tiny figures visible in doorways toppling out like so many miniature rag dolls. Clusters of parachutes blossomed in groups.

Terrain flitted past aircraft doors as jumpers caught by the slipstream were whipped out of sight, momentarily glimpsing other transport aircraft flying parallel alongside. They flew in 'V'-shaped formations of threes. Schulz dived out of his aircraft with the bullhorn klaxon tooting shrilly in his ear. There was a brief glimpse of wing, fuselage bottom and tail-plane flashing overhead. Ground and sky careered at a crazy angle until the shock of his opening parachute abruptly halted his 50-metre dive and brought him up sharply in his taut harness. Heavier weapons containers were already below, descending more rapidly. He caught his breath; the slipstream 'was as hard as a board', he recalled. 'Over me the billowing white bell of my 'chute ruffled over my head like a sail in the wind.' Nervousness was replaced by a cold-blooded focus on landmarks, what was happening and the need to ensure a good landing. Descending paratroopers flailed about with outstretched limbs to try and turn into the preferred forward landing, feet and knees together for a judo-roll. 'Machine gun bursts and rifle shots whistled past against us, but the enemy fire was definitely less than we had all feared,' Schulz realised.

Hitting a parachutist jumping at 120 metres with the RZ-I parachute was next to impossible. As soon as the parachute opened the paratrooper oscillated from side to side, a difficult shot for an inexperienced rifleman unlikely to assess the correct range. Tests revealed that it took an average of 1,708 rounds fired at 350 metres to achieve a single hit. It still took as many as 185 to be on target even closer, from 150 metres. Dutch defenders, surprised at the awesome spectacle that unfolded above and having little impact on it, soon lost control.

Aircraft represented a bigger target and flak had dispersed many of the formations on the run-in. Some paratroopers plunged into the harbour adjoining the airport. Few had the presence of mind or indeed time to unravel the complicated harness which took on average 80 seconds to release. Twenty pounds of equipment and 17lb of parachute took them swiftly to the bottom. Another stick had the misfortune to drop across the blazing hangars and joined the hapless Dutch reserve funeral pyre. Parachute silk soon shrivelled and scorched and dropped wildly flapping figures into the fiery conflagration below. Thumping reports from grenades and crackling ammunition going off in bone-sack smocks cut short strangled cries.

'Even so, there are comic interludes,' recalls Schulz, observing heavy fire coming from around the perimeter. 'Some of my men landed slap bang on the backs of cows, which up to that moment had been peacefully grazing.' Horses bolted as more paratroopers came down, released their harnesses and began to splash through water-filled drainage ditches to get to their objectives. The drop at Waalhaven went broadly as planned. 'Within thirty minutes of the start, the aerodrome is firmly in our hands,' states Shulz. The entire perimeter defence was wiped out or taken prisoner in a short vicious action. 'The Dutch people fought very bravely, harder in fact than one would expect from a people which had not been at war for over a hundred years.'

To the south, the bridges at Moerdijk and Doordrecht were secured from both ends by a force of 700 men, including 400 Fallschirmjäger from FJR 1. Both sites became hotly contested. They were vital to link up with ground forces coming from the east. Key to breaking into the built up area of Rotterdam was the capture of the four bridges, north and south of the Noordereiland. Twelve Heinkel 59 sea planes ferried 120 infantrymen and engineers under Oberleutnant Schrader after landing along the Maas River and taxiing to the north bank by the Willems bridge. Astonished Dutch workmen helped the bemused Germans ashore from their dinghies, assuming they were British. Fifty Fallschirmjäger under Oberleutnant Horst Kerfin dropped inside the South Rotterdam Feyenoord football stadium on the main road to the city centre. They commandeered city trams and drove madly through the streets with loudly jangling bells, crossing several bridges before disembarking and occupying houses on the north bank. Bluff, daring and ruthless aggression were enabling these men to occupy the city's defences before Dutch forces could arrive.

Crucial to German success was the seizure and detention of the royal family and government in order to paralyse the Dutch will to resist. This was reliant upon successfully seizing the three airfields commanding all routes into The Hague by parachute assault followed by the rapid air-land of Generalleutnant von Sponeck's 22nd Division. His soldiers had specially prepared route cards outlining the quickest and most direct roads to the royal palace. The aim was to encircle The Hague with some 9,300 troops by nightfall on the first day. Graf von Sponeck was flying to Ypenburg with a bouquet of flowers on his lap. He intended to present to them to Queen Wilhelmina at the moment of arrest, but it was not to happen.

The northern group of aircraft began dropping paratroopers between 30 to 40 minutes ahead of the main air-land around the three objective airfields. The three companies of FJR 2 employed were taken aback at the intensity of flak they encountered when their 41 Ju–52s descended to 120 metres for the final run-in to Ypenburg airfield. 'During this last manoeuvre three of our Ju–52s were hit,' recalled the lead pilot. 'They caught fire and crashed to the ground.' Riddled with fire, pilots slumped over controls and co-pilots struggled to maintain control as well as trying to identify the distinctive airport runway. 'Every single one of the remaining planes was hit,' the lead pilot observed. One segment of the stream veered off and 60 men jumped south of the Delft suburb, well south of the airport. Other aircraft diverged to drop their loads two miles further north. 'It was only because of the robustness of the "Aunty Ju" [as the aircraft were affectionally nicknamed] that we could keep the planes in the air and prevent a total catastrophe even before we reached the drop zone.' Parachute sticks that landed in the open on the airfield were cut down by the 700 Dutch Grenadiers defending, others descended in the middle of Dutch positions on the east side of the runway. Only on the north side, battered by the preliminary Luftwaffe bombing, could some paratroopers get inside airport buildings.

The fly-in to Ockenburg was similarly broken up by flak. Only 35 of the 160-strong force landed with any degree of accuracy. Half the company jumped nearly eight miles away, south-east of the Hook of Holland, while another platoon landed at Katwijk, near Ockenburg. At Valkenburg, the third airport, 160 paratroopers were immediately locked in a desperate battle with the Dutch defenders. Parachuting under fire was proving a terrifying and disorientating experience, but the most vulnerable time was immediately on landing, which the determined Dutch, having studied the Norwegian experience, were quick to exploit. It took more than a minute to get out of the encumbering parachute harnesses, whose four fumbling release points had yet to be modified. Landed Fallschirmjäger were sitting ducks, armed with only pistol and grenades. Dispersion during the descent meant 12 paratroopers from each aircraft would spread across 600 to 700 yards. Somewhere along the drop line was the all-essential weapons container with machine-pistols, rifles, machine guns and ammunition. Depending on the aircraft configuration on dropping, an average platoon of 36 men might be spread over seven hectares, or 30 times the area they could realistically be expected to defend. At best speed a paratrooper stick could gather within 10 to 15 minutes. It took a battalion an hour or more to consolidate, longer on difficult terrain if they could not find their containers.

The German plan, precise in detail, unfolded like a railway time-table. Only 30 minutes were allotted for the parachute assaults before immediate reinforcement by air-land infantry. Fifteen soldiers were jam-packed into their Ju-52s with heavy weapons, motor-cycles, light vehicles and infantry trolleys ferrying the second wave regiments of the 22nd Air-land Division. The ground situation was far from clear. General Student's operational flow calculation was based on the assumption that shock, surprise and awe at this extraordinary vertical envelopment would overcome all. At Ypenberg Dutch Grenadiers had fought the scattered Fallschirmjäger assault wave to a standstill. Its 20mm low-level flak remained intact and only two of six Dutch M-36 six-wheeled armoured cars with their 37mm guns and three machine guns were disabled during the preliminary air bombardment. They knew precisely what would happen next and began to line up on the runways as a deep drone signalled the approach of the next air transport formation from the east.

The 38 Ju-52s of Kampfgruppe z.b. V.12, carrying elements of Infantry Regiment 16 and the 22nd Division headquarters staff, had already lost three aircraft even before reaching Utrecht. Their awful predicament demonstrated the vulnerability of 15 fully equipped infantry crammed in the back without parachutes. Luftwaffe crew members who managed to bale out described their pitiful fate: 'shocking' was the verdict of the terse squadron after-action report. Their fate, however, was to pale into insignificance as the first Staffel of eight machines made its final approach to Ypenburg airfield.

Dutch Corporal G. Mommaas, commanding armoured car PAW 602, recalled, 'they were magnificent targets as they landed at a ponderously slow speed.' Inside, German soldiers anxiously scanned the airfield surrounds for signs of enemy activity. Fire was opened almost immediately. 'Our almost continuous firing caused some overheating problems but Hummel [his co-driver] very efficiently managed to clear the jams.' Mommaas's other driver, Ale Fikkers, jumped about and 'operated the machine gun on the turret like an ape while I fired my first shots with the 37mm gun'. All hell broke loose inside the aircraft as huge holes were punched out of the corrugated metal sides, lacerating the helpless infantry packed too close to move. Burning fuel ignited and exploded the grenades and ammunition carried on the men's equipments. Within minutes each of the eight aircraft had burst into an oily slurry of flame. With crews dead or wounded, slumped over controls, some machines halted while others taxied aimlessly off the runway streaming fire and smoke. Corporal Mommaas, with the 20mm flak and dug-in infantry, poured in the fire. The second Staffel of eight aircraft was already committed to its landing and drove into the swiftly developing inferno. As German infantry scrambled out, shrieking and on fire, they were scythed down in a storm of cannon and machine gun fire. Mommaas was soon out of ammunition: 'Because the range was short we had first fired anti-tank shells, then the HE, our last five rounds being fired at a Ju-52 which had come to a stop in front of the bombed hangar. It was so close that I had to aim the gun through the open breech.'

Huge palls of oily black smoke boiled up from the jam of Ju-52s piled up along the runway length, further reducing landing space. Only three of 200 soldiers trapped in the burning fuselages survived. The third Staffel, unable to land amid the tangled wreckage, overshot at low level, losing three more machines in the process. They had to look for alternative landing sites. Some touched down on the coastal dunes and fields nearby and sank in sand or mud. A few aircraft came down on the main Delft to Rotterdam road where civilian cars were soon dodging round them.

Leaping from taxiing planes, elements of the III Battalion Infantry Regiment 47 air-landed at Valkenburg to the north. Here, the transports were mired up to their axles in the soft airfield turf. Unable to take off again, the Dutch defenders shot them into flames. The next wave carrying the II Battalion, denied room to land, had to turn away. Ockenburg was blocked by machines destroyed in a British air attack. General von Sponeck, unable to land at Ypenburg, was greeted by this dismal scene on arrival at Ockenburg. Shaken by flak bursts and holed by strikes, his aircraft – like many others – force-landed nearby in a small field. He managed to establish tenuous radio contact with Student, who advised him to break out south towards the German forces in Rotterdam. The discarded royal bouquet was never delivered.

Only Waalhaven remained an air-land possibility. The III Battalion of Infantry Regiment 16 touched down within 30 minutes of Hauptmann Schulz's parachute assault. It was a spectacular entry.

Petrol streamed from holed petrol tanks and one JU-52 trundled along the runway with both engines on fire. Doors opened and out poured the first two infantry platoons. They were the advance air-land group. Still under intermittent artillery fire, more Junkers transports taxied to a halt and the infantry emerged pulling trolleys loaded with heavy equipments. They moved off in the direction of Rotterdam city centre to link up with the sea-plane and tram-borne coup de main elements already holding the bridges north and south of Noordereiland. 'The howl of aero-engines and ammunition exploding in the hangars was deafening,' recalled newly landed Oberstleutnant Dietrich von Choltitz. This was accompanied by 'the crash of mortar fire and the rattle of machine guns plugging the planes' as he gathered his battalion together. 'Speed was the thing!' General Student flew in with a skeleton staff and attempted to coordinate his far-flung division with the few radio sets at his disposal.

In stark contrast, Oberleutnant Diedrich Bruns languished at Münster-Loddenheide airport in the Reich. His I Battalion was waiting to be flown into the airhead. He spent the entire morning queuing with his motor-cycle, to get it included as part of the air load. Programming was difficult because there was no way of knowing what gaps there might be among the returning aircraft. Newly landed crews talked about murderous flak. Air fleet losses were to be so heavy that 5,000 men of the Air Land Division were destined never to leave the ground at all. Bruns managed to fly out during the afternoon.

As they descended at Waalhaven airfield, telltale bursts of smoke indicated it was under intense and accurate Dutch artillery fire. Several Ju-52s were hit and began to blaze furiously even as they touched down. Brun's men were scrambling out the back even before the aircraft stopped rolling. They ran for the perimeter with shells howling and exploding, coating them all with dust and fine debris. Bruns managed to get his motor-cycle off, helped by his orderly and sped off to find headquarters and get his orders. This was not quite what they had anticipated.

The situation of the northern group around The Hague by evening of the first day was catastrophic. Only one-third of the anticipated force of 4,900 men had managed to land at Ypenburg and only 200 were still resisting. Six hundred of 1,000 had flown into Ockenburg but 500 were badly dispersed; similarly only 1,400 of 3,300 got into Valkenburg with a fragmented 950 men still in action. The feeder for the break into Fortress Holland remained Waalhaven, Rotterdam, which was earmarked to receive 3,200 men but landed 3,700.

Bruns discovered the situation in Rotterdam to be precarious. His company, loaded onto captured Dutch trucks, was soon fighting around the 650-metre long swing-bridge at the Old Maas River. Although the Moerjidk bridge was still hanging on further south, the road and rail bridges at Dordrecht were changing hands amid intense fighting. Martin Pöppel remembered his room-mate Dinkel from Bamberg was killed during an assault on the nearby Dutch barracks. 'We find his body lying twisted on the ground. We have seen our first men killed,' he reflected. More were to follow as they stood before them in silence. Any illusions Pöppel may have had about war were dispelled in the intense fighting that followed over the next few days. He had to sleep among the wounded. 'The place reeks of sweat and blood,' he recalled. 'One of them draws his last breath almost beside me. It will be a very long time before I can forget the appalling inhuman sound.'

Despite German failure at The Hague three Dutch divisions were committed to defending Fortress Holland by an increasingly confused Dutch Army Command. The price paid by the air-land division was heavy: 42 per cent of the officers and 28 per cent of the committed units were to be lost in five days. The II Battalion of Regiment 65 near The Hague and the III Battalion Regiment 16 at Waalhaven lost 50 per cent of all ranks. Roughly 90 per cent of the Ju-52s in the initial assault waves never returned, costing skilled aircrew. Nevertheless, the airborne corridor established between Rotterdam and Dordrecht to the south was precariously held, an area roughly ten by seven miles bordered by the great waterways of the Old and New Maas. There was still no sign of assistance from the powerful advancing ground forces for three long and anxious days.

On 13 May Von Kleist's massed German Panzergruppen suddenly broke out into the French plains. On the same day the Dutch government fled from Holland to England just as General Hubicki's 9th Panzer Division linked up with Fallschirmjäger Regiment 1 at the Moerdijk bridge. The desire to crack Dutch resistance on the northern flank of the German *Blitzkrieg* after the failure to apprehend the Dutch royal family and government resulted in the controversial Luftwaffe bombing of central Rotterdam. Half the bombing force was waved off at the last moment, but the devastating fire-storm that followed resulted in the capitulation of Holland on 14 May. It was a close-run thing for the 7th Flieger Division, who were at the limits of their endurance.

Holland had a cauterising effect on the Fallschirmjäger and air-land troops not reflected in the *Sieg im Westen* epic German propaganda film released shortly after the campaign. Martin Pöppel bitterly reminisced: 'Later on we heard a lot of drivel about the heroic remarks dying soldiers were said to have made. You know, all that stuff about "Farewell, my Führer, farewell my Fatherland, give my love to my parents, may God have mercy on me." I never heard anything like that. I only saw them die.'

He was still at Dordrecht with a 'situation far from rosy' when the panzers broke through from the south. 'There's great jubilation,' he later recorded, 'we've held on, and we've done it.'

The psychological impact of the sudden vertical envelopment of Fortress Holland reduced the Dutch military to confusion. Despite the aggressive counter-response that slammed the door to entry at airfields around The Hague, the foothold at Waalhaven was a canker that destroyed defence cohesion. The Rotterdam fire-storm raid was the final blow. With the royal family gone, surrender was the only option. The bloodily repulsed coup de main achieved its objective after all. The Dutch listened horrified as all this unfurled on their radios. Belgium capitulated on 28 May and seven days later the last British ships had left Dunkirk.

The German Luftlande had transitioned from company-size raids in Scandinavia to Student's strategy of vertical envelopment at multi-division operational level in one month. Despite technical shortfalls, it demonstrated that airborne forces inserted via the third dimension – air – outflanked everything. This new mode of battle required unique, resourceful, technically aware and independently thinking soldiers. Initiative was sorely tested by misdropped parachute insertions, and aircraft losses resulted in leadership dilemmas and changes of plan. Far from accepting the surrender of the Dutch royal family, the Commander of the 22nd Air-land Division found himself cut off, fighting for his life in hostile territory. General Student, the Commander of 7th Flieger Division, was wounded at a crucial point when negotiating the Dutch surrender. Always expect the unexpected had never been proved so true.

Soldiers arrived on the new airborne battlefields disorientated and in small groups. They anticipated encirclement even before operations commenced. Cut off, they were trained to fight against overwhelming odds with only light equipment. This was not conventional warfare. It needed to be prosecuted with ruthless determination. It needed different men.

There were already differences of perception within the airborne forces themselves, between those who jumped to battle by parachute or flew in vulnerable assault gliders and those ferried and air-landed by transport aircraft. The Fallschirmjäger and glider-borne Stürmtrupps regarded themselves as the elite of the elite. Frictions were later to develop within the airborne arm. The fact that Fallschirmjäger were in effect Luftwaffe Special Forces aided air cooperation. This same sympathy did not exist with the air-land elements of 22nd Division.

The new warfare was cheap by the established norms of 1914–18, but costly when viewed from an overall twentieth-century perspective. In August 1914 it had taken eight brigades numbering 60,000 men 11 days to batter the Belgian forts into submission at horrific cost. In May 1940, 414 paratroopers towed by 42 transport aircraft in 42 gliders and dropped by six planes captured Fort Eben Emael and two of three bridges. Within hours a fighting bridgehead was established across the Albert Canal, enabling a rapid penetration by the 4th Panzer Division. The cost was 38 killed and 100 wounded, having inflicted over 900 casualties and capturing 700 prisoners. The vertical envelopment of the Low Countries was conducted on an unprecedented scale and, despite shortcomings, was a truly dramatic step in a largely unresearched operational area. The Germans opted to expand the 7th Flieger Division into the XI Flieger Corps.

The Allies were stunned. 'There are no longer any islands,' reflected Jäger Martin Pöppel, 'and England is near. Now a parachute drop on England would be really something, damn it!'

4

WE NEED A CORPS OF PARACHUTE TROOPS

PLAYING CATCH-UP

The Paris newspaper *Le Figaro* had warned the day before the attack in the west that 'we are justified in fearing, like the Dutch, that small groups of daring parachutists will try to seize landing fields during the night and to sow disarray behind the lines'. Events, however, unfolded on a massive and unpredicted scale. 'One cannot stress too strongly,' its readers were warned, 'that every parachutist and every transport plane that lands at night in isolated spots, should be considered suspect, regardless of what uniform or costume is worn by the occupants.' Dutch radio had reported: 'German parachutists have landed in the Netherlands, some of them wearing Allied and Dutch uniforms. The Dutch people are urged to exercise extreme caution and vigilance.' England received alarming Dutch reports about paratroopers dropping disguised as nuns, women and policemen. Press reports vied with each other to publish the latest bizarre facts. The *New York Herald Tribune* claimed German parachute troops with five-winged bird insignia on their tunic lapels were making contact with fifth columnists. 'Four-birders' were landing beyond their objective to backtrack, mopping up resistance on the way; 'three-birders' captured gasoline and supply depots; while 'two-birders' seized landing fields and so on. The article concluded: 'These highly coordinated tactics reflect years of study and training. No wonder captured prisoners have maps showing a new Germany even before that objective is attained.'

There was acute alarm in Europe. The Swedish *Svenska Dagbladet* reported on 12 May a mysterious 'secret weapon' that the German

Wehrmacht High Command claimed was used to seize the strongest fort held by the Belgians at Liege. 'Strict silence is being maintained about the nature and use of the new weapon, which was strong enough to compel turn-over of the fort with its 1,000-man garrison.'

Not to be outdone by Hitler, Stalin launched four air regiments of 170 TB-3s carrying two Soviet airborne brigades across the Soviet-Romanian border. Hundreds of Soviet twin-parachutes blossomed above Izmail airfield in Bessarabia on 30 June 1940, spearheading the Soviet ground occupation of eastern Romania. Two days before, air-landings had secured Bolgrad. The parachute insertion after a 225-mile flight was designed to secure key points along the Romanian Army's agreed withdrawal routes before the arrival of Red Army ground units. Stalin ironically applied the 'Deep Battle' doctrine expounded by his murdered rival Marshal Tukhachevsky, similar, but not as dramatic with the absence of opposition, to the German *Blitzkrieg* model. Stalin's purges had decimated the creative leadership of the Soviet airborne arm. Shortage of aeroplanes and command competence had reduced it to a mobile infantry husk of its former self.

British Prime Minister Winston Churchill, barely 12 days in office, issued a memo to General Ismay at the War Office on 22 June stating: 'We ought to have a corps of at least 5,000 parachute troops.' Britain stood alone, vulnerable to invasion with insufficient resources to defend itself, let alone consider offensive measures. 'Advantage must be taken of the summer to train these forces,' he recommended, 'who can, none the less, play their part meanwhile as shock troops in home defences.' He asked for a War Office note on the subject. Staff were dismayed because there were not even any aircraft.

More importantly, there was not a man in the country who had any experience of training parachutists. Apart from pilots who had baled out in emergency, the only knowledge held was among air pageant show-jumpers. Large numbers of German parachutists were captured in The Hague, but they were saying nothing, awaiting rescue by their colleagues. Captured equipments at least were available for analysis. Captain Martin Lindsay recalled Major John Rock RE was just back from Dunkirk when he was sent for by the War Office and told to 'start parachute troops' at Ringway. There was little to draw upon. 'He was given no directions, except a German parachutist's boots and a smock suit from Holland.'

Six Whitley bombers and crews were allocated following the Prime Minister's direction and a thousand parachutes ordered from the manufacturers. 'There are very real difficulties in this parachute business,' wrote one senior RAF officer charged with tackling the problems: 'We are trying to do what we have never been able to do hitherto, namely to introduce a completely new arm into the service at about five minutes' notice and with totally inadequate resources and personnel. Little – if any – practical experience is possessed in England of any of these problems and it will be necessary to cover in six months the ground the Germans have covered in six years.'

Pilot Officer Louis Strange, an ex-1914–18 colonel, was appointed to go to Manchester, where there was a half-built airport with one runway, to investigate the possibilities of training paratroops. There were a few offices, administration buildings and hangars still under construction. After a hasty inspection, accompanied by 'the usual cold stares which greet a new junior officer on arrival at any RAF station', he reported back to the Air Ministry and the group captain in charge of combined operations training. 'You'd better get back as quickly as possible, and get the place organised,' he was told. 'You are in charge of a new unit called Central Landing School.' Remonstrating he was too junior to 'go around giving orders', Pilot Officer Strange was quickly transitioned to Squadron Leader Strange and returned to Ringway airport, Manchester. The first trainee parachutists belonging to Number 2 Commando arrived to begin parachuting in July.

Three days after Winston Churchill's directive and even as the French were signing the instrument of surrender in the railway carriage at Compiègne, the adjutant general in Washington ordered that a Parachute Test Platoon be set up. It was to be formed from volunteers from the 29th (US) Infantry Division stationed at Fort Benning, Georgia. As fighting raged in the Low Countries in May the United States completed the development and testing of the T-4 parachute, enabling an armed infantryman to jump from aeroplanes with a static line at low altitudes. The 28-foot diameter canopy, like earlier Russian models, was to be jumped with a smaller reserve parachute.

The 29th Infantry Regiment was paraded at Fort Benning in the pre-dawn light of 26 June 1940 and given a totally unexpected call for volunteers. 'The First Sergeant must have gone crazy if he thinks I'm gonna volunteer for an outfit that's goin' to be jumping out of aeroplanes,' was one immediate remark. 'I'm for keeping my two dogs right here on the ground where they belong,' was another characteristic comment. Twenty men immediately volunteered. Physical requirements were demanding: each man had to weigh no more than 185lbs, be in excellent physical condition and have completed a minimum of two years' infantry service. 'Because of the high degree of risk associated with parachute jumping, all those volunteering must understand that duty with the Parachute Test Platoon is strictly voluntary,' directed regimental headquarters. 'It will require frequent jumps from airplanes in flight at various altitudes, which may result in serious injury or death.' Most had only ever seen stuntmen parachuting. Only unmarried men were allowed to volunteer. Few takers were anticipated, but by 0830 over 200 men had put their names forward. The final platoon was honed down to four squads of 12 members. This was achieved through written exams and commanding officers submitting outstanding, rugged and athletically inclined soldiers, who also showed leadership potential. The 48-strong platoon commanded by Lieutenant William T. Ryder began training in early July 1940.

Various factors influenced the origin and recruitment of the first Sky Men. Two totalitarian nations, Russia and Germany, clearly led the way. They had been 'volunteered' in a pre-emptive sense with whole units selected and transferred to an airborne role. Appeals were made to ideology, party and state, convincing because nobody wanted to be seen as apart. To decline could impact on their uniformed status and the social standing and privileges that went hand in hand with membership of a politically sponsored elite. Communist Komsomol and Hitler Youth organisations encouraged allegiance to a state that wanted their youth to engage in daring and adventurous activity, offering useful martial by-products. Media trumpeting of Fallschirmjäger accomplishments in Holland and Belgium soon attracted ready volunteers in Germany.

Japan began training paratroopers in the summer of 1940, influenced by the same successes. German parachute instructors began to arrive and by the autumn up to 100 were in country. At the end of the year 9,200 Japanese Army and Navy paratroopers were in training at Shimonoseki, Shizuoka, Hiroshima and Himeji. British intelligence reported 500 parachutists jumping 'daily' at Canton aerodrome and that '5 deaths and 12 cases of broken limbs are reported as having occurred within 15 days in this form of training in Formosa'. Evidence suggested 'that both the military and naval Japanese Air Forces are not only taking seriously this form of attack from the air, but are accelerating the training of considerable numbers of parachutists'. Japan was not yet in the war, but reports concluded: 'It is natural to suppose that this is being done with the object of using them, or at any rate having them ready for use . . . in the not too distant future.' Objectives might be the Chinese at Kunming, the French in Indo-China, or the British in Hong Kong. The two democracies: Britain and the United States were playing catch-up. Totalitarian nations could order soldiers to transition to parachute units. Where would appreciable numbers of volunteers be found within the democracies?

British veterans in their understated way rarely invoke patriotism as the reason for responding to Churchill's call for parachute volunteers. The vast majority of the initial intakes for No. 2 Commando, the first British airborne unit to form up, did have this at the back of their minds. Surveys reveal the sense of emergency that prevailed. Britain was 'standing alone' now that France had fallen. Most volunteered so they could choose their arm of service, unlike conscripts. Entry to airborne forces meant they had to volunteer a second time. 'We were a motley crowd, English, Welsh, Irish and Scotch etc,' declared former bus driver Arthur Lawley, 'and belonged to all classes of life, ages ranging from eighteen to forty years, but all had one burning desire, and that was to have a go at Jerry.' William Elvin, later to serve with the 6th Airborne Division, claimed 'the youth in those days wanted to fight for their country'. Another parachutist, Ralph Cook, felt 'this was the best and quickest way to get to grips with the enemy'. Early intakes into No. 2 Commando and the first parachute battalions could be described as gladiatorial: they volunteered to fight. 'The one thing that was required to become a parachutist in those days was *guts*,' declared Arthur Lawley. 'We were never medically examined beforehand, neither did one's age matter – what a difference to the procedure of selection today.' In this nationalistic and patriotic sense, they were no different from the Fallschirmjäger and Soviet paratroopers.

Boredom and dissatisfaction with static guards awaiting an invasion that never came was another factor encouraging volunteers to join No. 2 Commando, which later became the 11th Special Air Service (SAS) Battalion. 'Some time in June 1940 at the time of the fall of France, a notice appeared in the mess,' recalled Second Lieutenant Ian Smith, 'asking anybody who could swim, play the rougher sort of sports, was very fit, and looking for adventure to apply.' Smith, 'being bored teaching disinterested recruits the joys of arms drill and feeling well out of things', was attracted. 'I asked that my name go forward.' He was amongst the earliest to parachute with the fledgling force. Corporal Ernie Chinnery transferred from the 17/21st Lancers, declaring, 'I volunteered for parachuting as I did not relish spending the rest of the war in a training establishment as a gunnery instructor, whilst others were getting all the action.' Lieutenant Tony Hibbert with the Royal Artillery remembered at the height of the invasion scare, 'if the Germans could only put two divisions ashore we were finished.' He therefore resolved to join No. 2 Commando. 'We were wasting time,' he complained, 'and should do something before the Germans arrive.' 'Nothing was happening,' agreed Lieutenant John Timothy with the Queen's Own Royal West Kent Regiment on hearing the call for parachute volunteers. 'Well, as the war wasn't coming to me, I thought I'd better go and meet it.'

It was appreciated from the very inception of No. 2 Commando that special men would be needed. Parachuting was very unusual. Ordered to report to the George Inn at Knutsford, Tony Hibbert noticed the car in front was distracted by a low-flying plane and 'eight little blobs came out'. At the appearance of these parachutists the car drove into a ditch. 'It was the most extraordinary unit, all *individualists* of the highest order,' he declared. 'Many had already fought in Spain, China and other places.' Common to all was 'complete disregard of discipline in the traditional sense'. It was replaced by a different sort of focus, to excel in all aspects of infantry warfare. Sergeant Eddie Hancock, an early volunteer, appreciated that: 'While discipline is essential, how it is applied is equally important. It must not stifle initiative.' Self-discipline, he felt, was the vital element in a crisis. 'Front line troops seldom subscribe to the dogma, "If it moves salute it, if it doesn't, whitewash it".' Combat efficiency became the new airborne discipline. Hancock recognised that, 'civilians who volunteer to serve in time of need have different attitudes.' More perceptive than the average conscripted soldier, 'they are unlikely to willingly tolerate moronic instructors'. They were a different breed of men requiring a different type of leadership approach than that associated with the traditional county regiment infantryman.

'In the early days the idea was to use us as a guerrilla force, dropping behind enemy lines and causing as much mayhem as possible,' remembered Second Lieutenant Ian Smith. 'All our training was to this end and was therefore of an individual nature . . . working in small groups, practising sabotage and concealment in the countryside.' There was also a cold-blooded desire to close with the enemy.' Grenadier Guardsman Reg Curtis was motivated by memories of 'the carnage of Calais' and 'British prisoners of war belonging to the Warwick Regiment who were herded into a field just outside Dunkirk and machine-gunned to death by the Waffen SS'. The blitz made Curtis's war very personal. 'I thought of my home being blown to smithereens, and how Jerry had prevented me from carrying on my ambition of becoming a London policeman.' He did not hesitate on being asked to volunteer: 'I abruptly took a pace forward before it was too late.'

Four weeks of intense physical training was followed by parachuting at Tatton Park near Knutsford, the Central Landing School's drop zone six miles south-west of Ringway. Six weeks' field and mountain training followed at the commando school in Scotland. 'At Ringway we lived hard,' recalled Lieutenant Anthony Deane-Drummond with 2 Commando: 'Before breakfast each morning we went for a three mile run, followed by thirty minutes' PT. After breakfast we normally had a 12 to 15 mile "parachute march". This meant covering at least 11 miles every two hours and it took some doing while carrying full equipment.'

Corporal Reg Curtis remembered the hard physical selection. 'Some conditions were abominable,' he recalled, but he regarded it as a challenge. 'For everyone it was a test of strength, coordinated with guts, sheer cunning and determination to win through.' They were guinea pigs, constantly evolving new methods, not just to prepare for parachuting, but also to cope with the unequal conditions they would face jumping into vulnerable combat situations. 'We were taught to persevere to the end, and to be able to endure great, if not impossible fatigue.' Physical robustness inculcated a sense of aggressive well-being. 'It was emphatically stressed never to accept defeat, even when against overwhelming odds,' Curtis pointed out. Sky Men would always be outnumbered and surrounded on entry into battle, but, he went on, 'Even when the cards were down with nothing less than a miracle to sort out a situation that extra flair and determination would come to the rescue and save the day.' This was what would differentiate airborne soldiers from normal line infantry.

'As nobody had any experience of parachuting everybody had an individual and unusually diverse idea of how to best train for the leap ahead,' recalled Second Lieutenant Ian Smith, assembling with early jumpers at Ringway. On 11 July 1940 pilots and instructors were hurling 200lb dummies through a three foot two inch hole opened in the floor of a Whitley bomber to try out training parachutes. About 100 men from No. 2 Commando watched the first live demonstration two days later. 'How to land?' Smith pondered. 'One school favoured the legs apart method, another the front roll and some . . . thought we could best learn by jumping off a high wall.' Two types of aircraft exit were shown; jumping through the Whitley floor, or former bomb bay, and pull-offs from a platform where the rear-gun turret had been removed. Pupils watching these stunts from the ground were hardly encouraged by what they saw.

Harry Ward, who had re-entered the RAF after show jumping, was appointed the chief parachute instructor at Ringway in November. He condemned the 'pull-off' method as 'absolutely useless', because tactically only one man could be released at a time: 'You had to crawl down to the end of the Whitley, go through the little aperture to get onto what had been the gun turret, which was now an open platform [on the tail-plane], and for the character to stand there and get under the bar hanging out at the back of the Whitley, just hanging on the bar with one hand, pulling the rip-cord and being dragged off.'

It was not far removed from show jumping. Sergeant T. Dawes recalled being second in line to jump during the live demonstration. 'I saw the number 1 hanging on grimly with glassy eyes, then suddenly there was a flash of white silk and he had gone.' His Flight Sergeant Brereton advised him to relax as they circled again to approach the Tatton Park drop zone. 'With a great effort of will I dared to look down on my first bird's eye view of the English countryside,' where to his consternation he saw 'five hundred feet below a tiny stretcher with a dark motionless figure being lifted onto the blood wagon [ambulance].' The number 1 had accidentally knocked himself out. Appreciating the discouraging effect this must be having on Dawes, Brereton assured him, 'There's nothing to worry about' and for good measure, 'I'll pull the rip-cord for you myself.' 'Just tell me what to do,' responded Dawes, feverishly clutching at the bar. 'Watch my hand and when you see it fall, pull the handle upward and outward,' explained the flight sergeant, shouting above the noise of the buffeting slipstream.

'OK,' Dawes said, 'You mean like this?'

'Not now you bloody fool!' But it was too late, he had gone! Three hours later the search party found Dawes six miles away, helplessly hanging in a tree by his parachute. Learning was proving painful.

'Some tried to hold on,' recalled Second Lieutenant Smith, face into wind, 'a singularly useless exercise and very sore on the arms!' 'Unfortunately we usually pulled it either too soon or too late, and so landed almost anywhere in Cheshire,' declared Captain Martin Lindsay at Ringway, 'which was good for our geography, but tiring.' Not only was the method tactically impractical, it was dangerous. 'One of the 'chutes caught in the slipstream blew back inside the fuselage, and we nearly had a nasty accident,' revealed Lindsay. 'After that it was decided that we should go straight through the hole' of the Whitley bomber, an equally tense and unpleasant affair.

Smith's first exit was through the floor of a Whitley. 'When the red light changes to green close your eyes and go,' he was kindly informed by his RAF dispatcher Warrant Officer Warburton, arm around his shoulders and face close up. 'I glanced at his face and noticed the complete absence of teeth, and was very aware of an overpowering stale beery smell.' Hung over from the night before, this was his first ever jump. 'I was only too pleased to leave the aircraft. It was this combination of noise and morning-after breath, that accelerated our exit to the fresh air at 300 feet.' Veteran accounts speak of the trial and error nature of these early jumps.

'Various bright sparks,' Smith explained, 'had theories as to the best way to land.' Innovations could verge on the bizarre. 'One inventor thought it best if we all wore under our boots a series of clip-on springs, about the size of bed-springs.' The special boots were stained yellow and the enthusiastic inventor jumped with his brightly visible brain-child. A gust of wind swept his legs from beneath him and the 'wretched inventor landed painfully on his backside'. So far as Smith and the other bemused observers were concerned 'he could have landed barefoot for all the good his boots proved'.

'The one thing we all agreed on,' Smith emphasised, 'was that we had to know how a parachute worked.' They closely watched and assisted the Women's Auxiliary Air Force girls packing their parachutes. This 'was taken very seriously indeed, though there were many jokes about 'chutes opening and showers of hair pins and lipsticks falling out.' In time the hazards of parachute trialling were to come back and sober them all.

In the United States a strenuous programme of callisthenics, hand to hand combat, tumbling and a daily three-mile run was combined with parachute instruction to prepare bodies and minds for the hard knocks of jumping and landing. Volunteers were 'doubled' wherever they went. Ground training taught them how to fall, distributing the shock of landing throughout the body, rather than directly on feet and legs. They practised dropping from slow moving trucks.

US parachute training was conducted via a harsher instructor ethos than the British. From the start the US Test Platoon was subjected to punitive discipline. This characterised British selection, but ceased on arrival at RAF Ringway, where it transitioned to a more 'civilised' and relaxed teaching style. At the conclusion of often spittle-punctuated, long-winded shouted instructor critiques, American students might be required to perform ten push-ups for an imperfect tumble. Scant sympathy allied to remorseless pressure inculcated immediate and unquestioning response to orders at every phase of training. Ten push-ups could be awarded for errors and ten more for an insipid response. This created the future ethos underpinning American jump-training. Should the student not quickly 'switch on' and perform it was assumed his ignorance or carelessness would result in broken bones or loss of life. British parachute instructor Flight Lieutenant John Kilkenny once corrected a sergeant major 'of some standing' at Ringway for awarding 50 press-ups for incorrect falls. What are you doing that for?' he enquired: ' "If 'e doesn't do it right, I 'urt 'im'." This is true. So I said, "Wouldn't it be wiser if you gave him another two or three of the things to do and told him to do it without sticking his elbow out or something like that?" ' Kilkenny remembered the hard-bitten sergeant major's response to his intervention. 'He thought I was just a twit.'

'I went to the American schools,' Kilkenny recalled. 'There was a lot of it if they didn't do the thing correctly.' His view was 'put him right' rather than punish. It reflected a difference in national temperament. 'Of course there's something in the philosophy but not to me,' Kilkenny explained. 'It doesn't suit me.' A paratrooper, in the American view has no time for mistakes. Former US airborne officer Gerard Devlin observed: 'If a paratrooper's main 'chute fails to open at the usual jumping altitude of 1,000 feet, and he is not quick-witted enough to get the reserve parachute open immediately, he will hit the ground only eight seconds after leaving the plane. And then he will be very dead.'

Like the British, the US Test Platoon was thoroughly psyched up to view their first test demonstration with a dummy, prior to jumping live the following week. All eyes were on the approaching aircraft and open door as the dummy exited at 1,500 feet. As one observer recalled, 'The dummy dropped with all the speed and grace of a ton of bricks and slammed into the ground less than fifty yards in front of the wide-eyed platoon.' Confidence evaporated. They were assured by their Warrant Officer Harry Wilson the reserve parachute would have saved the dummy's life if he had been human. They reassembled a day later, with understandable foreboding, to witness Corporal Laurence Wallace conduct a live jump, which resulted in a perfect landing. He stood up and ceremoniously bowed to his impressed audience. The platoon's confidence was restored, but with some reservations.

The big day arrived for the first platoon descent. Its historical significance was appreciated and a bidding war broke out to auction the Number 1 position, after the platoon commander Lieutenant Ryder. Numbers were taken from a helmet and the winner, Private John Ward, was offered $50 by frustrated bidders for his place, twice the rate of monthly pay. Again in one of those incongruous historical moments the officer jumped but Ward froze at the door. There was some tense re-jigging inside the aircraft, which was only dropping a single paratrooper on each pass. The next-in-line, Private William 'Red' King, took Ward's place in history.

Even during peacetime the US Test Platoon commanded funding and facilities superior to RAF Ringway in England, then under the threat of German invasion. They jumped from the Douglas Dakota, a custom-made parachute delivery aircraft, superior even to the German Junkers 52, both converted airliners. Two parachute towers, formerly used for the 1939 World Fair at Hightstown, New Jersey, were pressed into service to provide controlled descents on the lines of the Soviet 1930s training towers. After a successful demonstration before General George C. Marshall, the US Chief of Staff, in August 1940 the platoon was disbanded. One group became specialised in technical parachute rigging and maintenance, while Lieutenant Ryder formed a parachute-jump training unit to provide the nucleus for the first battalion: the 501st Parachute Infantry Battalion, established in September. Two months later the War Department announced that three more battalions were to form in 1941. By January 1941, one month after America's entry into the Second World War, the bulk of the 501st was already parachute qualified. America was playing catch-up at the same pace if not faster than her under-resourced British ally.

The good luck experienced by the Test Platoon during its training and experimentation in 1940 was in stark contrast to that experienced by the British pioneers. Despite particularly high casualties subsequently suffered by the US parachute battalions beginning to form up, every member of the Test Platoon was to survive the war. Several were wounded but none were killed in action. In England the first deaths were occurring as her airborne forces struggled less against the enemy, but more against official Royal Air Force and War Office inertia.

FIRST BLOOD

'We arrived at the drome, all raring to go,' recalled Sergeant Arthur Lawley, anticipating his first descent. 'We noticed, however, that all the RAF personnel seemed very subdued and we were told that we would not be jumping that morning.' A fatal accident had occurred among the first batch of drops, but they were assured that it was 'one in a million'. Lawley claimed, 'a few days later a second man was killed the same way.' Corporal Ernie Chinnery recalled Driver Ralph Evans was jumping ahead of him during their fourth jump through the hole in the Whitley floor. 'When a jumper leaves the Whitley he is completely out of sight, there are no windows in the fuselage', so nobody can monitor progress. As they circled for Chinnery's turn, 'We were told,' he recalled, 'that a red Verey light had been fired by the DZ crew, that the last jumper had had an accident and that we were returning to Ringway airfield.' They were lined up in the hangar and told that Driver Evans had been killed. Jumping was suspended until further notice. Sergeant Lawley remembered the grim details 'amid a deathly silence'. It was explained 'a young chap had got into a spin when only about eight feet of his 'chute had been pulled out of its pack, this wrapped around him, the tie-pin between the apex of the 'chute and the rigging line broke, and he was killed'. 'There were a number of fatalities, sadly,' remembered Flight Lieutenant John Kilkenny, later posted to Ringway, and 'they immediately set a hum on everything throughout the camp.' The two troops C and D of No. 2 Commando engaged in parachuting were immediately dispatched to Scotland for field and explosives training, while the jump instructors and experts tried to find what had gone wrong. The weather in Scotland reflected their mood. 'It rained practically the whole of August,' Chinnery recalled.

A safer parachute opening sequence was designed and this resulted in the introduction of the X-Type Irvin Parachute. On jumping, the parachutist's bodyweight pulled his rigging lines from the pack first, reversing the previous unsafe sequence, which meant the canopy deployed free of snagging lines. Primitive cord static lines were discarded and replaced by a web line. Arthur Lawley recalled the frustration and unease of being grounded 'owing to these accidents' because 'as yet none of us had done our first jump'. Newly formed A and B troops from 2 Commando were given the opportunity to door-jump from a Bombay bi-plane. This was a temporary stop-gap and less frightening than jumping through the Whitley hole.

Lawley's description of his first jumps offer a revealing description of the modest way new parachutists held their nerve during these trying early days. Eight of them boarded the Bristol Bombay, which had a static line attachment to a handle fixed on the fuselage structure left of the door. 'I noticed that after the first three had jumped the handle had become very loose,' Lawley remembered, as the weight of each man pulled at the handle to open their canopies. 'But no one would say anything about it,' he explained, 'as they were all too scared at what would be said if they did.' This was within days of fatalities. 'There were no "jibbers" in that stick!' Lawley emphasised.

By 21 September 1940, 21 officers and 321 soldiers had passed selection to undergo parachute training with No. 2 Commando. Squadron Leader Maurice Newnham, who was eventually to take over the parachute school, was much involved in its evolution and recalled: 'Of this number 30 had found themselves unable to screw up the necessary determination to jump; two had been killed through parachute failures; and 20 were either unsuitable or had sustained injuries which rendered them medically unfit.'

With such a substantial fall-out rate there would be real problems achieving Churchill's stated aim of 5,000 parachutists. It was not simply a question of courage. 'We were all shaken when two promising young Captains, from the Royal Marines and Royal Artillery, asked to be RTU [returned to unit], not being able to take it,' remembered Captain Martin Lindsay at Ringway. The former was killed later in circumstances of great gallantry at Dieppe, while the latter went on to command an artillery regiment. 'Most of the men' who had fallen by the wayside, explained Newnham, 'were of a very good type and were a loss to the Commando'.

Minutes of Royal Air Force and Air Ministry meetings reveal the extent to which official inertia was dogging progress during the months after Churchill's call to action. Fear of German invasion and the approaching climax of the Battle of Britain was distracting attention. 'To drop 600 or 700 parachutists would absorb all the aircraft (at 8 per machine) in the Whitley Group,' complained the author coordinating an Air Staff note on the subject. 'The position is that [parachutists] are now being trained at Ringway and can be turned out at the rate of 100 per week, so that the figure of 5,000 will be reached in about 12 months' time.' It was suggested the Prime Minister ask the Dutch government in exile to rent six Douglas DC Dakota aircraft belonging to the KLM airline that had fled to England. 'I am strongly of the opinion that the Whitley machines are thoroughly unsatisfactory,' wrote an RAF officer. 'They can only carry 8 men, who would have to sit throughout the passage overseas, huddled up in the bomb tube in great discomfort, and then drop through the middle of a small hole, with no margin for error in poise. Conditions which are calculated to damp the light-hearted enthusiasm with which these young men volunteered for a hazardous adventure.'

Some of these adventures were as bizarre as they were under-stated. Guardsman Frankie Garlic became entangled by his static line when his pack snagged on the strop of the previous jumper. He was left dangling helplessly beneath the hole and could not physically be hauled back inside. Despite him flapping about close to the belly of the Whitley in the slipstream, the pilot Edward Cutler had no choice but to land. This meant certain death for Garlic. Cutler attempted a slow careful approach over grass, keeping the tail of the aircraft as high as possible in the air. Garlic had the presence of mind to get on his back and the back of the 'chute acted as a sledge when he touched down, disintegrating as friction stripped off layers of silk. Corporal Reg Curtis watched the landing. 'Frankie just slid out from under the Whitley, unlocked his 'chute harness and calmly walked away looking none the worse for his unusual parachute landing.' The aircrew who had jumped down were unable to find him and began to fear they had lost him on the approach. Garlic had meanwhile wandered over to the Women's Voluntary Service NAAFI wagon to calm his nerves with a cup of tea. Lieutenant Tony Hibbert recalled his indignant reaction: 'It's bad enough to be left hanging,' he complained, but on landing 'nobody took the slightest notice'.

Parachute training continued to labour in the face of Air Ministry and senior army torpor. By September 1940 there was a sneaking suspicion that perhaps the German Luftlande had already shot its bolt. 'The success of the past airborne operations was primarily due to the absence of opposition,' concluded the chairman of Military Plans during one meeting. 'Where even minor opposition had been encountered, notably in Holland, very heavy casualties had been suffered both by the aircraft and parachutists.' Now that the element of surprise in terms of tactical handling was lost, 'there was little prospect of successful airborne operations of the type practiced in the past', especially 'if it was intended to capture an aerodrome'. Debate suggested gliders, which 'could be landed in any open space of the size of an ordinary field', offered infinitely greater possibilities. Parachutists should be employed in limited numbers to assist glider landings.

'Rotorchutes', a form of rotary steerable parachute that could manoeuvre in the air and land in a given position, anticipating the helicopter, were given a sympathetic hearing. The fact that Mr Hafner, the inventor of this project, 'was at present in an internment camp' gave some clue of the academic nature of the debate being conducted. Orders for only 12 gliders were placed, as the manufacturing provision for 700 more would follow once experience had been gained with these. It was, however, decided to begin training 360 army glider pilots. These were to be air-trained by the RAF and ground-trained by the army. There was a palpable lack of urgency permeating discussions. Development could be likened to Nero playing his fiddle while in the background London burned in the Blitz raids.

Ignorance about gliders, seemingly the more promising option, replicated the dismal knowledge and experience of parachuting. In June 1940 the design executive of General Aircraft Ltd met with the Ministry of Aircraft Production and agreed: 'We want a glider capable of casting off from a present plane at 20,000 feet, and able to glide 100 miles to its objective, carrying a crew of eight – one pilot and seven others.' There was a loose assumption that a tug-plane operating from a south coast airfield could release a glider at some fantastic height and it would drift, with luck, to within 20 miles of an enemy objective. Available gliders in England were sport machines with abnormally low wing loads, designed to soar rather than carry. Something more practical and robust was required to carry loads with high aerodynamic efficiency. This formed the basic design of the Hotspur, the first British military glider. Nobody at this stage foresaw how glider-borne airborne troops might eventually be used in tandem with parachute soldiers.

'It was the gliders who were the glamour boys in the early days,' declared Ringway Chief Parachute Instructor Harry Ward. He shared a hangar with the nucleus of the unit that was to become the Glider Pilot Regiment. 'Most of the flying was carried out on [civilian] sailplanes only,' he recalled. Four appeared in August 1940, driven in by road, preceded by a group of civilian pilots flown in by obsolete Avro 504s and Tiger Moths, which were to be used as tug-planes.

Michael Maufe, a flight lieutenant in the RAF Volunteer Reserve, was told to report to the Central Landing School at RAF Ringway 'which I was told was a highly secret organisation – something to do with gliders'. He found his new unit included over a dozen pre-war glider pilots, several of whom he knew. 'Apparently, we were the "founder-members" of a future airborne force to be formed by Winston Churchill when he heard that the Germans had captured a vital fort in Belgium using glider-borne troops.' The newcomers' difference of approach was highly incongruous. Maufe recalled 'the atmosphere at Ringway was more like that of a civilian gliding club than a normal service unit', friction occurred with stiff regular-service officers. All the available aircraft were requisitioned privately owned or club gliders. 'It was a sad day,' Maufe remembered, 'when all those beautiful clear varnished gliders were painted in dull green/ brown camouflage.' Gifted amateurs overseen by uniformed and unimpressed regular service professionals produced a volatile mix not conducive to rapid progress. 'When the pilots, who knew quite a lot about gliders, tried to pass them out as airworthy themselves,' Maufe explained, 'they were told they must only be done by qualified technical personnel who at that time knew nothing about gliders!'

The first prototype Hotspur arrived in November 1940, following a brief 14 week gestation from drawing board to delivery. The first test flight demonstrated the rough and ready nature of glider development. It was towed by a three-ton truck but could not take off for its maiden flight, checked by the combination of rain, mist and low cloud that typified English November weather. 'On Friday the aircraft was taken out again,' wrote the chief engineer, describing its unorthodox test flight, 'towed behind a car – and just lifted' before the tail skid bent. A new skid was fitted the next day when the glider was finally winched up before progressing to the towing aircraft. It was then decided to modify it for parachute descents.

'I got three 200lb dummies fitted with 'chutes and took them into a Hotspur,' recalled Harry Ward. 'Just before approaching Tatton Park [the drop zone], I took the door off the starboard side of the Hotspur, and it was immediately whipped out of my hand and jammed up against the leading edge, acting as a brake.' His pilot, Flight Lieutenant Robert Fender, lost control and immediately cast off from the tug aircraft: 'Immediately we turned over and went straight through the top of a huge tree in full leaf, which tore the wings off, and we finished up in a heap of plywood on the ground, a 200lb dummy lying across my chest. Bob Fender shouted, "You all right, Harry?" I said, "I don't know yet. I can't move." '

It was decided to stick to basic glider training for airborne forces.

Gliders had to follow their towing aircraft at night or in poor visibility. Nobody at first even knew how long the tow rope should be. Hemp ropes lying outside in wet weather had a propensity to snap, with uncertain consequences, until the first nylon ropes came from America. Night flying could be especially tense. 'To keep position on tow at night we had three torch-lights, one on each wing tip and one on the tail,' explained Robert Fender. 'You flew the glider entirely on the lights – it was like sighting a rifle.' Fender remembered the arrival at Ringway of Major John Rock, a Sapper who 'set the pace for the army'. Rock is seen as the founding father of the future Glider Pilot Regiment. 'He was coming up with all sorts of ideas', and much involved with night flying developments until he was tragically killed in a night-flying glider accident.

The human experience of what it was like to fly in the back, the whole point of delivering soldiers to battle, began to emerge. 'Army passengers were being towed around the area for a few hours at a time by the Development Unit,' recalled glider pilot Bill Johnson, 'in an attempt to find the answers to many questions such as what clothing did the glider soldier need or was he going to be air-sick?' One Hotspur defect was the intense heat generated inside by the Perspex hood. 'It was worse than a Turkish bath,' recalled one observer, 'and troops would stagger out after a flight dripping with sweat.' 'Yes, he was going to be air-sick because he could not see out of a Hotspur,' remembered Bill Johnson. Claustrophobic conditions inside were not conducive to dispersing the stench or alleviating nausea. 'Some portholes were put in and the problem was largely cured,' Johnson recalled.

There was no residue of tug-towing experience to draw upon. The Air Ministry had banned towing civilian gliders before the war. Bill Johnson confessed he was in awe watching tug-pilot training at Ringway: 'First, the tug slows down – a lot! The glider dives forward and ahead, if you please, of the tug. Still diving, the tug now formats on the glider, using the throttle – not to be recommended, especially the inevitable twang when regaining level flight.'

'Normally, one reduces power in order to descend without gaining speed,' explained Johnson; now he had to land on the spot without an engine. Close shaves by gliders with tug-aircraft in the air were legion. Initial attempts by tug pilots to fly in formation and then descend with a glider in tow 'must have given the tug pilot an embolism', he commented. Seconds after reducing power, gliders might be vertically above him on a tight tow rope, or a few feet astern of the tug with the tow rope dangling in a huge potentially dangerous loop. Once the glider's inertia was taken up by operating the throttle: 'the resultant twang could remove the nose of a glider or the tail of the tug. The trick was to push violently forward on the stick at the precise moment just before the rope went taut.' This required skill and did not always work. Many casualties resulted from these deft dances between tug and glider.

'A fully loaded Hotspur was crashed at this time, or a little earlier, near to, or on the airfield. There were very serious injuries and some killed among the soldiers. Some of the injuries were caused by loose equipment flying about on impact and so racks were made for rifles etc as a result – a lesson expensively learned!' Eight soldiers died, but casualties incurred during development were accepted as an unavoidable evil. 'There was also, so help me! One tug for two gliders,' recalled Johnson. 'I have mercifully forgotten what happened to that monstrosity.' The process inexorably continued because 'they were all basically good ideas and might have worked. Practically nothing in wartime is too stupid not to be worth a try.'

Theory needed to be put into practice against the enemy. The first semi-public exercise was mounted on Salisbury Plain on 3 December 1940. Two sorties of two Whitleys dropped 32 men from No. 2 Commando with weapons containers during a 5th Corps exercise. Sergeant Arthur Lawley recalled, 'as each one of us landed we were pounced on by brass-hats who fired all sorts of questions at us.' B Troop mischievously commandeered a grand car belonging to HRH Prince Olaf of Sweden, viewing the exercise, while en route to their objective. Two days later Planning Staff at the Ministry of Air decided on an airborne raid against the Tragino aqueduct in Campania province, near the heel of Italy. It was too precise a target to be tackled by conventional air attack. On January 11 1941, Operation Colossus, the first British parachute operation of the war was officially approved.

Arthur Lawley remembered: 'Fifty of us were told that we had been picked for a special demonstration for which we would have to train and live on the 'drome at Ringway.' The Tragino aqueduct carried the main water supply for the province of Apulia, feeding Taranto, Brindisi, Bari, Foggia and other towns supporting Italian operations in the Mediterranean and North Africa. It was hardly strategic. In reality it was a live fire experiment to identify the potential range of parachute operations and test equipments under combat conditions. Could the RAF take them across a vast distance from the UK mainland and deliver on target and on time? Still controversial, the parachute force was being given the chance to vindicate its existence, practically and demonstrate to the world that Britain had a parachute capability, which despite setbacks, it was prepared to use aggressively.

No. 2 Commando had meanwhile transitioned to the 11th SAS Battalion. In early January 1941 a sudden whisper went around its camp. 'By this time we were all getting very bored with all the fun we had had,' announced Sergeant Lawley, 'and were impatient in wanting to do something real, especially when we saw the results of the London, Manchester and Sheffield blitz.' A specially selected team labelled X Troop assembled at Ringway. 'Eventually we were told that we were going on a job,' Lawley recalled. 'The job was a sabotage one, that of blowing up an aqueduct.' It was the first combined operation. The RAF would deliver the Army parachute raiding force and the Royal Navy would extract them by submarine. X Troop was to be commanded by Major T.A.G. Pritchard, the 11th SAS second-in-command. An officer-heavy group of seven officers and 29 men was selected.

Mounting for this first airborne operation was rudimentary. Half of X Troop were Royal Engineers, the remainder of the force was there to protect the demolition element. Exact information about the construction of the aqueduct was scarce. Only one picture was available, taken 13 years before by the London engineering firm that built it in 1928. A full scale mock-up of the section to be attacked was erected at Tatton Park, but the final full scale night rehearsal before the raid was a fiasco. Lawley never forgot it: 'There was a 40 mph gale blowing.' Lieutenant Anthony Deane-Drummond remembered: 'About half the aircraft dropped their loads in the wrong place, so that the wretched parachutists landed in the trees along one side of Tatton Park.' Others hit the roof of Tatton Hall and landed in the oaks around it. 'Practically everyone hit the ground very hard, resulting in a number of broken limbs,' claimed Lawley. All were reduced to chasing arms and explosives containers 'bowling along at a brisk 10 or 15 mph over the ground', Deane-Drummond sombrely noted. The top-brass were unimpressed, particularly as the local fire brigade had to be called out to rescue those hanging in the trees.

The eight Whitley Mark V bombers needed for Colossus formed a composite flight from Numbers 51 and 78 Squadrons from RAF Dishford, detached from bombing duties for the raid. At dawn on 8 February all eight aircraft arrived at Luqa airport, Malta, much to the surprise of the RAF planners who had expected one or two not to make the 1,400-mile journey, much over occupied France. Raid security appeared intact. The paratroopers thought the target was Abyssinia, while the air crew guessed Yugoslavia. There were cheers when it was announced the target was Italy.

'You are pioneers,' Pritchard, the raid commander, announced as they climbed aboard during the early evening of 10 February, 'or guinea pigs – and you can choose which word you prefer.' Few expected they would get back. Their CO, Lieutenant Colonel Charles Jackson, told them from the start that extracting survivors would be unlikely. Sir Roger Keyes, the Chief of Combined Operations, sending them off at Mildenhall was equally pessimistic. 'A pity, a damned pity,' one trooper overheard him whispering to himself as he turned away. Eight aircraft took off between 1740 and 1817; six loaded with raiders, explosives and weapons containers and two with bombs for a diversionary attack on Foggia.

'We got to the target without incident,' recalled Arthur Lawley, 'and started dropping at roughly 9.30 pm.' Six men and containers exited at various intervals from the six aircraft. 'Through the hole at my feet some houses and then a river flashed by in the moonlight,' observed Anthony Deane-Drummond. 'Green light! A sudden jolt into reality.' He jumped number 5, one after the containers dropped in the stick middle. 'The first thing I noticed was the silence after the incessant drone of the engines,' interrupted by the slight jerk of his parachute opening. 'We had been dropped rather low, from not more than 500 feet, which gave us about 15 seconds before we touched down.' He found the surrounding countryside illuminated by moonlight 'far wilder and tilted at far sharper angles than we had expected'. Lawley 'found myself floating steadily down in beautiful moonlight and everything was deathly silent'. They both came down in a ploughed field on the side of a hill about 100 yards above the aqueduct. 'For a second I listened intently,' Lawley recalled, 'but could only hear the distant drone of the planes and the bombing carried out by two others further up the valley to distract attention.'

The air drop occurred in dribs and drabs because aircraft were dispersed by flak over Sicily. Deane-Drummond and Lawley's aircraft dropped at 9.42 pm, while the others did not show up until about 10.15. Five dropped reasonably accurately but one aircraft dropped one and a half hours late two miles away in the next valley to the north-east. Always expect the unexpected once again, as a string of setbacks occurred. Lieutenant Paterson, the senior Royal Engineer officer to reach the objective, was perplexed to discover the aqueduct piers were constructed from concrete not brick. Explosives had been prepared and loaded for the latter. Some containers were missing and others could not be found in the dark. Local inhabitants were pressed into service as bearers carrying explosives from their landing spots to the piers but only 800lbs of the 2,240lbs earmarked for the job could be found. Paterson improvised: instead of blowing three piers he packed what he had around the westernmost pier with 160lbs for an adjoining abutment.

At 12.30 the main charge exploded, followed 30 seconds later by a smaller bang under the small bridge nearby, leading to the aqueduct. This was a tense moment. '*Whoomf*! Our bridge went up in a clod of flying concrete, iron rails and bits of masonry,' recalled Lieutenant Deane-Drummond. 'I had never expected so much debris, and we were showered with blocks of concrete and bits of iron.' Lawley listened intently. 'To hear the water rushing down the mountainside like a raging torrent was music to our ears.' They had done it.

The raiding force split into three groups to rendezvous at the coast with the submarine HMS *Triumph*, but were all captured by the Italians. The submarine had been compromised in any case and was not there. One of the raiding aircraft hit by flak had announced by radio it was to ditch in the same bay. The paratroopers spent five nights covering 60 miles to evade the enemy. One man was killed, another wounded and the whole force lost for a result of little military significance. Within two and a half days the aqueduct was repaired. Only Lieutenant Deane-Drummond escaped with the story and got back to England in August 1942.

Britain was seen to possess a parachute force. But in the absence of any survivors there were doubts whether the raid had been successful. It took ten days and media pressure for the War Office to release a short guarded report about the action, while alarm and consternation reigned in Italy. Lessons were learned: air photographic reconnaissance was seen to be insufficient and night dropping procedures had taken longer and were more complex than anticipated. Container release gears and the concept of separating dropped weapons from fighting troops needed to be urgently reviewed. Despite the disastrous pre-raid rehearsal, 11th SAS Battalion's earlier training was vindicated. The determination, resilience and initiative displayed by the force on arrival, ignoring or coping with unexpected setbacks, was exactly the aggressive response their training was supposed to imbue. They would always be outnumbered, there would always be surprises and reversals, but they should never give up. They launched knowing they were unlikely to return. Fortunato Picchi, the SOE Italian-born interpreter who jumped with the group, was shot as a spy.

One small raid was of no strategic consequence. Resources remained at an all time low. 'The word "priority" had been used and abused to such an extent that it had almost lost meaning,' recalled a much harassed Squadron Leader Maurice Newnham, tasked at Ringway with fleshing out the bones of Churchill's concept. The army complained it was short of men and weapons and where would the aircraft come from? The RAF was reluctant to release bombers for an air transport role. Newnham recalled: 'The idea of raising and training a large airborne force in readiness for the re-occupation of Europe raised only frosty sceptical grimaces on the harassed faces of many whose help was necessary to its success.' Volunteers for 11 SAS reduced to a dribble while wastage through injury, sickness, refusal to jump and other causes diminished its strength. A complete troop had been lost in Italy. The ironic backdrop to official obfuscation was frenetic activity to raise anti-glider poles and block runways to deter the very type of force the Air Ministry appeared reluctant to sponsor.

Prime Minister Churchill visited Ringway on 26 April 1941, to review progress for himself. He was accompanied by General Ismay and Air Marshal Sir Arthur Barratt, the head of RAF Army Cooperation Command. Expecting to see after a year of development something approaching a functioning airborne force, he was presented with a partly trained parachute force numbering less than one-tenth of his stipulated requirement and only half a dozen gliders. The weather was miserable, with winds gusting beyond the 25 mph limit. Five-old-Whitleys loaded with paratroopers waited in the corner of the aerodrome for the winds to abate. The visit was highly staged; Ringway staff knew they had scant opportunity to get their message of insufficient resourcing across. An intercom system had been set up in the control tower to enable the Prime Minister to listen into proceedings. Wing Commander Nigel Norman, the senior air staff officer, radioed the Whitley formation leader with commendable self-assurance to enquire whether they were ready to take off. Back came the loud metallic response after a pregnant pause: 'No, I'm not ready to take off – five of the blighters have fainted.' Sheepish grins were met with a broad smile from the Prime Minister when the aircraft eventually took off. The incident visibly relieved tension and broke the formality of what became a productive exchange of ideas. Forty paratroopers were dropped and reinforced by a further 100 for the ground exercise.

'All that we could show him at that time were paratroopers dropping from the five ancient Whitley bombers and a few gliders,' recalled Flight Lieutenant Maufe, a Ringway glider pilot. 'The demonstration as a whole could not have impressed him and he took drastic action to get things moving faster when he returned to London.' Parachute Instructor Harry Ward heard his parting comment, '*We will have an airborne division* and then where we had met opposition before from the Army, they all jumped on the band wagon!'

Two days later General Ismay, who had accompanied Churchill, received a terse note in London. 'Let me have this day the minute which I wrote in the summer of last year directing that 5,000 Parachute troops were to be prepared.' The Prime Minister accepted there were difficulties but he wanted action. 'Let me have all the present proposals for increasing the Parachute and Glider force together with a timetable of expected results.' He took four weeks to digest the material, a process interrupted by news that a German airborne corps had landed on the island of Crete. The very force level to which he aspired was fighting an unprecedented strategic level vertical envelopment. Crete would change everything.

5

CRETE: A STRATEGIC GOAL

PRELUDE: THE FIRST AIRBORNE CORPS IN HISTORY

The 50,000-strong Anglo-Anzac expeditionary force under Lieutenant General Sir Henry Maitland Wilson had been conducting a skilful controlled retreat south through Greece since the middle of April 1941. It had been outflanked by the German invasion through Yugoslavia. Hard-fought troops were exhausted. Athens was abandoned and the dusty columns of men were retreating across the 60-metre high bridge spanning the Corinth Canal separating Attica from the Peloponnese. They were to be evacuated by sea from Piraeus and other southern disembarkation ports. This four mile wide land bridge bisected by the canal was easy to pick out from the air.

Eyes anticipating yet another of the endless Stuka dive-bombing attacks detected the menacing silhouettes of approaching aircraft in a brilliantly blue early morning sky. Troops scattered in all directions either side of the dusty road as clanging air alarms were punctuated by the cracks of flak and bursts of machine gun fire. Foreseeing high diving planes, nobody noticed the low-flying gull shapes until the last moment. Momentary shadows swished overhead, wheeling past like huge birds with outstretched wings. Barbed wire encrusted skids on the nine DFS 230 gliders snatched at scrub and whipped up huge clouds of dust as they bumped and skidded into loud wood-splintering scraping halts. One crashed directly into the canal bridge ramp, seriously injuring the pilot and many of the German assault engineers inside. Cockpits and side hatches were discarded and Fallschirmjäger in their distinctive baggy smocks poured out, some still reeling from the aftershock of landing. The bridge was rushed from both sides.

One group shot and grenaded startled defenders with short bursts from machine pistols. Others clambered all over the precarious bridge superstructure, slashing wires and pulling off demolition charges.

The background drone of the approaching swarms of Ju-52 transports rose to a crescendo roar as they passed overhead, spilling paratroopers. Wave after wave of 140 aircraft dropped the I Battalion Fallschirmjäger Regiment 2 (FJR 2) north of the Corinth Canal bridge and the II Battalion on the southern bank. Oberst Alfred Sturm directed this first combined glider and parachute assault of the war on a single objective.

Company Commander Leutnant Arnold von Roon was relieved on leaving the aircraft that there were not crowds of British troops waiting to disembark on the nearby quay at the canal entrance. As he kicked his legs to turn into wind he saw the long column of Allied vehicles on the road. 'They halted at the moment we jumped,' he recalled. Drivers were dashing through scrub next to the road seeking cover. 'Soldiers in khaki were running all over the place, as were many civilians, seeking cover behind fences and under bushes and trees.' As he floated down 'a desultory fire opened up'. Leutnant Häffner's reinforced glider-borne assault pioneer platoon had captured the bridge minutes before the arrival of the main parachute force. It was early morning of 27 April 1941.

Von Roon, commanding the 3rd Company and jumping with the first flight recalled how bizarre this first parachute insertion since Holland was turning out to be. As one of his young officers, Leutnant Kühne, crunched into stony ground near a ditch, two young Greek girls aged about 17 or 18 set about him 'and tried to give him a good snog. Clearly, they wanted him to know they were not hostile!' He saw flak starting to burst ahead of the third flight of Ju-52s bearing down on the objective. These distracting puffs of smoke caused men to jump too soon, and 'one didn't want to get too near the bridge', he thought. Inevitably 12 jumpers straddled the 60-metre deep canal cut through the rocks with three plunging into the eight-metre deep water, weighted down by helmet, parachute and equipment. Two of them slipped beneath the surface before help could arrive. 'Same place, same time and less than 100 metres apart,' thought von Roon, reflecting on the irony. The whole stick had floated between 'euphoria and misery, luck and fate, life and death; which in war are inextricably intertwined'. Their 'soldier luck' had run out.

Savage fighting broke out around the bridge. One of von Roon's men, Oberjäger Schröder, pursued New Zealand truck drivers into the bush. One enraged Kiwi turned behind a fence and fired a complete pistol magazine at him, striking his arm. He defiantly flung the pistol high into the air when called upon to surrender. 'They all fought until their ammunition was exhausted,' recalled von Roon.

At this point the bridge erupted with a sharp crack; briefly rising up and falling into the canal beneath a huge pall of black smoke. Several startled Fallschirmjäger and a war correspondent, von der Heide, went with it. He had been filming the successful action for the newsreels from the bridge span. The attackers were now very vulnerable to countermeasures, having split their strength between both banks. Von Roon appreciated that 'explosives were more valuable than gold to engineers' and their trove of explosives was hit by a chance round, or a direct shot from a stubborn English soldier. Whatever the verdict, the bridge was gone.

Oberstleutnant Schirmer pursued the retreating British with captured trucks on the Peloponnese side. A mixture of daring and bluff enabled him to capture 72 Allied officers and 1,200 prisoners. His regimental commander Oberst Sturm, left behind to capture Corinth with a much reduced force, was less impressed. Schirmer was both 'congratulated, then shat upon', as Sturm later confided.

General Student, the commander of the newly expanded XI Fliegerkorps (Air Corps), was unaware that this attack, especially ordered by Hitler, was about to happen. Relocating FJR 2 and its assets in place and on time amid the roll-out plan to invade Russia had, nevertheless, been a masterpiece of resourceful logistic organisation carried out by the unrepentant staff of Luftflotte 4.

Hauptmann Friedrich Freiherr (Baron) von der Heydte, commanding the I Battalion FJR 3, was coincidently moving by train with his unit, bound for the Balkans. 'What was that? Was I hearing right?' he recalled, overhearing a chance radio broadcast. 'Was I hearing right? In a daring attack from the air German paratroops had occupied the Isthmus of Corinth.' His response was the same as all the other Fallschirmjäger regiments on the move. 'Damn! We weren't there. Were we too late?' The Fallschirmjäger arm had not seen combat since the year before. 'We did not grudge it to others, but we also wanted to experience it for ourselves.' Everyone now knew that German paratroopers were in the Balkans and in strength.

'To parachute down over England! My God, that would be something,' recalled Jäger Erich Reinhardt, echoing his contemporaries. Fallschirmjäger were due to spearhead the German invasion of England as part of Operation Seelöwe (Sea Lion) in the summer of 1940. Preliminary planning envisaged the 7th Flieger Division forming bridgeheads on the south coast of Britain, backed by sea-landed elements from von Rundstedt's Ninth and Sixteenth Armies. This was scaled down to landings on the South Downs and north of Dover. Friedrich von der Heydte recalled that aerodromes were to be the initial targets and he had one selected 'somewhere between Oxford and Cambridge'. It was finally decided that paratroopers would secure a crossing and defend along the line of the Royal Military Canal extending across the Romney Marsh from Kent into Sussex, to protect Sixteenth Army landings between Worthing, Folkestone and Dover. Parachutists would seize the iconic white cliffs.

Von der Heydte received his orders on 25 September when the parachute regiments were assembled in Goslar. His battalion would fly from Saint-Quentin aerodrome in France. 'Advance parties had already left for France,' he remembered, and 'in Goslar all preparations – packing of equipment etc – were made.' However, Sea Lion was deferred on 12 October. 'Two or three days later the whole operation was called off,' recalled von der Heydte, 'no reason was given.' An attack on Gibraltar was next contemplated and prepared. Von der Heydte remembered 'it was to be carried out by a reinforced battalion landing on the Rock in gliders', supported by a corps ground attack from La Linea, having crossed Spain. Both options were rejected as too risky. The Royal Air Force and much-respected Royal Navy could still cause irreparable damage.

Despite heavy losses in Holland and Belgium, the battle-winning contribution of the German airborne arm resulted in the very expansion to corps level that Churchill sought for the British Army. A third Fallschirmjäger regiment was added to 7th Flieger Division and losses made good. The glider-borne contingents of the Assault Group Koch that performed so admirably at Fort Eben Emael was expanded into a full *Stürm* (assault) regiment of one glider-borne and three Fallschirmjäger battalions. Recruit intakes came from the Luftwaffe and army. Corps troops formed up with flak, medical, signals, transport and reconnaissance units and heavy weapons anti-tank and mortar companies for the division. Luftwaffe air transport groups were allocated to the division as a separate formation. All these capabilities conferred greater ability on the airborne to operate independently of ground forces. XI Air Corps was formally established in January 1941 under the command of the newly promoted Generalleutnant Student. Within one year it had expanded from five parachute battalions and specialised companies to four regiments with division and corps airborne assets.

With the Balkans occupied and much of south-east Europe in German hands, contingency plans to assault Malta and Crete were discussed by the Oberkommando der Wehrmacht (OKW). OKW favoured assaulting Malta, whereas Student believed Crete a more suitable objective for his fledgling corps. The build up for Operation Barbarossa, the forthcoming invasion of Russia, was swallowing resources. Crete might enable the RAF to threaten vital Romanian oilfields at Ploesti. Despite misgivings, Hitler supported Student's plan, fully backed by Göring who, following the Battle of Britain setback, saw laurels to be won from the first strategic vertical envelopment in history. The operation, a purely air force affair, was unprecedented: a whole island captured by air alone.

The transition to corps status meant an expansion from 8,250 parachutists to 11,000 between 1940–1. Where were these men to come from? The first wave of Fallschirmjäger recruits was 'told' to volunteer. The Hermann Göring paramilitary police battalion and first army company formed around established units and were then transferred to the airborne role. After the excitement of their unveiling at Hitler's birthday parade in 1939, recruits poured in. The flow became to a torrent after exciting newsreel coverage of the Scandinavian and western campaigns. Jäger Erich Reinhardt was seduced into volunteering by the village teacher's two pretty daughters who told him about 'the existence of a German paratrooper force, which I was told had just paraded in front of Hitler in Berlin'.

Media publicity played a part. Heavyweight champion boxer Max

Schmelling joined the paratroopers and the press made a huge fuss. 'The only thing to it was to avoid getting "cold feet" at the first jump,' the popular *Adler* airforce magazine reported him saying. 'Once that stage has been got over, parachuting is a fine sport that only needs a little courage and good nerves.' Schmelling was a recruiter's gift. 'I enjoy it quite as much as boxing,' he claimed. 'Only real men are with them,' proclaimed another article, offering seeming practical and convincing advice to sign up. One 23-year-old technical draughtsman from near Würzburg claimed he joined the paratroopers 'to be with soldiers with the most chance of survival'. A married 32-year-old doctor from Bremen with children rose to the idealistic challenge of being 'where the impossible must be achieved'. He did not want 'to be just a doctor, but like many of my other wartime colleagues, remain where bullets are whining.' The press loved the paras, describing how a shopkeeper from Schwerin joined after three years' Luftwaffe ground service 'to finally get involved in a combat mission, with all that involves'. It was precisely the propaganda the National Socialist regime wished to inculcate among its fighting men. One farmer's son who failed flying selection transferred from ground personnel to become a para 'and be able to fly earlier at the enemy'.

Fallschirmjäger battalion commander Friedrich von der Heydte described these 'idealists' as he called them, 'the most difficult to handle'. The average age of his men on the eve of the invasion of Crete was 18 and 'without exception they were volunteers'. He disliked idealists because 'quite a lot of them who had been in the Hitler Youth, were saturated with national slogans'. Von der Heydte sought soldiers with knowledge, endurance, toughness and self-control, remarking 'in all these cases the type of man who broke to pieces under the inexorably gruesome hardness of a soldier's war was the fundamentally soft idealist'. The other type he disapproved of were the 'ambitious', quite often party functionaries or overly staid military types. These men 'were a latent danger to the feeling of comradeship and, therefore, to the morale of the troops'. If he could, he avoided selecting them.

Jäger Max Bloom transferred from the army alongside 88 volunteers from Infantry Regiment 89. Most of the idealists fell out during the paratrooper selection course. 'Only four were deemed good enough to go,' he recalled. Underpinning the elitist ethos permeating the Fallschirmjäger arm was its Ten Parachutist Commandments (See Appendix I), personally approved by Hitler, a strong supporter of Student and his paratroopers. It extolled Wagner-like warrior ideals of caste superiority, emphasising each man was selected to be part of an elite. Every soldier was to be offensive-minded and physically highly tuned. Teamwork was lauded because it was recognised they would land in conditions where there would be no support. Weapon handling therefore became a vital skill, as also the need to conserve ammunition. Personal security was key to achieving the shock impact that came with surprise. Initiative was to be ruthlessly asserted to exploit every opportunity in tenuous circumstances that had to be overcome by a fierce and adventurous spirit. Special men were sought, eminently suited to the faster tempo required to operate across two conflicting dimensions, from air to ground. 'Never surrender' was the maxim. 'Death or victory must be a point of honour.'

Von der Heydte identified the main difference between the para-chute and line-infantry soldier as being the speed at which they entered battle. Infantry observe enemy positions and the ground over which they will manoeuvre beforehand and identify the main danger areas. 'The parachutist on the other hand, is taken on a short flight directly from his base-camp and, without any middle act, is plunged straight into close combat with his adversary.' This required certain intangible qualities which had to be brought out during selection because 'he starts fighting in a situation which most infantrymen would regard as hopeless, for he ventures voluntarily, without tanks or artillery, into total encirclement.'

Although the National Socialist regime sought unquestioning Wagnerian stereotypes, the qualities sought by the Fallschirmjäger spawned the unconventional rather than austere Prussian virtues of obedience and hard work. Jäger Feri Fink with the Stürmregiment was convinced he was part of 'the elite of the elite', but admitted 'in everyone of us there existed a bit of *Schweinhund* and it all depended on the individual how much that inner characteristic manifested itself.' Fink and his men regarded themselves as 'rebellious patriots'. They assiduously served Germany, but used their heads in so doing. 'As a consequence Fatherland and Folk was not totally ahead of the rogue.' In short, they were soldiers 'with a new face'. Those uneasy with this unconventional approach peddled rumours that the Assault Regiment was a type of penal unit. 'Many of us, it was claimed, had criminal records and were serving the rest of our time.' Jäger Erich Reinhardt with FJR 1 could understand these sentiments. 'I hoped my simple country soul would find some understanding with the paratroopers,' he confided, 'which would certainly not have been possible in the old Prussian military system fostered in Hitler's Germany.' He was no traditionalist. 'I felt an aversion towards both the officers and soldiers.'

Communists and Socialists served with Fallschirmjäger units like exiles absconding to the French Foreign Legion to break with the past. Erich Reinhardt's father was an anti-Nazi. 'The Nazis have a screw loose,' he told his son, 'how on earth can the leader allow such a ridiculous cult to exist?' Nevertheless, his view was tempered by nationalism. 'Even my father wanted Germany to win the war together with 99 per cent of the German nation.' OKW had intelligently perceived the adventurous spirit that permeated Fallschirmjäger recruits and stipulated that *all* applications submitted were to be accepted, whatever the individual's background. Obergefreiter (lance sergeant) Jochen Hüttl was a Jewish paratrooper, who was awarded the Iron Cross 1st Class. He remained with his unit until 1943 when the regime even combed paratrooper units for Jews. It was a company commander decision whether they were retained and Hüttl's proved unsympathetic. Arno Spitz, another Jew, volunteered in 1941 by neglecting to put a cross in the box marked 'Aryan' on his application. He went on to win the Iron Cross 1st Class in Russia and was captured fighting with his unit on the outskirts of Berlin during the last days of the war. Unteroffizier Ball, a famous Jewish ice hockey player, volunteered because 'the only way to secure decent living conditions for Jews in Germany in the case of a Hitler victory was to have fought particularly bravely during the war'.

'I liked the adventurers best,' admitted battalion commander von der Heydte with FJR 3. 'You could go horse-stealing with them, but you could also take them on any patrol – they were born parachutists.' They were individualists often at the peak of their military profession. 'Ludwig Pernpeintner was a real specimen, a brawny and rebellious oaf from lower Bavaria,' recalled Jäger Martin Pöppel with FJR 1. 'But you couldn't get anything on him, since he already had the highest grade for non-officers as a lance corporal or Stabsgefreiter.' They were bright enough to run rings around their occasionally more stolid superiors. Willi Lojewski, one of Pöppel's friends 'was a real mercenary'. In his youth he had been with the East Prussian Border Guard, then the Reichswehr, and had fought in the Spanish Civil War 'and was now with us'. 'He was proud to be the only man among us to wear the Spanish Cross,' and was a formidable drinking partner. 'He knocked back schnapps like the rest of us drank water.' 'Many of them had committed some offence, only to become honest with us,' explained von der Heydte, 'others had run away from home solely to prove themselves men.'

Jäger Heinz Austermann summed up the stark differences between the Fallschirmjäger and other more conventional soldiers in the summer of 1940:

They came from all over Germany, from all units of the Wehrmacht. The eternal mercenaries and the young adventurers, who believed all their dreams would come true in the paratroops. The politically unsound, who fled from the Gestapo, were here. There were men who came with such a long civilian or military criminal record that they believed that only by serving in the paratroops could their records be cleared. Demoted officers and NCOs here saw the best opportunity to be promoted quickly to their old rank again. In no other unit were there so many colourful characters, so many individualists.

'As diverse as my soldiers were, I liked them all,' declared von der Heydte, 'whether good or bad, they had grown into my heart. I lived with them, and for them.' These were the men who were to be launched against Crete.

Student presented his plan to Göring on 5 April and to Hitler on the 21st. Operation Merkur (Mercury) was not accepted until 25 April, leaving only 25 days for planning. Overall control of the operation was in the hands of General Löhr commanding Luftflotte (Air Fleet) 4, but the actual parachute and glider assault was the responsibility of 7th Flieger Division commanded by the newly appointed General Süsseman. Student was coordinating and directing at XI Corps level. With such short planning parameters and with the bulk of Student's units and specialised equipments requiring to be moved 1,500 miles from central Germany to the Balkans, Luftwaffe signals transmissions markedly increased. The British listened intently. 'Ultra' encrypters working at Bletchley Park in Buckinghamshire began to decode and sift the signals traffic.

This was the first corps-size airborne operation in history, mounted when the majority of German resources was being directed to support the imminent massive German invasion of the Soviet Union. Radios were scarce, having been required to direct armies for the out-march to Germany's eastern borders. Transport aircraft were mustered from all parts of the Reich. 540 Ju-52s were placed at Student's disposal but this was sufficient only to carry his force in two waves. Many aircrews had no parachute dropping experience. Airfields in southern Greece were insufficient for their needs, the best having been taken over already by the VIII Air Corps, providing 160 medium bombers, 180 fighters and 150 Junkers 87 Stuka dive-bombers for the assault. Much of the Luftwaffe ground crew and airfield command infrastructure had already been committed to Operation Barbarossa. Transport Geschwader (squadrons) were based on 'desert' airstrips where dust obscuration became an immediate problem. The 22nd Air Land Division could not be extricated from the Barbarossa roll-out and 5th Gebirgsjäger (mountain) Division was superimposed at barely 20 days to go. Many of its soldiers had never flown before. Tropical uniforms were unavailable in the stifling Mediterranean heat and the whole enterprise was dependent upon a single tanker carrying the required aviation fuel docking in time, but it was held up by the collapsed bridge in the Corinth Canal. The fuel required for at least three sorties per aircraft only arrived the night before the proposed launch.

The mountainous island of Crete is 160 miles long by nearly 40 miles across. Ultra had already identified the three airfields and 100 miles of coastline as key objectives. Student's plan was to land Gruppe West, the four battalions of the Stürm or Assault Regiment, commanded by Major General Meindl, at Maleme airport to the west of the island in the first wave. Gruppe Centre was to consist of the main bulk of the 7th Flieger Division under Lieutenant General Süssmann and was tasked to secure the Suda Bay and Cannea area and the airport at Rethymnon. Gruppe East was a four-battalion strong force commanded by Oberst Bruno Bräuer, earmarked to capture the most easterly airfield and the important port facilities at Heraklion. Maleme and Cannea were the first-wave dawn objectives and Rethymnon and Heraklion would be assaulted eight hours later, after turning round the same aircraft. The attack was to be conducted by 15,000 Fallschirmjäger with some 8,500 Gebirgsjäger stood by to air-land. This was the first vertical envelopment in history not supported by a planned ground link-up.

Student was duplicating the 'oil spot' strategy he had successfully applied in Holland. Cannea was seven or eight miles away from Maleme, Rethymnon was about 38 miles and Heraklion nearly 45 miles distant. All the strategic objectives were to be seized on day one, with 15,000 lifted by air and two sea transport convoys bringing in a further 6,300 men and heavy equipments to land at Maleme on the first night and Heraklion the second evening. As von der Heydte explained: 'These reinforcements would serve to exploit the para-troopers' gains and would widen the perimeter on all sides – like a spreading oil spot – until finally the various bridgeheads were linked and the whole island occupied.'

German intelligence was inaccurate, assessing the enemy at between three battalions of infantry to two full brigades. It assumed there were no Greek troops and that the Cretan population was pro-German and would not resist. In fact there were 32,000 British and Dominion troops with General Freyberg's CREFORCE and 11,000 Greek troops, 43,000 in all. German estimates were out by a factor of at least three. Freyberg was only selectively fed Ultra information for fear of compromising the source. Despite appreciating the threat against his three airfields he was as equally disturbed by the sea-borne invasion threat; a misappreciation. The Royal Navy was more than adequate to deal with the motley collection of caiques and fishing boats transporting Student's heavy weapons and equipment. Airfields were the deciding factor, the key to vertical envelopment.

Auftragstaktik, or mission command tactics, lay at the basis of the oil spot strategy. Commanders were given a mission and the resources to achieve it. How they executed the mission was not prescribed by senior commanders who relied upon independently thinking junior commanders to fulfil their objectives. Developing airborne tactics was totally unlike conventional infantry shock tactics. Company commanders chose their own drop zones, accepting dispersion in the face of strength to produce a different type of shock, the unexpected as a force multiplier. The tactic did however fragment the attacking force, accepting geographical dispersion even before wind, terrain and anti-aircraft fire produced the same outcome. Hauptmann von der Heydte, having experienced the impact of such dispersal in Holland, elected to jump his battalion as a single group. He had seen what could go wrong. Fierce resourcefulness snatched victory from the jaws of defeat. Oberst Bruno Bräuer, due to jump at Heraklion, commented on 'the almost super-human sensation of the parachute jump'. It produced battle winning self-assurance. The jump, Bräuer explained, 'compresses into the space of seconds feelings of concentrated energy, tenseness and abandon: it alone demands a continual and unconditional readiness to risk one's life. Therefore the parachutist experiences the most exalted feelings of which human beings are capable, namely that of victory over one's self.'

Von der Heydte, soon to jump at Cannea, reflected, 'Psychologists may ponder whence that sense of power and courage is derived once a parachutist has gained terra firma after a successful jump.' It generates a cocktail of emotions powered by adrenalin and euphoria, 'a sensation almost of intoxication'. German commanders appeared to factor this awareness into their command decisions. Generalmajor Meindl commanding the Stürm Regiment due to assault Maleme airfield felt there were two attack options. Either the regiment jumped complete behind the aerodrome in an offset assault to avoid enemy flak and attack from the rear or he simply dropped into the middle of the enemy's defences, relying upon shock, surprise and the fighting quality of his soldiers to win through. He elected to do the latter. Von der Heydte explained that on landing the paratrooper 'feels himself a match for any man and ready to take on anything that comes along'. Both men were confident their fierce unexpected attacks would carry the day. Meindl was unaware that his force of 1,860 glider men and

Fallschirmjäger were to jump in amongst 11,859 defenders. Von der Heydte's battalion formed part of Gruppe Centre where 2,460 men were to land among 14,822 Allied troops. At Rethymnon 1,380 men in the second wave would be pitted against 6,730. Bruno Bräuer's FJR 1 Gruppe of 2,360 men would need all the superhuman qualities they could muster against 8,000 well dug-in British and Dominion troops.

The 'Fallschirmjäger Lied', or song, encapsulated the spirit and vigour of the way the paratroopers expected to conduct the coming assault:

> Fly on this day, against the enemy!
> Into the planes, into the planes!
> *Kameraden*, there is no going back! . . .

They were facing average odds of six to one against, relying simply on combat effectiveness as a force multiplier.

'TOUCH AND GO': THE FALLSCHIRMJÄGER EXPERIENCE ON CRETE

Fierce though they were, the average age of von der Heydt's men in FJR 3, a factor of rapid expansion after Holland, was just 18 years, 'scarcely more than boys' he reflected. Awaiting them on the fortified island were hard-bitten New Zealand, Australian and British veterans evacuated from Greece or brought in from the Western Desert. These were tough men, urban children of the Great Depression and farmers from the outbacks of Australia or New Zealand. During the fiasco of the unsuccessful Greek campaign they had been out-manoeuvred and caught off balance, rarely able to close with the enemy. After being dive-bombed along the dusty roads of southern Greece to the evacuation ports, Crete represented a paradise on arrival; a beautifully rugged Mediterranean island free from the ravages of war.

The 28th Maori Battalion had lost 150 men in Greece without being allowed to stand their ground. Unlike many they got out with their weapons but had to part with some of these on arrival at Crete. Company commander Major Humphrey Dyer observed no Maori would readily give up any weapon he had fought with. Captain J.H. Marriott with the 2nd Royal Leicestershire Regiment, a mechanised unit, recalled occupying 11 different defensive positions during a 20-day retreat in the Western Desert at the beginning of 1941. They were given six hours' notice to hand over their vehicles to the 4th Indian Division and 'after a very rough sea voyage and 50 hours after we had left the desert we tied up at Heraklion harbour'. They occupied positions around the airport with 14th Brigade, newly roled as dismounted infantry.

'We were bombed and strafed daily, usually at meal times,' recalled Marriott and, 'at first we shot back.' The softening up process had begun with Luftwaffe air attacks from the middle of May. 'Soon brigade realised that this shooting was an ineffective waste of ammo and that it was better to conserve and keep our positions concealed.' 'We really kept ourselves hidden,' recalled Lieutenant Sandy Thomas with the 23rd Battalion at Maleme. 'We were terribly careful, we wouldn't even drop an orange peel or anything at all.' Apart from occasionally rehearsing counter-attacks, 'we stayed really hidden to get surprise.' Marriott remembered, 'the attack we were told was expected on 20 May.' This date is cited in many veteran accounts. The enemy was anticipated and he would come by parachute. Lieutenant Colonel George Dittmer briefed his Maori 28th Battalion officers to anticipate bombing attacks followed up by parachute drops onto clear areas. 'The Maori were expected to leave the protection of their pits to deal with the threat.' Rehearsals were carried out. 'All Tommy guns would go with the first wave so as to permit riflemen to get in with the bayonet.'

At dusty landing strips in the Athens area, at Topolia, Megara, Tanagra, Dadian and Corinth the Fallschirmjäger made ready amid hastily erected tented camps. During the previous month they had moved by train from Germany through Austria and Hungary and then by vehicle through Romania, crossing the line of great armies moving east for the invasion of Russia. They had not seen action for nearly a year, preoccupied with planning for Sea Lion and dealing with the bureaucratic and administrative hurdles of reorganisation and expansion to Corps status. Now they were immersed in packing and loading weapons containers, parachute preparation, equipment checks and calculating aircraft jump order to reflect the tactical plan. It was an endless round of test weapon firings, briefings and platoon and company tactical rehearsals. Aviation fuel arrived the night before and required nearly three million litres of petrol to be transferred into 15,000 200-litre drums which then had to be hand-pumped into aircraft tanks. Paratroopers who should ideally have been resting prior to the operation were instead rolling drum after drum of fuel to their respective aircraft. Confidence was tinged with apprehension at the approaching unknown.

'On 19 May we received our orders for the next day – a parachute drop on the island of Crete,' recalled Oberjäger Martin Pöppel. 'We reckoned that such a small island wouldn't be a problem for us.' That evening the normal loud soldier songs were superseded by sensitive and nostalgic tunes. 'For most of the men it would be the first parachute jump in action,' Pöppel reflected, 'and only a few – such as myself – knew what death in action was really like.' 'According to the situation reports the invasion should be child's play,' recalled Gefreiter Adolf Strauch with the II Battalion of FJR 2. Success, they were assured, would come on the first day of the insertion. Strauch, who had jumped at the Corinth Canal, reflected: 'Maybe, but we have our particular experience and our own opinion.'

'The orders given by [company commander] Goette were so optimistic; it seemed that the British really did shoot with beans,' remembered Jäger Erich Reinhardt, due to jump at Heraklion, his first time in action. 'I was concerned that perhaps the drop would be made in daylight and not at dawn, as it would take at least two hours flying time to cover the 185 miles.' Nobody was happy with the insertion across so many miles of sea. Nevertheless, 'we had discovered that we belonged to the second wave and were pessimistic in that we thought that by the time we arrived in Crete, there would be nothing left for us to do.'

The air-land soldiers with the 5th Mountain Division would have the longest and therefore tensest time to wait. An airfield had first to be secured by the paratroopers and their aircraft sent back. One Jäger with the Krakau Regiment 85 recalled being briefed by his platoon commander about the totally unfamiliar conditions they would experience inside the Junkers 52 transports. 'The best was you don't get air-sick and you would be able to swim for it' in an emergency 'because the Ju would float for 20 minutes on water.' The problem was that the vast majority of mountain soldiers, coming from the land-locked Alps, were non-swimmers.

The initial shock of the landings at Maleme would be taken by the glider men of the Stürm Regiment. Glider soldier Ferdinand 'Feri' Fink remembered the pathos of their final briefing by the company commander von Plessen, who was not to survive. They silently stood around him in a square when he suddenly appeared to sag, lost for words, after giving the detail of the briefing. 'After a pregnant pause von Plessen straightened himself and finished his speech with some banal words about soldier's luck and similar stuff.' The final bivouac amid small fires under the sinking red sun was the poignant setting for songs about comrades who had been killed earlier, sung hesitantly, as if by children attempting them for the first time. 'Much was said, everything conceivable was spoken about, but not a word about the coming day.' Fink had a fitful night's sleep and nobody felt like breakfast when the steadily escalating noise of loading and preparation woke them up. Everything had to be queued for as usual: a breakfast they didn't want and last-minute hand-outs of equipment and rations. 'Hardly a word was spoken,' remembered Fink.

By 0400 the roar of taxiing aircraft drowned out everything at the mounting airfields. The first light of dawn eerily penetrated the huge red dust clouds whipped up by the propellers of the slow moving aircraft, hanging like a dense fog over the airfields. 'We're starting,' said Fink's pilot quietly as the glider tow tightened. They could hardly see through the dust but felt the perceptibly increasing roar of the Ju-52's three engines. 'We rolled faster along the ground, but for a longer time than we were used to.' All the gliders were heavily laden, packed with their ten men and equipments. Slightly uneasy, they strained to listen for a change in engine note. Finally the glider rose and then bumped down again, rose and settled again. 'That was very unusual!' Fink thought. 'Shall I throw my bicycle out?' he called out in a vain attempt at humour. No one responded. Slowly and ponderously they gained height and suddenly cleared the dust cloud when they were 'bathed in silver morning light' as they climbed higher and higher.

Presently his friend Horst, sitting forward on the bench, complained about the stifling heat. They were wrapped in the same bulky 'bonesack' smocks stuffed with ammunition and grenades that had been worn in Norway and Holland. He slit a hole in the flimsy glider wall and levered it open with the barrel of his rifle to let in a blessed draught of cool morning air. Horst lit a cigarette, reached back and slapped Fink on the shoulder, holding it in front of his face.

Down below Fallschirmjäger Regiment 3 was taking off. Hauptmann von der Heydte could just make out the shadowy outline of the control sentry through the dust. His torch showed green. 'We started to move, the wheels knocking hard on the bumpy ground, faster and faster until suddenly the knocking ceased,' he recalled, 'and gave place to a gentle sensation of gliding as the machine lifted itself from the runway and rose in a wide sweep upwards.' Taking off in formations of three in dust was hazardous and barely negotiable. Looking down from above, pilots saw aircraft suddenly change direction into pairs or veer around approaching dust palls. Von der Heydte gazed at the dust cloud 'which blustered and boiled like a dirty sea'. Except for the aircrew, not one of the 13 men seated alongside uttered a word. 'One after another the aircraft lifted themselves out of the reddish-grey fog until they had all collected like a flight of huge birds and turned in column towards the south,' he recalled. Transport Geschwader were taking over an hour to gather into unit formations. Fuel concerns impelled them to set off before the stream had a chance to fully gather. Concentration over the drop zones was therefore compromised, even as they took off. 'Everybody was glad once we were in the air,' von der Heydte remembered. 'It was early in the morning and the sun was rising and it was a wonderful picture.' Everyone inside was preoccupied with their own thoughts. 'When there is no going back, most men experience a strange sinking feeling,' he recalled, 'as if their stomachs had remained on the ground.' He was soon asleep.

Flying over the brilliant blue Mediterranean Sea at low level and in formation required intense concentration from pilots. Many were unused to flying the *Kette* formation of three aircraft in a 'V' shape in stream columns. Gunners manning the dorsal machine gun towards the rear of the fuselage test-fired over the sea. Most Fallschirmjäger slept once the magnificent early morning spectacle of the Athens Acropolis passed them by as the formations droned out to sea. Crammed inside knee to knee, chatter subsided and most dozed off taking advantage of the anticipated two-hour flight, lolling into whatever space could be found.

Feri Fink jerked widely awake in his glider when he saw a seemingly stricken glider plunge beneath them. He peered down through the plexi-glass window until the aircraft righted itself, disappearing beyond his restricted field of vision. 'A glider has cut loose,' he called, louder than intended. 'That's the third,' came a voice from the front. 'Poor swine, they're off for a bath, hope nobody drowns,' was the essence of the uneasy murmuring that came back from the front bench. A premature release over the sea was everyone's unspoken fear. Lieutenant General Wilhelm Süssemann's overloaded glider crashed 19 miles south-west of Athens, coming down over the island of Aegina. The commander of the 7th Flieger Division was dead alongside four of his staff before the aerial armada even arrived at Crete. Two gliders made emergency landings en route, while two more were lost at sea; they were 40 men down.

'In the early hours of the morning we heard the aircraft coming over,' recalled Lieutenant Haddon Donald commanding 14 platoon 22nd Battalion, overlooking Maleme airfield. 'We looked out over the sea and the sky was black with aircraft.' The bombers and fighters of VIII Flieger Corps under General der Flieger von Richthofen had arrived, 30 minutes ahead of the transports. Over 200 medium bombers and up to 180 fighter aircraft swooped down to strafe and bomb Maleme, Cannea, Rethymnon and Heraklion. After 20 minutes 150 Stuka dive-bombers bombarded the anticipated drop zones. 'We had been bombed every day before that, but this was a real concentration,' recalled Haddon Donald, 'there was hardly a square yard where there wasn't a crater.' Attacks were intimidating. 'We didn't expect the vast number there was,' remembered Fred Irving, also at Maleme. 'We were so frightened we were having a wee every few minutes.'

With Crete now clearly in sight, almost 30 DFS 230 gliders began to cut away from their tug-aircraft with 12 miles to go. Almost immediately there were control problems as gliders sought to avoid each other on the crowded run-in. Fink was momentarily blinded by the sun as they curved eastward from the south-west to line up on Maleme airfield. 'Only a few minutes separated us from our objective, we knew it.' He could sense the quickening of breath from the men ahead already wincing at the prospect of incoming fire. They prepared for the landing: 'We put our leather gloves on and some started checking and rattling their weapons.' Dry coughing sounds signified the arrival of the first flak, some bursting with an unexpectedly loud ring amongst them. 'A steel splinter whirled evilly straight through the hull in front of my knee and through the spokes of the folding bicycle.'

'We're carrying on,' intoned the pilot up front. They whooshed along a valley at low level, recognising Hill 107 to their left; a bridge and road flashed by beneath them. 'I'm not going to get over the trees in the way,' shouted the pilot, more urgently this time as a tree-covered embankment swept up. 'Then under!' barked the section commander. 'Get ready,' called the pilot and the section commander jettisoned the cockpit cover while Fink and his friend Horst loosened the side hatch. Trees and vineyards flashed by. '*Achtung!* Watch Out!' cried the pilot as everyone ducked their heads as low as possible. Thick red-brown dust enveloped the glider which bounced, trailing streaming debris and ploughed to a scraping halt in a vineyard. A cry came from forward, 'Damn we're under fire,' thought Fink. 'As the dust dispersed we were all surprised to see everything within the glider covered with a fine film of earth, weapons, equipment and clothing were coloured red-brown.' Quickly releasing their harnesses, they leaped out. They had landed about 1,000 yards from their objective, the airfield, in the dried up riverbed of the Tavronitus.

Brigadier Howard Kippenberger commanding the 10th New Zealand Brigade in the Galatos area in the valley south-west of Cannea saw the first four gliders passing overhead. 'The first we had ever seen, in their silence inexpressibly menacing and frightening.' This was Sussemann's staff, landing without their general.

Kurt Seiler, swooping in, recalled the totally unexpected 'infernal din of firing' which was an enormous shock. They thought they were achieving complete surprise. 'There were bullets actually zipping through our glider in the few seconds it took us to get down,' he remembered. 'We could see nothing at all from our cramped positions, and then we hit the ground in a terrible crash and the pilot was killed. We fell out of the wreck and were enveloped in shooting; there were bullets flying at us from all directions and two men were hit at once, and their cries soon ceased.' They were pinned down and made a break for cover, but two more men went down and Seiler was wounded. He was to lie there the whole morning.

Twenty-two gliders belonging to Oberleutnant Kurt Sarrazin's 4th Company landed on the plateau on both sides of Hill 107, overlooking Maleme airfield, two of them snagging guylines and ripping through tents in the New Zealand encampment. This was the centre of the 22nd New Zealand Battalion's defended locality. Ray Minson, watching them coming in, recalled how 'very flimsily built' the gliders were and how 'this one peeled off and hit an olive tree.' He said: 'The men started to come out of the door – and that was all there was to it. They came out one by one and we shot them one by one. It was too easy. It was like duck shooting.'

Sarrazin was killed and Major Walter Koch, the battalion commander and victor at Eben Emael, received a severe head wound. The 3rd Company with Fink landed in the dried up River Tavronitus and overran a flak battery but Oberleutnant Wulff von Plessen, his company commander, was killed. Stosstrupp Braun landed nine gliders in loose formation near the bridge in the dried-up riverbed but Major Franz Braun with the Stürm Regiment staff was killed. General Meindl, the regiment commander and leader of Gruppe West, was seriously wounded shortly after landing by parachute.

Arnold Ashworth, defending nearby, recalled 'a pathetic looking German trying to drag his bullet-riddled body behind the glider for a refuge it could not offer'. A field grey uniformed arm kept pathetically trying to wave a white handkerchief a few inches from the ground. Ashworth moved out to deal with the glider to their left, still firing back, when he was distracted by 'a most agonising voice, panting over and over again *schotten, schotten*, which translated into English means shoot me, shoot me'. The critically injured glider soldier had managed to crawl away from his comrades with half his hip torn away by the heavy calibre bullet of their anti-tank rifle. Ashworth found himself reflecting: 'A short while before he had been a fine specimen of manhood, as of course were all these airborne troops, all specially chosen with a high standard of physical fitness, and now here he lay at my feet pleading with me to put an end to his horrible suffering and wasted life.'

He picked up some personal photographs of a smart young man from a corpse with what appeared to be his two children picking flowers. 'I could not help looking down at his horribly distorted form and wondering if maybe tomorrow someone else would be standing over me gazing at the few photographs which I carried.' They had achieved success for the moment, but, 'it was a sobering thought and it didn't cheer me up at all.' The shock glider assault was unravelling, but both sides had yet to comprehend it had failed. New Zealand soldier Ray Farren had been stunned by the savage bombing of their positions overlooking Maleme airfield. 'We couldn't see a thing for at least a quarter of an hour or 20 minutes after the bombing ceased,' he remembered. They were momentarily confounded by the enormous concussive effect of the explosions. 'Because of all the smoke and dust some of us had temporary black-outs and it took a little while to recover from this.'

Justus von Schutz flew with the first wave of approaching Ju-52s. 'I was quite confident it would be all right,' he remembered, 'and besides this I was very tired so I slept in my aeroplane.' Crete was in sight. 'I asked my boys to wake me up in time, so I could take some pictures.' Battalion commander von der Heydte was awoken: 'We are nearing Crete, sir,' he was informed. Looking out, his first impression was that his aircraft was hanging virtually motionless over an emerald blue sea bathed in sunlight. 'I could see our target – still small, like a cliff rising out of the glittering sea to meet us – the island of Crete.' The tension quickened.

'Slowly, infinitely slowly, like the last drops wrung from a drying well, the minutes passed,' von der Heydte remembered. Pilots were expending 98 per cent of their attention at this stage simply trying to stay in formation as flak began to burst ahead. Follow-on aircraft were buffeted by the slipstream of those in front struggling to main-tain the tight concentration needed for the approaching drop zones. Navigational landmarks clearly stood out: Hill 107 at Maleme, the line of the dirt airstrip and the rough scar of the dried riverbed alongside it. Rising thermals were making aircraft wave up and down as they came over land, unbalancing Fallschirmjäger nervously poised to jump from open doors. Pilots had little scope to evade fire because they were hemmed in by the narrowing stream of aircraft, fearful of colliding with those alongside. In levelling off at drop height they throttled back and slowed down in the teeth of ever-intensifying bursting flak. 'There is nothing so awful, so exhausting, as this waiting for the moment of a jump,' recalled an agitated von der Heydte, standing as number 1 in the door. 'In vain I tried to compel myself to be calm and patient.' A thin ribbon of surf passed below. The fly-in was from the west, based on a calculation that the sun would then be in the defenders' eyes.

Arnold Ashworth at Maleme detected a heavy droning noise and looked high in the sky, but his friends attracted his attention and gesticulated out to sea. A sea invasion, he surmised, looking to scan the horizon for telltale boat silhouettes. Nothing, and then when he raised his eyes above the surface, 'I saw them crawling like noisome giants toward us, their undercarriage appearing to be sweeping the placid sea. Troop carriers, they were coming in waves, the blackness of them adding the sinister to the fantastic; they were easily the largest planes that we had ever seen.' New Zealander Alan Queerie with 5th Brigade recalled: 'It seemed unreal for a few seconds, it was a weird sight, we'd never seen a parachute drop or anything like that.' As the aircraft stream roared over doll-like figures started to tumble out. 'It was only a matter of seconds,' observed Ashworth, 'a most demoralising experience – there were men and equipment falling everywhere.' The sky was alive with descending attackers. 'They just floated down,' recalled New Zealand soldier Clarrie Gordon. 'They were not high up, two or three hundred feet, I suppose. I don't know how long, the first minute, ten seconds, I wouldn't know,' declared Gordon. 'All of a sudden somebody pulled a trigger and she was on, the whole thing was on!'

Leutnant Freiherr von Könitz, flying a Ju–52 transport, was repeatedly hit flying over Maleme. 'A machine gun burst struck behind the co-pilot's seat, severely wounding the aircraft engineer Feldwebel Schwörer in the head.' The crew further realised that 'the tyre of the right-hand wheel must have been shot through.' This was to result in a one-wheel touch down and 'hop' when they got back to Megara. Oberfeldwebel Helmut Wenzel, the veteran of Eben Emael and now a platoon commander in one of the lead aircraft, recalled how 'the clacking noise of bullets and little holes in the aircraft tell us we are already under fire.' Contested drop zones were to become every paratrooper's nightmare. 'The chap behind me is hit and curls up on the floor,' he noticed, 'probably dead – there is no time left to see to him.' The drop zone was coming up and 'we have to get out and jump!' To his consternation he realised on jumping out that they were in the midst of established enemy positions. 'Infantrymen stand up firing at us with all they have.' With frustrated anger he wrenched his shoulder strap aside to free his pistol and fired back. Bullets began ominously snipping at his trouser braces, scorch-marking his smock and cutting away his binocular strap. 'Damn dogs!' he shouted in fear and frustration. Another bullet entered near his right armpit and exited from behind his neck as he crashed into a vineyard. He fired back and hit two 'Tommies' with his pistol before a machine gun burst spun him to the ground, ripping open his haversack and disintegrating his water bottle in a burst of spray. Incoming fire ceased and switched elsewhere. They thought he was dead.

'We just kept firing at those that were still moving,' claimed New Zealander Wally Wakahuru, a Maori with 5th Brigade. 'The ones that were dead were coming straight down and they were so close you couldn't miss them.' They were meting out terrible punishment upon the totally vulnerable descending parachutists. Karl Pickert summed up the German position: 'I know I cursed the fools who had told us what an easy job we would have, and myself for not bringing more water and rations. The heat seemed terrific, and I wondered how we would last the day.'

Over 200 Ju-52 transport aircraft and fewer than 30 gliders dropped the three and a half battalion force of Gruppe West into a fire-storm. Flak and cross winds scattered the force over an area of 20 square miles, some even landing in the sea. The III Stürm Battalion was delayed by dust on take-off. One minute intervals had been calculated for each plane to take off but it took five minutes each time for the dust to clear. When the battalion arrived two hours late it flew into a totally alerted cone of fire. 'I think I'll never forget the screaming of the parachutists who thought they were landing in an unopposed area as they came down,' recalled Lieutenant Sandy Thomas with 23rd Battalion at Maleme, 'passing through this tremendous fire.' The battalion commander was killed suspended beneath his parachute before reaching the ground. Virtually every officer died during the landing or shortly after. Within two hours the 600-strong battalion was reduced to a scattered 200, hiding behind stone walls, lurking in olive groves and dried out watercourses and ditches. Prevented from reaching their weapons containers, they could only fight back with pistols and grenades.

Only the II and IV Battalions, dropping mainly to the west of the airfield, got down broadly intact. General Meindl, the force commander, was soon wounded, as also the Ist Battalion commander. Regimental headquarters took three hours to even open radio communications after the drop. The first situation report based on fragmented information was sent to Corps at midday. Dispersed units attacked where they were able, but the first directed regiment attack order did not come on air until 1300. The wounded Oberfeldwebel Helmut Wenzel was pinned down for the entire day. He could not move until nightfall.

Hauptmann von der Heydte, jumping with FJR 3 in Prison Valley south-west of Cannea, barely escaped drowning in a reservoir in an area ironically completely devoid of water. Later sticks of *panzerjäger* (anti-tank) and mortars did land in the lake. Gruppe Centre's first wave was scattered by flak and poor navigation across 15 square miles. Von der Heydte, who snagged a tree with his parachute at the water's edge, remembered an overwhelming feeling of loneliness and isolation once on the ground. He had jumped with hundreds of parachutists, yet 'I could see no soldiers anywhere'. The 3rd Regiment drop was dispersed among rugged and tree-covered hilly terrain; the II Battalion was frantically searching for weapons containers that had disappeared among the olive groves. Staggered start times in Greece meant companies arrived at intervals of 20 to 30 minutes. Two companies of glider troops which had attacked flak positions around Suda Bay found themselves totally isolated and under siege. The III Battalion, like its sister unit in the Stürm Regiment, dropped among New Zealand and Greek defensive positions and was annihilated. Many of the heavy equipments landed in the reservoir and the heavy weapons company commander was killed. Vegetation and broken ground impeded visibility. Von der Heydte's I Battalion had attacked the prison complex in the valley, but shortly after landing they had linked with nobody else. 'Apart from the drone of the returning aeroplanes, there was no sound – no human voice, nor even a rifle shot,' he recalled. He set off to find the rest of his battalion.

The unexpected was at the forefront again. The first wave was totally surprised at the strength of resistance and having to fight for their drop zones. Not only were Greek troops present in strength, they were fighting back despite the occupation of mainland Greece, and the Cretan population was joining in too. Terrain and the nature of the ground was a further unpleasant surprise. Vertical air photographs had not revealed the 'castle' heights they encountered in Prison Valley, or undulating broken ground and dried watercourses around Maleme airfield. Water shortages were anticipated but the wave of heat that met them was also unexpected, and temperatures of 104 degrees were commonplace. 'We were all drenched with perspiration,' recalled an irritated von der Heydte, blaming 'some brain-wave of the planners' resulting in their 'wearing the same sort of clothing as had been worn by German parachutists only six months previously when jumping over Narvik, close to the Arctic Circle'. Veterans described the drop zones as 'dressing rooms' strewn with discarded tunic jackets. Dry preserved rations, packaged for operations in north-west Europe, melted in the heat 'constituting an extraordinary pot-pourri of melted chocolate, smoked bacon, spiced sausage, and rock-hard rusks,' complained von der Heydte. Days later, and with no re-supply, they ate it gladly. The Fallschirmjäger had anticipated a short sharp action with a surprised enemy. The unexpected was more pronounced for them than the enemy.

'A VICTORY THAT WASN'T A VICTORY': THE SECOND WAVE AND AIR-LAND EXPERIENCE

As the aircraft returned to their mounting airfields in southern Greece it became apparent that seven of the 493 committed Ju-52s had not made it back, although many were considerably damaged. General Student, still in Athens, assumed in the absence of news to the contrary that the landings had been successful, although no radio communications had been received. At midday he had no idea that the Stürm Regiment was effectively rebuffed at Maleme and its commander severely wounded. Fallschirmjäger Regiment 3 was blocked south-west of Cannea and the commander of the 7th Flieger Division was dead.

The parachute insertion plan, linked to close air support from Fliegerkorps VIII's bombers and fighters, had to run like a railway timetable to maintain momentum. More aircraft dropped out with serviceability problems than were shot down. Preparations at the mounting airfields became tinged with an aura of chaotic and hurried activity. Oberjäger Martin Pöppel at Tanagra observed the huge clouds of dust thrown up by the returning aircraft taxiing in for maintenance, 'some with large bullet holes in their wings and fuselage.' After fitting their own weapons containers, he remarked, 'if you didn't laugh you'd cry – we have to fill up the Junkers' petrol tanks by hand!' Hand-pumping, an hour-long process in the intense midday sun, had not been factored into planning timetables. 'The reports from the aircrew was not so very optimistic,' remembered Jäger Erich Reinhardt at Topolia. It appeared 'the majority of the British were not so hypnotised by the first drop of paratroopers'. Gefreiter Erich Strauch, waiting to emplane for Heraklion with Gruppe East, recalled the Ju-52s returning. 'They were not all there, our fears were confirmed'. Before they were able to fit new weapons containers 'the first dead were lifted out of the damaged machine – the aircraft chief didn't say much.' At Topolia Dr Eiben, the medical officer flying with FJR 1, observed about 100 vultures fluttering down around the airfield periphery, creating an ominous backdrop.

'It appeared to be complete chaos in the heat,' recalled Erich Reinhardt. Aircraft shortages meant there was insufficient space for everyone in the second wave. Quarrels over seniority and priority of places broke out. Reinhardt observed his company commander come first to their aircraft and then turn away for another. He never saw him again. All of Dr Eiben's aircraft lost their places and his medics were left behind. He managed to purloin a seat next to the company commander Oberleutnant Voshage to jump as number 2. This produced a spat with Leutnant Proff, a platoon commander on his first live operational jump, who wanted the place. Eiben refused:

he was the senior and did not want to tempt fate. Proff jumped third and was killed soon after landing, as was everyone else who jumped after Eiben. Pöppel in the second wave managed to fly out at 1300 when Dr Eiben was still boarding his aircraft; Gefreiter Strauch did not fly until 1400. The plan was clearly going awry.

'We could not see any sign of an escort,' remembered Reinhardt once under way. Eiben began to feel distinctly uneasy watching swarms of Me 110 fighter aircraft flying past in the opposite direction at the halfway point. 'Had they already used up all their fuel? Have we got fighter protection?' he thought. Most could not care less: drained by the heat and last minute activity before boarding, they slept, relishing the fresh air coursing through aircraft once they were over sea. Eiben remained uneasy: 'A flight into action raises many lively thoughts, reflections about one's whole life, touching on life and death. There are moments when one must kill the inner *schwein-hund* that emerges. The men are also busy with their own thoughts. Some who would otherwise be noisy are somewhat silent. Such a flight produces enormous inner tension, but they are all burning to get into action.'

Reinhardt's Ju-52 suddenly dropped out of formation and conducted an emergency landing on Milos. 'I had the quiet suspicion that the engines were in no way defective.' He inferred, 'It was clear that the first flight over Crete had badly disturbed our pilot and perhaps he thought five minutes of cowardice is preferable to a lifetime of death.' Reinhardt was to parachute in much later.

The defences at Rethymnon and Heraklion had been alerted to the morning's events at Maleme. 'At 1600 hours the sky filled with aircraft, Dorniers, Heinkels, Me 110s and the Ju–87 dive-bombers,' recalled Captain J.H. Marriott with the Leicesters at Heraklion. 'The father and mother of an air attack then started.' He remembers that, 'although the sky was still full of aircraft we had a twenty minute lull, perhaps the para aircraft were late.' At 1800 hours, 'looking out to sea, I saw what looked like a thousand stars twinkling beyond the island in the bay.' He soon realised 'this was the sun playing on the blisters of the para aircraft'. Three streams 'flying in Vics' appeared overhead and 'as the sky filled with parachutes of all colours we began to witness the best and most thrilling air display of the century.'

The early arriving serials of Gruppe East, dropping to the west of the town of Heraklion, landed reasonably intact, including Pöppel and Strauch. Later serials, notably Fallschirmjäger Regiment 1, dispersed during the launch, were heavily punished. 'Even before reaching the coast we received heavy fire,' recalled Dr Eiben. 'In a short time I counted 12 to 13 holes in my vicinity in the fuselage that were not there before.' A frantic exchange ensued between the company commander and the pilot because, being to the left of the formation, they were drifting too near the town. 'Further right,' he called, but too late. As Eiben jumped out he saw two other aircraft already streaming smoke. Gefreiter Adolf Strauch watched the awesome aircraft run-in from below. 'The English flak and artillery shot out of every barrel, burning diving machines!' he recalled. Heavy casualties inside meant 'only isolated jumpers were tipping out of the doors, pilots held their aircraft steady until they crashed – a battalion was annihilated.'

'We were regaled with the sight of burning planes and parachutists plummeting to earth,' Marriott with the Royal Leicestershire Regiment gleefully recalled. 'One aircraft achieved the impossible of having a wretched parachutist caught on each wing.' Flak and the staged arrivals resulted in a catastrophic dispersal of Fallschirmjäger Regiment 1 across 45 square miles. The 6th and 7th Companies had only three survivors. The drop at Rethymnon by FJR 2 was equally catastrophic, spread over six to seven square miles, directly over prepared defensive locations. Lew Lind with the Australian 2/3rd Field Artillery saw descending parachutists firing machine-pistols clamped between their knees, 'landing everywhere'. 'Many had been hit and their bodies on striking the ground gave a flip like a clasp knife.' Three more 'whose parachutes had not opened, crashed with crunchy thuds'. Furious fighting developed around their gun pits. 'The companies with orders to go for any DZ within 15 minutes reach were off like hounds unleashed,' recalled Marriott. 'It was largely a case of individual fire and movement by sections to pick them off wherever the poor wretches were trying to conceal themselves, often underneath their parachute canopies.'

By the end of the first day Student's situation was critical. Piecemeal company parachute drops at Maleme to support Gruppe

West proved disastrous. A tenuous foothold was achieved but attacks against Hill 107 dominating the airstrip had been beaten off. Gruppe Centre's situation in Prison Valley six to seven miles away was equally tenuous, while landings around Rethynmon, nearly 40 miles distant, were a total failure. Gruppe East some 45 miles further eastward was barely hanging on. Freyberg's CREFORCE was more than holding its own, but its First World War fixation with holding ground was in stark contrast to the aggressive fighting responses from the greatly diminished and often surrounded paratroopers. Gruppe West was still attacking, whereas Centre and East hung on. Gefreiter Strauch confessed in his diary: 'We have few hopes of victory, but we're not going to give up.' The British and Dominion defence had been unsettled. They were unable to assess the strength of the landed units and were not under the same enormous pressure as the attackers to do something.

Hill 107 overlooking Maleme airfield became the key to the developing battle. The 5th New Zealand Brigade sent too small a force to fight it free. Freyberg, commanding forces in Crete, remained wary of seaborne landings. With telephone lines cut and intimidated by constant Luftwaffe air attacks, Hill 107 was given up. On the map it looked like a mere straightening of the line, but it meant the best chance of retaining Crete was lost. Platoon commander Lieutenant Sandy Thomas regretted the uninformed decisions taken at that decisive point ever after. 'If only we could have held on, gone forward instead of back.' He felt they should have won. 'It was just touch and go,' he declared, the same could be said for Student.

Student had committed 7,000 men by air at this point and had less than 1,000 Fallschirmjäger in reserve; a whole airborne division had been expended and little to show for it. Not until a lone Ju-52 landed amid fire at Maleme early the following morning did Student appreciate Hill 107 was in German hands. He changed the plan and shifted the *schwerpunkt*, or main point of effort to the west. Crete would be rolled up eastwards from Maleme airport. Six Ju-52s were ordered to crash-land with ammunition and weapons and the first 600 mountain troops placed on stand-by to land later in the day.

The Luftwaffe meanwhile kept the defenders of Crete off balance. New Zealander Fred Irving at Maleme described the intimidating extent to which they were obliged to fight with one hand tied behind their backs: 'The spotter planes came over and circled round and we were ordered not to shoot at them. They went round and round just above the large trees. They must have realised we had annihilated their whole unit and they came over and fired just about everything they had at us. They machine-gunned us, bombed us and really just tore us apart. The effect on morale was quite terrific, you prayed, you literally prayed, whether you were religious or not.'

Captain Marriott remembered: 'They always had an aircraft of sorts watching us in daylight hours, capable of bringing down an air strike and directing it.' Air dominance alone was to ensure the eventual conquest of the island.

On the second night the Royal Navy intercepted the first convoy of Greek caique vessels, carrying about 100 men apiece and much of the heavy artillery and equipment the paratroopers needed. They were just 18 miles short of their objective, north of Cape Spatha. The flashes and deep rumbling at sea were noted by the exhausted besieged paratroopers at Maleme and from the heights in Prison Valley. It was a massacre. Boats were rammed, shot up and ploughed through by heavy warships, prompting the remnants to scatter. One thousand men ended up in the water, 300 perished and a further 100 were wounded. The Royal Navy was constrained from operating south of Crete by day due to Luftwaffe air superiority and had slipped in to scan the northern waters by night. Twelve caiques and three heavier vessels were sunk and none got through. German air power was still holding the struggling island of Crete in its grasp and was to finish the job. Key reinforcements were dropped by parachute at Maleme at 0830 on 21 May. This was the last of the parachute reserve commanded by Oberst Ramke, who replaced the wounded General Meindl. Many 37mm anti-tank guns and machine guns mounted on motor-cycle combinations were included within the drop. They proceeded to fight the airstrip clear, but it remained under artillery fire. It was, nevertheless, decided to air-land the first mountain battalion.

'When are they finally going to need us?' remarked a Gebirgsjäger with Oberst Krakau's 85th Regiment. 'This question came up, time and time again.' The air-land troops of the 5th Mountain Division, like those of the 22nd Division that had preceded them in Holland, grew increasingly anxious watching plane load after plane load of paratroopers taking off in the blinding dust. They were granted only three weeks to prepare after 22nd Division, caught up in the Barbarossa build up, was taken off the Crete order of battle. Subtle differences emerged going to war in aeroplanes. 'Rucksacks were not full,' recalled the jäger, 'only the essentials are packed' to lighten air loads. In any case 'it would be hot there, very hot', not the Alpine climate conditions they were used to. Like the paratroopers before them, 'nobody spoke about the coming operation, everyone rummaged through former war experiences in Norway, Holland, Belgium and Corinth to isolate the best things.' Being veterans there were few illusions about what was to come, except hardly anyone had flown in airplanes before. 'The uncertainty was ever greater, the waiting unbearable.' Then during the afternoon of 21 May 'suddenly and unexpectedly' they received the word – 'we're off against Crete!'

Once the formations were under way for the two-hour flight, having waited to see the Acropolis, like the paras, most men were soon asleep. Before long the huge blue silhouettes of the Cretan mountains began to emerge from the sea. A leutnant with Regiment 100 commanded by Oberst Utz recalled the order 'Helmets on!' as Crete hove into sight. Rucksacks were handed out and grips tightened on rifles. 'The unloading had to be quick, more so if there was artillery fire on the airfield,' he rationalised. Kurt Neher, flying with the Gebirgsjäger, remembered they were 'flying at an altitude half that of the island' as they descended for the approach. 'Machine gun bursts skim the water below us – but fall far too short.' Pilots called 'Hold tight' and suddenly inside the fuselage the ground was above the windows. There was nowhere to land and Neher's aircraft lifted and flew in a wide curve out to sea again. 'Brown fountains erupt and cover the transport aircraft already landed with earth, smoke and dust.' The landing strip was under artillery fire.

The leutnant with Regiment 100 observed 'a huge reddish dust cloud showed the landing strip'. Everyone's nerves were stretched taut, he felt 'it was too short and hardly anything to see in the clearing dust'. 'Hang on,' the pilot called and with a sudden curving descent he was down. In amongst roaring aircraft engines the thuds of enemy artillery strikes could be discerned. 'They were coming in very close to our aircraft,' recalled the leutnant as they taxied along. Quick-firing cannon reports and the whine from machine gun bursts could be heard puncturing holes in the fuselage side. Petrol streamed from fuel tank strikes as they feverishly evacuated the aircraft.

Glider soldier Feri Fink with the Stürm Regiment defending Maleme aerodrome watched the first formation of 60 Ju-52s bringing in the advance guard of Regiment 100. 'From now on, we're over the worst of it,' he declared with some relief, because from this point onward they were likely to win. He described the erratic landings under fire with dust-strewn multiple crashes and near misses as a virtual 'wild boar hunt'. Other aircraft were seeking to take off amid the clouds of dust and black oily smoke boiling up from burning transports. He recalled the bizarre image of a Luftwaffe hauptmann in dress-white tunic emerging from one of the first flights. He urged him to quickly take off before more artillery strikes came down. The officer responded haughtily, 'First I will collect my Staffel and then take off in close formation.' Fink was incredulous. 'Didn't this bird of paradise realise,' dressed in his popinjay uniform, 'what artillery shells are about?' At this point the hauptmann's third aircraft taxied up, caught its wheel in a hole and swung round to crash into the first two flights. The exasperated officer was still shouting 'Whoa, whoa, whoa' as artillery shells howled in among the entangled aircraft. Fink dived for cover in amongst the perimeter trenches, closely followed by the figure in white.

Kurt Neher's pilot made another attempt to land under fire: 'Now he grits his teeth. To hell with it – the bird must land. The Ju just manages to clear a vineyard, touches the ground, rears up and digs one wing into the ground. Grinding under the huge pressure, the wing snaps apart in the middle, ripping the fuselage as it half turns to the left.'

Inside, pandemonium reigned as 'men, packs, life jackets and ammunition are thrown forward, torn and tightly squeezed. No use holding on to anything. For a few seconds we lost every bit of control over our bodies. The Ju came to a halt, half standing on its head. We still grip our rifles.' Amazingly no one was hurt. '*Out!*' someone called.

Their air-land experience was not that far removed from that of the paratrooper. 'War! And we stand suddenly in the midst of it,' declared a gefreiter from Regiment 85: 'Heavy enemy fire was drumming down onto the airfield, grey-brown clouds of smoke whirl high. The air around us shook and reverberated under dull muffled explosions.'

Jäger Fink was amazed to see groups of Gebirgsjäger emerge time after time from the wall of smoke and dust, often trotting with heavy weapons or towing trolleys off the runway, 'all with their distinctive rucksack – no sign of panic from the lads'. Within a short time over 20 or so wrecks littered the airfield, two or three in flames. By nightfall a complete mountain battalion was down and forming up in the dark. Transport aircraft were strewn along the beaches next to the runway where some had crash-landed in shallow water. Fink remembered they lost 22 men and 17 wounded, 'the majority from belly landings off the aerodrome'. By the following day three battalions of mountain troops had landed at Maleme. For the first time at a local point on the island the force ratio swung two to one in favour of the German invaders. Over the next few days 8,500 mountain troops landed at the western aerodrome, the entire 5ᵗʰ Mountain Division. An immediate flanking move to the south stopped the artillery fire coming down onto the airstrip.

General Student flew in on 25 May as the break-out and eastward advance began to pick up momentum. The crisis was not entirely resolved. Of 2,000 paratroopers dropped at Heraklion, the British had counted 1,450 corpses. Brigadier Chappel commanding 14ᵗʰ Brigade claimed: 'By May 23ʳᵈ, we had buried 800 German dead, piles amounting to 300 had been left unburied by the Greeks and there were a considerable number lying about scattered in the out areas.' Civilians were attacking the Germans with everything they could lay their hands on. Captain J.H. Marriott recalled, 'The Cretan women certainly decapitated four paratroopers to my knowledge.' At Rethymnon Oberst Sturm, the German commander, and his staff were captured by the Australians. All this was, however, to no avail. The arrival of the air-landed units had sealed the island's fate. As the Germans advanced east many of the defeated British and Dominion troops avoided them by retreating south across the mountains to Sfakia.

For many paratroopers pinned down or cut off, defeat appeared to stare them in the face for the first time in this war. 'I have lost a lot of blood and am physically weak,' recalled Oberfeldwebel Helmut Wenzel. 'My chest wound has not been bandaged – nor seen to all day and is emitting a pungent stink.' He spent the remainder of the first day after landing crawling hundreds of metres in his weakened state to avoid capture. Veterans still retain memories of unadulterated horror. Cretan civilians were very much in the line of fire during the assault and ground fighting and took revenge at every available opportunity. Hauptmann von der Heydte came across one peasant youth approaching his men as if clutching at a heavy load. His chalk-white face distorted with pain revealed a terrible sight. 'His stomach had been ripped open by a shell splinter; and what he was holding in his hands, what he was trying to press into himself, was his own bleeding mass of entrails.' Compassion for the opposition lessened when Fallschirmjäger were found hanging from their parachute harnesses in trees. 'Two of them had their faces evilly disfigured,' recalled Dr Eiben at Heraklion. 'My impression was it seemed one of them had his eyes punctured.' Franz Rzeha's 5th Company FJR 2 had suffered heavy casualties at Corinth, so was not inserted until the second day, during one of the futile reinforcement drops near Maleme. He cradled the head of a mortally wounded Fallschirmjäger who 'looked at me with big eyes and murmured "Mamma, Mamma".' He covered the face with a dirty rag, realising 'his mother would never hear her son's words nor see his terrible and lonely death'. His company had been virtually wiped out.

The Fallschirmjäger experience at Crete was a searing exposure. They encountered foes as fierce as themselves on unequal terms. Galatas village in Prison Valley was cleared of paratroopers by the New Zealanders in bitter hand to hand fighting. 'This was the first time that bayonets really came into it,' recalled Lieutenant Sandy Thomas with the 23rd Battalion. 'The thing about bayonets is that they seemed to go in with a hesitant ease, I never realised until that moment how effective their training [on straw-packed dummies] in Burnham had been, and how like it was to the real thing, with these bayonets going into these chaps.'

A pitched battle with rifle, bayonet and grenade developed in the

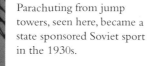

Parachuting from jump towers, seen here, became a state sponsored Soviet sport in the 1930s.

s form
xercise
1935.
were
sted.

village square of Galatas when a Fallschirmjäger counter-attack was unexpectedly struck by a New Zealand bayonet charge. 'We had the advantage of perhaps three or four seconds and went in,' recalled Sandy Thomas:

> In no time again we had this pitched battle, with us so close to them that we were right in amongst them. There were some Germans behind me, some of our chaps in front of me and it was bayonets and firing and bayonets. I can remember someone saying, 'Those chaps on the roof – Watch out!' I glanced up and saw a man throw a grenade and it registered in my mind, but at that particular moment there was a fair-haired chap coming straight at me. He had his rifle right at me, his bayonet on it as well. I fired and at the same time I felt this tremendous jar in my thigh and it lifted me up and in the same instant feeling this tremendous numbness and sickness.

The shrapnel peppered his back, 'possibly more painful than the main wound and I fell on the ground'. Such close-in fighting had a salutary effect on the Fallschirmjäger. 'In Crete,' battalion commander Friedrich von der Heydte recalled, 'we encountered for the first time an enemy who was prepared to fight to the bitter end.'

Von der Heydte's Iˢᵗ Battalion was not relieved by mountain troops from Maleme for five days. They had no food and very limited ammunition. Meagre rations, the unaccustomed heat by day and cold at night undermined their physical resistance. 'The faces of some of them had grown taut, almost shrunken,' he recalled, 'their eyes lay deep in their sockets, and their beards unshaven now for five days, accentuated the hollowness of their cheeks.' Some suffered acutely from diarrhoea, having been forced to drink stagnant water. They had reached the limit of their endurance when a leutnant from the mountain troops came to his hilltop command post. 'It was an appearance from Heaven, a gift from Heaven,' he recalled. Galatas was re-occupied after hard fighting on 26 May and Cannea fell the next day.

On 27 May the decision was taken by the British to evacuate the island. Both sides had fought fiercely, but the inexorable build up, stemming from the vertical envelopment at Maleme, demonstrated the German edge in organisation, resources and leadership. Of 22,000 men, 750 landed by glider, 10,000 by parachute and 8,500 air-landed. The remainder came by sea. Soldiers on both sides were reluctant to give up. New Zealand infantryman Clarrie Gordon was surprised to receive the evacuation order: 'We didn't believe it. We thought we would be going back tomorrow to have another go. We were dog-tired certainly, but I think most of us would have got the handle working to have another lick all right.'

When the word came to retreat to Sfakia, 'I think it just knocked us off our bottoms a bit, we sort of got much tireder than if we were going forward'. There was no turning back. Rethymnon was reached by the Germans on 29 May and Heraklion occupied the next day. British and Dominion troops were evacuated from there on the 28th and some 13,000 troops taken off by the Royal Navy at Sfakia. Twelve thousand Allied troops were left behind on the island. The British tried to hold ground and were never under the same urgency as the Germans to react. Vertical envelopment was do or die. The means to achieve this were strewn about Maleme runway. There were 134 aircraft wrecks. The 493 transport aircraft flying on day one were reduced to 185 by the day the British evacuated.

'Our comrades lay there still, their parachutes behind them, mown down in the order they had jumped,' observed Oberjäger Martin Pöppel, marching into Rethymnon. 'It was said that others had been mutilated. Thank God, I never saw any.' Of 11,000 Fallschirmjäger inserted into the battle, 156 officers and 3,339 were killed, with 91 officers and 2,237 wounded. 'Every third Fallschirmjäger is dead, every second wounded,' remarked Gefreiter Adolf Strauch, 'a victory that wasn't a victory.' The Stürm Regiment, the first assault, lost 70 per cent of its men, 699 officers and 1,166 from the 1,860 men committed. Vertical envelopment at the corps level had come at a crippling price. Fifty per cent of the Gebirgsjäger air-land element became casualties and 12 per cent of the committed aircrew. Some 117 transport aircraft were lost or written off and 115 damaged. 'There was a disgusting stench of decomposition in the heat,' recalled Erich Reinhardt, who managed to parachute late in the battle, 'and for the first time I was made aware of the insanity of war.' They became

Three CH-47s, as sho[w
noise during Oper.

Leonardo da Vinci's 1483 sketch of
a parachute figure.

Above right German First World
attached to parachutes in the bucket
Considerable nerve was required to go back up

The 'crucifix' position, adopted by each German paratrooper jumping through the door, is demonstrated for recruits during ground training.

An amateur Dutch civilian photographer in Rotterdam's suburbs took this image ᵗ‸e unsuccessful German parachute assault on Ypenburg aerodrome on 10 May 1940.

An unfortunate exit for this British paratrooper through the hole in the floor of an obsolete Whitley bomber.

The American Test Platoon which started training in July 1940 had the advantage of being better resourced than the British and could door-jump from Dakota aircraft.

An American trainee exits his aircraft. Nobody ever forgot their first jump.

h paratroopers mock-charge during training in 1940. 'In the early days the idea was to
us as a guerrilla force, dropping behind enemy lines', declared a parachute officer.

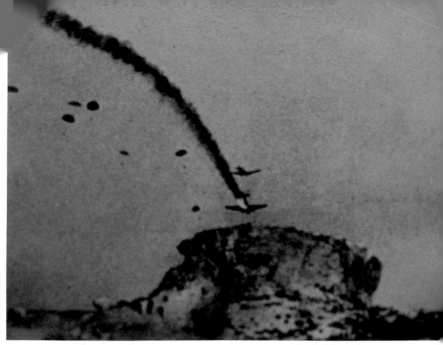

The second wave of German parachutists at Heraklion, Crete, jumping from aircraft on fire. 'Every third Fallschirmjäger is dead, every second wounded,' commented a surviving German paratrooper, 'a victory that wasn't'.

German mountain troops anxiously await the order to emplane for Crete, they were t the balance from failure to success in the first few days.

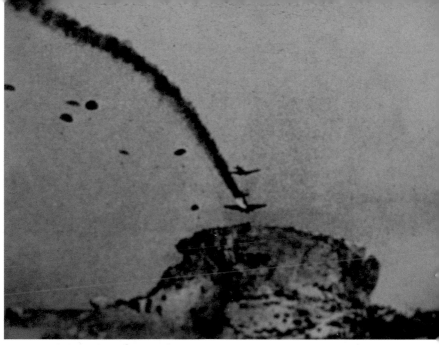

The second wave of German parachutists at Heraklion, Crete, jumping from aircraft on fire. 'Every third Fallschirmjäger is dead, every second wounded,' commented a surviving German paratrooper, 'a victory that wasn't'.

German mountain troops anxiously await the order to emplane for Crete, they were to tip the balance from failure to success in the first few days.

An American trainee exits his aircraft. Nobody ever forgot their first jump.

British paratroopers mock-charge during training in 1940. 'In the early days the idea was to use us as a guerrilla force, dropping behind enemy lines', declared a parachute officer.

village square of Galatas when a Fallschirmjäger counter-attack was unexpectedly struck by a New Zealand bayonet charge. 'We had the advantage of perhaps three or four seconds and went in,' recalled Sandy Thomas:

> In no time again we had this pitched battle, with us so close to them that we were right in amongst them. There were some Germans behind me, some of our chaps in front of me and it was bayonets and firing and bayonets. I can remember someone saying, 'Those chaps on the roof – Watch out!' I glanced up and saw a man throw a grenade and it registered in my mind, but at that particular moment there was a fair-haired chap coming straight at me. He had his rifle right at me, his bayonet on it as well. I fired and at the same time I felt this tremendous jar in my thigh and it lifted me up and in the same instant feeling this tremendous numbness and sickness.

The shrapnel peppered his back, 'possibly more painful than the main wound and I fell on the ground'. Such close-in fighting had a salutary effect on the Fallschirmjäger. 'In Crete,' battalion commander Friedrich von der Heydte recalled, 'we encountered for the first time an enemy who was prepared to fight to the bitter end.'

Von der Heydte's Ist Battalion was not relieved by mountain troops from Maleme for five days. They had no food and very limited ammunition. Meagre rations, the unaccustomed heat by day and cold at night undermined their physical resistance. 'The faces of some of them had grown taut, almost shrunken,' he recalled, 'their eyes lay deep in their sockets, and their beards unshaven now for five days, accentuated the hollowness of their cheeks.' Some suffered acutely from diarrhoea, having been forced to drink stagnant water. They had reached the limit of their endurance when a leutnant from the mountain troops came to his hilltop command post. 'It was an appearance from Heaven, a gift from Heaven,' he recalled. Galatas was re-occupied after hard fighting on 26 May and Cannea fell the next day.

On 27 May the decision was taken by the British to evacuate the island. Both sides had fought fiercely, but the inexorable build up, stemming from the vertical envelopment at Maleme, demonstrated the German edge in organisation, resources and leadership. Of 22,000 men, 750 landed by glider, 10,000 by parachute and 8,500 air-landed. The remainder came by sea. Soldiers on both sides were reluctant to give up. New Zealand infantryman Clarrie Gordon was surprised to receive the evacuation order: 'We didn't believe it. We thought we would be going back tomorrow to have another go. We were dog-tired certainly, but I think most of us would have got the handle working to have another lick all right.'

When the word came to retreat to Sfakia, 'I think it just knocked us off our bottoms a bit, we sort of got much tireder than if we were going forward'. There was no turning back. Rethymnon was reached by the Germans on 29 May and Heraklion occupied the next day. British and Dominion troops were evacuated from there on the 28th and some 13,000 troops taken off by the Royal Navy at Sfakia. Twelve thousand Allied troops were left behind on the island. The British tried to hold ground and were never under the same urgency as the Germans to react. Vertical envelopment was do or die. The means to achieve this were strewn about Maleme runway. There were 134 aircraft wrecks. The 493 transport aircraft flying on day one were reduced to 185 by the day the British evacuated.

'Our comrades lay there still, their parachutes behind them, mown down in the order they had jumped,' observed Oberjäger Martin Pöppel, marching into Rethymnon. 'It was said that others had been mutilated. Thank God, I never saw any.' Of 11,000 Fallschirmjäger inserted into the battle, 156 officers and 3,339 were killed, with 91 officers and 2,237 wounded. 'Every third Fallschirmjäger is dead, every second wounded,' remarked Gefreiter Adolf Strauch, 'a victory that wasn't a victory.' The Stürm Regiment, the first assault, lost 70 per cent of its men, 699 officers and 1,166 from the 1,860 men committed. Vertical envelopment at the corps level had come at a crippling price. Fifty per cent of the Gebirgsjäger air-land element became casualties and 12 per cent of the committed aircrew. Some 117 transport aircraft were lost or written off and 115 damaged. 'There was a disgusting stench of decomposition in the heat,' recalled Erich Reinhardt, who managed to parachute late in the battle, 'and for the first time I was made aware of the insanity of war.' They became

Three CH-47s, as shown here, flew at tree-top level over the Sierra Leone jungle to cloak noise during Operation 'Barras', the heliborne British rescue mission in 2001.

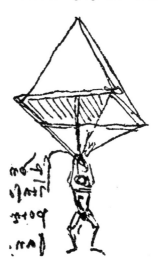

Leonardo da Vinci's 1483 sketch of a parachute figure.

Above right German First World War balloon observers attached to parachutes in the bucket container at top right. Considerable nerve was required to go back up after being shot down.

Parachuting from jump towers, seen here, became a state sponsored Soviet sport in the 1930s.

Soviet paratroopers form up after a mass exercise descent at Kiev in 1935. German observers were highly interested.

British paratroopers
attack in North Africa.

An aircraft exit trainer
in the United States
with an audience of
dubious students
waiting to go.

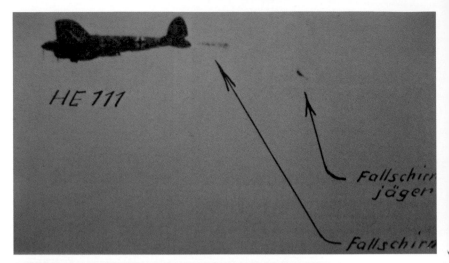

HE 111

Fallschirm
jäger

Fallschirm

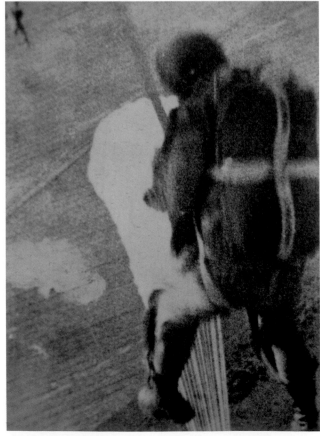

Above A rare photograph of a German parachute training accident at Wittstock Parachute School in 1942. The soldier towed by his parachute can be seen below to the right. He was rescued by being pulled inside the cockpit of another aircraft.

This hapless American trainee paratrooper has snagged his parachute strop beneath his left arm. This will be broken or dislocated when the line, attached to the aircraft, snaps taut with his body weight.

indifferent to it after a few days, but were scarred psychologically for life. 'Of the original ninety-three soldiers of our company who first jumped over Heraklion only four, I repeat, *only four* had survived.' It was suspected the paucity of prisoners may have had something to do with the Greek soldiers and civilian non-combatants. Greeks found with German weapons were executed. 'I hope the civilians knew why they were being shot,' Reinhardt reflected. Perhaps not, because there were no interpreters.

General Student's star was no longer in the ascendant. The 'father' of the German Airborne Forces was obliged to report to General Halder, the Chief of Staff, that the combat strength of 7th Flieger Division was down to three and a half from nine battalions and that the famed Stürm Regiment had virtually ceased to exist. Hauptmann von der Heydte remembered him at Athens during the pre-operation briefings. 'I would say he was a man full of strength, full of confidence when he gave his orders.' In Crete he had fundamentally changed. 'This battle made him years older, he looked like an old man, like an ill man.' He was awarded the Knight's Cross by Hitler, who later told him he thought 'the day of the parachutist is over'. More Germans were killed each day during this ten-day battle than had thus far been lost in the war.

The Blücher male family line, Wellington's rescuer at Waterloo in 1815, ended this May 1941. Leutnant Wolfgang Graf von Blücher from Holland, already a Knight's Cross holder, was killed. He was the oldest brother at 24. His younger bother Lebercht, a gefreiter, also died, alongside his little brother Hans Joachim Graf von Blücher, aged just 17 years. The mother's grief attracted newspaper publicity, but the full extent of Fallschirmjäger casualties was kept hidden from the German public.

Hitler told Student that 'without the element of surprise there can be no future for airborne forces'. They would be deployed on limited air operations but their future role would be elite shock infantry. The Allies came to precisely the opposite conclusion.

6

ALLIED SKY MEN

ALLIED EXPANSION

'How we at Ringway writhed in our chairs as we listened in May 1941 to a broadcast by an official Air Ministry commentator,' recalled a frustrated Wing Commander Maurice Newnham, 'in which he asserted that Crete would never be captured by airborne assault.' Churchill's hectoring at the lack of progress with his airborne corps, which only numbered 500 and a handful of gliders, rose after his fact-finding mission to RAF Ringway and the apparently significant German airborne success on Crete. 'This is a sad story,' Churchill admitted in a return note to General Sir Hastings Ismay, the Military Secretary to the Cabinet, 'and I feel greatly to blame for allowing myself to be overborne by the resistance which was offered.' The press had scoffed at the effectiveness of the German parachute arm and it was assumed the Home Guard would be more than a match for men required to take pills for fear their parachutes might fail to open. Crete took some explaining. 'We are always behind-hand with the enemy,' Churchill lamented. 'We ought to have 5,000 parachutists and an airborne division on the German models, with any improvements which might suggest themselves from experience.' The Air Ministry and War Office were instructed to get on with it. 'A whole year has been lost,' Churchill reminded Ismay, 'and I now invite the Chiefs of Staff, so far as is possible, to repair the misfortune.' Churchill was looking at future areas of conflict where they might be employed 'in the wide countries of the East and North Africa'. Captain John Frost, newly recruited into airborne forces, remembered, 'had it not been the insistence of Winston Churchill it seems doubtful if our airborne forces would ever have been formed.'

In September 1941 it was decided to form a full parachute brigade with an engineer squadron with four battalions and another battalion raised in India. Volunteers aged between 22 and 32 were called for from existing British units. Only the fittest and the best were to be accepted for parachute training. 'From the first, any weakling was ruthlessly cast out of the ranks,' declared Major General Frederick 'Boy' Browning, appointed to oversee the formation of airborne forces. A new wave of recruits was now required to populate this expansion beyond the original No. 2 Commando, which had transitioned first to the 11th SAS Battalion and then the 1st Parachute Battalion. Two more were earmarked to form alongside it.

The new airborne organisation was located at Hardwick Camp near Chesterfield in Derbyshire. Hardwick Hall (named after the Elizabethan mansion situated in the grounds) became the nucleus for parachute training and physical selection for airborne forces. Browning was determined to form a corps d'elite from the outset. They were to wear special uniforms with a distinctive new headdress, a red beret, introduced in 1942, and Browning retained 'the right to throw them out at any moment'. The conundrum was where to find the talent required to build a force that would be numbered in thousands rather than hundreds. By August 1942 a complete division was to be formed within which a Parachute Regiment was established as part of a newly created Army Air Corps, including two glider air–land battalions. The initial flow of volunteers in the second wave of entry after No. 2 Commando was sufficient to create four battalions. Thereafter it was decided to convert nominated existing infantry battalions to the parachute role. Who were these men and how did they differ from the first gladiatorial pioneers?

'Did you volunteer? Why did you volunteer? What do you think life will be like in a parachute battalion?' These were the fundamental questions asked of each parachute recruit, recalled Eddie Hancock, an early arrival in the 2nd Parachute Battalion. Only three of the eight men who travelled with him passed selection. 'Yes, it can be a bit rough up here,' his driver informed him on arrival at Hardwick Hall, passing two men hobbling past on crutches and others with arms in slings. Private Bill Kershaw thought Hardwick Hall was 'like a concentration camp – everything was done at the double'. Life was hard: 'Up at the crack of dawn, whatever the weather, and you daren't drop out.' Private James Sims was asked, 'Why do you hate your mother?' A weak: 'Good Heavens, what on earth gave you that idea?' meant you were out, Sims recalled. Better to put on a show of fury, he was advised. 'Better still, you should reach across and make a grab at the psychiatrist' to make the point. 'Then you were sure of a rifle company.' Despite the call to send the most willing, adventurers and the super-fit, many units, according to Captain John Frost, filtering arrivals, 'had taken the opportunity of unloading mostly those men who would be missed the least'. Hancock, accepted as a sergeant and wise to the military penchant never to miss an opportunity to unload dross, recalled 'the lame, the unwanted miscreant, and those who hadn't volunteered had to be sent straight back'. But, as he indicated, 'the record speaks for itself', selection and robust physical preparation soon 'united men from many different regiments into an effective fighting force'.

Physical selection for parachute training developed into a mind over matter combination of intense circuit training with gymnastics to develop athletic suppleness and field exercises to develop stamina; both of which included elements of the unexpected. A cross-country run might end with a sudden call to march 20 miles with full equipment. 'What an eye-opener this was,' declared Private Geoffrey Morgan, later to join the 2nd Battalion. 'Six weeks of toughening training. Six weeks of not being allowed to be seen walking within the camp. Six weeks of being with the toughest instructors imaginable. Assault courses with live ammunition. No sign of a parachute. If you could stand this training you could stand anything.'

Any man that fell out was returned to his unit. 'Milling', or boxing with over-size gloves toe to toe non-stop for two minutes, was introduced to identify controlled aggression. All this was interwoven with weapons handling, tactical training and shooting. 'From the outset it had been stressed that parachute soldiers were, first and foremost, first-class infantry, with the added advantage of travelling in luxury, *by air to battle*,' explained Sergeant Eddie Hancock. This was to prove 'the understatement of the century', he discovered, after having been introduced to the claustrophobic Whitley bomber, which 'hardly constituted opulent travel'. To get even this far required the unremitting physical and psychological grind of pre-parachute selection, later termed 'P Company'. Hancock described the uncompromising physical stress: 'It was a long hard slog as we surmounted false crest after false crest. On arrival, after we had eaten hard tack rations, our bedding was a ground sheet and a gas cape, placed on the concrete floor of an unheated Nissan Hut. "How lucky we are to have cover" quoted the company commander.'

Rifle shooting preceded the demanding return trek. 'Most of us were suffering from blisters and the aches and pains accumulated on the way out' but 'nobody dropped out,' Hancock observed. 'I passed the course,' Geoffrey Morgan recalled, 'but to even start parachuting required a 40-mile forced march to Ringway, Manchester, from Hardwick Hall.

Lieutenant John Waddy in India was addressed by a brigadier with a leg in plaster in September 1941, accompanied by his brigade major, also encased from his armpits to his hips. 'You may think we are not good advertisements for parachuting,' they told them, 'but we have come here to ask you to volunteer.' Waddy until then had only heard about parachuting from the German perspective. 'We were stuck in this station at Maltan, known as the hottest station in the British Empire,' he recalled, 'and after two years of war we didn't see any prospect of getting out of it.' He was among 15 officers and 300 men of the Somerset Light Infantry who volunteered. 'Let's get out of this hell hole and get into the war,' he declared. Only he and another officer passed selection with 80 of the men. Alex Reid joined the 2nd Parachute Battalion 'to escape the deadly monotony of army life on the Home Front'. Bill Kershaw described his home life as 'terrible', his mother had died, the Blitz was on and 'you had to do something to stop these buggers', so he joined up 'to kill two birds with one stone'. When his battalion was broken up to convert to tanks, he decided to join a parachute battalion instead, which he assumed to be 'more adventurous and demanding'.

Later second wave arrivals joined for a multiplicity of reasons, reflecting the normal vagaries of human behaviour. Although scared of heights, Captain Philip Burkinshaw was attracted to training at Hardwick and Ringway because he would be nearer his family 'and importantly the girlfriend'. There was also the glamour of a red beret.

George Price 'was unhappy with the idea of running around in a bren gun carrier loaded with highly inflammable jelly', so he transferred from the armoured corps to a parachute battalion. Parachuting 'appealed' and he thought it would be less dangerous. Although the financial reward was not particularly high, Sergeant Tom Wood responded because 'I had a wife, Sally, and a son, Don, and it meant another three shillings and sixpence a day to send home to them.'

The attack on Pearl Harbour in December 1941 and the significance of the German airborne achievement on Crete the previous May hastened the training of airborne battalions in the United States. 'By the middle of 1942, there appeared within the Army a hero-figure closely approximating the stature of the fighter pilot: the paratrooper,' recalled Kurt Gabel, a naturalised German. 'He was my salvation, I could not become a fighter pilot, but I would become a paratrooper.' He was to join the 513th Parachute Infantry Regiment (PIR). In January 1942 it was announced that four army parachute regiments were to be formed. By the middle of the year two US airborne divisions, the 82nd and 101st, with one glider and two parachute regiments each, were activated. The United States was already overtaking the United Kingdom in terms of scale and resources to meet expansion targets. C. Carwood Lipton remembered: '*Life* Magazine had run an article on paratroopers sometime in early 1942, and it told about the training they'd got and the difficult physical requirements.' He was to join the 101st Division. 'I just got interested in seeing if I could become a paratrooper,' he recalled.

Like the British, American parachute regiments were recruited nationally and not regionally in county or state units. The 82nd Airborne was known for example as the 'All American' division. Recruits were young, born since the Great War, white and segregated from black soldiers and many were hunters and athletes from high school. They came from all walks of society: poor and middle class, farmers, coal miners, mountain men and many others from the Deep South. Patriotism was important. 'It was just what you had to do,' remarked Lester A. Hashey with the 506 PIR overcoming reservations about the army. 'Something was wrong with you if you went into the service in those days,' but now the United States was at war. If you had to join, then his view was make any army time a positive, learning and challenging experience. 'Nobody forced you to do this,' declared Lieutenant Richard Winters with the 2nd Battalion 506 PIR, 'you volunteered and it was the notion *you* wanted to do something.' 'You wanted to be with the best,' he explained, 'apart from self-satisfaction, objectively one's survival rates improved.' Don Malarkey serving with the same unit determined: 'I wasn't going to be in the infantry – I knew that – I was going to be in some kind of top unit, or I wasn't going to be in the army.'

These men had lived through the Great Depression. 'My mother had ten children so you had to work to survive,' remembered William 'Wild Bill' Guarnere with the 101st Division. 'That's what it was, just survival in the streets of Philadelphia.' Money therefore played a role. 'What the hell is the airborne?' Bill Maynard asked. 'No one had ever heard of it.' 'These are the guys who jump out of aeroplanes, you've got all your army equipment [with you] to fight the enemy,' he was told. 'Go to hell,' was the uniform response. Nobody put their hands up. 'You get paid $50 a month more, so that made it $100 bucks,' they were informed. Bill raised his hand. Clarence Ollam was given a similar 'gung-ho speech about jumping out of aeroplanes' during infantry training. There was hardly a spark of interest until 'the speaker said we would be paid more money for doing it'. They were all attention. 'We all looked at each other and raised our hands,' Ollam recalled and volunteered for the 82nd Airborne Division. Many soldiers had been poor and had struggled, taking on any job to live. This made them resourceful, self-reliant, and inured to hard work and ready to obey orders without question, simply to hold down a job. Such skills were easily transferable to the military.

The hard-knocks unquestioning obedience demanded from the original Parachute Test Platoon was now part of the American airborne's training ethos. 'Chicken-shit' behaviour, the remorseless application of apparently mindless and repetitive physical selection and training methods, was deliberately invoked to produce a tough image. 'No one asked you to come here,' Kurt Gabel was told on arrival for selection, 'you will not be welcome until we decide that you are fit to become one of us.' The reception station at the parachute school at Fort Benning was nicknamed 'the Frying Pan'. Push-ups and running at double time between training and anywhere within the barrack circuit were airborne staples. Constant press-ups were for regular fitness circuit training and any infraction, 'real, imagined or manufactured', Gabel explained.

Failure and fall out rates were every bit as merciless as in the British experience, reflecting the same physical standards and mental resilience sought. 'They weeded off so many,' recalled Paul 'Buck' Rogers with the 506th PIR. 'They'd be there one day and gone the next.' During 1942 it took 500 officer volunteers to produce the 148 that made it through to parachute training and 5,300 enlisted volunteers to achieve 1,800 airborne soldiers for his regiment. The 2nd Battalion marched an epic 118 miles with full equipment in 75 hours with only 12 men of 586 falling out. 'Some of us lost as much as 40lbs, but I didn't have nothing to lose,' declared a lightweight, 'Popeye' Wynn with the 101st. 'I weighed about 130 lbs. If I lost 40, I wouldn't have been big enough to stand.' Kurt Gabel's unit selection for the 513th PIR lost almost 50 per cent of the original volunteers that formed up in his barrack block in the first three days. Soldiers could opt to fall out at the start with no penalty, but to 'quit' later meant transfer to 'Dog' Company, where Gabel was told: 'You will clean barracks and latrines and work in the kitchen all day and you will live in separate barracks because you will not be fit to live with troopers. You will have become a dog. And when we no longer need you after training, we will kick you out into other parts of the army, with that quit-slip forever on your record.' Like with the British system, progression from selection and basic training to parachute training was a blessed relief.

American parachute training was in four stages. Stage A was physical conditioning and selection, B included synthetic and ground training using apparatus to simulate the aircraft jump, parachute flight and landing. As they had to pack the very parachutes they would use close attention was generally paid to rigger instructor training. The next stage C, involved controlled and actual parachute descents from 250-foot jump towers, adapted from the Soviet experience. Kurt Gabel recalled witnessing a dummy drop from a tower to prove the utility of the reserve parachute, which the British did not have. It only opened partially: 'For a few seconds the unopened dummy ploughed into the ground at 150mph. We watch wide-eyed, as it bounced three times and came to rest just outside our spectator semi-circle, the skirt of the limp canopy partially draped over its legs.'

There was a stunned silence interrupted by the drawled explanation from the instructor who suggested, 'Well, it usually opens.' Naturally it would have 'worked OK' with a little wind but there was no time for a repeat act. It was never revealed whether or not this was black humour. This dubious spectacle was demonstrated just before the fourth stage, the actual aircraft descents. Five jumps were needed to qualify: two solos, a collective third jump, then with equipment and the final descent happened by night. Gabel's course resulted in two killed and 12 hospital injuries.

'Parachuting is really a conflict between one's rational and emotional self,' claimed British Parachute Regiment Captain Peter Lunn. 'Rationally one believes that there is no very great risk; emotionally one is convinced that to jump out of a flying aeroplane means certain death.' Little was known about the psychology of fear. Some demonstrably tough and courageous soldiers found parachuting nerve-wracking, others accepted it calmly. Flight Lieutenant John Kilkenny, an experienced parachute instructor at Ringway, saw how the different attitudes manifested themselves in the aircraft. 'There must be hundreds of little psychological tussles,' he later reflected. 'Some of the chaps perspire like mad as they're approaching their turn; even coming down to the hangar to draw their parachute and go into their line.' 'The chap going in to bat at cricket,' Kilkenny explained, 'he sweats.' Creating parachute divisions encouraged the consideration of methods to allay fear, jumping en masse with equipment, often at night and low-level and under fire. As with combat training, concerns have to be identified and systematically addressed, but this experience was not available to the early pioneers.

'Parachuting should be "debunked"; it must become an everyday affair,' concluded Wing Commander Maurice Newnham at Ringway. 'To do this we've got to build up confidence; stop line-shooting and the blood-curdling tales that are spread about.' A sober training approach was required, not the style of a gladiatorial commando battle course. 'Only yesterday there was a paragraph in one of the big national papers saying that paratroopers were so tough *that they drank blood and crunched glass.*' There was recognition that assimilating drills would help to overcome fear. The less the man had to think the better. 'The drill must be made repetitive – automatic,' explained Kilkenny. Physical instruction, films, posters and training aides were all directed to this end, to inculcate a frame of mind. 'The *will* to jump as a natural drill' introduced within a training school environment was the solution as outlined by Maurice Newnham. Constant visual and aural reminders encouraged the soldiers to mimic them. Kilkenny observed this, 'was just what we wanted them to do, if they did this physical thing, they would get away with their jump every time.' Each nation adapted a systematic approach of their own choosing, a structured progression of frequent practising of the basic skills needed. 'This was rammed into people's heads,' explained Kilkenny. Responses had to be automatic if they were to be performed under the stress of actual parachuting.

Early Russian parachutists dealt with fear by promoting patriotic and ideological party fervour. The young were encouraged to participate in risk-taking sport. Veteran jumpers were deliberately mixed with novices to settle nerves because experimental trials took a quota of fatalities as the bizarre was separated from the workable. The Soviets transitioned from jumping dozens to thousands in just five years. Like the British they were hampered by the lack of a suitable aircraft and had to adapt exit points on bombers: hatches, bomb bays, machine gun cupolas and even wings, that had not been envisaged for parachutists. Jumping such aircraft with a rip-cord self-releasing device was not ideal at low level. Novice paratroopers might be gripped by a mind-numbing terror and were known to forget pulling the ripcord. Captain Ilya Grigoryevich Starinov jumping in the early 1930s recalled fatalities and serious injuries from students who 'didn't pop [their] chute in time'. One of Starinov's female partisan jumpers was the first to offer to jump from the first available aircraft 'after the tragic death of one of our parachutists, when others had lost their nerve'.

The first Fallschirmjäger Parachute Commandment extolled elitism from the very beginning: 'You are the chosen fighting men of the Wehrmacht,' it proclaimed. Fear was not an issue. 'You will seek combat and train yourselves to endure all tests.' Parachuting was simply a method of going into battle. The end result was the point: 'To you the battle shall be fulfilment.' German parachute training preceded the American style of unquestioning obedience to orders. Immediate compliance meant less accidents. Jumping from the door of a Ju-52 ex-airliner was easier and a lot less frightening in any case than clambering across the wing of a Tupelov bomber in full flight. Nevertheless, fear – like that experienced by the Allies – had still to be overcome.

On 20 September 1937 Gefreiter Selbach with the Heer Parachute Infantry Company was jumping over the Mecklenburg training area. One of his rigging lines snagged the rear wheel of the Ju-52 transport as his canopy opened and he was towed along through the air. Major Richard Heidrich, on his first parachute course at the time, recalled the incident, stating his training had 'got off to a bad start'. He was watching the exercise. Another aircraft flew near to attempt some form of rescue but it was decided eventually to cut Selbach loose at 500 feet over a lake. It was hoped the canopy might yet fully deploy on release, but the line was entangled too near the sheet. He plunged into the lake on being cut away with a flat sheet spiralling uselessly above his head and was killed on impact.

Rumours and stories of parachuting mishaps were avidly followed by all ranks. Hauptmann Ludwig, the adjutant of the parachute school at Wittstock, recalled a spectacular rescue in 1942. Obergefreiter Zimmermann was jumping from a Heinkel III bomber, a faster alternative to the aging Junkers 52, considered for the attack on Malta. Jäger Robert Frettlohr recalled having to jump through the bomb door during training. 'It was like a little opening,' he recalled and more scary to jump from than the Ju-52. 'You had to go down a couple of steps and you jumped through like a bomb.' Because it was faster, 'you can imagine what your back felt like when the 'chute opened!' The problem for Zimmermann was that his caught on the bomber's tail wheel as it opened. Zimmermann had been the last to jump and the pilot flew on blissfully unaware he had a parachutist in tow and came in to land.

Frantic activity ensued around the airfield and a red flare was fired up into the air to warn off the pilot, out of radio contact, from landing. Ground personnel and anyone else who could be found were lined up on the runway to spell out the problem in letters visible from the air to the mystified pilot, indicating: *Man Behind You.*

Zimmermann, fully conscious throughout, realised the aircraft would have to come down eventually, started to unbuckle his harness, thinking to try and drop clear, perhaps on the grass. Once his breast buckle was released it began to slap him in the face, caught in the slipstream. This caused swelling and acute pain. In order to reach him it was decided to fly an old twin-engine Dornier 23 with an open cockpit immediately below and haul him in. Meanwhile as the aircraft edged cautiously together, a rope of rip-cords wound together was lowered from beneath the Junkers but proved too high for the virtually blinded Zimmermann, beaten about the face, to reach. Eventually the Dornier got close enough for one man to stand up in the open cockpit and hold him while his rigging lines were cut through with a knife. On release one of the Dornier's propellers sucked in the parted lines, causing it to immediately veer away and go into an emergency landing. Zimmermann, fortunately, was on board. Despite the spectacular rescue and the demonstrable feat of flying skills and courage, Zimmermann died of a heart attack in hospital a few days later.

The type of aircraft being jumped had an enormous impact upon the fear factor. Door exits from the German Ju-52 or the American Douglas Dakota were much easier than jumping through a British Whitley bomb bay. Fear of the unknown was still a factor. 'What you worried about most was your 'chute – did you pack it right?' remembered US paratrooper Rod Strohl during the parachute course. 'You'd pack it one day and jump the next,' which meant, 'you had all night to think about it – all kinds of ideas of what you might have done wrong.' Nobody in any case would admit fear. 'There was bravado and all that, but you didn't want to be afraid – you kept that out of your mind.' The main issue for many American parachute trainees was they, like many of their international counterparts, had never flown. 'My first flight, up I jumped,' announced US paratrooper Lester A. Hashey, 'that was years before I ever landed in an aircraft and for most of the fellow troopers, it was the same story.' Reactions varied between thrill and uneasiness about what may happen. 'As I went out the door I was blank,' confessed 101st paratrooper Tony Garcia, 'I cannot remember leaving the plane until after the 'chute opened – my God! But after that it wasn't as bad.' Forrest Guth, also under training, regarded it as a thrill, 'a roller coaster – you get off and you wanted to get right back on again.'

The British were labouring with the obsolete Whitley bomber, unanimously condemned by instructors and student jumpers alike. Aircraft fitter G. Abbot recalled 'dry lipped, white knuckled young men' boarding Whitleys for parachute training runs. Flying in the open tail gave a unique view of exiting paratroopers. 'Only feet below the tail, the exiting man would suddenly appear travelling rapidly backwards, arms and legs flailing, every facial expression visible – usually one of fear, if not his first jump acute apprehension, for the static line hadn't tightened to open the chute.'

'Jumping through the hole was a stupid idea,' thought parachute instructor Harry Ward. Sergeant PTI Gerrard Turnbull, also serving at Ringway, was convinced it required 50 per cent less training to go through a door compared to a dubious hole in the floor. Flight Lieutenant John Kilkenny agreed with the later arrival of the Douglas Dakotas. 'Instead of swinging round off your seat and out of a hole like a gymnast, you jumped from the door. It was marvellous!' he enthused. 'It was almost play.' Major John Timothy with the 2nd Parachute Battalion immediately recognised the benefits of jumping the open-door Dakota. It was no longer a question of 'bunny hopping' when 'if you didn't judge your jump through the hole correctly you were liable to get a broken nose or smashed up face'. The more spacious Dakota could also take twice as many paratroopers as the Whitley and 'they were a damn sight more comfortable as they were fitted with bench seats and you could get up and walk around.'

The scarcity of resources heightened the concerns of British paratroopers, very much aware they were in the guinea-pig role. Lieutenant John Waddy recalled the primitive facilities made available to them at the Air-Landing School set up in November 1941 at Willingdon airport, New Dehli. 'The apparatus consisted solely of 14 orange 'chutes, one harness hung on wire from a hangar and a massive contraption with a hole' for practicing exits, which Waddy explained was 'known colloquially as the Thunderbox [army slang for toilet].' The dearth of equipment meant that the 14 instructors sent out from England arrived with a parachute each as hand luggage. They were much sought after. 'There was always an undignified rush to the packing sheds' to secure the so-called 'Blighty 'chutes', Waddy explained. 'You could see the Indian 'chutes because the stitching used to go along and miss out about two inches and go on a bit further on.' His first jump was a decidedly nervous affair from a twin-engine Valencia bi-plane 'made in 1925 but of definite 1914 style'. They were unceremoniously nicknamed 'flying pigs': 'These planes seemed to flap their wings to take off in about 200 yards, and then flew to the drop zone at 50 mph. One could tell when the red light was due, for the whole plane shook and the wires hummed and quivered as the plane reached its maximum speed of 60 mph.'

'We jumped from 500 feet, no reserves, no helmets,' except 'this canvas thing with rubber round it' and of course through a hole in the floor. John Waddy recalled a formal visit by King George VI who echoed their concerns by regally asking, 'Why can't we have an aircraft with a door?' Anxiously looking down through the hole during take-off Waddy reflected on this first jump, 'Well, there's only one way out now.' He admitted, 'I've got a terrible head for heights, I can't even climb up the top of a ladder.' Nevertheless, the exhilaration of a successful jump was undeniable, sobered somewhat by five fatalities on his course. 'To encourage the others they decided the officers would do a demonstration jump to prove that the 'chutes all opened.' The slightly uneasy officers survived but ten more fatalities occurred within five months until expertise was despatched from England to resolve the problems.

Jumping from platforms on tethered barrage balloons was universally unpopular and generally feared. It was a cheap, yet effective British improvisation to provide practical parachuting continuation training despite aircraft shortages. Parachute instructor Harry Ward pioneered the method at Ringway. 'I took an army bod with me, a captain,' he recalled, 'who was scared absolutely witless.' After heaving out some dummies Ward jumped, followed after a long pause by the captain, who declared, 'I'm not standing for this ballooning business; I'm going to put in an adverse report about this.' He was eventually persuaded to change his mind after being plied with drinks in the mess.

Balloon jumping was totally cold-blooded, requiring considerable individual motivation standing in virtual silence on an unstable platform 800 feet in the air, with just the sound of the wind whistling through the cables. The basket or 'cage' was suspended on a single cable to an anchor vehicle with a winch. It provided a stark contrast to the normal noisy bustle of a typical aircraft exit where the scramble through the hole or door was a mindless community activity impelled by signal lights and a simple 'Go!' which galvanised even the faint-hearted. An immediate slipstream blast took away any falling sensation, whereas the parachutist exiting a balloon dropped some 200 feet before his parachute opened. This represented a thrill for some, but was detested by many.

Parachute training refusals were closely monitored and official inquiries conducted between 1942–4 reveal a number of interesting observations. A spate of refusals at battalions after departure from Ringway suggested that the understanding and professional training exhibited by the RAF was not necessarily followed through at unit level. It was decided to temporarily attach RAF Parachute Jump Instructors (PJIs) to assist them. Anxiety neurosis occurred when 12 men refused to jump a balloon at night, the fear proving contagious and influenced further by the concern of wives and girlfriends. Parachute unit commanders regarded psychiatrist reports and opinions with scepticism. One boffin, keen to examine the effects of a refusal on accompanying jumpers, flew in disguise with a Whitley stick and 'refused' to jump at the critical moment. 'A portly little gentleman,' Harry Ward recalled, he was unceremoniously thrown out, volubly protesting, by the RAF dispatcher whose action was more in keeping with the robust school's approach to 'anxiety neurosis'. Inquiries reveal a compendium of reasons for refusal: fear of cold-blooded balloon jumps, spurious delay winding up tension and changing back to Whitley holes after Dakota door jumping. Overall it emerged that regular jumping made refusals less likely.

The fear that applied to graduated unit parachute training was not comparable to the cold-shower immersion endured by agents, trained at Ringway to drop into enemy-occupied Europe. A certain 'Mr Y' might arrive from Manchester with an escort or interpreter, complete two hours of ground training, and then drop onto Tatton Park with a portable radio transmitter or sabotage equipment. There would be a repeat performance and he or she might be gone within a day. Dutch agent F. Th. Dyckmeester recalled his accelerated training programme caused by 'short notice' having to quickly take off with fellow 'victims' and left 'sitting there terribly afraid' contemplating the hole in the Whitley floor. 'We called them E Syndicate,' remembered Flight Lieutenant Kilkenny at Ringway. 'We gave them the first of everything. We didn't enquire what they were, who they were or anything.' They included female agents, much to the embarrassment of one parachute instructor bursting for a pee, who relieved himself with some panache through the hole in the floor. He was not to know until later that the number 1 watching so inquisitively in the stick was actually a female member of E Syndicate, indistinguishable in the same smock and rubber helmet. 'One chap taking his wife with him,' recalled John Kilkenny during a special agent sortie, 'found she couldn't jump and so he threw her out and then went after her.' 'There are some people who are like that,' Kilkenny explained, brave people who nevertheless do not possess the nerve to exit. This applied to many of the hastily trained agents. Some actually asked to be thrown out, departing with a weak '*Merci, monsieur*' as they went through the hole.

British paratroopers wore a distinctive camouflaged jump smock. This set them apart from the rest of the army along with the special badges and the soon highly regarded maroon beret and new rimless airborne helmet. The British soldier's penchant for irreverence in the face of authority was asserted when the red beret was initially introduced. Lieutenant John Waddy recalled, 'soldiers put them on top of their heads like pancakes.' Waddy was with the 156th Parachute Battalion in the Middle East and the soldiers rather liked their distinctive bush hats with the parachute badge. The new division commander began his welcome address on arrival by scolding the soldiers and insisting, 'Before you join my division you must learn how to wear your red berets properly.' Inevitably a shrill and anonymous voice piped up from the rear ranks: 'Well, fuck your red berets!' Ironically, the commander was to be killed in Italy 'sticking his head up over a wall with his red beret on' despite the warning 'Watch out, sir, there are some snipers around.' There was always a scramble to sew on the coveted parachute wings on completion of the parachute course. Parachute padre Joe Downing recalled: 'It was said to be some time before a new-fledged para-boy abandoned the habit of walking crab-wise, with his right shoulder thrust visibly forward.' Newly qualified Bill Kershaw 'saw one of the blokes in London after the course who had wings on both arms and chest as well!'

'Once you got in there you was proud to be,' declared US para-trooper J.B. Stokes. 'We was proud of our boots, we was proud of our shoulder patch and we was proud to be paratroopers.' US para-troopers were issued with a two-piece jump suit with baggy trousers and voluminous pockets. They were soon nicknamed those 'devils in baggy pants'. Jacket pockets were sloped downwards to enable access even when a parachute harness was worn and the two large pockets in the trouser legs were stuffed full of everything from socks to hand grenades, doubling as a veritable combat pack. A streamlined high jump boot was added to prevent snagging lines on opening para-chutes. These boots became the paratroop symbol, even more than jump qualification wings. Much sought after by non-parachutists, the warning 'You'd better not let a paratrooper catch you wearing them jump-boots' was to prove a universal initiator to countless fist-fights and soldier brawls. 'Through these portals pass the toughest para-troopers in the world,' announced the sign adorning the entrance to the parachute school at Fort Benning. Punitive discipline created highly aggressive soldiers who regarded the rest of the infantry as simply 'Legs'.

Image was all-important in inculcating an aura of elitism. Walter Gordon with the 101st Division recalled the delight of being able to 'blouse', i.e. tuck the baggy trousers into jump boots. 'It doesn't make much sense now, but at the time we were all ready to trade our lives in order to wear these accoutrements of the Airborne,' he claimed. 'We had a lot of physical training and a ton of ego building,' recalled Clarence Ollam with the 82nd Airborne Division: 'The combination of the two made us believe that we were the best, toughest soldiers in the military, and every time we left post someone would try to prove it. Youth, physical training, booze fuelled any number of scraps with other units willing to question our superiority.'

Colourful though the new emerging Allied elite might be, they were as yet unproven, whereas Axis airborne units appeared to be expanding from strength to strength.

RAIDERS TO AIRBORNE BATTALIONS

The oil refineries at Pladjoe, east of the town of Palembang and Soengai Gerang on the Moesi River in south-east Sumatra, were still partly obscured by smoke from the high-altitude Japanese bombing. At 1830 on 14 February 1942 the first waves of transport aircraft approached. At first there was little cause for alarm as the 70 Lockheed Hudsons with convincing-looking RAF markings hove into view until parachutists began tumbling out. About 350 Japanese paratroopers dropped from each wave astride the Moesi River as a storm of anti-aircraft fire rose up.

Stricken aircraft began to stream smoke on the run-in at about 600 feet. It seemed about seven to nine men jumped from each. As aircraft crashed the survivors began groping for more height to avoid the clusters of flak bursting ahead. Many of the pilots had never been under fire before and the drop became increasingly scattered as Japanese paratroopers, landing under fire, ponderously assembled into groups. Two aircraft were dropping containers and heavy equipments, one of them spiralled down, part of the total of 16 that were shot down. Fighting that night was confused and inconclusive. Paratroopers landing inside the Pladjoe refinery were liquidated by the Dutch defenders and others landing alongside the fence enclosing the Soengai Gerang refinery were shot down even as they landed. Muffled explosions illuminated by massive fire-balls began to erupt within the refineries as the demolition started. More paratroopers landed at 1000 and 1400 the next day near the aerodrome, which was soon occupied, heralding the arrival of the Japanese seaborne contingent that captured the town of Palembang. It was over, but the oil refineries were ablaze.

One week later on 21 February about 350 men dropped from some 20 to 25 Douglas type transport aircraft on Koeping in Dutch Timor. They jumped at 0830 hours on two successive days. Defenders were distracted by a feint attack with five aircraft dropping parachutists on the southernmost tip of the island. This time heavy strafing as well as bombing was employed to neutralise the air defences. Each aircraft jumped 15 to 25 Japanese paratroopers dressed in green uniforms buttoned to the neck, armed with light sub-machine guns and LMGs. They shouted in the air, 'You are my prisoner, Australians!' as they floated down, further yelling to instil panic. They secured an area one and a half miles from the Allied defensive positions and were relieved by an 18,000 strong seaborne force the next day.

These were Japanese raiding regiments and two of these battalion-size units constituted a raiding brigade. They were the progeny of the German instructors who had been training them since the summer of 1940. Anti-aircraft fire severely limited the effectiveness of the drops which were dispersed. Follow-up aircraft could only drop equipment loads haphazardly. Operations were, however, improving with frequency. Japanese paratroopers took few prisoners. Company raids had preceded further battalion-size insertions by naval parachutists in February at Menado on Celebes Island in the Dutch East Indies.

The Allies appeared unable to match either German corps-size airborne envelopments in the Balkans or Japanese battalion-size drops in the Far East. After Crete, Wing Commander Maurice Newnham escorted a staff officer concerned with future airborne development to watch a training descent at Tatton Park. 'What absolute nonsense,' the officer remarked, 'they'd all be shot before they reached the ground even if the aircraft managed to reach the objective.' Underlying official inertia was still dragging progress, but Newnham's aspirations were soon to receive a boost.

On 28 February 1942, 12 huge black Whitley bombers were outlined in the moonlight at Thruxton aerodrome near Andover. A company group of over 100 paratroopers and engineers under the command of Major John Frost of the 2nd Parachute Battalion emplaned shortly after 2200 hours. 'I find it hard to analyse my feelings at that moment,' recalled Flight Sergeant C.Cox, a radar technician accompanying the raid, 'but I remember wondering whether my luck would hold.' Five preferred moon and tide days had already been lost through Channel gales and there was now snow on the ground at their objective at Bruneval, 12 miles north of Le Havre. Major Frost remembered how the day before, then the last chance, the raid programme was extended another 24 hours. 'We were all miserable,' he reflected. 'During this last phase we had time to brood.' Maintaining secrecy for another month would be virtually impossible, there could be no leave. Would the raid have to be abandoned? He found himself asking. 'The key word for that raid was security,' remembered one of the soldiers, 'there wasn't a whisper, when it was coming, where it was going and when it was going to happen.' Cox, looking about the airfield before take-off, was reassured by John Frost's soldiers 'who struck me as very tough chaps whose view of life was "come what may – I'm OK".' At 2214 the dark Whitleys began trundling down the runway and lifted into the night sky.

The objective 'was a small blob' that a Spitfire pilot had photographed on a cliff north of Le Havre. Professor R.V. Jones, a radar expert, had identified it as a likely *Würzburg*, the first observed example of German radar, an equipment that looked just like an enlarged electric fire'. As Jones recalled: 'Although the equipment was on a cliff nearly 400 feet high it was not very far from a landing beach and I wondered whether we might nip in and pinch some of the equipment.' Raiding was the only agreed activity considered appropriate for British airborne forces at this stage, with Headquarters Combined Operations still undecided how to take their future employment and doctrine forward. The establishment of an airborne division suggested a conventional role at the end of an unconventional air insertion into battle. Unlike the German Luftlande Corps, there was little agreement yet between the British services, particularly the army and RAF, how this might be done.

Major John Frost, the raid commander, was already rankling about over-prescriptive higher headquarters control on how his raid was to be conducted. It was a far better planned combined operation than that mounted at Tragino the previous February. Air Force Whitleys were to drop the force, the army would conduct the raid and the navy would extract them with armoured landing craft and motor torpedo boats (MTBs), with a fighter escort provided for the return journey. But these were not German *Auftragstaktik*, mission command, tactics. Frost was directed to divide his company into three main components, one to capture the radar, another to fend off likely reaction from the German garrison nearby and another to secure the beach for the extraction. Insufficient attention, he felt, had been paid to his need to have a larger company headquarters element to control the separate groups. 'When I protested, I was told that if I did not accept the plan, division HQ would find someone who would,' he recalled, 'so I shut up.'

Airborne command in battle was an unknown. The new commander of the British Airborne Division forming up was an 'impeccable Guardsman', Major General 'Boy' Browning. His active service experience was as a patrol officer in the trenches of the Great War. Brigadier Richard Gale, commander of the 1st Parachute Brigade, was an ex-1914–18 machine gunner. He had in turn nominated Ted Flavell to command Frost's battalion. Flavell had been Gale's machine-gun commander and TA, not regular, during the inter-war years. These traditionally grounded soldiers were being nominated to direct an entirely new form of airborne infantry soldiering. They were to succeed, but were totally unlike the 'do or die' unconventional and free-thinking soldiers leading the German Fallschirmjäger.

Frost's soldiers were, however, supremely confident at their tactical level. One remembered: 'The briefing was very good, it was exceptionally detailed, we had a beautiful model of the ground and we had a very large number of photographs from all angles.' Despite the flashing and banging of flak as they passed over the coast, Flight Sergeant Cox recalled, 'we did not pay much attention to it for we were kept too tense watching for the red and green lights in the roof above the hole.' They jumped low. 'I think it was only 250 feet,' recalled one soldier, 'and you were no sooner out than you were on the deck.' Cox landed with a gentle bump on the snow-covered earth. 'The first thing that struck one on standing up was how quiet everything was and how lonely I felt.'

They expected some 30 Germans to be around the radar post and maybe another 100 in the buildings at Le Presbytère north of the villa serving the post and likely 40 more garrisoning the village of Bruneval below the cliffs to defend the beach and man strongpoints. The drop was broadly accurate, landing a half mile from their objective, enabling the paratroopers to quickly secure the radar site. 'The whole thing was in the open,' recalled one soldier. 'There was a little cabin where the man sat in, but inside there was only room for him and the display, the rest of the gubbins was in a container in the back.' A short, vicious fight broke out. 'Our orders were to take only the experts prisoner and to kill the remainder,' recalled Frost. Lieutenant Young killed five in situ and was condemned by his remonstrating sergeant as 'a cruel bastard'. One wounded German radio location expert fell ten feet down the cliff and was hauled back and taken prisoner.

Intermittent firing broke out as the groups attempted to secure their associated objectives. Cox and the engineer detachment swarmed all over the apparatus seeking to dismantle it with screw-drivers and hastily lever bits off with crow-bars. Loud protestations came from covering paratroopers when vital pieces were hack-sawed apart by flashlight. 'I was asked to take flashlight photographs of the antennae in front,' recalled Cox, 'and this definitely produced an increase of the fire.' It was nerve-wracking work.

As Frost had predicted, they were soon assailed by the unexpected in the midst of the success their sudden and shocking appearance created. The radar group, having struggled to heave their vitally important heavy pieces onto a wheeled trolley, began to trundle it down the steep slope to the beach as they withdrew under increasingly heavy fire. 'As we were moving down to the beach to be, we hoped, taken off by the navy,' Frost recalled, 'we heard that the beach assault party had been partially misdropped, so the defences were not yet in our hands.' At that moment the Germans also attacked the rear-guard defending the beach retreat. 'I saw little bits of grass trembling at the impact of the bullets almost at my feet,' remembered Cox during this headlong rush towing the trolley. They tried to keep the pieces of apparatus on board as the cart bounced along with bullets dully splattering against the metal radar parts. Cox saw, 'one went through part of the apparatus in my hand.' Ominously, there was no sign of the Royal Navy and the beach was not yet secure. Frost confessed, 'by that time I was a little doubtful and wondered if we should be killed or taken prisoner.'

Just as the plan was unravelling the misdropped party arrived in the nick of time. They surprised the advancing Germans in the rear and were able to roll up the beach defences. This group had passed through Bruneval village en route silently knifing three Germans to ensure a quiet transit. 'In general, the paratroopers were very keen on their knives,' admitted Frost, 'so much so that I saw several of them plunge them into dead Germans.' Although they gained the beach, Frost was labouring with inadequate radio equipment and trying to coordinate his disparate groups with only a skeleton company head-quarters group. With no radio contact with the navy 'it looked as though we were going to be left high and dry,' he glumly reflected, 'and the thought was hard to bear.'

Just over two weeks before, the Channel dash by the German battleships *Scharnhorst* and *Gneisenau* had illustrated how precarious a Channel extraction might be. Indeed, the rescue force had been obliged to heave-to in darkness and wait as a German destroyer and flak ship passed them by. It was with some relief that Frost heard the shout, 'The boats are here! God bless the ruddy navy, sir!' Extraction was hectic, under fire while wading out and vulnerable to being grounded by the receding tide. 'All the equipment and the wounded went on the very first boat,' recalled a soldier, 'and they rushed that equipment back to England; the scientists wanted it for something.' The raid was a success, but like so many airborne operations, the line between success and failure had been touch and go. 'The Germans had an armoured division about 50 miles away,' one of the para-troopers said to press reporter A.R. Humphries aboard one of the landing craft. 'As we left the beach I saw a column of headlights coming toward us though still some distance off.'

Major General Browning was ecstatic: 'You have put airborne forces on the map,' he told Frost. 'From now on we should be able to get all sorts of things that have been withheld up to now.' Frost lost two killed and six wounded and missing. 'I think we killed about 40 Huns,' he declared. Positive publicity was generated at an especially low point in the war. WE FIGHT AGAIN IN FRANCE, news-paper headlines declared, and the raid received coverage in America, Canada and New Zealand. The Germans were equally impressed, and a post combat report stated 'although attacked by German soldiers they concentrated entirely on their primary task' which 'was well planned and was executed with great daring'. General Student sent one of his staff officers to study lessons from what he regarded as an impressive achievement.

Operation Torch, the Anglo-American landings in Morocco and Algeria on 8 November 1942, took the German High Command completely by surprise. The following day, however, the Germans began to reinforce through Tunis and Bizerta, two ports not included in the invasion, and began forming a rudimentary bridgehead. The purpose was to cover the retreat of Rommel's severely mauled Afrika Korps, defeated at El Alamain the month before. By 15 November the British First Army under General Kenneth Anderson had crossed the Tunisian border and was heading east for Tunis and Bizerta. The 1st Parachute Brigade was placed at his disposal. Lieutenant Colonel James Hill, commanding the 1st Parachute Battalion in that brigade, recalled Anderson 'was a nice enough chap, but he knew nothing about parachutists'.

The British 1st Parachute Brigade had embarked by sea in October, 'a fit, tough, combative unit eager to move against the enemy,' recalled Sergeant Eddie Hancock. A press officer observing the 2nd Parachute Battalion was struck by the variety of occupations reflected in its ranks: commercial artists, an upholsterer, and factory and ship-yard workers. Their age was mostly in the early twenties and they had been recruited from all over the United Kingdom. The 2,000 men of the brigade had been specially selected at Hardwick Hall and 85 per cent of the outgoing force was destined to become casual-ties. The target discussed on the ships was an airborne assault on the aerodromes at Tunis, but 'a message came through on the wireless that the Germans had landed 10,000 parachute troops at Tunis,' Hill recalled, 'so that was the end of that idea.' No firm policy had yet been developed for employing the brigade, which would require the cooperation of all the available Allied air forces. In fact, Lieutenant Colonel John Frost, promoted to command the 2nd Battalion after Bruneval, observed once the initial concept of a brigade drop to capture Tunis was forestalled by the arrival of the Germans 'there seemed to be no ideas at all'.

On the day before Torch an American parachute task force of 39 C-47 aircraft transporting 556 paratroopers of the 509th Parachute Infantry Battalion took off from England on the first leg of a 1,490-mile flight to Africa. The US airborne effort had expanded from test platoon to two divisions in 26 months. Major General Mark W. Clark, the deputy to the Torch commander, General Eisenhower, was keen to use this first parachute battalion newly arrived in

England. It was uncertain whether or not French (Vichy-led) troops in North Africa would fight, so there had to be a 'peace' plan with an airport landing or a 'war' airborne assault. The objective for this unprecedented long-distance projection of airborne combat power was Tafaraoui, south of Oran. Fuel limitations meant the force would have to land on the mud flats east of Oran. Navigation for such an intimidating long flight was to be provided by a Rebecca-Eureka guidance system. But by the time the lead aircraft was over Spanish Morocco 200 miles west of Oran it was flying alone. One large group of 21 C-47s separated from the force managed to gather over the Mediterranean but then flew into unexpected heavy flak over La Senia airfield, east of Oran. Although the option was now clearly war, when the force launched, the last signal it received was confirmation of unlikely French resistance.

French fighters caught three C-47s coming in to land at Tafaraoui airfield and mercilessly raked the transports, killing and wounding helpless paratroopers within. All three aircraft made forced pancake landings and the survivors scrambled out to shoot back. Seven men were killed and 20 wounded. Two plane loads damaged by anti-aircraft fire force landed near La Senia and the occupants were taken prisoner. Two more landing at Fez aerodrome in French Morocco suffered the same fate and the occupants of four aircraft that came down in Spanish Morocco were hustled off to Spanish prisons. This was an inauspicious start to American airborne operations. At least the recently inducted civilian airline and transport pilots, unused to flying in formation, had got the main part of the force into theatre. The remnants of the 509th were warned off for further operations on 15 November.

Meanwhile, the British 3rd Parachute Battalion launched from Gibraltar on 11 November in American C-47s to capture an airfield near Algiers landed at Maison Blanche. First Army, taking advantage of the lack of French opposition, occupied it before they arrived. The battalion was promptly ordered 250 miles further east to capture Bone airfield the next day. As they began to tumble out over their hurriedly selected drop zone a similar formation of German Junkers 52 transports veered off on sighting the drop and flew back to Tunis. It had been that close. The 3rd Battalion was relieved by ground forces, having established a pattern of exploiting detected enemy gaps and overrunning airfields in the path of the First Army ground advance. On 15 November there were two American parachute landings on airfields at Tebessa and Youks le Bains. The next day the 1st Parachute Battalion flew to seize the airfield at Souk el Arba, 60 miles southwest of Bone. Once again the commanding officer selected his drop zone from the air and led the remainder of the formation by dropping on to it. Immediately the battalion pushed on a further 30 miles to Béja, requisitioning transport and engaging German armoured car units coming from the opposite direction. These flexible air-mobile operations rapidly executed by parachute after selecting drop zones from the air were the precursor to the sort of rapid helicopter insertions that were to occur 20 years later during the Vietnam War.

'I was given 32 American Dakota aircraft,' recalled 1st Battalion Commander James Hill, 'and these aeroplanes had never dropped a parachutist before.' This was a form of free-booting battalion-heavy parachute raid, never done before, during which concepts and methods were improvised as they went along. 'I was given the most marvellous orders,' Hill declared, which were essentially to secure roads and objectives for the approaching ground forces and get the prickly French on side. This was no mean task, because they were commanded by Admiral Darlan 'and we had blown up his fleet'.

Resources were primitive. Aircraft were fitted for parachuting but they had no intercom between aeroplanes. 'I was able to beg from somebody a quarter inch to the mile French motoring map of Tunisia,' Hill explained and using this, 'we decided roughly the area we would drop.' Because there was no radio, 'when they saw me jump out of the first aircraft, the remaining 32 aeroplanes would then come in and let their chaps out.' At the first attempt they were blocked by a cloud system over the Atlas Mountains and the stream had to uneasily watch a dog-fight when four German Me 109 fighters were fought off by the US Lightning escort. 'That was exciting,' Hill confessed. They flew back to Algiers, having traversed 390 miles. General Anderson was not impressed: 'If this happens the next time, you go,' he insisted, 'the nearest place to the enemy.' A few days later they dropped at Souk el Arba aerodrome near Béja. Four hundred paratroopers were confronted by a French brigade of

1,200 men. Hill bluffed his way into their confidence by marching his men into the town first with helmets and then again later wearing red berets. German staff representatives in Béja threatened the French with Stuka attack if the British were allowed in. The French disdainfully ignored the threat and the war was back on. 'So that was our entry into Tunisia,' declared Hill.

The flexible air-mobile phase was short-lived because the Germans began to push out of their swiftly established Tunisian enclave. The 2nd Parachute Battalion had been on stand-by for further operations at Maison Blanche near Algiers since 29 November. They were first warned off for a parachute assault on the Pont du Fahs aerodrome, south of Tunis, to destroy enemy aircraft and then move on to Depienne airstrip 12 miles to the north-east to do the same. John Frost, the battalion commander, became increasingly frustrated. 'I had to undertake two quite useless aerial reconnaissances' and now his battalion was earmarked to drop 40 miles deep into enemy territory 'with the task of destroying non-existent enemy aircraft on airstrips already evacuated by them'. Improvised reconnaissances by fire with parachute battalions were becoming increasingly inappropriate in the face of an increasingly stable German defence. The ensuing pace of order and counter-orders with different objectives was not appreciated by the soldiers obliged to react to them.

'A first-class example of disorganised chaos,' complained Sergeant Eddie Hancock, engaged in the activity preceding operations with the 2nd Battalion at Maison Blanche airfield. 'Around us was SNAFU [Situation Normal All Fucked Up],' which was 'a far cry from the quiet orderliness of the RAF' experience back in England. Overnight rain had transformed their dusty airstrip into clinging mud. Aircraft were parked indiscriminately, there were no perimeter roads, dispersed bays and hard runways and no control tower. 'We'd met another challenge,' he complained. Aircraft were straggled all over the aerodrome and troops had to wade across a sea of mud laden with parachutes and containers to find their correct plane and load it. They were also not encouraged when they met the American aircrews. 'We've just left Stateside,' announced Hancock's crew-chief. 'It's the first time we've met British troops, the first time we're going into combat, and, the first time we've dropped paratroops.' Slightly perplexed to hear that a month ago their pilots were delivering mail and cargo across the United States, they were next informed, 'when you go out of this here baby, you'll be christening her.' Take-off for a combat jump was barely three hours away.

As the stream flew over Pont du Fahs it was realised there was no enemy. Many of the battalion did not even know the location had changed when they jumped at Depienne, picked out from the air by the CO, who jumped first. Hancock took great pains to explain the differences between British and American parachute delivery to the US crew-chief. Americans flew low and then surged up to 1,000 feet to gain height for the reserve 'chute, whereas the British glided in from high level to between 600 and 800 feet, before throttling back to jump. Specially lengthened strops were needed to open British canopies on Dakotas otherwise men could get hooked up on the tail wheel. Major John Timothy recalled five or six men being lost on test exercises in the UK this way. The aircraft tail had to be lifted just before the drop.

Strange aircraft brought new tensions. There were small portholes next to the Dakota windows to fire out of if attacked. 'If you fire, don't hit the other aircraft and for God's sake don't hit our engines,' said the crew-chief. Hancock quietly resolved, 'If we met that sort of trouble we'd bale out'. There was always a myriad of concerns. 'Greater worries transcend the lesser ones,' Hancock appreciated, beginning to focus on the likely enemy reaction to their arrival. After the hurly-burly of airstrip preparation and the last-minute change of objective 'jumping was going to be the easy bit'.

They parachuted with the maximum of ammunition because they would not be re-supplied. 'If Joe Goldsmith had been allowed to have his way,' Hancock remembered, 'he would have jumped with a pair of loaded Bren magazines as ear-rings.' One of their supply-container parachutes failed to open properly and landed with 'a puff of dusty dirt and stones' as the basket disintegrated. That cost 25 per cent of Hancock's platoon reserve ammunition. 'We spotted one Roman Candle,' he recalled, a bad start, 'the first fatal casualty.' An approach march to the Oudna Valley, to capture the next airfield in sight of Tunis, was made across rugged terrain that night.

The assault on Oudna was to prove a searing experience to

Hancock's platoon, reduced from 32 men to eight on its first baptism of fire. No matter how well they had been trained and selected, they were all the same flesh and blood when a storm of artillery fire came down: 'The Germans were dead on target. I glanced behind at my runner. He had been slower than I to get down. A spurt of blood gushed forth as he was hit in the throat. I looked to the left. Another series of crumps, explosions and the swish of bullets. I saw Gyp, resolutely facing the front, going forward, briefly silhouetted in a flash, then headless, his lifeblood spurting from his neck.'

Hancock struggled to regain composure. 'Self-discipline and hours of constant repetitive teaching came to my aid.' The British paratroopers now learned what the Fallschirmjäger had had to endure at Rotterdam and Crete and which cannot be taught. On the ground they were poorly resourced light infantry, virtually naked in the fight against concentrated machine gun, mortar and artillery fire and powerless to react against the German panzers who emerged during the attack on Oudna. Dick Ashford, his company commander, admitted, 'the Colonel says we've taken on much more than we can chew and paid the price.' Hancock prayed as his men increasingly went down: 'Please God give me the strength to do what I must do. If I am to die, let it be quick, or if I am to be wounded, don't let it leave me crippled or a useless hulk.'

The 2nd Battalion was marooned 56 miles behind enemy lines once it was appreciated that the British First Army, stalled by unexpectedly heavy opposition, would never reach them. The paratroopers could not be re-supplied and had only the weapons and ammunition with which they had jumped. Resources were insufficient. The wounded Eddie Hancock had to be evacuated on a locally requisitioned donkey and was captured. A two-day epic withdrawal back to Allied lines followed for the remainder, in contact with the enemy, assailed by tanks, armoured cars and aircraft attacks the whole way. Frost lost 16 officers and 250 men en route. 'Throughout this time,' the enraged commander reflected, 'neither First Army nor 5th Corps made, or caused to be made, even one gesture to find out where we were.'

Mercifully a 3rd Battalion parachute operation to capture the port of Sfax in southern Tunis was shelved. German resistance and the approaching winter nullified any hope of an early end to the campaign. The free-booting air-mobile phase was over. After a brief period of rest and recuperation the 1st Parachute Brigade went into the line as light infantry, fighting a series of long and hard defensive battles in the Tunisian hills, often facing Fallschirmjäger units likewise employed as line infantry. Both sides were beginning to appreciate an intangible by-product of parachute training. Raiders made first-rate shock-infantry fighters. They could operate as conventional infantry after landing and concurrently possessed the skills to revert to raiders if units fragmented, when they could fight on or exfiltrate in the event of setbacks, as at Oudna. These skills were now applied to static defensive fighting in the Tunisian hills throughout the winter of 1942–3.

'The coldest I have ever been yet,' wrote A.C.V. Menzies, the padre with the 3rd Parachute Battalion in his diary on 6 January 1943. His hut doubled as the regimental aid post and the floor was covered with fleas. 'Casualties began to arrive with shrapnel and bullet wounds from 0030 hours onwards. The wounds looked like great dobs of raspberry jam on the men's arms and legs. The soldiers were all cheerful though naturally apprehensive about their wounds: it seemed amazing they could survive with such gaping holes in their bodies.'

A company attack had failed. 'We were all tired shivering and sweating,' attempting to sleep, he remembered, on the 'abominably cold' earth floor. 'Dreamed my flea-bites were spouting fountains of blood.' The winter fighting was costly and cold. 'Tunisia was nothing more than an expanse of *Hammada* [desert] waste, surrounding hills and projecting crags,' recalled Corporal Reg Curtis with the 1st Parachute Battalion. Images of that winter fighting were to haunt him forever. 'I was horrified,' he recalled during a lull in the fighting, 'to find an enormous brute of a pig munching away at a dead German.' Death and mutilation pervaded all else at Djebel Mansour in early February 1943 when his battalion suffered 105 casualties. 'Lofty', one of his previous No. 2 Commando friends, called to him passing through the regimental aid post, 'It's nice to see someone alive.' He had been shot five times through the calf, thigh, forearm and one bullet had gone clean through the end of his penis. Eddie Hancock remembered that with 1,700 casualties from the cream of the 2,000 selected at Hardwick Hall 'few of the original members survived'.

'Some of the actions we were involved in were too horrific to put into words,' claimed 20-year-old Private Geoffrey Morgan with the 2nd Battalion. 'This was really where I changed overnight from being a boy to a man.' Guard duty at night could be perilous. 'Can you imagine what a young fellow's mind does when he actually goes forward to his first guard relief and finds that the two mates he is to relieve have been killed with their own fighting knives?' A note was attached to the corpses stating 'This fate will befall any we find with fighting knives.' They were withdrawn.

Menzies' North African diary is punctuated with lists of the dead, interspersed with bleak comments about physical hardship. 'Geoff Ellis not dead but a prisoner with wound in the head,' he wrote on 14 May. 'Only 18 unwounded or slightly wounded now left in A Company, Captain Bob Stevenson and Lt Freddie Norton killed, Lt John Batty died of wounds.' The brigade had blunted a threatened German-Italian break-out in the Tamera Valley in March. 'Most miserable night ever: blankets, tunic, wet through, feet encased in wet boots, rain oozed in from ground and walls of tent.' Savage fighting amid the clay-red mud with the tail of the parachute smock flapping behind earned the mud-smeared paratroopers the nickname 'Red Devils' from the Germans. Red berets were not worn in battle. Soldier traditions emerged in this maelstrom of fire. *Who-ooh-Ma-hamed!* became the 1st Parachute Battalion war cry, picked up from the local Arabs calling to each other in the foothills. 'Whatever the jabber was, the Paras adopted it,' recalled Corporal Reg Curtis. Sergeant Eddie Hancock thought it far more sensible than 'We died for the Führer.'

The Red Devils regarded themselves as a particular elite, making individual reinforcement a problem. 'We couldn't take men from the Infantry Replacement Training Depots, because the Toms [colloquial for "Tommy Atkins"] would not have accepted them,' explained Major John Timothy with the 2nd Battalion, 'since they weren't paras.' It was bad enough assimilating trained paratroopers with no battle experience. One young soldier approached Timothy and complained, 'My corporal won't speak to me,' explaining his corporal section commander had told him to 'get some hours in under shell-fire before you speak to me'. This was hardly practical as they were living cheek by jowl in trenches together for 24 hours a day. The problem was resolved when Timothy took the young-ster on patrol himself, but as he sadly recalled, 'they were both dead within a month.' Casualties became so heavy among corporals (often patrol leaders) that soldiers were reluctant to be promoted. 'The reinforcements we did receive couldn't stand up to our losses as the fighting was so intense,' Timothy explained, 'and we were up against it pretty much all the time.' When the battalion finally emerged from the Tunisian mountains there numbered only 14 officers from 24 and 346 soldiers still on their feet from 588 who had gone in, despite 230 reinforcements received in January. Casualties were running at 80 per cent.

There would need to be a major refit prior to any further airborne operations and heavy casualties had dictated this would be from a low experience threshold. The 1st Brigade had conducted three major airborne operations and took part in more battles than any other formation with the First British Army, capturing 3,500 prisoners and inflicting 5,000 casualties on the enemy. The Red Devils' nucleus had, however, been decimated in the process.

7

THE BLUNT INSTRUMENT:
SICILY TO D-DAY

FORGING THE AIRBORNE INSTRUMENT:
THE MEDITERRANEAN

In 1943 Allied airborne expansion overtook the previous lead enjoyed by the Soviet Locust Warriors and German Fallschirmjäger. Hitler, dismayed at the Luftlande casualties on Crete, increased his parachute divisions but employed them as crack mobile infantry. Air mobility with light scales meant their proven shock capability could best be expended on fire-brigade rapid reinforcement missions. Serious consideration was made during April and May 1942 for a vertical envelopment of the island of Malta. The Ramcke Brigade of four battalions of Fallschirmjäger was to be dropped and air-landed with the Italian Folgore Airborne Division, a panzer regiment was available for support with a sea-landed Italian infantry division and a gebirgsjäger division was placed on readiness. The operation, due to be launched on 15 August 1942, was cancelled in July, ostensibly because of German and Italian disagreement over the island's future occupation. Hitler's reservations about Italian resolve under pressure persuaded him not to risk another possible Pyrrhic airborne victory, which the presence of the Royal Navy power, despite local Axis air superiority, made questionable.

Russia's five airborne corps, caught widely dispersed at Kiev, Minsk, Leningrad and the Ukraine, were in the throes of major reorganisation when the Germans invaded in June 1941. Most of the 800 bombers, many of which were dual-roled as air transports, were destroyed on the ground, leaving less than 200 by the end of the year. Lightly equipped and configured for offensive operations, the VDV Airborne units were inserted piecemeal as conventional infantry and burned out. By autumn the badly mauled 4th and 5th Airborne Corps had been pulled back to Moscow, two corps were annihilated near Kiev and a third was put into the line as a rifle division. There was in any case no airlift. A brigade air-land at Orel in early October was conducted by a mix of TB-3 bombers and PS-84 civil airliners. In January and February 1942 the Locust Warriors were reduced to battalion size or shuttle-lifted weak brigade groups and employed on partisan operations during the Soviet winter offensive at Vyazma near Moscow. Stalin quickly appreciated the quality of man that resulted from parachute training and transferred complete airborne corps units across as elite Guards Infantry Divisions in the summer of 1942. Poor coordination between the Red Army and Air Force, shortage of airlift, and poor navigation skills by pilots resulted in scattered drops with fearsome casualties. Some missions even dropped soldiers into snow-drifts without parachutes.

In September 1943 the 1st, 3rd and 5th Guards Airborne Brigades were committed to support the Red Army crossing of the Dnieper River. Foul-ups occurred assembling the 180 aircraft and 35 recently developed gliders. By take-off time on 24 September only 48 of 65 assigned aircraft managed to lift off for the first insertion near Dudari. Heavy flak forced the aircraft to drop at 1,800 feet, a long time for a descending parachutist. The 5th Guards Airborne Brigade jumped directly over 19th Panzer Division armoured columns coincidently transiting Dudari at the time. As many as 50 per cent of the jumpers were killed in the air floating down through a mass of concentrated tracer sent up from every tank and half-track in the division massed below. The debacle tangibly demonstrated the poor planning and insufficient air support that dogged Soviet airborne operations. Soviet paratroopers fought to the death once on the ground as 2,300 men were scattered across a 25 square-mile area. In a sense they replicated a poor attempt at Student's 'oil-spot' strategy in that they attracted countermoves to prevent their consolidation and spread, thereby fragmenting the defence effort. They could not be ignored and invariably fought on as partisans despite defeat. The Dnieper operation was the final serious Soviet airborne operation of the war. These battalion-size piecemeal insertions assisted ground operations in a tactical sense, but rarely beyond the level of localised, if unexpected, protracted raids.

On weekends in 1942 the public at Stoke Orchard in England used to stand on the perimeter road at the top of the hill watching airfield flying. 'We used to make a dive approach into the valley below,' recalled glider trainee Lieutenant John Prout, 'and then climb directly below and behind the spectators and scare the living daylights out of them by coming in silently from behind them and approaching just over their heads.' In September 1941 it was decided all British glider pilots were to conform to RAF selection procedures and elementary flying training. By March 1942 the first 40 volunteers finished their course and commenced further training to evolve basic glider techniques. At the end of 1941 the Glider Pilot Regiment formed within the newly established Army Air Corps. Some 2,500 pilots were to be trained by the end of the war.

Crete was the swan-song of the German glider as an assault vehicle. German gliders were now used to ferry heavy equipments or troops in an airmobile reinforcement capacity. Huge Gigant gliders, developed to carry light armoured vehicles, were now fitted with engines. The Allies saw the glider as an assault and reinforcement vehicle, able to land groups of airborne soldiers and their heavy equipment in one place, rather than have them spread by the wind. The new Horsa glider was introduced: the Mark I variant carried 28 fully armed soldiers exiting from a port-side ramp door and the Mark II had a hinged nose to carry vehicles and guns. Rear fuselages could be dropped off for quick exits. The Americans developed the Waco CG-4A glider called the 'Hadrian' by the British, a fabric-covered wood and steel construction able to carry freight and 15 fully armed troops, leaving through a hinged nose. As the German glider effort contracted the Allies' expanded. Like parachuting, a particular type of individual was needed to pilot or fly inside a glider.

Gliding was dangerous and from inception the British decided pilots would train and fight as soldiers on the ground within the so-called Total Soldier concept. 'As soon as you landed you became a soldier and you fought with whoever you took over,' explained Sergeant Arthur Shackleton. 'So if you took the infantry you fought as an infantryman. If anyone got shot you could become the platoon commander.' Likewise flying artillerymen meant 'you fought with the guns, if signallers, then one might operate radio sets and lay line'. Transporting medics generally meant 'you would probably be a stretcher-bearer'. The Glider Pilot Regiment was trained to fight with any weapon used by airborne troops and taught to be signallers and liaison officers, as all were officers or senior NCOs. They could often be earmarked as an airborne division reserve on landing. Like paratroopers, they faced rigorous selection and tended to attract like-minded individuals.

John Prout when interviewed declared: 'I wasn't very keen on jumping out of aeroplanes so I would prefer gliders,' and, if acceptable, 'I would like to be driving it.' Arthur Shackleton joined through boredom. 'We were training with nothing to train with – if you can understand – make believe,' he explained. He was particularly attracted because 'the OC [Company Commander] couldn't veto it'. Commanding officers often rejected transfer requests so as not to lose their best men. Sapper John Kingdon wanted 'a bit of action, a bit of excitement perhaps' but 'everything else we volunteered for was stopped'. 'We never got anywhere but he couldn't stop this one,' Kingdon commented. It was not an easy option because 'it was a very tough regiment', claimed John Prout, 'very tough'. Shackleton found only ten out of a 100 passed the initial examinations conducted at Oxford. 'So I was called up to Tilshead on Salisbury Plain where they tried to break your spirit,' he recalled. 'We had bags of marching drill, rifle drill, run-marches, assault courses, and they pushed you to the limit because they wanted you to go beyond the limit really.' Of every 100 that went through 'Hell's Gate' at Tilshead only 15 emerged for flying training.

Flying gliders was as physically demanding as it was dangerous. Controls were basic: an air-speed indicator, a turn of bank indicator, a dual-control stick with the co-pilot and a red knob lever in the centre for the tow-cable release. The cockpit was 'like a greenhouse really', described Staff Sergeant John Kingdon, 'fully glazed about six feet across I suppose in width' and blisteringly hot in sunlight. Take-off could be tricky as the glider rose before the towing tug-aircraft, 'and you would be hovering up and down,' Kingdon explained. 'You wouldn't come up too much because you didn't want to lift his tail or anything.' Intense concentration while battling the tug slipstream was required in flight because 'you had to manoeuvre in such a way that the tow rope remains straight'. This was particularly difficult flying in formation with other aircraft. 'If the tow rope dropped to the side and then it suddenly turned up again, it would just snap.' Should this occur over sea or rugged terrain, disaster beckoned. Equal quick-thinking and concentration were required to land. 'You chose the right moment, pulled the "tit" as we called it and released yourself and turned into the landing.' There was no going back. 'You had to think quickly but you didn't get much choice', because from release at 2,000 feet 'it doesn't take long to get down'.

There was a myriad of things that could go wrong. Gliders might undershoot, stall and dive, prematurely release or become trapped in an involuntary spin. Pilots clearly appreciated the hazards, seeing 30 men killed in 28 accidents in 1942 and 19 lost through 14 mishaps the following year. Sergeant Harold Lansdell lost his first two instructors to crashes and witnessed a fatal smash at Burnaston, which convinced him 'what a dodgy game I was in and that I ought not to expect to survive the war'. His fiancée was 'not at all pleased about the glider pilot business', but Lansdell continued amid 'a serene fatalism' that it would not be him.

Operation Freshman was the first British glider raid of the war and conducted against the Norsk Hydro Plant at Vermark in Norway. It was a harbinger of hazards yet to come. During the night of the 19/20 November 1942 two Halifax-Horsa glider combinations flew a force of 30 skilled airborne engineer soldiers into an isolated valley 80 miles beyond the coast and 60 miles west of Oslo. The objective was to sabotage a heavy-water plant thought to be linked to the production of a German atomic bomb. Only the Halifax bomber was then capable of towing a glider 400 miles and returning to base. Guided by a Rebecca-Eureka radio location device, the group, commanded by Lieutenants A.C. Allen and D.A. Methuen, were to be led by Norwegian guides for the final leg to their target. After blowing it they intended to get out via Sweden. The weather was marginal and ice formed on the tow rope of the first combination that reached the objective. It snapped and the prematurely released glider crashed into a mountain side. The second tug and glider completely disappeared and was later found to have crashed near Helleland. Just one Halifax returned.

Only after the war was it discovered that the survivors had been shot on the spot by the Germans and the severely injured poisoned in hospital under Gestapo supervision. The first British glider operation of the war demonstrated the reach and versatility of glider missions but also the tenuous line dividing success from failure. Back in England glider squadrons were being mobilised for more conventional infantry insertions, but as Sergeant Arthur Shackleton recalled: 'This was all experimental.' 'We had no yardstick to go on,' he emphasised. The capability still very much resembled a blunt instrument. 'Everything we did had never been done before so you were groping and learning by mistakes,' he explained.

The first American glider unit was the 88th Glider Infantry Regiment, formed in May 1942, the first of 11 such regiments created by the US Army during the war. They were smaller than the three-battalion parachute infantry regiments which numbered 1,958 men, because they were constrained by the numbers of gliders. Regiments formed with just two battalions with 1,605 soldiers. German glider men, the heroes of Eben Emael, had regarded themselves as the elite of the elite. So much so that Jäger Feri Fink questioned the need for non-jumpers to conduct parachute training before the invasion of Crete. American paratroopers by contrast did not regard their glider counterparts as equals.

Unlike the paratroopers and British infantry glider battalions, they were not volunteers. Physically fit men were routinely assigned and expected to accept a glider role. Soldiers did not complain but were piqued by the lack of hazardous flight pay and envious of the distinctive insignia and badges worn by paratroopers. Rivalry caused by this shot-gun wedding to flesh out more infantry for airborne divisions was pronounced. Paratroopers saw glider soldiers as second-class, but instinctively appreciated it took guts to ride flimsy gliders under fire. Glider troops had no reserve or a second chance because glider release was a one-shot do-or-die action beyond their control. The inequitable pay situation was remedied in July 1944 but not before many men had died. A popular song, 'The Glider Riders', colourfully expressed their frustration to the tune of 'That Daring Young Man on the Flying Trapeze'. One verse chanted:

> We glide through the air in our flying caboose,
> Its actions are graceful, just like a fat goose,
> We hike on the pavement till our joints come loose,
> And the pay is just the same.

Posters of crashed and burned out gliders hung on the walls of their barracks, proclaiming: *Join the glider troops! No flight pay. No jump pay. But never a dull moment!*

British glider infantry battalions were also re-roled but there was a volunteer and selection element. British paratroopers could be equally dismissive until they went into action with the first air–land brigades. 'If to go into action by parachute is worth two shillings a day extra pay, then to go into action in a glider is worth four!' declared a paratrooper with the 1st Parachute Brigade. All the glider soldier could do was crouch in his flimsy wooden fuselage and hope he was not hit by unseen fighter aircraft or heavy flak. 'The first glider I ever saw cast off in the air at 5,000 feet, immediately nose-dived to earth and killed the entire passenger load,' declared the same paratrooper. 'Trusting myself to an apparatus constructed mainly of plywood did not appeal to me in the least!' commented Sergeant Eddie Hancock with the 2nd Parachute Battalion. Two Hotspur glider flights was all it took to 'cure me of wishing to be glider-borne'. Just one more flight would have earned him the badge 'but I never sought it'. 'We missed a few thermals,' he recalled, 'and the unexpected sheer drop which left the stomach suspended way above, made me retch.' From that moment on, 'I decided it was safer to descend by parachute.'

Glider infantryman Patrick Devlin with the 1st Battalion Royal Ulster Rifles remembered 'parachutists' wings were more highly regarded', whereas the small glider badge worn on their battle-dress sleeve fell into disuse. 'I don't think anyone bothered to wear it.' 'There was a definite difference between us and the parachute brigades,' he insisted. It was a case of 'expert silent killers' versus 'only glorified infantry', he pointed out with a hint of sarcasm and 'anyway paratroops got an extra two shillings a day, parachute money, whilst we got one shilling . . . so we were downgraded.' Nevertheless, they had the advantage of unit cohesion on landing, 'not scattered all over the place trying to make contact with each other'. 'There was nothing to it,' he insisted, 'but I did not think it was suitable for flying into battle, I wasn't at all impressed.'

In March 1943 Lieutenant Colonel George Chatterton, commanding the newly formed Glider Pilot Regiment, was ordered to despatch two companies of glider pilots numbering 200–300 men to North Africa, and proceed there with the first of them. He was met by the new commander of the 1st British Airborne Division, Major General 'Hoppy' Hopkinson, who had replaced Browning. He animatedly informed him on arrival in Algiers that: 'I've a very interesting operation for you to study.' Churchill and Roosevelt had approved the invasion of Sicily as a preliminary to putting Italy out of the war. General Montgomery's Eighth Army was to land near Syracuse on the island's east coast; General Patton's Seventh US Army with the American 82nd Airborne Division on the south coast. Chatterton was told by a clearly enthusiastic Hopkinson that Montgomery had agreed to use gliders in a night landing ahead of the main forces. D-Day would be 10 July. Chatterton thought he must be joking, it was after all 1 April, All Fools' Day. But Hopkinson's office wall was adorned with aerial photographs of the Sicilian coast showing all too clearly the rocky outcrops, cliffs and small fields enclosed by stone walls. He was serious. There were neither towing planes nor gliders in Africa but Hopkinson assured him the US Air Force would provide both.

Sicily was a rugged mountainous and inhospitable triangular-shaped island of 9,926 square miles, not unlike Crete. Space to land would be tight. Chatterton's pilots had on average achieved eight glider flying hours in six months, which did not include night landings. Few were even rated as experienced day pilots. They would also have to master the intricacies of a different glider, the Waco CG4, and the Waco tended to float farther than the Horsa, which could land in a more confined space. Moreover, the available Wacos were 200 miles to the west strewn around an airfield in large crates. Chatterton demurred but was only given half an hour to either accept the scheme or relinquish command of the glider mission. Hopkinson, like Student before him, wished to make his airborne mark. Lieutenant Colonel John Frost, one of Hopkinson's veteran parachute battalion commanders, rated him as 'another amateur soldier' whom he described as 'a glider enthusiast' who 'managed to insist that the glider-borne 1st Air Landing Brigade undertook the initial assault'.

Chatterton and his pilots tracked the crates down and, consulting the handbooks, put them together themselves, living in the crates to shelter from the fierce heat as they were emptied. Time was short. Self-taught, they had to ferry the strange planes 600 miles east to take-off strips in Tunisia facing Sicily; just about the only familiarisation flight they would have.

The Wacos or 'Hadrians' could not carry a jeep and gun so some Horsas had to be especially flown from England for the operation because time and shipping space precluded other options. The distance was 300 miles longer than the accepted 1,000-mile range for a Halifax-Horsa tow. Experiments were made and Halifaxes run dry to identify the extra fuel needed to improvise something to bridge the gap. Marauding German Ju-88s could be expected over the Bay of Biscay and it was accepted that gliders would have to cut away and ditch in the event of an attack. The first duo that flew snapped their cable and had to ditch hours from land. The flight to Africa was ten hours, a veritable marathon of concentration and close control for glider pilots. One crew that ditched spent 11 days and nights, often unconscious and delirious in a deflating and partially swamped dinghy prior to rescue.

John Prout recalled the preparation for his flight. 'First of all we would go on a ten-hour flight around England to get used to flying the glider for ten hours, because it's very heavy work flying a glider on tow and we had to have three pilots so that you could change every 20 minutes or so.' They were supposed to have a Beaufighter escort but 12 German Ju-88s turned up instead, leaving no alternative but to release from the tug. The Halifax was shot up but inflicted damage on the attackers and just managed to arrive severely damaged in Africa. Prout and the crew were abandoned 240 miles from land in the Atlantic. An aircraft managed to guide in the Royal Navy sloop HMS *Crane*, which picked them up the next day. They were lucky; the ship was passed a location that was 50 miles out. During the return journey the captain informed Prout: 'I have had a message that another glider has come down but I am too far off my course now.' He was sorry he could not turn south to look, 'but I thought I would let you know,' Prout recalled. The missing glider crew were never seen again.

The majority of the Horsas and all but ten of the 350 gliders arrived at the bleak Tunisian airstrips facing Sicily. The next challenge was a 300-mile haul to the island at dusk and in darkness. Most pilots had still not flown more than four hours and perhaps only 30 minutes at night. None had been in action before and neither had the American Dakota tug crews.

Operation Husky, the invasion of Sicily by some 200,000 Allied troops, was to be preceded by four separate airborne operations on 10 July, two American and two British. Colonel James Gavin's 505th Parachute Regimental Combat Team was to conduct a three-battalion parachute assault into a large oval-shaped area between Gela on the coast and Niscerni, ten miles inland. This was to block the roads leading to the landing beaches earmarked for Patton's Seventh Army on Sicily's southern shore. Another three battalions with the 504th Combat Team would drop to reinforce the following night. Hopkinson, determined to demonstrate that glider airborne assault was as effective as any other, planned to land 1,600 men of the British 1st Air Landing Brigade at the Ponte Grande, a bridge just below Syracuse. This was to enable Montgomery's Eighth Army landing on the south-east coast to break out into the Catania Plain. Senior parachute commanders with the 1st British Airborne Division had their doubts whether gliders should lead alone. This was to be the first mass glider assault without parachute troops, dwarfing the German effort on Crete, but conducted with a fraction of the exper-tise. 1st Parachute Brigade would attack the Primasole Bridge further north four days later to maintain the break-out momentum of sea-landed ground forces heading for Catania. The glider force would precede the American parachute drop by one hour. This was the first Allied mass vertical envelopment of objectives to support a seaborne invasion.

'All I'd been shown was a night map with a field marked on it near Syracuse,' recalled Staff Sergeant Glider Pilot Victor Miller. 'I had no idea who we might meet.' As he was going to be flying with an officer he was not overly concerned. 'I reckoned those who had planned it must know their job,' he rationalised. Air-land infantry climbing aboard the unfamiliar and very fragile-looking American gliders felt vulnerable. Lance Corporal Joe Hardy with the 1st Battalion Border Regiment dropped his torch just inside the door on boarding and it fell straight through the canvas onto the ground below. Not much protection there from hostile fire with this makeshift construction, he thought. 'I will be very glad to get back on the ground,' he decided. Conditions on the launch night of 9 July were hardly encouraging. Waves were already leaping and foaming offshore in a steadily rising wind. Pilots saw the spume spraying from wave tops over low flying tugs ahead. The formation flew low-level in echelons of four to avoid radar contact, following the leader up ahead who was navigating. British combinations navigated themselves.

They flew east to Malta, which was due to appear after two to three hours and then would bear north to Cape Passero on south-east Sicily and on to Syracuse. Take-off had been at dusk and arms were soon aching clutching control columns to keeping cables taut while avoiding the worse of the slipstream from the tug aircraft thundering ahead. Eyes straining through the gloom produced headache and eye throb. Staff Sergeant Mills could see from the buffeting ships were getting below that the wind was rising even further. Glancing behind he saw the troops were simply sitting and steadily munching barley sugar, rather quietly it occurred to him. Victor Miller's passengers were passing around the whisky and he accepted a swig. Soldiers fought back air-sickness as they bumped along in the turbulent slipstream. The absence of noise inside the gliders was remarkable. Soldiers could converse instead of attempting the shouted exchanges inside the roaring propeller-driven Halifaxes and Dakotas. Under certain wind conditions the passage of air across the wings produced a deep humming, which rose to a mild roar during the descent. Much could go wrong in a glider and it was unsettling to consider the myriad of technical mishaps that might occur over the sea. Dakota pilots had switched on their rear facing wing lights. Exhaust glow was also discernible; but it only took a momentary lapse of concentration to slip out of position. Lieutenant Colonel Chatterton's attention was sharply focused with adrenalin when he saw the outline of his tug, flying in a moon beam directly alongside. Hitting rudder and aileron he carefully jockeyed back. Six searchlight beams rising out of the gloom of Malta below provided some relief as the combinations banked into the final navigation turn that would bring them on course for Sicily. By the time they reached the enemy coast about a quarter of the glider combinations had lost their intercom communication with the tug pilots.

The wind had risen to such gale proportions that offshore blasts had cloaked the outline of the approaching coastline behind a wall of dust. Glider combinations had to take evasive action to avoid aircraft suddenly visible through the haze groping about for Cape Passero, their first anticipated landfall. Some clue was provided by searchlights and flak opening up from the Italian coastal defences. Less anticipated and totally disorientating was the storm of flak and tracer that suddenly spat up from below. The Allied invasion fleets began to engage their own approaching aerial armada. Half the pilots could not even discern the coastline; none could pick out their individual landing zones. 'We were winding our way across the darkening Mediterranean, bodies encased in a flimsy aircraft of canvas and metal studs,' recalled glider pilot D.E. Baker, 'a slender nylon tow rope between us and the drink.' They were afraid. 'Sicily coming up and suddenly the night was lit by searchlights and rows of little red spots . . . curling up towards us.' Baker realised, 'our flight of no return lay through this barrage' and he cast off.

Still uncertain, the tugs started to release their combinations over the black sea. George Chatterton, piloting the brigade commander, let go but admitted to his co-pilot, 'I can't see a damned thing.' Harry Lansdell, carrying a part platoon of South Staffords, was flying with an American pilot still in communication with the tug. A 'scratchy' conversation ensued 'which I did not understand but Kinney seemed to, and bang we were off'. The action appeared incomprehensible amid the bursting flak. 'Being the last glider of all and subject to the most offshore drift there was not the slightest hope for us to reach land only just to be made out in the distance.' He gave the order to prepare for a ditching.

Despair and gut-wrenching fear in the back was the precursor to descending towards black nothingness, punctuated by a brief glimpse of white caps as they came in. Attempting to land a glider in a turbulent sea, with a descent rate of between 60 and 100 mph, was akin to attempting to skid-land across an uneven icefield. The inability to pick out the horizon in the blackness with nothing to assess wind drift made the enterprise dubious in the extreme. 'Actually, it's amazing how hard water is, it's like running into a brick wall at 80 mph,' described Captain John Tillet in the 2nd Ox and Bucks. The initial impact generally stove in the nose of the cockpit, injuring or killing the pilots and washing people out of their seats to the back of the fuselage. A belly-flop sinking might be arrested by the wings which, despite the fuselage quickly filling with water, could hold the glider on the surface. Shifting vehicle loads on impact or one wing clipping the water prematurely caused the aircraft to spiral or cartwheel through the water, breaking up and scattering the occupants across the surface as if coming down over land. The water was too choppy for many to survive. Of the original fleet of 122 gliders approaching Sicily, 68 went into the sea, many with no trace, leaving only 54 to face the hazardous night landings feared by Chatterton. Both the division and brigade commanders ended up in the sea, including Chatterton. They survived but 326 soldiers drowned.

'He's dropped us!' shouted glider pilot Staff Sergeant Reed, flying with C Company 1st Battalion the Border Regiment, having heard the characteristic release bang. They were over sea; 'Prepare to ditch!' Reed shouted. J. Swan, sitting in the back of the fuselage, recalled: 'What a rush, equipment off and under our feet, opening emergency exits, putting our weapons under our feet as well and then before I could do anything, *smash*, we were down.' There was a frantic rush for the exits in the darkness: 'I struggled to get through the emergency exits under the wing and out to the surface, gasping for air, looking around, bodies swimming around everywhere, clambering onto the wings.'

Two men failed to appear. 'We listened for any kinds of "Help" but nothing.' They had to wait, standing on the wings, watching the intermittent flashes of battle above the dark horizon of the shoreline. Having 'ditched about 9 o'clock, by 12 o'clock the wings were beginning to really get waterlogged and sagging,' Swann uneasily recognised. With increasing dismay they realised they were well off track and remained floating on the water, dreading abandonment. Nine hours later they were picked up.

As Sergeant Harry Lansdell's glider gently descended toward the black water he knocked out the Perspex window next to him with his rifle butt as his co-pilot demolished his with a revolver butt. 'As we struck the surface at 2330 hours the water broke through the soft under-nose of the glider and cascaded over our heads.' It was completely dark. 'Within half a minute there was only a foot of air space between the roof and the water.' They got out, but one corporal was missing. Lance Corporal Joe Hardy, sitting in the back of his glider with a Border Regiment platoon, recalled: 'The tugs naturally wanted to get away from that flak as quickly as possible. It was decidedly unhealthy. Who was to blame, I do not know.'

They sensed they had been gliding for an overly long time and ditched about 200 yards from the shore. An air pocket inside the fuselage enabled most to get a gulp of air before pulling themselves out. They had landed in a precarious situation beneath a defended cliff face. 'If we ducked, there was a fair chance of getting drowned,' he remembered. 'If we didn't there was a very fair chance of getting shot.'

D.E. Baker's glider was descending swiftly into inky blackness and he could see nothing at all at 100 feet until 'suddenly a darker mass loomed up and before any action could be taken we hit with a horrible rending sound'. They had been checked by a huge bush which they struck at about 90 mph, bursting open the fuselage sides at the arrested impact. 'We gathered ourselves, our wits, and felt ourselves all over to make sure we were really whole.' They were under Italian fire, but still moved off toward the Ponte Grande. Gliders were landing blind all around, careering in over unseen rocky ground and smashing into solid banks and walls. 'A weird whistling noise then broke the night,' recalled Baker, 'and turning towards this new menace we perceived to our horror an immense shape tearing toward us.' It was another glider which 'hit the wall with a terrible crash' and 'cries of agony filled the air'.

Intermittent landings occurred throughout the fighting that quickly enveloped the bridge objective. Glider Pilot Staff Sergeant T.N. Moore's Waco glider struck a rock that stove in the nose and broke his ankle, pinning his legs beneath the cockpit seat. Within seconds Italian grenades were bouncing onto the canvas roof, which caught fire amid the bursts. Flaming patches of fabric fell inside the ammunition hand-cart in the centre of the glider, loaded with phosphorous grenades and mortar bombs. It exploded even as the sixth man was scrambling out, killing another one 100 yards beyond, seeking cover. Garrett, Moore's co-pilot, managed to get him out even though his left elbow had been scythed off by the explosion. They were alerted to a plaintive cry 50 yards away. One of their corporals was pulling himself toward them on his back, pushing himself with his elbows. 'He had been struck between the knees by an exploding grenade' and they attempted to dress his wounds. 'It was almost hopeless, for the hole in each knee was larger than a field dressing.' They were eventually recovered.

Grimly determined isolated groups continued with the mission. One platoon of the South Staffords captured the Ponte Grande which was held, reinforced by stragglers, until the following day. German troops pushed them off but seaborne troops arrived within an hour to recapture the bridge, having landed virtually unopposed behind a much distracted enemy. More than half the glider troops who survived the debacle of the fly-in became casualties: 279 were killed or wounded and 57 glider pilots killed. Only one man in 15 from the brigade and none of the guns carried by the gliders got into action at the bridge. Back at Sousse in North Africa came slow realisation of what had happened. 'This was a severe blow to the division,' recalled Lieutenant Colonel John Frost with the 2nd Parachute Battalion. 'The 1st Air Landing Brigade no longer existed as a fighting formation and could take no further part in the campaign.'

As the Dakotas were revving their engines prior to the take-off of the US 505th Parachute Regiment Combat Team, an airman from the weather station ran up to the commander Colonel Gavin's aircraft and yelled: 'I was told to tell you that the wind is going to be 35 mph west to east,' adding, 'they thought you'd want to know.' Training jumps were generally called off at 15 mph to minimise injuries. Few had jumped at more than 25 mph and nobody at 35 mph and certainly not over the rugged and broken terrain they anticipated. 'There were many other hazards of greater danger in prospect' than the wind, Gavin reflected, but it was not encouraging.

Gavin's 266 C-47s were soon blown hopelessly off course, many of the pilots missing the signal lights at Malta. They also had to run the flak gauntlet of the invasion fleet, as well as the enemy, as the dispersed formation homed in on the drop zone east of Gela on the island's south coast. They came from every direction. There were 12 Italian divisions manning Sicily, six on static coastal defence and only two German divisions. The Hermann Göring Fallschirmjäger Panzer Division directly menaced the American coastal sector. American aircraft hit by flak off the coast stood little chance of survival as they were unarmoured and had no self-sealing fuel tanks. Over the drop zones there was small arms fire; some units encountered heavy resistance while others landed unopposed. Strong winds scattered the aircraft and the drop 20 miles east of the objective and spread them over an area of 100 square miles. Only one-eighth of the 505th Combat Team landed on the correct drop zone from the 3,405 troops that departed Africa. Gavin could only personally muster 20 of his men four hours after the jump. Nevertheless, most of the combat team did at least land between the landing beaches they were due to cover and the very confused Hermann Göring Division. Most of the paratroopers were thoroughly shaken up by heavy landings on trees, buildings and rocky hillsides, causing many casualties. 'The thing I remember most about the jump is how quick I hit the ground,' recalled Clarence Ollam with the 505th. 'We must have been really low.'

Ironically during the ensuing fighting just one battalion, the 3rd, accomplished all the missions assigned to the entire regimental combat team. In the event of uncertainty, the men were still directed to jump because it was directed only pilots and crews were to return to North Africa. Whereas there was doubt in the minds of the American paratroopers whether they were in Sicily, Italy or the Balkans, the enemy was equally confused, convinced they had been attacked by a parachute army. Not only were telephone communications badly disrupted, paratroopers attacked enemy columns wherever they found them. Substantial actions where artillery positions were attacked and tanks fired at by bazookas coincided with low-level skirmishes. The enemy were harassed and confused.

General Matthew Ridgway, commanding the 82nd Airborne Division, had been apprehensive about friendly fire even before the operation began. He was shocked to learn that Admiral Cunningham, the British Naval Commander, was not prepared to risk allowing friendly aircraft near his ships. Three years of intense naval warfare and horrific losses to aircraft permeated his view. He was persuaded to desist so long as the airborne transports followed a prearranged flight path at least seven miles distant from his ships. Colonel Reuben Tucker's 504th Parachute Infantry Regiment Combat Team arrived over the coast of Sicily on the second night to conduct the agreed first wave reinforcement.

Having failed to halt the Allied invasion the previous day, four major Axis air attacks came in against Cunningham's ships on 11 July, including an attack by 30 Ju-88s that bombed Gela. Supply ships, including a hospital ship, were hit and the USS *Robert Rowan*, an ammunition container, had exploded spectacularly with devastating force. A massive bombing attack was launched starting at 2210 that night. As it died away the transports packed with Tucker's 504th flew along the coast and turned left, to disgorge the first serial of paratroopers. Succeeding serials arrived off-course and as the first of these commenced its run to the drop zone the invasion fleet opened a desultory fire which steadily increased in volume and intensity until all guns were blazing, including from ships farther out to sea.

On shore Generals Patton and Ridgway, observing the debacle, were aghast as the slow-moving transports, an easy low-level target, were subjected to a withering fire. Machine gun bullets and shells tore through the floors of the crowded jump planes, killing and wounding paratroopers hooked up and waiting to jump. Six blazing aircraft spiralled to the ground with paratroopers unable to climb the steep angle to reach the doors and get out. Two crash-landed in empty fields alongside, while several others immediately turned eastward to drop in the quieter British zone. Eight planes bringing up the rear turned sharply out to sea to avoid the disaster looming ahead. Tucker's plane, despite repeated hits, disgorged its load and he landed near tanks firing at the aircraft with their 50mm machine guns. Still wearing his parachute he ran between the tanks shouting, 'Cease fire! Cease fire!'

'All hell broke loose in the direction of the beaches,' recalled Colonel James Gavin near Gela. The low steady drone of the anticipated reinforcements could be heard. Everybody grabbed their weapons to engage but were cautioned to wait 'until we understood what was going on'. 'Suddenly at about 600 feet the silhouettes of American C-47s appeared against the sky – our own parachute transports! Some seemed to be burning and they continued directly ahead in the direction of Gela. From the damaged planes some troops jumped or fell, and at daylight we found some of them dead in front of our positions.'

The next morning Colonel Tucker had only an artillery battery and a rifle company with him and 550 men of the 2,000 that had taken off in Africa accounted for. Thirty-seven badly damaged planes riddled with holes and floors running with blood made it back to the landing fields around Karajan; some of the dead and wounded were still inside wearing their parachutes. Of the 144 aircraft that took off, 23 were never seen again and 318 paratroopers and aircrew were killed or wounded.

Two nights later the British 1st Parachute Brigade jumped over the Primasole Bridge to gain a bridgehead across the River Same to achieve entry to the Catania Plain. They were understandably apprehensive. Private Geoffrey Morgan with 2 Para had already heard about gliders crashing into the sea and the heavy flak from their own invasion fleet. 'We found this out just before we went in,' he recalled. Twenty-nine of the brigade's 116 aircraft failed to drop at all and only 39 dropped their men on or within half a mile of the drop zones. Lieutenant Colonel Alastair Pearson, commanding 1 Para, went into the American crew compartment with his pistol to motion the pilot through the intimidating flak to reach their objective. Lieutenant Colonel John Frost dropped accurately, confident that 'this American squadron had always managed to drop us accurately on the exercises we had done before'. He felt the 52nd Troop Carrying Wing would do likewise for Sicily but 'this was easier said than done'. 'For thirty minutes our plane dodged everything they flung at us,' recalled Corporal Reg Curtis with 1 Para. 'It was a sickening half hour, as we were helpless to do anything.' Like all the other Sicilian insertions the brigade ran a gauntlet of friendly and enemy fire. 'A tracer bullet clipped one of the 28 rigging lines to my parachute,' remembered Curtis and, 'it collapsed lazily over my shoulder as I landed heavily on a road.'

Only 20 per cent of the force arrived in place. Frost saw no aircraft flying in formation anywhere and of those he could distinguish most 'were going flat-out and some were weaving through the air in desperate evasive action'. They watched one duo with bated breath tearing towards each other from opposite ends of the drop zone. 'A really sickening crash seemed inevitable,' but they tore past, 'perhaps not even knowing how near they had been to disaster.' Soon after landing they began to realise they had just missed a drop of reinforcing Fallschirmjäger on the same drop zone. This had occurred hours before and Germans were still combing the area in the dark looking for weapons containers. Fallschirmjäger Regiment 3 and other German parachute units had landed during the night of the 12/13 July. 'We must have brushed shoulders!' declared Reg Curtis. 'They were parachutists!'

The Primasole Bridge was captured by the much reduced force in situ, but it was soon pressed hard on three sides by Italians and German Fallschirmjäger. A three-day battle developed with success bloodily ebbing and flowing as German infantry and panzer attacks battered the defenders until the Eighth Army vanguard arrived in the nick of time to finally secure the heavily contested objective.

'Sicily had been a sobering experience,' reflected Colonel James Gavin when the island was finally overrun on 17 August. Lessons were immediately apparent. Soldiers in the future would need to jump at minimum with weapons and ammunition attached to the man. Pathfinders and other navigational aids needed to be introduced, alongside more training for aircrews.

Approbation was heaped on the pilots of the US Transport Command, who had more aircraft shot down by the Allied fleet than the Axis defenders. British Dakota pilot James Quinn with the 216th Transport Command Squadron recalled British paratroopers 'refused point blank to be dropped by Americans – they said, "No dust",' because 'half of them were dropped in the sea', while 'several more were dropped away in the north coast of Sicily where there was little defence.' John Frost, annoyed that less than one-third of his men achieved the target, declared, 'it was difficult to claim that the fireworks round the Primasole Bridge were invisible from anywhere out to sea.' Future night operations would be jeopardised by 'American shortcomings', he felt, and 'it was essential that they be invited to make good their navigational deficiencies.' US aircrews were on the same steep learning curve as their parachute cargoes.

Anguish over losses and the difficulty of appreciating the extent of damage caused by friendly fire obscured the positive contribution made by the Americans who devised the mass glider marshalling procedures worked out at the Sousse airfields for the first time. Glider Pilot Regiment Lieutenant John Mockeridge believed the American 54th Troop Carrier Wing were 'as well trained in flying skills, if not better than we were' and 'the majority of the American pilots had many more flying hours than we had', being civil pilots before the war. 'Both armies' staffs had at that time little airborne experience,' he remembered and, 'consequently some peculiar decisions as to what was possible were taken.' Casualties among the gliders pulled by RAF Albemarles over Primosole, Mockeridge recalled, were proportionally the same as those sustained by those gliders towed by American Dakotas over Syracuse.

The 82nd Airborne Division returned to Sicily in late August while the badly mauled British 1st Airborne Division remained in North Africa. The impending collapse of Mussolini's Italy led to serious consideration of landing the 82nd Division in the Rome area as part of the negotiations to split disaffected Italians from their German allies and swiftly occupy the Italian mainland. General Ridgway despatched General Maxwell Taylor on a secret fact-finding mission to coordinate with Italian Marshal Badoglio about the practicality of an apparent suicide mission. There were six German divisions based in or near the city, all beyond Allied fighter range. This represented the first considered example of diplomatic pressure being applied by the threatened projection of an airborne capability since Göring's air-land operation in the Sudetenland in 1938. American paratroopers were sitting in their C-47s on Sicilian airfields when the cancellation order came through.

Italy accepted unconditional surrender on 3 September, which was timed to coincide with the Canadian and British landings on the toe of Italy around Reggio and Anglo-American landings at Salerno. Ignominiously the 1st British Airborne Division landed by sea at Taranto Harbour. 'No aircraft, no aircraft at all,' was how Major

General Hopkinson had broken the news to the disillusioned men of 156 Para according to Captain John Waddy. HMS *Abdiel*, carrying 400 men from 6 Para, struck a mine in the harbour, losing 58 men killed and 154 injured. Hopkinson was killed by a sniper soon after in ground fighting at Castellaneta.

On 12 September the 82nd Airborne Division was given eight hours to react to an urgent call from General Mark Clark, the embattled Fifth US Army Commander, clinging to a tenuous ridge under furious German counter-attack at Salerno. The 504th and 505th Parachute Infantry Regiments were dropped into the hard pressed beachhead near Paestum and Albanell on the 13th in an airborne reinforcement that tipped the balance in favour of the Allies. It had been impossible to conduct the normal highly detailed and complex briefings that were the prerequisite for airborne missions. One soldier described the detail passed down at infantry squad level: 'The Krauts are kicking the shit out of our boys over at Salerno. We're going to jump into the beachhead tonight and rescue them. Put on your parachutes and get on the plane – we're taking off in a few minutes for the gates of hell.'

This was not far removed from the fate of the 2nd Battalion 509th dropped around the town of Avellino in the mountains 20 miles inland from the Fifth Army beachhead. The mission was to utilise the rugged terrain, totally unsuited for parachuting, to block German reinforcements reaching the beaches. Many of the 64th Troop Carrier Command aircraft missed their dropping zones and scattered the 640 paratroopers over 100 square miles; the battalion commander landed in the middle of a German tank park. Desperate tactical situations often necessitated this sort of calculated expenditure of life. There was no possibility of relief by ground forces. All but 130 of the troopers fought their way out, mining roads, blowing bridges and ambushing elements of the diverted German defence. The paratroopers did not surrender. Once the conventional ground holding role became impractical they were sufficiently tenacious to revert to a raiding mode. The significance of this was lost on senior airborne planners seeking tactical solutions to conventional infantry missions. Student's untidy 'oil-spot' strategy of vertical envelopment worked, but it was costly.

The airborne capability appeared to be an unwieldy and often blunt instrument. Much of the fault lay with the planners, unused to manoeuvring sizeable airborne units. At the Primosole Bridge only four of 19 gliders departing Africa accurately landed, at Syracuse only 16 of 137 made it and only 13 reached the ground without casualties or damage. Parachute commanders had felt a company-size parachute raid would have been more appropriate than a mass glider envelopment, hardly worthwhile in terms of the expended resources. Airborne operations were ruinously expensive in manpower and aircraft and infinitely complex to manage. The objective had to be worth the effort. Months of preparation assembling 150 glider tug crews and 300 glider pilots and immense ground work was expended to deliver less than 90 men on the Ponte Grande. There were problems of aircraft navigation, delivering unit cohesion on target, indeed even finding suitable size landing sites. High incidental crash rates with human loss occurred even before units were under fire. It was questionable whether the high casualty rates, often caused as much by friendly as enemy fire, made vertical envelopment a viable tactical option. 'It was a nightmare, the whole thing,' declared one glider pilot describing the Syracuse operation.

General Dwight D. Eisenhower, the Supreme Commander and earmarked to lead the anticipated invasion of France, instituted a painful introspective review. Writing to General Marshall, the US Chief of Staff, he declared, 'I do not believe in the airborne division.' He recommended, 'I believe that airborne troops should be reorganised in self-contained units, comprising infantry.' His view was that a division 'would require a dropping over such an extended area that I seriously doubt that a division commander could regain control and operate the scattered forces as one unit'. British parachute commanders suspected the army had never seriously supported or believed in airborne forces. Brigadier Hackett's 4th Parachute Brigade, warned off to maybe support the Salerno landings across the Straits of Messina, called them 'mere puddle-hopping operations'. 'Sicily was yet another humiliating disaster for airborne forces,' argued Lieutenant Colonel Frost with 2 Para, 'and almost enough to destroy even the most ardent believer's faith.'

General Marshall conducted a huge airborne manoeuvre in the

United States in December 1943 to test the 11th Airborne Division and the airborne concept. At stake was the potential break-up of five established American airborne divisions and the future of airborne support to assist the projected invasion across the English Channel, anticipated in 1944. The exercise was successful but called for greater coordination between ground and air assets. A more precise instrument was required for D-Day.

CROSSING THE ENGLISH CHANNEL

Staff Sergeant Roy Howard piloted the sixth glider in the stream, having taken off for the Normandy coast at 2255 hours on 5 June 1944. Shortly after midnight five glider-borne platoons of the Ox and Bucks numbering 180 men were released over the Orne Estuary, their objectives were two bridges crossing the Orne River and Canal. Roy Howard's dilemma was how 'to navigate various courses on a 45° angle of descent, dropping at the rate of 2,000 feet per minute, in the dark and without aids of any kind'.

Extensive army airborne and air force joint training followed the debacle in Sicily. Parachute pathfinders teams were formed and trained to mark drop zones and glider landing sites. Selected aircraft crews had received specialist pathfinder training to find designated drop zones by dead reckoning, map reading and radar aids. Eureka beacons were placed on the ground by parachuted pathfinders to guide aircraft monitoring their beams with Rebecca homing devices. Precision, however, was dependent upon the accurate dropping of the first markers.

All Roy Howard possessed was a gyro compass illuminated with a dimmed torch and map. 'So far we had seen nothing,' he recalled, 'not even the coastline over which we had released.' A parachute flare burst ahead, briefly lighting the sky around, but blackness soon descended. They were at the point of no return and 'falling like a brick and steering a course at the same time of 212°, to be held for 90 seconds as Fred checked the map and his stop-watch. This covered the first two miles and we turned again onto 268° which we held for 2 minutes 30 seconds, covering a further 3.3 miles.'

They were playing a form of blind man's bluff in the dark, totally reliant upon their compass, judgment, a stop-watch and sharp eyes. 'Still not seeing anything of the ground but continuing our half-way-to-the-vertical dive with only the hiss of the slipstream to be heard among all the now silent men [in the back of the glider] we turned our third course of 212° for the final run-in.'

At 1,200 feet with less than a minute of flight remaining, 'there below us the canal and river lay like silver, instantly recognisable.' It looked exactly like the model they had spent hours poring over and calculating angles of approach for weeks before. Howard landed within yards of the bridge. He was supposed to be the last to land but actually arrived first and alone. 'With a drumming and crash of army boots along the floor of the glider', the platoon commander, as surprised as he was delighted to be in the right place, 'disappeared into the night', Howard recalled, 'to shoot up the Germans guarding the bridge'.

Four other gliders crash-landed in and around the fortified locations protecting the Orne River and Canal bridges, one nosing into the barbed wire emplacement on the canal bridge periphery. Both bridges were captured during a brutal 15-minute skirmish before the German defenders appreciated war had returned to France after a four-year lull. The navigation and precision flying that climaxed with a swiftly executed assault made it one of the outstanding glider actions of the war. Enemy reinforcements now faced a six-hour detour through Caen in order to cross the Orne to reach the invasion bridgehead.

Supreme Commander General Eisenhower had nursed doubts concerning the controlled efficacy and precision of what he considered a blunt airborne instrument. The successful 11th Division Test Exercise in the United States had allayed some his concerns after Sicily but predictably he chose to visit the US 101st Division on the eve of D-Day. 'They looked so young and so brave,' recalled Kay Summersby, his official driver. The general walked around and looked directly at every man he met, wishing them success, confiding to Summersby afterward how 'it's very hard really to look a soldier in the eye, when you fear you are sending him to his death.'

Two American and one British airborne divisions were to spearhead the invasion of Normandy on D-Day, 6 June 1944, and protect the flanks of the seaborne landings. The US 82nd Airborne Division to the west of the invasion was to drop both sides of the Merderet River around Sainte Mère Eglise, north of Carentan, to deny the road axis for German reinforcement to the Contentin peninsula. Its sister division, the 101st, was to seize beach exit routes from Utah and the Douvre River crossings, the only useable road above defensive flood obstacles. 'You're going to be jumping behind enemy lines – what do you expect?' Lieutenant Richard Winters with the division asked himself. 'You have no idea – that'll make anyone stand and search his soul for a few minutes.'

On the opposite eastern flank, the British 6th Airborne Division was to capture the Orne River and Canal bridges at Benouville, destroy the heavy German Merville battery overlooking the river estuary and blow bridges across the flooded River Dives to prevent German reinforcements from reaching the invasion beaches. Eisenhower was swayed to use the airborne because of the need to get eight Allied divisions ashore on D-Day to face an anticipated five German. Flying three divisions over the Atlantic Wall improved the odds significantly, particularly as 500 ships between 100 to 15,000 tons were needed to land one division with its weapons by sea. Neither Eisenhower nor the paratroopers due to drop underestimated the challenge. 'Remember,' recalled Brigadier James Hill commanding the 3rd British Parachute Brigade, 'the country was strange to us – infested by Germans and it was a dark night as well – no mean task.'

On the night of 5 June six American parachute regiments took off from nine airfields with 822 aircraft loaded with 13,000 men, followed by 375 gliders. The British carried another six battalions of 7,000 men with 266 aircraft and 344 gliders that night, to be followed on D-Day by glider-borne infantry and heavy equipments. Eighty-nine British and 52 American gliders landed the first night.

Glider soldier Denis Edwards had landed with the coup de main assault against the Orne Canal Bridge, which gave him a grand-stand view of the mass parachute assault that followed. 'The first few planes flew over with little opposition but those that followed ran into heavy flak,' he observed, 'and at least one was hit, set on fire, and came hurtling down like a comet from about 3,000 feet.'

'Then the parachutists arrived, the sirens sounded, the anti-aircraft guns went into action,' recalled Lieutenant H.J. Sweeney, one of the Ox and Bucks platoon commanders watching the assault come in. 'The main para force was getting a hell of a pasting from ack-ack and the now fully alerted enemy ground forces,' described Denis Edwards, 'and I was quite thankful that we had come down first.' It soon became apparent that the assault was losing cohesion. Jubilation at the arrival of the aerial reinforcement was tempered by uneasiness. 'One disturbing factor,' Lieutenant Sweeney observed, 'was they seemed to be flying in all directions at once, quite unlike the steady stream we had seen on exercises.' 'The upshot of all the confusion,' claimed Edwards, whose unit was clinging onto the bridges against steadily escalating German counter-attacks, 'was that it was around 0230 hours before the first of our reinforcements arrived, and then only in dribs and drabs.'

The American stream flew west of the Contentin peninsula to avoid possible flak from the invasion fleet and then flew due east to their landing zones. They were disorientated by an unexpected cloud bank on the coast which broke up the formations which were further dispersed with the onset of heavy flak once the cloud cleared. As when the British crossed the coast at Ouisterham, intense anti-aircraft fire caused evasive manoeuvring and first the pathfinders, then the main streams, began to jump widely dispersed sticks. Disorientated by flooded river lines, many pilots, distracted and fearful of flak, dropped their sticks across the flooded areas. Miscalculations of the time taken to cross the Contentin peninsula and flak at the far side caused some sticks to jump out over the Channel, an unseen and lonely death for some. The 82nd Division dropped 20 separated sticks more than 25 miles away from their designated drop zones, the 101st scattered its loads over an area of 15 by 25 square miles. Only 1,100 men mustered on D-Day from 6,600 and 35 sticks were out by at least 20 miles. British errors were equally catastrophic. The British 5th Brigade dropping near Ranville achieved an accuracy rate varying from 40–60 per cent, with 52 of 85 gliders crash-landing in the darkness.

Glider landings under fire without the element of surprise hardly constitute an act of war. The fatal demise of all three gliders attempting to land on the Merville battery illustrated the fine dividing line between success at the River Orne and failure in the teeth of ack-ack fire seeking a hostile battery in the dark. Lieutenant Hugh Pond, riding one of these gliders, recalled 'one shell hit the flamethrower' which meant 'the glider and the unfortunate chap were on fire for the last few seconds of the approach'. They crash-landed about 150 yards away but were too late. 'As we all rushed out, except for the poor chap on fire, we heard shooting, which we realised was the battalion in the battery.'

Glider landings among the densely packed bocage hedgerows in the American sector could be catastrophic. Waco gliders were especially flimsy, held together by struts and canvas. 'We watched helplessly while one glider after another attempted to land in the fields around us and crashed,' recalled Lieutenant Charles E. Samman with the 505th PIR. 'When they hit something all the equipment inside tore loose and hurtled through the nose of the glider, killing or injuring the men in front of it.' The 101st's assistant division commander Brigadier General Don Pratt was killed instantly when his glider crash-landed. The wide dispersion was calamitous, it took hours to recover the few guns and supplies as German pressure perceptibly rose. US glider pilots had already dubbed the British Horsa the 'Flying Morgue' because of its tendency to break up during hard landings. One crashed and turned upside down just west of Sainte Maire-du-Mont, ironically 200 yards from the 1st Battalion 506th Regiment's medical-aid station. Eighteen dead and 14 seriously injured were extricated from the wreckage. 'I doubt if 10 per cent of the gliders landing on that field did so without crashing,' remembered Samman, 'and very few of the men who landed were in any shape to fight.'

Overall results of the airborne landings only slowly became apparent and were discouraging. By dawn the 101st Division could only muster 38 per cent and the 82nd 33 per cent of its strength. Dispersal reduced the 6th British Airborne Division to about 40 per cent of its established strength. In effect, Eisenhower, counting on three divisions, had only the equivalent of one-third of each broadly in place.

'As the time was getting closer I was getting nervous, getting butterflies in my stomach,' recalled Private George Alex with the US 82nd Airborne Division. Conditions deteriorated as aircraft flew low-level, bumping along rough slipstream corridors created by the aircraft ahead. Soldiers were jerked about by sudden stomach-churning evasive actions to avoid flak. 'Then one man gets air-sick,' recalled George Alex, 'and pulls his steel helmet off to heave into it. And then everybody else down the line follows suit. Everybody is heaving, dry heaves, waiting, waiting to get out of that aeroplane. We are all sick and the plane stinks and we are ready to get out any time . . .' An unpleasant experience, because as George O'Connor flying with 13 Para recalled, they were so crowded 'one wit asked the dispatcher if he had brought any olive oil with him, as we were packed in like bloody sardines'.

Physically weakened after air-sickness, troopers had to pick up and fasten heavy equipments to their harnesses. After Sicily the British had introduced leg-bag valises and the idea was shared with the Americans, to avoid the vulnerability of searching for separately para-chuted containers. 'The valise weighed around 65lbs,' remembered O'Connor and, 'I was hoping I wouldn't have to carry it too far, when I landed.' William 'Wild Bill' Guarnere jumping with the 101st remembered the tendency to overpack the new leg bags, an idea 'the British came up with'. 'You kept shifting everything you could get your hands on into them' which meant the designed weight soon soared to '40, or 50 or 60lbs'. Exiting aircraft sometimes acceler-ating up to 150 mph to avoid flak meant the slipstream ripped them off. 'Everyone who jumped with a leg bag of supplies – they lost it,' declared Guarnere. 'Most of the paratroopers who landed had nothing,' he exasperatedly recalled.

The transition from bumpy low-level flight to gyrating evasive flying was as dramatic as it was sudden. Jack Schlegel recalled paratroopers dozing as the 3rd Battalion PIR approached their drop zone, 'when a line of tracer bullets cut through the length of the fuselage of the C-47 causing men sitting on either side to pull their feet in closer'. Everybody was now fully alert to experience the next shock, which was a thumping blow into the port engine. Immediately Lieutenant John Evans their officer yelled 'Stand up and hook up!' A third strike took off part of the right wing instantly tilting the plane over to the right. 'Go!' Evans shouted and led the way. 'I recall I was the 24th and last to leave the plane,' Schlegel remembered, and the Dakota was going down. 'I moved as fast as I could to get out and, after baling out, saw the plane go up in a ball of flame.' Hardly a minute had elapsed between quiet dozing and total catastrophe. Evans was never seen again.

George O'Connor recalls, 'my thoughts were interrupted by an almighty thump on the plane's fuselage.' Looking out of the Dakota doorway: 'I could see what looked like little red bubbles gently floating up towards the plane, they appeared to be strung out in a line, as they approached the plane, they came towards us at terrific speed, some of the bubbles shot past us, but some of them exploded near us, I could hear pieces of shrapnel hitting the fuselage.'

They were pitched about and nearly thrown out the door by a blast of gunfire. He saw 'the rest of the lads were rolling about on the floor, they were so tightly packed together they were getting tangled up'. Dispatchers sought desperately to disentangle the muddle and ensure lines were still hooked up. They tumbled out amid tracer fire. On the ground O'Connor saw 'one para about to land, he was upside down, his feet caught in the rigging lines'. He landed completely winded by the impact but was fortunate; another was impaled by one of the anti-glider landing poles.

Paratroopers and glider men were vulnerable in the back of their aircraft and totally reliant on their pilots. Unlike the relationship between the Fallschirmjäger and their Luftwaffe pilots, the Allied airborne divisions did not have the same single service rapport. Flight Lieutenant Harry Chatfield, flying Stirlings with 512 Squadron RAF, described the gap. 'You're in the cockpit, there are a number of people, sort of "hustled" into the aircraft and you took off.' He admitted, 'quite frankly, as far as paratroopers were concerned you very rarely got to know them' and it was much the same for glider infantry. 'You were on the runway, there was a glider behind you, there was a tow rope in between you, somebody hitched the tow rope and somebody else said off you go.' They messed separately from the glider pilots. 'It was the intimacy we did not have. As a crew we did, but the link between the two services we never did have.' He admitted this had always been a cause of regret since the war.

It was much the same for the Americans. 'Finally the pilots,' recalled John W. Martin jumping with the 101st, 'I'm just starting to read their minds.' Their perspective was: 'OK, we've got just so much gas and we're gonna have to get back to England, so what are we going to do with all the guys back here?' he asked pointedly. 'You got to hit the green light sometime and we're standing there ready to jump.' The urge to survive might supersede the professional desire to achieve an accurate drop. Chatfield admitted, 'I suppose it's one of the feelings I've always had that I wished to heck I'd known who we'd taken, and on the other side you're not sure whether you'd want to know them.' Chatfield flew into a storm of flak during the daylight delivery of the Air Landing Brigade on D-Day. As they flew in low the lead glider combination just ahead was shot down in flames. 'Bad as it may be for us, once you turn round, you're on your way home, which is not a choice for most of the other people.' So far as the parachutists were concerned 'they had no flaming option. Once they're out of the plane, they're over there.' They could fly back to the officers' mess and await the next sortie.

On the ground the Normandy paratrooper and glider experience had one of two dimensions. The minority of between 35–40 per cent who were accurately dropped generally pressed on with their missions despite the obvious inversion of odds. The majority, some six men out of ten, representing the overwhelming Normandy airborne experience, had somehow to find their units. The former were surrounded but had the comfort at least of belonging to a larger body of men. The latter were equally cut off, but in fragmented small groups or alone. As a consequence of their specialist selection they reverted to the raiding role as irregulars until they could make their way back.

Whatever the scenario, the initial emotion on landing was one of loneliness and isolation, made worse landing either in the flooded areas or directly among the enemy. All this was preceded by the trauma of an uncomfortable flight and landing under fire. J.B. Stokes with the 101st jumped very low, which 'wasn't bad either, because you got to the ground quicker'. As he floated down 'you could see the tracer bullets burning holes through the parachute'. Private Donald Burgett in the same division saw shadowy figures plunging into the ground in the dark all around him. Seventeen men landed one after the other with sickening thuds and grunts with parachutes barely opening because they had jumped too low.

Over Sainte Mère Eglise the 505th Parachute Infantry sticks were dropping so low that the green lights could be distinguished in the aircraft doors from the ground. They immediately came under fire, oscillating violently above German soldiers shooting up, who had been supervising civilians trying to extinguish a blazing barn near the main square. Eleven men landed within 200 yards of each other among the Germans, who had already shot dead four men from an earlier 101st stick a half hour before. Chaos reigned again amid the fresh arrivals, two of whom hit the church steeple. One of these, Private John Steele, hung helplessly with his parachute caught on the spire, as a bloody skirmish erupted below. Another parachutist floated into the burning barn, setting off secondary explosions as his ammunition detonated cutting short agonised screams. Two more landed in trees; one was shot and left hanging while the other slashed his lines and escaped. Six or seven of the eleven were killed in the air or shortly after landing.

Not every man jumped alone: some dropped with man's best friend, specially trained dogs. 'I wonder what has happened to the Alsatian dog and his handler, Les Courtell?' reflected Private Sid Capon who had jumped with 9 Para. Parachuting Alsatians were trained to carry medical equipment and messages. 'They always jibbed at the first jump, but after being pushed out, invariably followed their handler on all further drops,' recalled Brigadier James Hill. Sid Capon remembered Les Courtell's dog Glen was used 'to sniff out the Germans', and despite humorous mischievous attempts by other soldiers to mimic his handler 'he knew only one master'. Glen was affectionately remembered 'as a lovely dog that would jump out of the aeroplane with no assistance from any of the occupants'. The dog had its own parachute and when he had landed Capon recalled he would 'obediently sit and await his handler when his 'chute had ceased to billow'. Courtell's friends sentimentally recalled 'Glen with his little red light attached to his harness so that his handler could see him. He had to have someone to release him, not like us that are capable of doing this ourselves.'

Jim Batey with 9 Para flew alongside the pair to Normandy and remembered how the dog sensed something was amiss during the pounding they received from anti-aircraft fire on crossing the coast.

He noticed that Courtell had to provide 'a little help' this time when they both jumped. Glen and his handler were probably killed that night by a friendly fire aircraft incident, which likely wounded James Hill and wiped out his tactical group. Their gravestone can still be seen at Ranville airborne cemetery today, in the sixth row from the rear, with a simple inscription: '*Glen* the pal of Les'.

Private Doug Tottle, a medic attached to 9 Para, landed alone in a field with tall grass. 'By now all the planes had gone and the ack-ack had stopped, there was a deadly silence. All I could hear was the wind blowing through the grass. This was the moment I was really scared. I expected to find the field full of my own mates. In my opinion silence is much worse than noise. We were told, that on landing to look for a church steeple. I couldn't see a steeple.'

Sapper Tom Barrett, also with 9 Para, overshot his drop zone by 30 miles. The aircraft was going too fast and too low and his overweight kit bag was snatched away in a slipstream in excess of 150 mph. He landed next to an orchard and after all the noise 'the night was now strangely quiet'. His Sten gun was gone and the only weapons he had left were a revolver, ammunition, grenades and a killing knife. 'I wondered where my comrades were but there was absolutely no sound save for the thumping of my own heart which was beating double time.' A dog barked. 'It sounded like a heavy gun and I immediately fell to earth. Then it was quiet again.'

Many paratroopers from the American 507th and 508th Regiments overshot their landing zones at the confluence of the Douvre and Merderet rivers and plunged into swampland along the flooded waterways. Exhausted from standing long periods hooked up and encumbered by heavy equipment, emotionally drained at being shot at, and often falling out of aircraft ensnared by their rigging lines, many were paralysed by splashing into icy cold water. They did not retain sufficient presence of mind or strength in their terror to disentangle themselves in water that many of them could have stood up in. 'I saw at least a dozen bodies of men who landed in water which could not have been more than two or three feet,' observed Brigadier General James Gavin. 'Because the parachute came right down on top of them, it sealed it to the water. And they were excited anyway, and they were being shot at as well. We lost a surprising number that way.'

'I was heading for a vast sheet of water,' recalled Brigadier James Hill shortly after exiting, 'and realised it was the flooded valley of the Dives.' He found himself wallowing in four feet of water. 'This entailed five hours' cold and very hard work negotiating the numerous underwater obstacles such as farmer's fences, dannert wire, blackthorn hedges and deep submerged irrigation ditches from 10 to 15 feet in width.' More and more people splashed into the water around him. They attached toggle ropes to each other and attempted to swim and wade out of the flooded area. 'Undoubtedly,' he remembered, 'a number of men hampered by their 60lbs weight of equipment drowned in their efforts to find a way out.' Padre A.L. Beckingham, jumping with 8 Para, saw men 'clambering to their feet, still I suppose getting over the shock of landing in water and finding how extremely heavy the water-logged equipment now seemed. They began the slow exhausting business of trudging through the water and swimming the ditches, heading towards the glare and sounds of distant firing.'

As these groups struggled to reach friendly units they encountered both friend and foe blundering about in the darkness. 'It became very tricky,' recalled glider soldier Denis Edwards with the Ox and Bucks, 'as people suddenly loomed up in the darkness.' Men had to close to within whispering distance and then call out the prearranged password. Germans were closing in as well. An unknown band approached Edwards' position on the Orne River Bridge and did not respond to the password. 'Our light machine gun opened fire and downed the lot of them,' Edwards recalled. 'At dawn it was discovered that whilst they had wiped out a German patrol, they had also killed two of the paras who had been taken prisoner by the enemy.'

'We were supposed to head for a green light,' remembered Signaller Harry Read who landed in the flooded Dives area. There were lights all over the place. 'I had come to the conclusion I was in the wrong place. I shouldn't have been in the water anyway.' He began to trudge and wade toward dry land: 'I just made my way through this water and disappeared down a trench, pulled myself up and continued, disappeared down another, pulled myself up and continued. Disappeared down a third.' Totally exasperated, he pitched the heavy radio accumulator he was carrying into the bog and carried on. With daylight he realised there were many other parachutes in the flooded area. 'The circle of silk on top of the water indicated quite obviously there was a bloke underneath.' His misfortune appeared the lesser as he regarded the ominous parachute blooms dotted around. 'So I was rather glad I just landed in a foot or two of water,' he confessed.

Most of the paratroopers were isolated and unsure where they were. 'I kept looking at my map and we were not even close where we were meant to be,' recalled 'Shifty' Powers with the US 101st Division. 'We did not know where we were – we was plumb off the maps that they'd give us.' They headed east, toward the invasion beaches; others simply followed the sound of firing. Joseph Lesniewski in the same regiment landed near one companion and started to walk around looking for more troops. 'We were running into Germans everywhere and we had to hide,' he recalled. 'If we didn't, we were dead meat.' Many had no weapons or equipment because they had been ripped off in the slipstream. 'There were four guys with me at D-Day who had nothing more than a jump knife when they landed,' remembered Lieutenant John Winters with Easy Company in the 506th Regiment. 'We ran across someone later who had been killed and we'd take his weapon, and that's how you get a weapon for D-Day,' he explained, 'haphazard.' 'It was quite a confused situation,' commented C. Carwood Lipton in Winters' company, 'but we were better prepared for it than the Germans were. The Germans did not know where we were.'

'The Hun thinks that only a bloody fool will go where we are going,' declared General 'Windy' Gale commanding the British 6th Airborne Division during a pep-talk prior to the invasion, 'and that is why we are going there!' Brigadier James Hill remembered 'the tremendous cheer he got' wherever he said it. It was true. One of the positive aspects of the dispersed drops was that the Germans, unable to identify parachute concentrations, could not drive into them. They did not have a clue what was going on. Despite this dispersal, virtually all the premier objectives were secured by the dawn of D-Day. Eisenhower achieved his aerial tri-division impact more by luck than design. Few planners had appreciated that widespread raiding could have a superior cumulative impact than conventional ground-holding. The airborne instrument after Sicily was still blunt, but the shock waves emanating from lesser blows were seriously unhinging and distracting the German defence. It was precisely the effect required but few of the tactical thrusts and blocks could be tangibly represented on a conventional staff map. Wherever paratroopers landed they fought, gathering into larger groups, dominating areas rather than ground and vindicating Student's 'oil-spot' strategy as more and more objectives were encompassed.

'These airborne landings began at about 0030 hours and carried on throughout the whole night and following days,' reported the operations log of the German 716th Division, about to be overrun by British and Canadian seaborne landings. 'Incident reports concerning parachute jumps and airborne landings arrived at division headquarters in timed intervals as the landings occurred, between 0040 and 0105.' Alarms were raised. Not until 0210 was it realised the Orne River and Canal bridges had fallen. The whole of the German reserve, including elements of the 21st Panzer Division, were directed east of the Orne to resolve this sudden critical development, away from the Allied seaborne landings scheduled at dawn. Confusion reigned when combat groups from the German 736th and 726th Regiments were directed at parachute landings reported near Bernières, directly behind Juno beach, the centre of the British amphibious landing area. One reinforced infantry company from Regiment 736 combing the area just inland was caught in the preliminary naval bombardment 'and annihilated'. 716 Division Headquarters reported: 'There were no eye-witness reports as all communications were broken, and of the units employed, not one man returned.'

Parachute landings behind the American Omaha and Utah beaches were first reported to the 352nd Division responsible for the eastern sector at 0145 hours. The commander of the 709th Division to the west covering Utah was absent trying to return from a cancelled map exercise at Rennes. Once again the landings siphoned off reserves not subsequently able to combat the beach landings. The Kampfgruppe Meyer of the 352nd Division was sent west with three battalions at 0420. The 91st Division, newly located at the base of the Contentin peninsula and whose arrival resulted in the last-minute relocation of the US 82nd Division drop zones, was tasked to coordinate the crucial counter-attacks from north, west and south of the roughly identified American landing areas. Its commander, however, Lieutenant General Falley, was killed alongside his chief logistics officer near his headquarters by misdropped American paratroopers. 352 Division, having felt it had the situation in hand, saw all its preliminary work unravelled, because: 'As was to later become apparent, this enemy came together, and demonstrated a particularly apt grasp of guerrilla tactics. In widely dispersed small groups, these paratroopers caused casualties among our inexperienced troops through sniping and bitterly contested hedgerow actions. The last paratroopers were not eliminated until late afternoon of 7 June.'

This was simply one area. Substantial elements of the 91st Division, which could otherwise have been directed against the thinly held Utah beach area, were regrouped and squandered on fruitless missions against an enemy who seemed always to combine elsewhere. All this had to be coordinated by a division HQ whose commander had been killed nearby and the whole unit was distracted, having to provide security in its own area. The 709th Division commander distracted by air attacks and having to deviate to avoid paratrooper pockets of resistance did not arrive until his division had already been split in half by the landings on Utah beach. Reserves consisted primarily of German infantry riding bicycles or requisitioned trucks. Once committed they were difficult to redeploy, subjected to Allied air attacks and constantly skirmishing with isolated groups of dispersed parachutists. Both of the key defending German divisions manning beach defences, the 352nd and 716th, had irrevocably committed their final local reserves to contain the airborne landings before they were engulfed by the massed seaborne landings. The only panzer reserve in situ, 21st Panzer Division, was committed to counter-attacks east of the Orne River against the British 6th Airborne Division, now forming up, whereas the amphibious landings were to occur west of the river.

On the Allied front, with six out of ten parachutists and glider soldiers landed in the wrong place, planned actions like the destruction of the Merville battery, the blowing of the Dives River bridges, the capture of Sainte Mère Eglise and the securing of the causeways crossing the flooded areas to the beaches were accomplished with a fraction of the conventional strengths thought required. 'My God, what a terrible sight,' recalled Doug Tottle when the 9th Parachute Battalion assaulted the Merville battery with only 150 of the 600 men thought needed. He was a medic and confessed: 'I thought I could stand anything, like dead men, arms and legs blown off, men crying for their mums. I couldn't. It made me feel sick and I am sure I was.'

'Landed! 20 miles behind the lines and in the wrong place,' wrote Major Brian Browne to his mother after D-Day. 'Immediately we ran into trouble.' He described an initial brush with a German patrol on bicycles. 'I shot three stone-dead and the others made off,' he recalled. 'Felt pretty good after that.' Thereafter he continued harassing the enemy, having collected '35 blokes in the same boat'. They had to disperse because they were too many to feed together. They were 'always soaked to the skin, eaten by mosquitoes and followed by Hun fire'. He was captured, escaped and carried on harassing the enemy until rejoining British lines on 19 August.

Private Tony Lycett's experience, having jumped with 7 Para and then spent 'six days adrift', was more typical. Returning individuals felt an unwarranted degree of guilt. Lycett was posted missing but got back six days later. 'I can only describe my experience as a scared animal desperate to rejoin the herd,' he admitted. 'As time went on it all seemed a bad dream, best forgotten.' He believed his remarkable experience to be uneventful: keeping off the roads by day, he moved through woods and fields by night, having to drink from muddy pools of water. Eventually he was helped to get back by the French Resistance.

Sapper Horace 'Tom' Barrett dropped 30 miles off course but managed to join up with two companions. 'The important thing to me was that at least there were two of us now,' he confessed. 'I felt less on edge,' because one of them had a bren gun. Their first shock was a chance encounter with a German motor-cycle rider, who they shot off the bike. 'I'll never forget that man, his back had been cut to ribbons by the bullets; his face and clothes were bloody and dirty.' The desperation of their situation was such that 'this wasn't the time or place for any feeling of sentiment'. German after-action reports referred to airborne and commando soldiers as 'belonging to a psychologically criminal level'. Airborne soldiers, it stated, were more 'prepared for a guerrilla bush war, for which the terrain is particularly suited'. There were claims they dressed in German uniforms 'or dark camouflaged jackets' and employed 'every ambush ruse'. One regiment described how 'our soldiers are attracted by calls in German, then stabbed to death with knives'. The Germans condemned them as representing 'a choice bunch of tenacious and versatile ambushers, possessing an instinctive disregard to the rules of war'.

Barrett and his companions inadvertently collided with a German officer on a bicycle, whom they overpowered. They felt he could not be released and as Barrett possessed the only killing knife, his companions looked to him. 'Although I didn't relish the job of killing him, I was a bit hardened by now.' But it developed into a nightmarish and grisly experience: 'I stuck the knife in his throat just below the left ear. I felt his blood gush out onto my hand; it was warm and wet and somehow it felt like treacle. Those things I noticed instantly. When I twisted the knife, the German with a horrible cry of pain, but with great physical strength born of that pain, got away from us and actually started running up the road.'

They had to shoot him several times in the back. The officer staggered, side-stepped and fell into a ditch. After 14 days on the run they were captured by the Germans, who immediately shot the French civilians who had befriended and looked after them. 'We turned away and sick in our hearts, were marched with our hands still over our heads for three miles.' They had got to within four miles of where they should have dropped two weeks before.

Atrocities begat worse acts, exacerbated by the isolation and helpless vulnerability of fighting alone. 'Give me three days and nights of hard fighting, then you will be relieved,' General Maxwell Taylor said to his 101st Division. Don Malarkey's platoon was told to fight with knives until daylight 'and don't take any prisoners'. This bullish attitude was not shared by the men. German soldiers began to suspect that paratroopers were not taking prisoners; any whose parachutes snagged trees were summarily dealt with. 'They were just left there hanging,' recalled Lieutenant Henry Lefebvfre with the 82nd Airborne Division, 'it was devastating.' Carl Cartledge, a lieutenant with the 101st, saw his medic Anderson completely entangled: 'Hanging in a tree by his feet, his arms down, throat cut, genitals stuffed in his mouth. His medic's red cross arm band was stained with the blood that had flowed from his hair.'

Men fought and died alone. Private John Fitzgerald with the 502nd PIR came across an isolated 82nd paratrooper who had occupied a German foxhole 'and made it his personal Alamo'. 'In a half circle around the hole lay the bodies of nine German soldiers. The body closest to the hole was only three feet away, a grenade in its fist. The other distorted forms lay where they had fallen, testimony to the ferocity of the fight . . . his ammunition bandoliers were still on his shoulders, empty . . . cartridge cases littered the ground. His rifle was broken in two.'

A peculiar courage and tenacity was required to fight like this, to the end, in total isolation. 'Being alone behind enemy lines is a unique, indescribable feeling,' confessed George Rosie with the 506th PIR. 'You just feel so helpless, so alone that there is nothing in your life you can relate to.' Guilt that they had somehow let their comrades down by not joining them impelled men to fight desperate lone actions. They spent hours ploughing through marshland and flooded ditches, still carrying their heavy weapons and equipment, to rejoin their comrades. When signaller Harry Read finally emerged from the flooded Dives valley and got back to the 6th Division Headquarters, 'I was just amazed how few of us there were.' Reinforcements were welcomed and without question. Sid Capon with 9 Para recalled, 'those that had survived from Merville and Le Plein now had men arriving that had been dropped far and wide and fought their own battles and reached us although two days late through no fault of their own.' Tony Lycett admitted 'there has always been a reluctance to give an account of this time' which he described as 'six days adrift'. 'I went "missing" which contributed little to the war effort and 7 Para's D-Day.' He need not have worried, Harry Reid described how 'chaps I hardly knew even though we were in the same section sort of greeted me like a long lost brother.' One-third of their men were missing. But Sapper Tom Barrett, taken prisoner by the Germans after evading them for two weeks, encapsulated the relative relief of capture after being on the run. 'There was no need to look over our shoulders, we no longer had to talk in whispers, there was no need to keep one's finger on the trigger whilst dozing, there would be no more lying for hours in sodden clothes, no more chattering teeth. All the suspense was removed from us and we fell into a deep sleep.'

Returning to their own lines decreased rather than increased chances of survival. As the front line coalesced after the initial confusing period, heavy German reinforcements appeared, desperately attempting to stem the invasion tide. In the days and weeks that followed D-Day airborne soldiers were kept in Normandy to fight as infantry. The 82nd Airborne Division were employed in 'hedgerow fighting' ground battles to push westward and cut off the Contentin peninsula; the 101st Division had to fight for the town of Carentan to effect a junction between Utah beach and Omaha farther to the east. Both divisions were required to block bitter German counter-attacks. 'I never thought I'd get through D-Day, let alone the next phase and next phase,' confessed William Guarnere with the 101st Division. 'I thought I was going to get killed instantly.' His Easy Company of the 506th PIR had jumped into Normandy with 139 men; only 74 were left 23 days later. His regiment lost one man in two. 'The chances of survival was very slim, extremely slim,' he confessed. During the second week of July with the Normandy beachhead secured and Cherbourg captured, the two American airborne divisions were moved back across the Channel. The 101st lost 4,670 killed, wounded or missing; its sister division the 82nd fared even worse, losing 5,245 casualties or 57 per cent of the original force.

The 6th British Airborne Division was reinforced by a sea-landed Special Service Commando Brigade on the evening of D-Day and was employed as line infantry securing the eastern approaches to the British beaches. Between 10 and 12 June 1944 the Germans launched a series of tenacious panzer and panzer grenadier counter-attacks at a gap in the line between the commandos and paratroopers at Breville, east of the Orne River, overlooking the Ranville drop zones. 'You just didn't see how we could get through the day to be truthful,' remembered airborne signaller Harry Read. 'They might come in the half-light of dawn or evening, they might come in the half-light of the evening, and both morning and evening. We did take an awful pasting.' They knew if the Germans broke through, they might destroy the invasion, so 'with our limited weapons we had to hold them off, and so that is how it continued'. Only limited glider-borne numbers of anti-tank guns and ammunition were available and they were dependent upon sea-landed tanks to match the approaching armour.

'What luck must one have in war?' asked Sid Capon with 9 Para, 'I have so far survived.' Reinforcements had landed by sea but not yet arrived. A German tank was rumbling towards them, emerging from an orchard. His friend Eric Bedford declared, 'well, there is only one thing we can do and that is throw everything that we have got at it.' Six men facing a tank, Capon pondered, 'and all this after what we had all been through.' The panzer swung left and fortuitously moved along the road where it became somebody else's problem. 'It was a let off for us but not those on the other side as we heard a terrific battle.' After such a day, Harry Reid recalled, 'You sort of said, "Gee Whiz, I am still here. I am still here," and I am sure the other fellows were much the same as me.'

The British airborne division was engaged in intense fighting as line infantry for a further month and a half after the US airborne divisions were withdrawn for reconstitution. There was bitter disappointment. The British airborne divisions had been expanded specifically for the projected invasion of France. The 1st was still held in reserve on the UK mainland. Troops especially skilled, selected and trained for complex airborne operations were expended in the line. Crippling losses of infantry could not be easily replaced. Manpower shortages were already resulting in the dissolution or combination of shattered British units. Padre Beckingham with 8 Para recalled wet weather, flooded trenches, ubiquitous mosquitoes depriving men of badly needed sleep and the constant emotional pressure of prolonged combat. 'There had been many rumours of the division being brought home,' he recalled, 'and when these were dashed to the ground, morale was inclined to drop.' They remained in the line until the break-out from Normandy in late August. Losses were as sobering as those of the Americans with 401 officers and 6,722 men becoming casualties.

The airborne instrument was proved blunt again, yet crudely effective, drawing off local German reserves that otherwise would have protected the invasion beaches. Allied planners were disappointed at the repeated inability of Air Transport Commands to drop cohesive units on target. D-Day airborne landings had been worth the risk. There was little appreciation of the force multiplier effect the scattered landings had upon the German ability to form up or even identify where the main airborne blows had fallen. American airborne divisions were quickly reconstituted while the 6th British Airborne Division was left intact but licking its wounds.

With the break-out from Normandy, the newly formed 1st Allied Airborne Army were pennies burning in the pockets of Allied planners, convinced there was going to be an overall German collapse. Sixteen airborne landings were cancelled at the last moment as swiftly moving ground troops overran their objectives. Normandy had demonstrated clearly the hopelessness of trying to deliver division-size formations at night. The conundrum dogging planners was the nagging doubt whether the enormous expenditure invested in terms of high grade fighting divisions and the costly logistic and air effort were worth the sobering cost.

8

PARACHUTISTS' SWAN-SONG

ARNHEM AND THE AIRBORNE SPIRIT

At first all that could be distinguished was a muted low-level hum, which rose in intensity to a deep rhythmic drone. It was a beautiful autumn Sunday afternoon in occupied Holland on 17 September 1944. Specks like insect swarms could be seen approaching the German front line in southern Holland. 'We suddenly discerned an unearthly droning noise coming out of the air,' recalled Leutnant Heinz Volz with the Fallschirmjäger Regiment Von Hoffmann, part of the 1st Parachute Army, covering the primary south–north roads toward Eindhoven. 'A huge stream of transports and gliders approached out of the enemy hinterland flying at an unusually low altitude.' So spellbound was the flak at this approaching mass and intimidated by the 'countless fighters' that swooped and wheeled over their area in 'minute detail' that they desisted from firing. 'Only in the hinterland did flak open up,' Volz remembered.

Two massive aircraft streams with 1,534 transport aircraft and towing 500 gliders flew a parallel northern and southern route from airfields around Grantham and Stamford and central southern England. A total of 1,113 bombers and 1,240 fighters flew in support of the streams, shooting up key targets around objectives and flak positions en route. Generaloberst Kurt Student, commanding 1st Parachute Army, stepped onto the balcony of his HQ at Vught, where he witnessed the northern stream diverging over S'Hertogenbosch. 'Wherever I looked I could see aircraft,' he remembered, 'flying quite low over our house.' They were unnerved by the roaring fly-past. 'Some flew so low that we ducked our heads.' The procession seemed endless. Three parallel streams passed over, one and a half miles apart. Student and his staff stared mouths agape: the parachute doors were open. 'They came in groups and as one disappeared into the distance another one followed – flight after flight. It was a spectacle which impressed me deeply.' The fly-past took 65 minutes to transit over his balcony and was oblivious to the desultory rifle fire his clerks and signallers shot up into the air.

Fourteen weeks after D-Day and the story of airborne development had turned a full historic circle. In 1940 Student had attacked east to west across 'Fortress Holland' in broad daylight with his newly conceived 7th Flieger Division. The Allies now sought to lay an 'airborne carpet' south to north going in the reverse direction in 1944. Three divisions: the US 101st and 82nd and the British 1st Airborne Divisions planned to cover the five main river and canal obstacles leading to the Ruhr and the North German Plains. The painful experience in Normandy had convinced them that accuracy could only be achieved in daylight. Qualitative and quantative technical improvements had transformed airborne lift capacities. Aircraft and gliders carried over double the 1940 Fallschirmjäger volumes and were escorted by longer range fighters and heavier bombers to suppress flak and enemy fighters. Student realised the Allies had at last dealt the 35,000-strong airborne army trump card killer blow that might shorten the war. 'At that particular moment I had no thought of the dangers it foreshadowed,' he reflected. His army was split in two by landings by the 101st Division around Eindhoven, the 82nd near Nijmegen and the 1st British Airborne Division 90 miles beyond the front line at Arnhem. 'I was only thinking of my own airborne operations in earlier days,' Student reminisced, 'if ever I had such resources at my disposal!'

In early September 1944 German forces had been in retreat on all fronts. Paris was captured on 25 August and Brussels on 3 September. Supreme Commander General Dwight D. Eisenhower was persuaded to compromise his own broad front strategy of encircling the Ruhr and invading the Saar in favour of General Montgomery's push on a narrow front, concentrating resources for a direct move on Berlin. The plan was to create an airborne corridor codenamed Market to be kept open by airborne landings conducted by 1st Allied Airborne Army to bounce the Rhine and break into Germany. The southernmost bridges at Son and Veghel just north of Eindhoven would be taken by the US 101st Division, the US 82nd would seize the bridges at Grave and Nijmegen to open the ground advance code-named Garden. This, led by XXX Corps, would push on to reach the final bridge across the Lower Rhine at Arnhem, the British 1st Airborne Division objective, 90 miles from the start line. Operation Market–Garden could conceivably see the war over by Christmas.

'All you could see and hear, as far as you could see, would be planes,' recalled Captain T. Moffatt Burriss, flying with the 82nd Airborne Division. British Staff Sergeant 'Bunny' Baker, piloting a Horsa, described the flight as 'the most amazing sight I ever saw'. He invited the 'live-loads' of infantry in the back of his glider to come up into the cockpit and see. 'Nothing was going to stop this lot!' he declared. Fighter bombers swooped down at any hint of flak. Dutch people hoisted the Netherlands flag and waved below. 'Truly it was going to be a piece of cake,' Baker concluded. 'Everything went more smoothly than on any exercise I'd ever been on,' remembered Major Tony Hibbert, the brigade major with the 1st Parachute Brigade.

The Allies were demonstrating their mastery of the complexity of airborne operations. Stirling Flight Engineer M. Mitchell, towing a glider to Arnhem, remembered, 'by this time we had got the whole thing off to a Tee – how to form up and so on in these long streams.' Pathfinders successfully jumped and marked drop zones and guided aircraft in with Eureka-Rebecca radio location aids. The 101st Division parachuting from 431 transport aircraft with 70 towing gliders achieved a copybook insertion. 'It was Sunday afternoon, noon time, only a slight breeze,' remembered William Guarnere, 'everybody got together and we all assembled very fast.' 'It was the most perfect flat jump field I've ever seen,' recalled Private David Webster, floating down onto a freshly ploughed field. 'Basically Holland is just a big glorified jump field.' The 101st Division later reported it was their most successful division landing in training or combat. 'The drop was perfect, a mass drop, everyone was dropping on the same field,' remembered Lieutenant Richard Winter in Guarnere's battalion. Only peacetime hazards appeared to apply. 'The most dangerous part about it was the fact that people were continually losing helmets and equipment and all this stuff is raining down,' he indignantly recalled. 'And if you get hit with this you're gonna be killed or wounded before you can get off the drop zone.'

The 480 transport aircraft and 50 tug glider combinations of the 82nd Airborne Division achieved similarly accurate concentrations on their drop zones. Troopers had speculated about the sinister spelling of the Grave Bridge but it was captured within an hour. 'I can remember looking down as we flew over from an altitude of 600 feet to see almost the colour of the eyes of the German anti-aircraft guys,' recalled Moffatt Burriss. 'You dirty Krauts, you just wait a minute and we'll be down there to getcha.' The expression on their faces spoke volumes, he remembered – 'Oh hell, we're in big trouble.'

Inaccurate navigation was severely punished and overall 35 Dakotas were shot down around the more heavily contested American drop zones. The British 1st Airborne Division achieved its most successful insertion ever, only seven aircraft were damaged by flak and 284 of its 320 gliders landed on or close to their planned landing sites. Stirling pilot Douglas Smith remembered the scene as he looked down after dropping his pathfinders at Arnhem. 'If Hitler could see what I can see now,' he remarked to his crew, 'he would throw in the towel, because it looked as if we were invincible.' At this furthest point of the airborne invasion 6,000 men with artillery, anti-tank guns and vehicles had successfully landed 60 miles into enemy territory inside 80 minutes. A remarkable accomplishment for a new service arm formed from scratch only four years before. The Allied airborne instrument had come of age.

Operational surprise was total. The Allies had never dropped by day and they were jumping into the midst of the German rear-combat zone, a two-hour car journey from the grumbling front to the south. Exploiting tactical surprise, however, meant a race against the clock. Five river and canal lines had to be taken and by nightfall on day one three had fallen: at Veghel, Grave and Arnhem. The bridge crossing the Wilhelmina Canal at Son was blown in the faces of the attacking 101st, as had been the Arnhem railway bridge when the British attacked. Minor crossing points would also be contested. The Germans still held the massive Nijmegen Bridge across the mighty Waal River.

However, few airborne plans survive totally intact and Market proved no different. Shortages of transport aircraft and night flying restrictions meant it would take three days to achieve the division's planned troop numbers at their locations. On day one the British were short of one parachute brigade and one-third of the glider air-land element. A planned three-day insertion for the entire airborne corps was to take six. The two American airborne divisions needed reinforcement and the Polish brigade had been expected on the third day. Vital re-supply further impinged on aircraft availability and poor weather began to unravel the complicated delivery plan as early as the second day.

More ominously, the Germans displayed far greater resilience than anticipated. After the sweeping Allied advances in early September it was felt the German defence would crumple at the first determined shove. In Arnhem it was belatedly discovered that the remnants of two SS panzer divisions were refitting in and around the town. Although badly mauled and at 30 per cent strength, they nevertheless had some two dozen tanks, which were immediately directed at the lightly armed British.

Meanwhile XXX Corps, the ground element, moving through the airborne corridor, had only advanced six miles before they were blocked by the first series of anti-tank ambushes. 'You couldn't take anything for granted,' recalled Frank Clark, fighting through with Grenadier Guards Sherman tanks. 'They took six tanks within minutes – boom, boom, boom.' The XXX Corps advance was constrained to a single vulnerable road, raised above dyke level on flat terrain. There was barely room for two vehicles to pass. 'As we came up to it,' recalled Clark, reaching the first ambush sites, 'we saw the debris at the side of the road of the knocked-out tanks and of course one knew that could be our fate as well.' It took until midday of day two before the first tanks reached the 101st Division outposts at the edge of Eindhoven. The bridge at Son was not repaired until the third day. Although the Arnhem Bridge had been captured, Allied tank units did not reach Nijmegen until the end of the third day. They were on the wrong side of the huge Waal River at the very moment they should have been in Arnhem. The typical experience of the airborne soldier fighting the Market–Garden battles was very much shaped by this losing race against an inexorable clock as the Germans steadily recovered from their initial tactical surprise. Frank Clark forcefully stressed: 'Never underestimate the German.'

The first imperative of airborne operations, having achieved surprise, is to use speed and aggression to maintain the initiative. Experienced airborne commanders considering bridges would opt to land directly both sides of the objective and trade heavy initial casualties off against lengthy stand-offs. 'Open space or not, we always wanted to jump on the target,' declared Colonel Reuben H. Tucker, commanding the 504th PIR. One company was ordered to jump the south end of the Grave Bridge while the rest of the 2nd Battalion landed at the north end. The bridge was quickly taken. 'We had no clear drop zones but landed on houses, churches, roads, ditches and wherever we came down,' he later reported. The sheer size and length of the structures spanning the Maas at Grave, the Waal at Nijmegen and the Lower Rhine at Arnhem commended just such an approach. The 1st British Airborne Division was constrained by RAF reservations about heavy flak to land eight miles west of the Arnhem Bridge. Lieutenant Colonel John Frost, an experienced parachute commander, sought to utilise both surprise and the confident gush of well-being that comes from a successful landing to prosecute an aggressive speed march to the bridge through woodland and into Arnhem's suburbs, bypassing the German resistance that began to fan out around the western approaches to block such a move.

Platoon commander Jim Flavell recalled it was 'a crutch-rot of a march conducted at cracking pace'. The battalion commander had also ordered 'no crouchy-wouchey'; they were expected to stand up and take risks. They had quickly formed up on the drop zone and left within an hour at 95 per cent strength. 'We had no time to spare for flank guards,' Frost determined, 'so trusting everyone to do the right thing if attacked, we pressed on.' Pace was all-important; only small parties were dropped off to cover important roads leading into their route and they moved rapidly through the crowds of welcoming Dutch. Frost refused to allow his men to become distracted and soon reached Oosterbeek village. 'Occasionally we heard the leaders of the vanguard in action,' Frost recalled, 'but we were not really checked again until the outskirts of Arnhem itself.' Flavell recalled the disappointed feeling that accompanied the 'gigantic thump' of the railway bridge being blown, even as members of C Company were trying to attack across it. They had been shooting up German lorries and picking up groups of German prisoners all the time as they moved along the houses lining the river bank, leading to the massive span of the Arnhem road bridge. Opposition was overcome by scrambling over garden fences and outflanking the resistance. Major Tony Hibbert, bringing up the rear of the advance, remembered General Urquhart, the division commander, calling out to him, 'For God's sake get your battalion moving faster.' This was easier said than done, Hibbert recalled: 'Walking with 80lbs on your back through a country which is so easily defended, with no reconnaissance, nothing'. A jeep-borne Recce Squadron coup de main directed against the bridge was ambushed en route and Frost's infantry were now in the lead.

The surprise engendered by an airborne assault is a two-edged affair. Attackers and defenders are confronted with mutually unexpected developments. Parachutists operate across ground familiar only from maps and air-reconnaissance photographs. The enemy is unknown and soldiers will always be mildly surprised at the idiosyncrasies of the terrain they have to speedily cross. German defenders, crestfallen at witnessing an awesome parachute landing involving hundreds of aircraft, rarely appreciate that it will take at least an hour, likely longer, before such a force can form up and move. Battle then develops into a series of unexpected meeting engagements. Frost capitalised on the tactical smothering effect such large-scale landings initially produce. Experienced German commanders were aware that despite the odds, such as the case of the German SS battalion coincidently exercising in the woods next to the drop zone when the paratroopers arrived, they had to immediately get stuck in. 'The only way to draw the tooth of an airborne landing, with an inferior force, is to drive right into it,' claimed SS Captain Sepp Krafft, which he proceeded to do. While he was hindering the initial advances of 3 Para into Arnhem, Frost slipped by, using the road beside the river to the south.

As the confusing situation developed it was the turn of the British to be surprised. Frost had been picking up SS Panzergrenadier prisoners en route to Arnhem and they should not have been there.

When he reached the road bridge at dusk he had to pause while an SS armoured column moved north to south heading for Nijmegen – the arrival direction for XXX Corps. This was not looking auspicious. The north end of the bridge was quickly captured because the German guards were watching this road direction also and did not anticipate. paratroopers suddenly appearing on the bridge parapet having scaled the steps below. Always expect the unexpected again. This was to be the British paratrooper and German experience fighting in and around the bridge for the next three days. Battle deteriorated into a series of chance meetings, as Captain John Killick described on reaching the bridge. 'In the dark we ran into a totally confused situation with Germans on the other side; one of my corporals got killed in an engagement on a spur just ahead of us.' They sheltered in a building to await developments.

A further characteristic of airborne operations is the sudden cold shower transition from peace to battle that every airborne soldier endures. There is not a gradual build-up like conventional infantry moving up into the line. 'There was no need to hurry over breakfast,' recalled Frost on the morning of the operation, due to the late take-off. 'I wandered along to the mess to find everyone else reading and smoking, all in the best of spirits and no worries anywhere.' At this stage it was 'just the normal beginning to an ordinary day'. Within 12 to 24 hours his battalion would be fighting for its very existence. 'We couldn't really believe that this was going to be it,' recalled Captain John Killick, soon to jump in with 89 Parachute Field Security Squadron on the first day at Arnhem. There was 'a rather nasty piece of fish' offered at breakfast, 'the idea being that you would be less sick in the aircraft if you only had fish for breakfast'. He also had a late start, 'so we sat around in the mess trying to read the Sunday newspapers and it seemed like any ordinary Sunday'.

Major John Waddy jumped with the 4th Parachute Brigade on the second lift at Arnhem, delayed by bad weather on Monday. On the way to their fogged-in airfields, 'I remember standing on the pavement watching all the population of Melton Mowbray going to work and I thought this is odd, they're going to work, we're going to war.' There was much hanging around and tea and buns provided by the Women's Voluntary Service at Saltby airfield. His American pilot had come on board and hung up his best tunic and trousers behind him. Responding to the quizzical looks he had inspired he remarked, 'Well, gee, we might have a weekend in Brussels.' The sun came out and the transition to war began pleasantly enough with a two-hour flight during which many paratroopers read newspapers commenting on the brilliant success of landings the day before. Waddy was flying in a stream of 36 aircraft that came into the drop in close formation, three groups of three aircraft flying in 'V' formation, four 'Vics' in a stream. Three such streams came in 30 seconds apart to deliver a dense concentration of 2,300 men, who could be down in six minutes.

Many soldiers in the 1st British Airborne Division, having missed D-Day, had either not seen action or had experienced it a long time ago. 'I remembered that this was my first jump since Sicily some fourteen months ago,' Frost recalled. This also has an effect on the sudden transition again to war. 'Two years is a long time to be out of action,' recalled Lieutenant Sammy Carr with 10 Para. 'When I have been resting, or way back out of operations for a long time, the gilt wears off the gingerbread and I am not so keen to risk myself as I was at the beginning of the war.' The sound 'as if someone was throwing stones against the bottom of the plane' began to focus his mind 'and as I looked I could see little white things coming up from below'. As the ack-ack fire became more pronounced the 'thought for excess self-preservation begins to rear its ugly head'. His life was about to become vulnerable once again.

When the streams passed S'Hertogenbosch and came down to 700 feet, 'this is where we started to get flak', Waddy recalled. Being number 1 he was able to lean well out of the door and watch the final approach. 'I could see this massive aircraft flying in front of me,' he recalled, as the slipstream pinched his cheeks, and 'the black puffs of flak, and the thing that fascinated me was that you saw a black puff ahead of you, it seemed to hang in the air and suddenly it whipped past your door.' Unbeknown to the approaching aircraft there was a battle already in progress for their drop zone. A Dutch auxiliary SS battalion was advancing across it, intent on clearing it of the glider infantry defenders who had landed the day before. 'Then we started to get machine gun fire and you could see the tracers coming up through the formations,' Waddy recalled. SS soldiers, realising they were about to be vertically enveloped by this oncoming mass of aircraft, began to frantically fire up at aircraft even now disgorging parachutists. 'As I was standing in the door I saw one of our aircraft pass beneath the door ablaze nose to tail as it went past port wing down and burst in a great ball of white flame. I thought to myself, *this is getting bloody dangerous.*'

American Captain George Merz, flying in the lead element of the next 36 aircraft, saw 'a smoking aeroplane tumble in out of control and crash straight in'. As he crossed the Rhine on the final approach he watched tracer flash past the windshield and strike the starboard engine. Smoke filled the cockpit and he switched off his engines and with wind-milling propellers swung away from the formation towards an open field. A mortar detachment from 11 Para in the back had begun jumping the moment the engine caught fire. The last few numbers in the stick and the crew jumped too low for their parachutes to open. Eleven aircraft from the third serial were now hit by fully alerted anti-aircraft gunners. One caught fire and began to dive, violently pitching all the 10 Para paratroopers inside forward into the aircraft interior. Its pilot Lieutenant James Spurrior was wounded and unconscious, but his co-pilot Lieutenant Edward Fulmer levelled the aircraft out despite being viciously scorched about the head and arms by flames shrieking, 'Get out, get the hell out!' Everyone jumped at low altitude but the last two had insufficient height for their canopies to open before the Dakota bellied in flames. Five aircraft were shot down on the run-in to the drop zone and another during the return flight, 17 American aircrew and 26 paratroopers were killed.

'You get the turbulence from the wash of the aircraft in front,' Waddy recalled, 'and because they were coming down to drop speed of about 90 mph there was quite a lot of yawing of the aircraft to keep in formation.' Pilots were flying in the middle of nine aircraft with a similar group density just ahead and immediately behind. They had to concentrate, despite the flak, on waiting for the precise moment to switch on the red and green lights. 'They had a lot to do,' explained Waddy. When he jumped, 'I could hear the crack-crack of machine gun fire.' Germans standing on the western side of the woods along the drop zone fired at the open doors. 'In fact my signaller who jumped just behind me, as soon as he left the door got a bullet straight through the radio,' Waddy remembered. Captain Bernard Coggins, navigating a 43 Squadron plane, later said, 'I don't know what hell looked like but I got a preview.' He had a grandstand view of the Dutch-German SS battalion caught on the drop zone. 'There were explosions all over the drop zone, which was now host to a bush fire.' 'When the last man was out of the door, the throttles were pushed to the fire wall, and we dove for home.'

Just hours before Waddy and his soldiers had been sipping 'tea and wads' handed out by the WVS at Saltby, hanging about waiting for the fog to lift. Their only concern was to avoid drinking so much tea that they may have to take their parachutes off to urinate in mid-flight. Nerves produced the same effect in any case. The shift from peace to war on arrival at the drop zone could not have been starker. 'One of my platoon commanders got hit coming down, in the legs,' Waddy recalled: 'He got hit in the pouches and he had a white phos-phorous grenade, which went off. He couldn't move because he'd been shot through the legs and was burning to death. This was when he was on the ground and he shot himself. After the war when I came back from prison camp his family kept writing to me asking me to tell them how he got killed. Of course I couldn't say.'

Transition to war for the airborne soldier could be a fickle or brutal occasion. Paratroopers overshooting the north end of the drop zone landed in trees and struggling in their harnesses were shot by the Germans before they withdrew. Those at the southern end of the mile and a half long Ginkle Heath DZ were less affected. Waddy came across his company second in command Hector Montgomery 'strolling up a path' moving towards the battalion RV. 'Come on, Monty, there's a bloody war on!' Waddy reminded him but, 'we didn't really know until the next day that things had gone wrong.'

As the plan unravelled at Arnhem, much of the paratrooper and glider infantry experience became that of street fighting. It was costly and difficult to control in the attack and an exercise of tenacity and endurance in defence. Lightly armed parachute soldiers were vulnerable in attack and totally reliant upon air-landed anti-tank guns and man-portable PIAT (Projectile Infantry Anti-Tank) spring-loaded weapons in defence against tanks. Street fighting was 'just fleeting', recalled Sergeant Arthur Shackleton. 'It was more like shadows running from house to house – so you were firing at shadows.' German fire appeared to him to be very methodical, five-second machine gun bursts followed by five-second intervals. 'So you would cross one street, rest, get your breath back.' Then there would be a fleeting figure across the road, 'so you would fire, but you never knew whether you hit him or not with it being dark.' Progress was by such measured leap-frogging. Costly and determined assaults managed to penetrate to within 900 yards of Frost's battalion, cut off at the bridge before collapse. The decimated attacking battalions were then forced to fall back on Oosterbeek. 'We had to run this gauntlet again,' recalled Shackleton. 'Five-second bursts – run, five-second burst, run!' By 20 September the Oosterbeek airborne perimeter was under siege from three sides with the Lower Rhine at their backs.

Airborne soldiers are only lightly armed. Before long some 2,500 paratroopers were surrounded by 24 German battalions with over 7,000 soldiers, supported by a mixture of 44 tanks, self-propelled guns and gun-mounted armoured half-tracks. Over 100 artillery pieces of calibres varying from 20mm to 105mm were ploughing up the confined airborne perimeter which measured barely one kilometre wide by two deep up against the river bank. Piecemeal reinforcement by 200 members of the 1st Polish Brigade dropped on the fifth day made little difference.

'Someone shouted out "Tigers"!' recalled Sid Blackmore, fighting near the Arnhem Bridge. 'You see these dirty big things coming through and you've got a little bomb like that sort of thing,' referring to his PIAT, 'and think what am I goin' to do 'ere?' The PIAT was heavy, ungainly, inaccurate and universally detested by the men required to serve them. It was so difficult to cock that the soldier had to stand it on end and use his foot to push the firing mechanism back against the spring. Getting the bomb into the cradle-shaped launch opening was fiddly and often had to be done when acutely anxious, with a tank approaching. There was considerable recoil against the shoulder on firing, which simply lobbed the projectile against the tank. 'It was like firing rubber against the wall, it was just useless,' Blackmore commented. Glider pilot Richard Long saw Major Robert Cain at Oosterbeek immobilise one tank kneeling and engaging before he was momentarily blinded and his face blackened and pitted by the blow-back of his fired bomb clipping a nearby wall. Such reckless tenacity unnerved the advancing Germans. Walton Ashworth, another glider pilot, recovered the wounded Cain and then 'was absolutely staggered' to see him back in action again. 'This chap came out of the copse with his face blackened and he got down immediately on the PIAT gun. I thought he must be a very brave man to be knocked out probably, then come back and take up the same position and still hit tanks. He was still firing when we left.'

The 2nd Para was pinned down in the houses at the north end of the Arnhem Bridge. After successfully beating off earlier attacks ammunition became critically short and the surrounding cellars became packed with hundreds of wounded and trapped civilians. 'All the Germans had to do was to stand back and bring up tanks with heavier guns,' recalled Major Tony Hibbert, 'and they literally burnt us out one by one.' 'As soon as you started firing out the window,' remembered Private Ron Youngman, 'they'd send a shell through', adding caustically, 'to warm you up like.' Frost's battalion held their ground with a ferocious tenacity that dismayed the Germans. Platoon commander Jim Flavell was convinced 'the Germans were frightened of us', because they were exceedingly jittery with any prisoners they captured. The heat from the rubble of the burned-out houses made it impossible to dig in, but the paratroopers stacked bricks for cover and re-occupied them first. There were more wounded than able-bodied soldiers left when the Germans began to systematically blast houses into rubble. 'First of all they put in high explosives to create holes in the wall and then pumped smoke shells through the holes,' remembered Major Tony Hibbert, isolated with his headquarters in the attic of a three-storey house. Smoke shells were phosphorous. 'People often think that, you know, bang-bang-bang and a lot of noise' was what constituted battle, John Killick explained. 'The frightening thing,' however, 'was when it went quiet': 'Then after a while you heard a tank engine starting up round the corner and the Tiger tank would come round and start coming down the road. You would see the turret swivel and the gun point towards the building you are in. That is when you get bloody frightened.'

By the fourth day XXX Corps had still not arrived. 'I was still hoping they was going to get to us,' declared Ron Youngman. 'They said in just two days we are going to get to yer. You're just hanging on thinking any minute they're going to come.'

At 1500 on 20 September an intensive bombardment by 40 Sherman tanks and 100 artillery pieces focused German attention on a sector well to the west of the Nijmegen railway bridge opposite the power station on the banks of the River Waal. American paratroopers with Major Julian A. Cook's 3rd Battalion of the 504th PIR began to splash into the shallows on the south bank carrying 26 flimsy canvas and wood assault boats. Among them was Captain T. Moffatt Burriss who later explained: 'Our mission was to save the British paratroopers at Arnhem and that was what we intended to do.' Arnhem was 10 miles beyond this last obstacle holding up the XXX Corp's advance along an airborne corridor, tenuously kept open by the battling battalions of the 101st and 82nd Airborne Divisions along its entire length. This assault river crossing, which has been described as one of the outstanding small unit actions of World War Two, encapsulated the fighting spirit of what has been recognised is a hallmark characteristic of airborne troops. The boats were inadequate 'pressed-out' improvisations lacking paddles and 'looked like something you wouldn't want to paddle a duck pond in, much less go across that raging river', declared Moffatt Burriss. 'No question about it,' he added, 'it was a suicide mission.'

Boats were propelled by paddles and a motley assortment of rifle butts, helmets, or anything to speed progress through the water. They got to about one-third of the way across before the incredulous Germans brought down a storm of fire. 'It actually looked like a hailstorm,' observed Burriss, 'with the bullet strikes kicking up little spouts of water.' German artillery batteries used up an entire allocation of 250 shells trying to suppress the assault. 'I'll tell you we were paddling like mad to get across,' described Lieutenant Thomas Pitt. 'Quite a few of the boats overturned; guys in a lot of them were killed.' The crossing seemed endless, 'it was a hell of a wide river' stretching for 175 yards. Most of the paratroopers had never been in a boat before and there was little paddle stroke coordination. Some boats started to go in circles. 'I had experience with canoes and rowboats,' explained Engineer Lieutenant John Holabird participating in the crossing. 'So

I took the stern and shouted, *Stroke! Stroke! Stroke!* as we wallowed across the Waal.'

'The adrenalin was flowing and every muscle in your body was all tensed up,' described Buriss. 'The casualty rate in the 15 minutes or 20 minutes – or whatever it took – to go across the river was probably close to 60 per cent. We lost a lot of men.' Anybody of any importance to Market-Garden watched this epic spellbound from the roof of the power station. Senior British officers observing with their American counterparts were incredulous. 'Unbelievable,' they muttered. 'My God, what a courageous sight it was,' declared Lieutenant Colonel 'Joe' Vandeleur whose Guards tanks had spearheaded the race through the airborne corridor and were rushing the Nijmegen road bridge. Bill Downs, an American CBS correspondent, gave his eye-witness impressions in a later broadcast, describing how 'enemy tracers shrieked at the boats'.

The fire at first was erratic, but as the boats approached the northern bank the tracers began to spread onto the boats. Men slumped in their seats – other men could be seen shifting a body to take over the paddling. One man rose up in his seat and fell overboard. There was no thought of turning back. The paddling continued clumsily and erratically, but it continued. One of the boats had so many holes in it that the men were baling out with their tin helmets – it was almost splintered when it reached the other side.

At river level Moffatt Burriss noticed his engineer helmsman's wrist turn red. 'Captain, take the rudder of the boat, I've been hit,' he said. 'Just as I reached out to take the rudder he caught a 20mm high explosive through his head and that blew his head completely off.' The psychological and physical effect of all this strain caused men to throw up and be violently sick as part of the nervous reaction when they grounded on the home bank. 'And I was one of them,' Burriss admitted. They rushed the German defences raked by machine gun and rifle fire the whole long distance. Consumed in the blood lust of the assault, no quarter was given to the old men and young boys defending the dyke road embankment. General Browning watching from the power station roof admitted, 'I have never seen a more gallant action.' Six more waves made the crossing with an ever decreasing number of boats.

The surprise assault river crossing in concert with a British Grenadier Guards tank attack on the road bridge, conducted at 1700, completely unhinged the German defence. The Waal bridges were secure by 1900. American paratroopers kissed the first tanks that crossed but became furious when it was realised they were not going to push on to Arnhem. Captain Burriss accosted Captain Peter Carrington commanding the lead troop when he told him, 'I can't go on without orders.' A storm of pent-up invective followed, a direct consequence of their appalling casualties. 'You get this tank moving,' Burriss muttered, cocking his Tommy gun, 'or I'll blow your damn head off.' Carrington ducked down inside and slammed the hatch. 'I couldn't get to him,' fumed the exasperated Burriss. There would be no Arnhem rescue.

What followed has often been labelled 'the epic of Arnhem'. 'We were just bloody determined not to give in,' declared Des Page with the 1st British Airborne Division at Oosterbeek. 'That was all it was – we were not going to be beaten by them.' Surrendering in any case was no easy task. Private Geoffrey Morgan recalled the dying moments of 2 Para, overrun the very night the Nijmegen Bridge, their rescue launch point, was captured from the Germans. 'Eight of us had broken into a house that evening and we had started to consider surrender,' he admitted. 'It's a difficult topic and there comes a time when pride has to be swallowed if you do not wish for certain death.' But with the continuous hum of Tiger tanks and machine gun fire 'we had to accept that they might not take us prisoners'. They were trapped in a basement and had only a filthy rag to poke and wave through the cellar grating. As soon as it appeared it was blown to smithereens by machine gun fire and a stick grenade rattled through the grating and bounced into the cellar. Someone had the presence of mind to pick it up and throw it through an open door. 'This was surely the end – no prisoners were being taken,' they surmised. Morgan jotted down some notes soon after to preserve the experience: 'Will our luck hold out? Mates are dying one by one, severed limbs; blown to pieces; minds are slipping. Eight of us no more than 22 years old. We've seen so much for men so young, we've been together through violent times . . . now like brothers like foxes we're trapped and the baying hounds are at our throats. Not one of us will let the other down. Is this the end?'

Morgan wrote on a piece of paper: 'If by chance this scrap of paper comes to light pass it to my mother. Maybe Mother, Dad would at last be proud of his wayward son. 25 September 1944.' Morgan looked around at the other survivors. 'I read their minds. Would we be burnt alive? Surrender is in no one's vocabulary.' Reality soon impinged on their meandering thoughts when urgent yells of *Raus! Raus!* came from street level, 'which meant *come out*'. They were menaced by two German machine guns and roughly frisked, then thrust into the back of an armoured half-track vehicle and driven off for interrogation.

Major Dickie Lonsdale briefed the survivors of his small group inside the Oosterbeek Laag church at the eastern edge of the airborne perimeter. 'You know as well as I do there are a lot of bloody Germans coming at us,' he said, emphatically adding, 'we must fight for our lives and stick together.' His final brief epitomised the uncompromising view of the trapped parachute commanders holding together the defence of Oosterbeek: 'We've fought the Germans before – in North Africa, Sicily, Italy. They weren't good enough for us then, and they're bloody well not good enough for us now. They're up against the finest soldiers in the world . . . Make certain you dig in well and that your weapons and ammunition are in good order. We are getting short of ammo, so when you shoot, you shoot to kill. Good luck to you all.'

'Things went from bad to worse' in Oosterbeek, recalled Staff Sergeant 'Bunny' Baker with the Glider Pilot Regiment. His enduring memory was the smell, 'a mixture of burning cordite and the sickly smell of death'. The other was: 'The feeling that we were completely on our own. We were in a mess, but while furious with the people who we felt had let us down, we couldn't go down without a fight.'

'Morning and evening we had to go round the sections of glider pilots,' recalled Arthur Shackleton, 'finding out in the morning who were killed during the night or, in the evening, killed during the day, and making sure that the trenches in their sector were manned.' They put two in here and there, 'so that there were people in the trenches and no gaps'. As with 2 Para at the bridge, there was no surrender, but a fighting withdrawal and boat evacuation across the fast-flowing Lower Rhine during the night of 25/26 September. A total of 2,323 men pulled out, leaving behind almost 6,400 of their comrades dead, wounded, missing or taken prisoner on the north bank. The Germans shelled the crossings, believing the operation to be yet another reinforcement. They could not believe the paratroopers would withdraw after so much blood had been expended. Johnny Peters, trapped in the Oosterbeek perimeter, recalled, 'We kept on saying *When is XXX Corps coming?* And the officer said, *Oh they'll be here tomorrow*, and again *be here tomorrow* and that's all we heard and tomorrow never came.'

Arnhem became a battle icon which suggested that there was something special about the fighting prowess of airborne soldiers. One incident that particularly impressed the hard-bitten veteran soldiers of the 9th SS Hohenstaufen Division was the unconfirmed tale of two English paratroopers who, running out of ammunition, attacked an SS section armed only with knives. Although unsuccessful, it became apparent this was not a matter of desperation or blood lust but a calculated act. True or not, the story was believed; the paratroopers were commanding enormous respect. Can such a phenomenon as superior fighting quality be explained in subjective terms?

Soviet Russia was the first nation to appreciate that the act of parachuting had intangible benefits. 'Isolated heroic men, men capable of brave deeds – there are many of them in the world,' claimed Voroshilov, the Russian People's Commissar of Defence in 1936, having identified the martial potential of parachuting. Capitalist countries had them in small experimental or show groups, he conceded, 'but there will not be found tens, hundreds, thousands of men who love parachute jumping as their near and necessary job' like in Russia. The German Fallschirmjäger had eclipsed the Soviet Locust Warriors by 1940 and also realised parachuting conferred a battle-winning edge of aggressive self-confidence. Hauptmann von der Heydte claimed each soldier who jumped with him at Crete in 1941 'felt himself a match for any man and [was] ready to take on anything that comes along'. So impressed were the Allies with Fallschirmjäger fighting performance, that they were convinced German paratroopers took pervitine drug stimulants before jumping into action. One British report pointed to the mixture of tea and rum found in their water bottles and concluded: 'It is probable that the proportion of rum was increased in the case of parachute troops.' Pervitine was used to keep soldiers awake when deprived of sleep over long periods, whereas *any* alcohol was a welcome distraction for the combat soldier. The Allies also subscribed to the conviction that airborne soldiers produced first-rate infantry. Nobody ever explained why this should be so.

Personal bonding forms a vital component of fighting power at the individual soldier level. The physical act of parachuting produced a feeling of togetherness that most veteran airborne soldiers allude to when explaining the phenomenon of superior performance. 'Is it the consequence of fear, to make one do an unnatural thing of flinging oneself out of an aeroplane?' asked veteran parachute soldier Colonel John Waddy. 'Is it the feeling that we are in this together, sitting or standing in a cramped aircraft in the dark, all geared up to that loony jump into the black slipstream?' The shared experience of parachuting undoubtedly created a bond. 'The one thing that we all had in common from the colonel to the private was that we had *jumped*,' recalled Lieutenant Martin Willcock, serving with 2 Para, 'a unique experience, which we would never forget.' It made them feel 'the battalion was something special and we were proud to belong to it'. Parachute Padre Joe Downing, unused as an officer to training alongside the other ranks, detected the social levelling implicit in 'all training together' and separating only to eat and sleep. 'I soon realised this arrangement was a stroke of genius' because 'it created a wonderful bond between us all.' The British Parachute Regiment recognised this during their early recruiting. 'They talked about joining their "band of brothers",' recalled Private James Sims, encouraged to join 2 Para. 'No one ever referred to you as a brother in the Royal Artillery.'

Parachute bonds transcended national boundaries and even included the enemy. Fallschirmjäger were respected by Allied airborne soldiers, who suspected they would be as ruthless and tenacious as themselves. John Waddy, serving with 156 Para, remembers German paratroopers captured in Italy banded together for interrogation, sitting in a ditch smoking and exchanging parachute stories with their captors. 'This fucker has only done five fucking jumps,' one of the escorts announced with a laugh. 'Instant camaraderie!' Waddy noted, leafing through their pay books and noticing that the last one had been on Crete.

Parachute jumping produced an adrenalin release that powered frenetic physical activity on the ground, even after the physical rigours of the flight and descent. Such energy is readily channelled into aggression. 'I felt like an eagle soaring through the sky,' recalled Private James Sims on landing. So intense is this emotional surge that after the elation a feeling of torpor can emerge, a form of hangover as the body's metabolism reasserts itself. The nervous fatigue that came with the first parachute descent was the equivalent of doing eight hours' hard work, according to wartime medical opinion. Correspondent Macdonald Hastings, jumping with British paratroopers in 1944, recalled the jubilation of a successful jump. 'I knew that I felt as jubilant as a song-bird, and as valiant as an eagle.' Once on the ground, 'you feel the tops and as a fighting man, by God you are the tops.'

Volunteer selection conferred a degree of excellence and edge recognised by peers as forming another characteristic of the airborne spirit, which was their awareness that they belonged to an elite. 'If a man did not make the grade, we could chuck him out,' declared Brigadier James Hill, recognising the training contribution this made for the Normandy drop preparation. 'This possible threat provided a salutary stimulant to all and sundry. I used to tell my COs that if we could not produce the goods under these conditions, let's collect our bowlers, pack our bags, and go home.' They had an intensely professional approach to war. Parachute officers sent on courses were expected to pass out top. 'You weren't expected just to scrape by,' recalled Captain John Timothy with 2 Para, 'you had to do well or there was hell to pay.'

The airborne spirit produced airborne initiative, a willingness to adapt to new ways. 'The joy about these experiments is that it got right down to the members in the battalions,' explained Captain Paul Bernhard with 12 Para, 'who were asked for their ideas and who were allowed to experiment on their own.' James Hill developed his own airborne tactical maxims, emphasising speed of decision-making and movement, simplicity of command and tight control of the limited parachuted support they took into battle. Fire effect had to be maximised because they could only carry limited quantities of ammunition. 'You keep going when other people stop,' explained signaller Harry Read. 'You just keep going. You can always do a bit more and that becomes ingrained in your character.' All these factors were battle-winning characteristics.

Veteran John Waddy recalled the offensive 'can-do' or 'press-on' feeling that personified the airborne spirit. 'If people had initiative you were allowed to use it,' he said. This was not the case with ordinary line infantry regiments, where excessive freedom of action was frowned upon. Waddy returned to his regiment briefly after the war, a period he described as the 'wilderness years' after being with the 'airborne family'. His commanding officer in Malaya was to later write in his annual confidential report, referring to his parachute background as 'too many weird ideas, most of which are administratively difficult'. He was regarded as 'the odd one out' and 'that bomb-happy parachutist'.

The shared paratrooper experience transcended regional and national boundaries, producing complete trust and loyal identification with like-minded fellows. 'If you had something they didn't have you gave them half,' explained British paratrooper Bill Kershaw with 4 Para. 'You broke a cigarette in half.' Private Thomas Simcox with 2 Para felt his 'generation will never have an equal', while Lieutenant Alan Jefferson with 9 Para said the bonding 'can only be equated with the feeling of being in love'. These were the ties that motivated men to fight for each other despite the likelihood of death. 'If I heard the battle cry *Whoa Mohammed!*' declared Staff Sergeant Andy Andrews with the Glider Pilot Regiment, 'I would try to get out of my deathbed to fight with them again.' Morale and black humour characterised their attitudes, encapsulated by popular paratrooper songs like 'The Man on the Flying Trapeze':

> He jumps through the hole with the greatest of ease,
> His feet are together and so are his knees,
> If his 'chute doesn't open he'll fall like a stone,
> And we'll cart him away in a spoon.

Edward 'Babe' Heffron with Easy Company of the 506th PIR recalled that his friend Jim Campbell 'might have been alive today if he hadn't said to me, "Heffron, you stay here with your gun – I'm goin' up."' As

231

he watched, Campbell advanced only to disappear beneath the huge mushroom of a powerful shell blast. 'I sleep on it, eat on it, I'll never, never forget that.' It left a powerful and indelible memory. 'He can't die,' he reflected. 'All your life you've got to remember what one guy did, because he thought it was his job to do,' because, with a sigh he admitted, 'he took a shot for you.' Lieutenant John Winters with the same company was equally emotional about one of his soldiers being wounded in the buttock by a German potato-masher grenade. 'He's behind enemy lines on D-Day,' Winter remembered. 'Does he holler help – no, he hollers, *I'm sorry, I goofed!* My God, it's beautiful when you think of a guy who was that dedicated to his company and his buddies that he apologises for gittin' hit.'

It was the same strength of feeling that impelled the 3rd Battalion 504th PIR to attempt their suicidal crossing of the Waal River to rescue their British airborne 'brothers' at Arnhem.

ACROSS THE RHINE

By the spring of 1945 Germany had lost the Rhineland and the flower of four armies in the west and the Russians were 45 miles from Berlin to the east. Despite the heavy losses incurred by the 1st British Airborne Division at Arnhem, the Allies still retained a massive airborne capability and it was no secret it would be used in support of a crossing of the River Rhine. War correspondent and photographer Robert Capa recalled the 17th US Airborne Division was crammed into long freight trains and 'shuffled all over France' as part of a deception measure for 48 hours prior to the drop. 'After two days of this hocus-pocus our generals decided that both the troops and the German spies were quite tired enough' as they arrived at an airfield 60 miles from where they had started. Airborne operations in the Pacific theatre had rarely been beyond battalion level so the massive impending drop was likely to be the last of the war. German soldiers defending the last great physical barrier to the Reich knew the war was already lost.

The salient features of the plan for Operation Varsity, the airborne crossing of the Rhine, were lifted from the shortcomings observed during Market-Garden, six months before. 'P-Hour', the moment parachutists jump, was to occur after ground forces had crossed the river and established initial bridgeheads on the east bank this time. Two airborne divisions, the 6th British and 17th American, were to jump alongside each other in a single drop. They would fly-in with 3,185 transport aircraft and gliders; over twice the number of aircraft employed the previous September and then over a three-day period. Gliders were to land tactically near specific objectives, rather than in a swarm, and the insertion would be supported by a massive artillery preparation from 658 artillery pieces, firing 45 rounds every minute for 120 hours. Drops were to be concentrated in an area six miles wide by three miles deep. In all, 21, 860 paratroopers and glider men would launch together in an unprecedented landing density.

The 6th British Airborne Division was to land to the left of the river crossing axis with 243 parachute transports and 440 tug glider combinations. To the right the 17th (US) Airborne Division would parachute from 298 transports and 616 tugs towing 908 gliders, some pulling two gliders. This was vertical envelopment on a scale beyond that even theoretically envisaged by Colonel Billy Mitchell over Metz in 1918. Major Lewis Brereton, his staff assistant then, was now the Lieutenant General commanding the First Allied Airborne Army whose XVIII Airborne Corps was executing this attack.

'We were told that we would land in the middle of the German Army to prevent them counter-attacking our ground forces making the river crossing,' recalled 21-year-old Private Paddy Devlin with the glider-borne Royal Ulster Rifles. Having experienced D-Day, he was not enthused at the prospect of landing in the face of flak. 'It was obvious that the enemy would shoot hell out of us as we came in to land and before we could get out of the gliders,' he surmised. The aim was to seize high ground overlooking the river-crossings in the Diersfordter Forst and the open country to the east as far as the River Issel, including Hamminkeln, to block any employment of German reserves. Fear of flak at Arnhem had resulted in landings too far from the bridge, with all the subsequent complications. Planners this time verged on complacency, while the airborne enthusiasts were prepared to take risks to achieve greater precision. The previous 25–40 per cent aircraft losses predicted at Arnhem became 5.5 per cent in reality over the entire nine days. Planning staffs thought this an acceptable return.

Soldiers were understandably less blasé. Harry Clark, boarding the Horsa glider *Irene II* with 26 of his men with the Ox and Bucks, recalled ten of them had been with him flying *Irene I* against the Orne River and Canal bridges on D-Day. 'The ten veterans knew what awaited them later that morning,' he observed and 'sat quiet and thoughtful', unlike the excited replacements blissfully 'unaware of the hell that was just a short time away'.

The 19th US Airborne Division had received its baptism of fire as line infantry that winter during the Battle of the Bulge. This was their first live airborne mission. Corporal Bob Krell could not sleep the night before the operation. 'You crawl deeper in your sack, but you can't get away from the noise,' he recalled. Over the roar of engines and the calling out of stick orders at dawn 'we will trudge out to the planes and climb in, not saying much about anything'. Emplaning before a large operation was always a time of reflection. 'Some had done it before; for others this is the first time,' he mused, but everyone knew 'that this jump across the Rhine will be the end of the Krauts'.

Paddy Devlin was woken up at 0245 on 24 March 1945 and by 0500 they had been driven out to their gliders which were lined up along both sides of the runway. Two hours remained before take-off. 'We removed our equipment and stood around chatting or kicking a football to keep warm.' It was still dark, but a fine morning was emerging, 'ideal for gliding', he recalled. Captain H.J. Sweeney, another D-Day veteran with the Ox and Bucks, was surprised to see that many of the glider pilots were dressed in RAF blue, a direct outcome of the heavy glider pilot casualties at Arnhem. 'Well, a lot of them didn't want to know,' remembered glider pilot Sergeant Arthur Shackleton, who had made it back. 'They had joined the RAF to fly, not to dig holes in the ground.' So not all of them took their infantry ground training seriously. 'When we crossed the Rhine a lot of RAF pilots were killed because they ran around like headless chickens panicking instead of digging in straight away,' Shackleton subsequently observed. There were wild parties and much hand-shaking the night before, Captain A.F. Boucher-Giles, a veteran of Sicily,

Normandy and Arnhem, remembered. 'This was the final party, a piece of cake, a quick end to the war and so forth,' he recalled. Although using the airborne corps might be likened to using a sledge-hammer to crack a nut 'most of us knew in our hearts that this would be a grim business, and the German would resent our intrusion into his homeland'.

There was last-minute letter writing and as Robert Capa described: 'cleaning of rifles and consciences'. Paddy Devlin had received communion from his Irish padre the day before, 'so I must have been in a state of grace when I set out on my murderous mission the following morning,' he concluded. One of Lieutenant Colonel Napier Crookenden's 9 Para lance corporals added to the tedium of letter censoring by insisting on sending 11 letters to 11 different ladies 'swearing deathless devotion to each of them'. Everyone appreci-ated what was coming. 'We were briefed and told that we would be jumping, together with an English airborne division on the other side of the Rhine,' Robert Capa recalled, 'right in the heart of the main defence line.' Casualties in parachute units were averaging almost one man in two, so there were considerable numbers of replacements jumping with less enthusiastic veterans. 'They'll sweat a bit, as any paratrooper sweats before making a parachute jump,' wrote Corporal Bob Krell with the 19th Airborne. 'They will get the same old butter-flies, but they'll jump.' This was Krell's last letter, 12 hours later he was killed in action.

XVIII US Airborne Corps combined the British 6th and American 17th Divisions and was attached to General Montgomery's 21st Army Group. Its task was to reinforce and expand the bridgehead that XII Corps, spearheading the river crossing, would create the night before. As the two aircraft streams converged over Brussels, the British flying from south-east England and the Americans from airfields around Paris, XXI Corps had already fought nine small bridgeheads onto the east bank; some of which were under considerable pressure. Ahead lay the six-miles-wide-by-three-miles-deep drop zones and landing sites in a triangle that encompassed the towns of Emmerich, Bocholt and Wesel. Inside this triangle were an estimated 712 light and 114 heavy flak guns. Vertical envelopment over such a concentrated fire zone was going to be grim.

Flight Lieutenant B.S. Evenden remembers flying across the Grand Place in Brussels and the people waving excitedly below. Another glider pilot David Reynolds saw a V1 Flying Bomb heading for England that attracted enormous attention as it 'crossed the stream at the same height but going a great deal faster'. It became increasingly hot and uncomfortable in the bubble-glass glider cockpits as they flew due east into the rising sun. Robert Capa, who had settled down among paratroopers with the American stream, was peering through his porthole window, watching as: 'Our shadows travelled on the roads and streets of the liberated countries, and we could see the faces of people waving to us. Even the dogs were fascinated and ran after our shadows.' The countless glider combinations 'looked as if someone had spun strings from the Channel to the Rhine'. It was an awesome sight.

Feldwebel Hermann Hagenberg's three 20mm gun crews belonging to Flak Regiment 21 were philosophical about their future. During the retreat, billeted on civilians, they had celebrated many 'farewell parties leaving the *Grossdeutsche Reich*' under the motto 'let's enjoy the war while we can, the peace will be terrible'. Now on the morning of 24 March 'the sky was darkened by countless aeroplanes appearing at a height of about 500 metres'. By relocating and camouflaging a new position between Hamminkeln railway station and the dyke of the autobahn under construction, they escaped the devastating bombardment that had lasted from the previous evening through the night and into morning. Now they could hit back.

Paddy Devlin had slept or dozed most of the three and a half hours flight in his glider. 'Never mind the silly war, but concentrate on the loot' became part of the aimless banter passed about to settle increasingly taut nerves. Devlin, who had been lucky on D-Day, was not so concerned. 'When you are 21 years old you believe it is always the other fellow who will get hit by the arrow and not yourself,' he philosophically suggested. In fact going to war by glider in his opinion was 'less nerve-wracking than advancing on the ground under shell fire as you were cocooned in the plywood fuselage by the slipstream from the outside battle noises'. They could see very little from the portholes. 'It was different for the pilots as they could see what was happening.'

'As we got closer and closer we could see a cloud of black smoke and dust in front of us,' recalled Captain Sweeny. 'Through it we could glimpse the flashes of the German anti-aircraft guns as they began to open up now on the parachute planes, which were now in front of us.' It was calculated it would take three hours to deliver the whole of the massive 3,000 aircraft stream and the parachute transports arrived in tight formations, nine aircraft across, 18 abreast with the two streams, before the gliders. Nearly 550 of them began to disgorge their loads in the midst of a dense and increasingly thickening belt of spluttering and bursting flak. 'I saw Chalk 68 was hit on fire,' recalled RAF parachute dispatcher Norman Goodacre, 'and Chalk 69 was also flying with difficulty ' His entire stick was abruptly tossed onto the floor when the aircraft pitched violently to one side. '*All out!*' shouted the crew chief. Goodacre thought he meant 'Abandon ship', but did not query it and jumped.

The drop zones were badly obscured by fires and smoke and dust from the artillery bombardment mixing with the smokescreen deliberately released to cover the river crossings. 'We came in at 300 feet,' recalled Technical Sergeant Charles Wendorf, dispatching paratroopers. 'There was a heavy smokescreen over much of the area and our men were jumping right into it and disappearing.' His pilot Lieutenant Ernest Hammerfahr, a D-Day veteran, called it, 'the worst yet – terrible.' Wensdorf saw that two of his complement of 29 paratroopers were staggering badly wounded as they approached the door. The men behind desperate at any delay 'just shoved them out of the door'. 'Bullets began to hit our plane like pebbles,' recalled Robert Capa. He jumped, managing to click the shutter of his camera as he descended. 'The first fear was over,' and once on the ground, 'we were reluctant to begin the second.' Some of his stick was dangling nearby from tall trees, completely exposed some 50 feet up. They were flailed by German machine gun fire. Capa swore in Hungarian, his parents' tongue, and buried his head in the grass, whereupon a young paratrooper nearby called out, 'Stop those Jewish prayers, they won't help you now.'

Trees snagged many of the descending parachutists. Sergeant Derek Glaister, jumping number 20 from a 7 Para aircraft, was the last man out. He and a group of others came down near a large farmhouse where a German 88mm flak gun was in action. They were way off target and invited immediate attention: 'Just before my feet touched the ground, a bullet smashed through my left elbow, so I lay on my stomach and pretended to be dead. I saw nine of the others come down, some into trees. The Germans shot them as they hung there helpless – it was a sickening sight.'

Five of the German crew approached him and he realised, 'I was in big trouble.' Despite being left-handed, he shot them all, firing his sten gun with his right, and threw a smoke grenade to cover his escape. He was swiftly shot in the back from ten yards by a tall German SS officer 'covered in boils'. The German looted what he assumed to be a body and left him.

The complexity of delivering 3,000 aircraft from 15 airfields in France and 11 from England into an area six miles by three began to have an insidious effect on the insertion. Faster parachute transports overtook slower glider combinations and passed beneath their streams to drop first. Seventy-two of the new American Commando C-46 aircraft were in the transport stream. Driven by more powerful engines, they carried 50 men, twice a Dakota load, which jumped doors either side instead of one. The first C-46 serials slotted in ahead of the gliders but the second, also moving faster, had to stack overhead at 2,000 feet, exercising quick thinking to clear the glider flow. Formations started to break up as they passed through multiple puff balls of flak bursting among and ahead of them. One C-46 stalled and literally fell from the sky dragging down its crew and 50 parachutists on board. When the stream turned to the right after crossing the Issel River 19 of their number were on fire, jumping parachutists as they went down. Fourteen of them were the new Commandos, found to be particularly flammable because of their wing fuel tanks and complex hydraulic systems.

'By the time we were a few minutes from the final run-in the orderly stream had become thoroughly confused,' recalled Flight Lieutenant David Richards. The glider stream, over 400 British to the left and 880 American to the right, began to get into difficulties. Air space became a premium commodity. 'Going into high tow on the final run-in we were harassed by a Dakota which was sitting too close and just above my tail,' declared Richards. 'It was extremely difficult for us in the Horsa to look back and see him, and I wonder if he could see us just below his nose.' Landing sites were completely obscured by smoke and dust below and the only clue provided was the telltale silver ribbon of the River Rhine. The RAF released high at 2,500 feet, while the Americans were casting off at 600 feet, just above the battlefield. Richards saw his group was 'a confusing mass of several combinations abreast of each other with more above and below' even before cast off. 'Just before pulling off we even saw a Stirling combination which must have been flying well above the stipulated speed.' 'I couldn't see the ground for fog or whatever,' remembered Sergeant Arthur Shackleton. 'There was no sign of our landing area, just one huge pall of smoke,' recalled Harry Clark, landing with a platoon of the Ox and Bucks. Many pilots managed to pick out the spire of the Hamminkeln church, which was poking out of the murk. 'I was trying to calculate where I would enter this smog when I felt a sort of bump and the wing went up and I found it hard to control the wheel,' recalled Shackleton. Half his tail fin and rudder had been shot away. He had no choice other than to 'fly straight forward and land as best I could'.

German gunners turned away from the difficulties of engaging parachute transport aircraft to target the rich feast that began to slowly and ponderously descend toward them. All guns were redirected at the gliders. Feldwebel Hermann Hagenberg's 20mm 12-gun battery was to claim five transport aircraft, two observer planes and 40 gliders that day. The distinctive slow pom–pom–pom of 20mm cannon amidst the sharper cracks of the high velocity 88mm guns reaped a grim harvest. 'Some gliders only needed some ten explosive shells,' Hagenberg recalled. Spare crew members fired up with rifles and machine guns. 'The standing order was to change the gun barrels after 50 rounds, but in this emergency we changed them glowing red-hot after 500 shots or more.'

German 88mm gunners around Hamminkeln held their fire and traversed as gliders began landing left to right and fired as soon as the aircraft ground to a halt. Lieutenant Colonel Napier Crookenden reckoned that 32 gliders were completely destroyed on the ground and 38 came under such heavy fire that their crews could not unload them. Hagenberg admitted: 'the 20mm explosive shells had a terrible effect upon the crews of landed gliders and the many parachutists, so the airborne troops could not form up.' 'They were like locusts,' reported another German gunner: 'You hit one and half a dozen took its place. Everybody was shooting, but they kept coming. Some must have flown themselves, for no one could have lived in them.' 'One of our gliders came over,' observed the wounded Sergeant Derek Glaister, and 'the 88mm cracked it open like an egg and the jeep, gun, blokes – all fell out. Point blank range – they couldn't possibly miss at 50 feet.' Hagenberg's battery managed to pull out under cover of smoke. They only lost one gun.

David Richards was being passed by faster moving tugs, who had released their gliders further back 'and the flailing tow ropes' they ejected after release 'were another hazard as we started to descend'. As he looked out: 'Turning north out of the sun's glare opened up a scene of confusion I shall always remember – the glider stream coming in steadily from our left with gliders at all heights circling, diving, some apparently being shot down and not making orthodox approaches – complete chaos.' It took 60 Horsa gliders to land a battalion of glider infantry and these were all aiming for the same objective area.

Whereas in Normandy the paratroopers had suffered the highest initial losses, it was the reverse at the Rhine crossing. Gliders received the almost undivided attention of the German gunners. Captain Sweeny remembered numerous machine gun hits alongside the fuselage that holed the petrol tanks of the jeep they were carrying 'and frightened us in the cockpit' as well as wounding the anti-tank crew in the back. Sweeny explained the difference between flying troops and heavy equipments. 'Those of us who carried in our gliders jeeps, trailers, ammunition and petrol were flying in tinder boxes,' he emphasised. 'If we were hit the explosives and petrol could blow us up in the air,' and there was nothing the men inside could do except wince and endure the punishment. Major Ted Lough with HQ 5 Brigade comforted his wounded driver Private Wolfe 'Wally' Jablitsky as they sat in a in a jeep inside their landing glider, ready to drive out. Bullets had slashed through the fuselage and hit the driver in the head, back and arm. 'Keep your chin up!' Lough encouraged just before a bullet struck him in the chin.

The worst casualties were among the heavy equipment loads: 50 per cent of the light tanks and artillery pieces and 56 per cent of the anti-tank guns were lost and between 44–46 per cent of all vehicles. 'Of the 50 per cent of my battalion' of 600 men 'who were killed, wounded or missing, 103 were actually shot down and killed in the landing,' calculated Captain Sweeny. Three bodies were left in the back of David Brock's burning Horsa he remembered. A seasoned veteran who checked it later described it as the worse scene he had viewed on any battlefield. All that was left of one of them were 'charred remains stuck in the ground with the iron tips of his boots being all that remained of his uniform, stuck to his heels'.

The Americans fared better, releasing their gliders at low level. American correspondent Ed Clark admitted it was difficult to take in a scene where 'too much happens too fast': 'To the left one glider, ripped through and through with ack-ack fire, crashes nose-on deep into the loamy earth. Not a man of the crew comes out. In a few seconds fire started by tracers roars through the fabric. The framework crumbles over and what used to be a glider joins the rest of the smouldering and charred wrecks.'

Practically all the 570 gliders landing in the early waves were hit by flak or machine gun fire. One hundred crashed rather than landed and 26 were so badly shot up on the ground they could not be unloaded. Low-level release gave few options and Ed Clark saw many gliders 'trying desperately to land before another hit finishes them'. It was a scene of indescribable chaos. 'Gliders came winging dangerously close to the ships and men already on the ground' seeking a place to land. 'The new arrivals smash through fences, rip through wires and crash into grounded ships.' Injuries were horrific and troops clambering out were immediately taken under fire. 'Most of the men,' Clark observed, 'belly-crawl to what they think is the right road.' They pass parachutes draped over trees and parachutists prostrate on the ground still wearing their harnesses. 'Some of the men look at the faces of the dead paratroops, others don't.'

'They say that only one in five gliders landed undamaged of the 400 or so used by our division,' recalled Paddy Devlin with the Royal Ulster Rifles glider battalion. 'I was in one of the undamaged, how is that for luck?' He was indeed fortunate and 'first out of that door like a jack-rabbit' but within the hour he was severely wounded by machine gun fire. Glider pilot David Richards felt the overwhelming array of targets that appeared over the objective caused by the last minute dislocation of the descending streams saved lives. 'There is little doubt that the original pairs of 10 seconds interval would have been easy targets,' he assessed, 'and the gliders would have been shot down in succession.' Mass vertical envelopment had worked, flying through fierce opposition for the first time in the history of airborne warfare. The defence was smothered by the density of men and material that came raining down. Landings were successful, despite the losses, and all objectives were secured by 1630 hours. Violent initial opposition dwindled rapidly in the face of determined counter-attacks by the newly landed airborne troops. Large numbers of prisoners were taken and by last light only isolated small groups of enemy remained within the XVIII Airborne Corps perimeter.

Paddy Devlin sat on the ground with hundreds of wounded British and Germans as medical orderlies came round ladling out tea from buckets. 'You took a couple of swigs and handed it to the nearest one beside you, in my case a German who drank from it and passed it on.' This was a surreal arrangement. 'We weren't talking to each other but as I waited I was thinking how only a few hours ago we were shooting hell out of each other and now it did not seem to matter.'

An anticipated German panzer attack was distracted by the bridge-heads already established near Rees on the east bank by the British XXX Corps. During the night the anticipated link-up was achieved with the XII Corps ground forces, which had crossed the river. The planned airborne break-out to the east, supported by a Guards armoured brigade got moving within 48 hours, driving for the Baltic coast. Forty days later the 6th Airborne Division linked with the Russians at Wismar and the war in Europe was over.

Operation Varsity had been the biggest airborne assault of all time, yet despite vindicating early airborne theories, it attracted less attention than the epic battles surrounding D-Day in Normandy and Arnhem. 'We lost many of our men, but this one was easier than Salerno or Anzio or Normandy,' claimed Robert Capa, who had experienced these theatres. 'The Germans of those campaigns could have murdered us here, but these Germans were beaten.' Bloody landings at Sicily, Normandy and southern Holland had resulted in the constant questioning of the worth of launching mass airborne attacks into the teeth of determined opposition. By 1945 the airborne arm had transitioned from a blunt instrument to a highly technical and precise capability.

The effectiveness of anti-aircraft weapons, more powerful, faster firing and assisted by radar direction and ranging devices, was altering the balance. Would the cost ever be commensurate to the operational gain? The official United States Army position in World War Two history suggested the capture of the high ground east of the Rhine in support of the crossing could just as effectively have been achieved by a ground operation, bearing in mind the speed at which subsequent bridges were erected. The overall loss was 1,185 dead and 1,308 wounded and 103 gliders and aircraft shot down. They captured about 4,000 enemy and killed 1,000. These were eye-watering losses pitted against enemy units at perhaps 40 per cent strength, broadly assessed as already beaten.

Robert Capa, having survived the jump on 24 March, simply stated: 'There's no future in this paratrooper business.' Jumping into the teeth of effective anti-aircraft fire no longer appeared to be a rational act of war.

9

THREADBARE PARACHUTING

'LES PARAS'

Once the threat of Japan was removed the United States cut its airborne strength from five to two divisions. The British followed suit, reducing to one and then to a single brigade in 1948. Technology was meanwhile transforming the face of airborne warfare; bigger and more powerful box-shaped tail-loading aircraft were introduced. Vehicles could be loaded through rear compartment doors and dropped with parachute combinations affixed to platforms. The American Fairchild C-119 Flying Boxcar demonstrated the new step forward in design. Introduced in 1949, it could drop 46 parachutists or carry 30,000lbs of freight out to a range of 1,770 miles and still utilise basic landing strips more commonly found outside Europe. By 1957 trials for the introduction of the C-130 Hercules aircraft had begun. This could carry 60 paratroopers or 44,000lbs of freight over 2,160 miles. With a reduced pay-load it could fly out to 4,460 miles. These developments heralded a new approach to airborne warfare. The C-130 was the ultimate in air transport. With a heated interior and pressurised hull the aircraft could fly at heights enabling the most economic cruising speed. On reaching its objective the aircraft merely opened its rear clam-like ramp door and could drop its load by parachute, close doors, regain height and fly back. Bigger aircraft however, meant vulnerability under fire to greater numbers of men, who in turn needed longer drop zones, adding further to the traditional ground dispersion dilemma.

In April 1952 the American Joint Airborne Troops Board declared: 'Gliders as an airborne capability are obsolete, and should no longer be included in airborne techniques, concepts or doctrine.' Britain had disposed of its wooden gliders, deteriorating since the war, the previous year. The awful casualties in the teeth of determined anti-air resistance sustained during Varsity in 1945 suggested daylight airborne assaults may not be a practical proposition. Crash casualties alone had been intimidating. The British Glider Pilot Regiment lost 111 men to 74 aircraft crashes during training exercises between 1941–5. The regiment was disbanded in 1957, having been reduced primarily to flying for artillery spotting,

Two regimental-size American airborne assaults were conducted by the 187th Airborne Regiment Combat Team in Korea in 1950 and 1951. Seventy-six of the new Fairchild C-119s, together with 40 C-47s, dropped 2,860 paratroopers and 301 tons of cargo during the advance to the Yalu River in 1950 and again ahead of a counter-offensive near the 38th Parallel when over 3,000 were dropped. It was a demonstration of how far forward airborne battle technology had advanced. Once again the mass deployment of airborne troops proved a rather blunt instrument, reduced to its traditional immobility once on the ground. North Korean and Chinese forces bypassed them with motorised forces and evaded the rudimentary blocking positions placed ahead of them. The French in Indo-China were meanwhile developing airborne concepts that exploited small numbers of parachute troops to maximum tactical effect. Bigger was not necessarily best.

Geography was the decisive obstacle to be overcome in the many conflicts that proliferated after 1945. When the French returned to Vietnam in early 1946 they were opposed by a well organised Communist-inspired national liberation movement under the leadership of Ho Chi Minh and his military planner, Vo Nguyen Giap. Operating from the remote mountainous region of north-east Vietnam and the Red River Delta the Vietminh escalated from intense guerrilla fighting to mounting a full-scale offensive against the French in 1950. Indo-China was a war without fronts and rear areas like the Second World War and 86 per cent of it was covered in growth and 47 per cent outright jungle. It was a stark contrast to the American and UN experience in the treeless expanses of Korea. The French adopted a containment policy of building strongpoints or forts, often dotted along major highways, the *Route Colonial* or RC. Many of these remote outposts required to be rescued under siege, as also the armed road-bound convoys that supported them. Parachutists were employed as a 'fire-brigade' to speedily deploy to threatened trouble-spots.

When France was overrun in 1940 her two existing parachute companies were dispersed. Survivors and Free-French infantry who fled to England were integrated into the British SAS Brigade. These were expanded to two battalions who parachuted into Brittany and central and eastern France to operate clandestinely in support of the 1944 Normandy invasion. A decision was made post-war to create an airborne division in France and North Africa and send a brigade to Indo-China. The SAS battalions were incorporated into expanded French colonial parachute battalions and three Foreign Legion airborne battalions were activated. Eight airborne battalions on average were serving in Indo-China between 1946–54 and were employed as a general reserve, capable of swift deployment anywhere in the country. Their Second World War SAS background bred techniques and an attitude of mind well suited to the unconventional demands of jungle warfare against the Vietminh. They were to be at the forefront of the fighting because it was realised that a small number of men quickly deployed in tactically sound positions can produce effects way out of proportion to the numbers employed. Indo-China was to prove the crucible for the painful evolution of Les Paras.

At a time when post-war inertia was removing the edge from veteran Allied divisions, like the British employed as light infantry on counter-terrorist operations in Palestine, the French were developing creative new techniques. These men were different, highly experienced soldiers who regarded themselves as quite distinct from the rest of the Metropolitan French Army. They even looked different in baggy tiger-striped camouflage fatigues with red berets – like the British – but worn at a rakish angle. Having experienced national humiliation in 1940, they were quietly determined never to see French honour sullied by defeat again. This in part contributed to a formidable performance. A British officer visiting a French airborne stand-by unit in Saigon in September 1950 recalled the high morale and combat experience of many of the ex-SAS officers and NCOs. The level of operations was intense. 'The average number of operational jumps per man is five or six, rising in the more senior ranks to eight or nine.' They were risk-takers; their ability to 'get away with it' produced a cavalier attitude to drop zone drills. 'Everyone regretted being in Saigon, when the fighting was in the north,' the report read.

Speed was the essence of each deployment, with troops launched on the briefest of verbal orders down to platoon commanders. Often the drop zone was picked out and confirmed by an aircraft flying ahead of a motley group of old German *Tante Ju*, or 'Aunty Ju', Junkers 52s and American C-47 Dakotas after 1952 and C-119 Flying Boxcars from 1953. If more than a company was needed, multiple lifts followed. Careful and detailed pre-selection of possible drop zones all over Indo-China were catalogued and followed up with the minimum of delay in an emergency. Much of the orders content was standard and relied upon the cumulative experience of officers and NCOs called out many times. Risks were taken by landing directly on the enemy to add to the shock of surprise, seemingly the only recourse against an increasingly numerous Vietminh. No attempt was made to reorganise on drop zones. Soldiers discarded their parachute harnesses and immediately attacked from the drop, relying on their impact to neutralise enemy fire. 'These measures enable the stand-by company to reach any threatened post throughout Indo-China within a few hours of an SOS being received,' explained the visibly impressed visiting British officer. 'The French ability to make do with very limited resources in equipment and aircraft may contain a lesson for British airborne forces,' he declared, 'in view of their tendency to insist on a 100 per cent scale of everything, before it can be used.' In essence, he considered their tactical handling 'gives the impression of being bolder and more robust, than the British practice'. Such élan, however, came at a cost as the Vietminh became increasingly numerous and more effective.

Once on the ground in the jungle, like the glider-borne air-land missions conducted by the Chindits in Burma during World War Two, operations developed at a snail's pace, with soldiers having to hack their way across unforgiving mountainous jungle terrain. Re-supply had to be by air. It could take exhausting hours to move from the drop zone by an isolated outpost to scale jungle heights to occupy vantage points to protect road convoys. Leslie Aparvary with the 1st BEP (Bataillon Étranger Parachutiste) in such a situation found himself unable to engage the main firing point of a Vietminh convoy ambush. 'We hastened to assist the others just as fast as we could.' They ran for a kilometre before they were pinned down. 'It was impossible to make headway, only by creeping and crawling, darting about, and taking cover if we could find it behind trees and bushes.' The difficulty was always to be able to site so as to exploit their superior fire-power, in this case '*Douze-Septs*' or 12.7mm heavy machine guns. 'By this time we could see the enemy clearly,' and as was increasingly the case, 'there were so many of them!' Eventually they beat back the ambush through fire-power alone as 'mortars and small cannon spread death everywhere'. Fighting within the close confines of jungle undergrowth against an implacable foe was a fearsome experience. 'Every now and then a man senses that the end is near,' recalled Aparvary, 'never in my life had the wings of death loomed so close.' Whole convoys with hundreds of French and allied troops were often totally overrun and wiped out by thousands of Vietminh irregulars.

Fourteen major airborne assaults were conducted during the French war in Indo-China and a host of tactical insertions. One included a raid that destroyed Ho Chi Minh's headquarters in the Red River Delta, but the communist leader escaped. In July 1953 74 C-47s dropped three battalions at Lang Son, who destroyed a communist supply dump including 10,000 weapons. The force was then faced with a nightmare two-day extraction march through 60 miles of communist-controlled jungle to safety. Some men perished with heat stroke. By the end of 1953 the parachute battalions had lost 5,000 dead, wounded and missing, more than 20 per cent of the airborne units fielded. French Legionnaire Lucien Bodard described how the end came to many solitary outposts overrun by hordes of Vietminh. 'The death throes were known only by a few radio messages,' he recalled, 'then came the great silence at the end.' The war was not going well and soldiers felt under-resourced and abandoned. 'That was what the war in Indo-China was like,' Bodard claimed. 'The fighting men died alone and the high command did not even know the manner of their death.'

Action rates for French parachute battalions far exceeded the Second World War experience. The 2nd BEP conducted counter-insurgency operations, raids and truck-borne actions with only one

Above US paratroopers waiting apprehensively on the eve of D-Day in June 1944, knowing they would land behind enemy lines. 'That'll make anyone stand and search his soul for a few minutes', admitted one paratrooper.

Paratroopers were so heavily loaded, like this American soldier, that they could barely climb on board their aircraft for the D-Day jump. Supreme Commander General Eisenhower expected few to survive.

British paratroopers and gliders land at Arnhem during Operation 'Market-Garden', the first daylight and successful multiple division jump of the war.

The 1st British Airborne Division mass parachute descent on the outskirts of Arnhem on 17 September 1944 caught the Germans completely by surprise.

Above: Operation 'Varsity' on 24 March 1945 was the biggest parachute assault ever – two parachute divisions jumped alongside each other from 3,185 aircraft in a single three-hour-long drop.

The paratroopers came down in an area six miles wide and three miles deep defended by 826 flak guns: 'the worst yet – terrible', remarked one American D-Day veteran.

The French paratrooper raid at Lang Son in Indo-China in July 1953, destroyed a Communist supply dump. The paratroopers then endured a nightmare sixty mile trek through Communist occupied jungle to get out, many soldiers did not survive because of heat exhaustion.

Below Piece-meal paratrooper reinforcements having emplaned for Dien Bien Phu in early 1954 look apprehensively at the camera. For some, it was their first ever jump.

Above British Commandos flown ashore during the Suez landings in November 1956. The first helicopter assault under fire coincided with the last parachute drop.

French paratroopers searching for insurgents in the Casbah of Algiers. Defeat in Indo-China hardened attitudes.

NATO employed its airborne troops in a reinforcement role during the Cold War. British paratroopers air-land with CH-47 Chinook helicopters.

The hover and step-off, shown here during intense air-mobile operations in South Vietnam during the late 1960s, could cause injury if heavy ammunition loads were being carried. 'Every time those turbines started winding,' remembered one soldier, 'I just thought *yeah*'.

A C-130 Hercules rescue aircraft lands at Lod Airport, Israel after the successful Entebbe rescue mission in July 1976.

French legionnaire paratroops jump under fire near the Old Town at Kolwezi, Zaire, in May 1978 during the surprise hostage-rescue mission.

'Now the Dragon is dead' announced one Mujahideen fighter, standing trophy over a downed Soviet helicopter in Afghanistan. With the advent of the Stinger AA missile system, 100 Soviet helicopters were shot down by insurgents in 1986.

British paratrooper vehicles under fire from Mujahideen rebels twenty years later. 'Before you go into an open area you get into a bit of a twitch', admitted one paratrooper pathfinder.

ten-day break midway between November 1952 and March 1954. On 17 March it was withdrawn from operations in Pleiku in the Central Highlands to Hanoi. From there it was parachuted piecemeal into Dien Bien Phu between 9–12 April, just over three weeks before its fall to the Vietminh. Men were just as liable to collapse and die from heat exhaustion in the jungle during typically 20-mile extraction marches as be killed by enemy action.

These air-mobile incursions had been mainly light. The Vietminh utilised their superior jungle mobility to mass and overrun strong convoys and strongpoints. The French sought to bring them to battle and destroy them with overwhelming firepower. To achieve this, two brigades with six parachute battalions jumped into a bowl-shaped valley at Dien Bien Phu between 20–21 November 1953. This fertile valley, ten miles long and five miles wide, was set in the Thai Highlands 185 miles from Hanoi and 95 miles from the Chinese border. It formed part of the primary Vietminh infiltration route from the Laotian border 12 miles away. It was only accessible by air to the French and was dominated on all sides by heavily wooded hills between 1,300–2,300 feet high. At its core was an old Japanese airstrip of compacted earth. Apart from imposing a block on a major infiltration route the Vietminh could not afford to ignore, the position, entrenched with strongpoints on the surrounding hills, offered the sort of topography that favoured a conventional defensive battle.

Infantry and Foreign Legion were brought in to garrison the location and replace the paratroopers. A series of escalating encounter battles was fought on the valley floor at the beginning of 1954. General Vo Nguyen Giap predictably picked up the gauntlet and blockaded the position with 28 battalions of Vietminh infantry. Unexpectedly he hauled 200 pieces of 75mm and 105mm artillery through the jungle and a 37mm flak regiment to join them. By mid-March a huge force of 100,000 men had penned in a garrison of 15,000 with ten tanks, two dozen 105mm guns and four 155m guns. On 13 March a massive artillery bombardment heralded an intensification of the battle with the sudden fall within 36 hours of two of the northern strongpoints: Beatrice and Gabrielle. The airstrip was rendered useless by artillery and two good French battalions were wiped off the order of battle. French morale was severely shaken.

By the end of March Dien Bien Phu was totally dependent upon air drops. 'Generally speaking where the earth showed was the French,' observed Major Paul Grauwin as he flew in with a surgical team, 'while the green belonged to the Viets.' Simultaneous Vietminh human-wave attacks were directed against five French hilltop positions, costing Vo Nguyen Giap 2,500 killed and three times that number wounded. Communist morale briefly faltered but the squeeze was maintained until by the end of May the garrison had lost 40 per cent of its territory and only 3,000 bone-weary French and Vietnamese paratroopers, Foreign Legionnaire and North African troops were left. They fought on through the mud and driving rain of the monsoon season with no realistic hope of relief.

Reinforcements could only come by parachute and mostly at night. Grauwin observed just such a drop by one of his relief surgical teams, who jumped over their position at 600 feet. 'The eight figures dangling from parachutes dropped right in the middle of the barbed wire, where shells were also falling.' The men had to run, doubled up and weighed down by heavy equipment to the nearest shelters. 'It would be sheer luck if they all managed to get out of there,' recalled a worried Grauwin. About 136 transports, including 24 C-119s flown by American crews, were theoretically available for re-supply. Many of their crews were logging 150 flying hours at the height of the battle in April 1954, three times the norm considered as heavy combat flying. Five parachute battalions were dropped in during the battle, in addition to 1,530 individual volunteers, of whom 680 had never jumped before. This piecemeal reinforcement kept going to the end with 94 jumping early on 6 May, the day before the fortress fell. Paul Grauwin recalled the inspiration these sacrificial jumpers brought the garrison. 'It was unbelievable, unprecedented; we could hardly believe our eyes.' The men at Dien Bien Phu were mistakenly convinced it meant 'that the higher command had decided to hold on to the end – until victory'.

Night jumps usually began at about 2100 when the first engine noises were discerned below and continued all night at intervals of 20 to 40 minutes. Men boarded in the calm of peacetime Hanoi until someone prepared them for action after a one and a half to two-hours flight. Someone said '*Go!*' and then as Grauwin described: 'pushed him into a black gulf at the bottom of which he saw flashes, explosions and the brilliant track of tracer bullets; after a sudden jerk of the parachute as it unfolded, he suddenly found himself among flares, whistling bullets, blinding flashes and the explosions of shells.'

Parachutists could not see the ground once the silhouette outline of the surrounding bowl valley slipped into blackness, and an unexpected collision with barbed wire entanglements confirmed Grauwin's arrival. Injury rates were surprisingly low, but newcomers arrived blind and completely disorientated. They groped their way into unknown shelters and trenches. 'Where am I? I saw a bit of light, so I came in,' announced one newly landed paratrooper to Grauwin. The new arrivals were instantly recognisable. 'We looked at their clean uniforms and their healthy faces which formed such an odd contrast to our own,' he recalled. 'Tommy guns were still gleaming with oil, their parachutes straight from the shop.' One unfortunate crashed into Grauwin's makeshift morgue. 'I fell on something soft; I didn't know what it was,' the paratrooper recalled. 'I made out a mouth, teeth, a nose – it was ice cold. Then I realised where I was.' Heavy shell fire had pinned him close to the ground, 'so I had to lie down on your stiffs,' he complained. Grauwin recalled he drank virtually the whole of his bottle of rum. Dien Bien Phu became the crucible; an icon like Arnhem had been for the British, to Les Paras.

Although the parachute battalions were reduced in strength to a few companies, Grauwin recalled, 'they have a part in every incident, in every attack, in every counter-attack.' Enthusiasm and confidence rose with each parachute reinforcement. 'France and the higher command are not going to let us fall,' they felt. 'They are sending us the best blokes of the lot.' This was going on even as unseen political negotiations over the future of Indo-China were being conducted in Geneva. Individual reinforcements jumped to be with their comrades at the end. One soldier explained he could not stay 'in my bolt hole at Nam-Dinh', a quiet sector, 'while the blokes promoted with me, the ones in my battalion and in my old command post get smashed up – so I've come to be smashed with them'. And he added, 'You know, I'm far from being the only one.' This again was the same airborne spirit so visible during World War Two. Medical conditions in dressing stations under fire with wounded lying in the mud were such that even amputees were among the walking wounded choosing to rejoin their embattled comrades. 'Volunteers, 6th Paras!' heard Paul Grauwin, the senior medical officer, and despite remonstrations some of the wounded began to laboriously trudge or stagger out. 'The other blokes are expecting us; now we know, we've got to go,' they said moving through stinking water-filled trenches. Dien Bien Phu fell during the early morning hours of 8 May, and still they left. 'If they're going to be wiped out, we'll be wiped out with them,' was the wounded's final response to Grauwin's plea to remain. The garrison did not surrender until it had been overrun.

The French suffered 7,693 casualties, of which more than 2,000 died and 6,500 were taken prisoner. Six parachute battalions were wiped out and 62 aircraft destroyed, maintaining the precarious air bridge and close ground combat support. They inflicted an estimated 22,900 casualties on the Vietminh, of which 7,900 were killed. It was a Pyrrhic victory, but the French were obliged to withdraw from Indo-China. Grauwin's cynical verdict after all the sacrifice was the bitter realisation that 'it was going to be June 1940 all over again'.

Achieving tactical air mobility by inserting quick-reaction 'fire-brigade' parachute units floundered at Dien Bien Phu. Once again strong anti-aircraft defences meant only piecemeal reinforcements were possible and at night. Airborne battalions had been constrained to light infantry reinforcement at an unfavourably sited fixed position. The lack of suitable drop zones amid jungle and scrub inhibited the flexibility that had been apparent in Europe. Helicopter technology was progressing to a degree that might open tactical access to difficult terrain denied to fixed-wing aircraft and previously only accessible to infantry on foot. Counter-insurgency conflict was pronounced after 1945 as nationalist movements sought to fill the vacuums created by colonial withdrawals or defeat during the Second World War. Insurgent forces sought to operate in forests, jungles, mountains and swamps inaccessible to parachute operations. Helicopters were beginning to offer surveillance and a limited troop-carrying capability across this type of terrain.

Leonardo da Vinci had produced some intriguing designs and models of wooden screw-shaped devices driven by a helical screw. Another machine showed a man pumping treads with his feet and turning a crank by hand to propel four wings. They did not fly, but Igor Sikorski, who invented the modern rotor blade, had been fascinated by the pictures as a child. A light machine was developed to drag air through blades, tilted to force the air down, and moving faster on the outside. The device produced lift and aerodynamic vortex ring and ground resonance difficulties were overcome, while a tail rotor prevented overall spin. The new machines could loiter and hover unlike fixed-wing, over any terrain and at low speed. Helicopters could deliver men and materials more precisely in time and space with less risk of injury compared to parachutes and gliders. This was virtual magic in terms of airborne tactical potential, but early machines had a very poor power to weight ratio which meant they could not lift much.

Helicopters were first extensively used for casualty evacuation and limited troop lift during the Korean War. Only about 19 were available to the French in Indo-China and only five of these were in action during Dien Bien Phu. Light air-cooled radial engines could only create low horsepower but a major technological breakthrough occurred in 1955 when French companies produced the Alouette II helicopter, powered by a gas-turbine engine. Turbo-shaft propulsion became universally adopted and speeded up the spread of the helicopter among military forces.

Algeria provided the scene for the first mass employment of helicopters. The French paratrooper experience in Algeria was to prove as character-forming as the crucible of Indo-China. Arab nationalism exploded into bloody violence in November 1954. Algeria had been part of Metropolitan France since 1848 and was extensively settled by European *pieds noirs* determined to maintain their favoured status and position. Algerian nationalists or FLN (National Liberation Front) provoked the *pieds noirs* with terror tactics resulting in brutal revenge attacks. Muslims seen supporting the French were slaughtered by the FLN, setting the stage for a brutal confrontation with the French military that was to last until 1962. An undeclared war was conducted with utmost savagery. Two airborne divisions were used as the main strike reserve, as in Indo-China, to repel infiltration into Algeria from safe havens in Morocco and Tunisia.

Many of the paratroopers were conscripts who were, nevertheless, 'moulded' by their regular officers and subjected to the same rigorous physical training that is uniform to airborne formations. 'Our officers were terrific,' remembered para conscript Gregoire Alonso. 'We got on well with them and didn't have this business of saluting all the time.' They were treated with the easy formality that comes with combat experience. 'If you had something to say, no problem,' claimed Alonso. 'These were guys who'd been in World War Two, in Indo-China, who'd seen it all, been wounded, some several times – they had a slew of medals.' The conscripts were quickly knocked into shape by veterans who appreciated they could only evolve with experience. When Gregoire Alonso came under fire for the first time he was carrying the radio for a very experienced platoon commander. When he immediately took cover the officer told him to get up and stand alongside him. 'The thing was, I just didn't know, hearing the guns and trying to shelter,' that they were out of range. 'Don't worry,' the veterans advised, 'you'll be all right.'

Physical conditions were bleak. The enduring memory of most veterans operating in the Algerian *bled* was of rugged mountainous terrain, stifling hot and dusty in summer, freezing cold with snow and mists in winter. 'We suffered terrible physical hardship the whole time,' remembered paratrooper Lieutenant Robert Andre, who lost a lot of weight, 'sleeping rough, living like dogs, gums bleeding if you brushed your teeth because we only had combat rations.' Helicopter insertions were followed by exhausting marches and tactical sweeps during the return to base. 'We'd move north, then south in a day,' Andre recalled. 'We baked in the southern desert in high summer,' and then, 'night after night of rain, fires forbidden.' Cumulative exhaustion and tedious operations, often without result, took their toll. 'You thought you couldn't go on, then next morning the machine started again.' Soldiers generally rested by day and patrolled at might.

Contact with the enemy was a rare event, conducted at long distance and often in pursuit, apart from sudden ambushes in close country. Gregoire Alonso was particularly fearful of FLN snipers firing Mausers over telescopic sights or English .303s and Italian Stattis 'which did terrific damage . . . Not many of them, but you'd hear the weird sound they made. And it was true that the bullets could take off a limb – they'd make a huge hole, you stood no chance.

People became really wary of them. If you heard the noise your ears flattened.'

The enemy was faceless. 'The supposed innocent inhabitants know everything, say nothing or tell you that they have never seen the *fellouze* even when they were sitting in an arms cache, complained Captain Antoine Ysquierdo, with a Régiment Étranger Parachutiste battalion: 'Everyone works for the rebels. The most insignificant shepherd knows everything. But to capture the bands, that is another story! We have sent out 5,000 to 6,000 men and who knows what material to kill a dozen poor fools and recover a pile of rusty shotguns.'

Fighting, when it did occur, was brutal with quarter neither given nor anticipated. Pierre Leuliette with the 8th BEP recalled how 'my poor friend V' who was wounded, 'lay howling on his bed of stones till morning'. He likely anticipated what was coming. 'He suffered unimaginably, both spiritually and mentally, a prey of mortal terror.' A rebel took hours to slither down to him before gouging out his eyes and slashing his Achilles tendons. 'He didn't finish him off, merely wanting him to have to lie still and suffer.' A sergeant lying a hundred yards away suffered the same fate and Leuliette realised there was little they could do, pinned down as they were, except to await the blessed dawn. Para Lieutenant Robert Andre, when asked if he had respect for the enemy replied, 'they came in all kinds.' There was an element of racism, explaining 'the image of the Arab then was a sneaky sort of pimp', but he then conceded, 'I faced some very brave men, I take my hat off to them.'

Atrocities might be for a purpose, but nevertheless spawned similar behaviour. One of Andre's sections was overrun by a lot of well-armed *felleghas*, ten minutes before they could be reached. 'They'd been stripped, it was really rough, emasculated – you get the idea?' he said. He detected a point to the bestial behaviour. 'Not sheer barbarism I'd say, but to strike terror into the imagination.' Scruples became an early casualty in this war. 'In battle there's no doubt a seriously wounded man might be finished off.' It was regarded as a form of mercy. 'But that's war for you,' Andre explained, 'alone out there, with half an hour to live, he'd stand no chance; so you'd hear the extra shots.'

Military success for the French came on the back of helicopter mobility; machines were integrated within combat units for the first time. Helicopter Intervention Detachments (DIH) were set up consisting of two light Alouette helicopters for reconnaissance, liaison and control, supported often by six CH-21s for troop and logistics lift. The Morice Line, an electrified fence built along the Algerian-Tunisian border in 1957, was fitted with numerous sensory devices which would initiate paratrooper interventions borne aloft by Sikorsky S-55 helicopters. Infiltrations were pursued by air-mobile platoon or company groups. Every helicopter was fitted with a 20mm cannon to provide mobile air suppression and the first ever armed Allouettes were created with SS-10 missiles. These could fire into the entrances of previously unassailable rebel caves. Robert Andre's parachute regiment spent 254 days in the field in 1958, losing 38 men killed, four officers and nine NCOs as well as 110 wounded.

Speed of reaction, coupled with light infantry helicopter air mobility, lay at the kernel of new tactics developed by the French. Ideas came from the veterans. 'Like all officers who served in Indo-China, everywhere I am struck by our slowness to adapt our methods to those required in a counter-guerrilla campaign,' complained Captain Pierre Sergent with the 1st REP. 'Army Staff HQ do not wish to admit that tanks are useless, as useless as these jets, which are too fast to be practical in hunting down an enemy who is on foot.' Sergent's view was: 'It requires a sort of "super infantryman" who is light, fast and similar to the paratroops or the legionnaires, of whom there are too few among the troops in Algeria.' Helicopters were still in their infancy. Commanders tended to regard them more as mobile gliders, flying 'truck-loads' of infantry, an uncomplicated role that could be conducted by any line infantry units.

The pace, however, of a helicopter insertion under fire is fast and furious. 'The *felleghas* cut the fence in several places and about 800 got in,' recalled Gregoire Alonso, describing the break-in from Tunisia in the wooded hill area around Souk-Ahras in April 1958. 'The 9th Paratroopers came in and a company was helicoptered right into the middle of it all – the choppers were under fire but no one was hit.' The rebels started to surrender, 'but unfortunately it was a trick'. At a whistle blast, those with their hands up dropped down and machine guns opened fire; 'most of the paras were mown down in the opening bursts.' Other airborne units, including the 1st REP, were flown in and over 600 FLN fighters killed or captured from a force of 820.

Alonso described the frenetic pace of combat. 'You kept your head down' until 'you start through that avalanche of bullets and stuff.' Such close combat was a series of rushes forward, movement covered by fire. 'You're hardly aware, you're sort of crazy,' recalled Alonso reliving the moment. 'Afterwards, once it's over, there's a great silence, people got killed you think, but *you* made it.' Pausing for breath he declared, 'you were lucky, because that's all it is − *luck.*'

The FLN was defeated in the countryside but the struggle continued in the towns, focused in and around the Casbah in Algiers. Defeat in Indo-China hardened paratrooper attitudes. They were not prepared to countenance a similar reverse in what they regarded as Metropolitan France.

SHOESTRING OPERATIONS: THE BRITISH

Britain's sole remaining 6th Airborne Division was stationed in Palestine at the end of the war in 1945 as an Imperial Reserve. This had less to do with parachute capability, more its ease of air-portability. The division could be easily transported by air because of its light equipment scales. It was soon drawn into frustrating low-level counter-terrorist police actions against Jewish extremists, trying to dampen violence between Arab and Jew over the future of the Palestinian Mandate. Jewish determination to establish a national homeland was inevitably directed against the occupying British security forces. Between 1945 and 1948 the 6th Airborne Division suffered 294 casualties of which 58 were killed.

'On the streets we were portrayed as the British Gestapo,' recalled an aggrieved Glyn Williams, serving with the division. Soldiers who had fought intense battles against the Germans in Normandy, the Ardennes and on the Rhine months earlier were very frustrated by the new 'hit and run' theatre of operations. 'The average soldier could not understand why British troops were hated,' Williams recalled. 'The British had liberated them from the concentration camps.' 'Small wonder that the troops' sympathy tended toward

"Johnny Arab",' remembered CSM Ron Kent with the Independent Parachute Pathfinder Company; 'however unprogressive he might have been in his 2,000 years of living in Palestine, he was not openly obstructive.'

Used to fighting conventional infantry battles at the company and battalion level, parachute soldiers had to improvise and learn to operate primarily at independent section or platoon level. Conditions were totally at variance to their previous experience. The enemy was not dressed in uniform and was rarely seen, explained Ron Kent. 'He would strike then disappear into the civilian background, actively assisted by the local population, women and children alike.' Conventional airborne operations were replaced by a new modus operandi of cordon and search, manning static observation posts, guards, convoy escort and clearance sweeps. The 1ˢᵗ Parachute Brigade on a typical day, 3 January 1947, was conducting cordon and search operations in two localities in northern Palestine, during which it screened 3,985 people and detained 34. Its sister brigade, the 2ⁿᵈ, detained 30 from 1,217 locals it searched. Jewish children were employed as shields and encouraged to stone British troops ferrying the cordons around suspect areas.

Soldiers were untaught in the new tactics so used their traditional initiative and resourcefulness backed by an innate aggression to improvise tactics to deal with the new circumstances. 'The main hazard was snipers,' recalled Air Dispatcher Patrick Maloney, attached to the division, and the response was robust. 'This proved to be a dangerous pastime for the terrorists, because if their location was a building,' he recalled, 'it was immediately blown sky high by the sappers.' Well used to reverting to raid tactics if required, airborne soldiers were comfortable operating in smaller, less supervised groups. 'A lot of it was patrolling at night for ambushing,' remembered Major John Waddy, serving with the 3ʳᵈ Parachute Brigade, 'but the Jews were always one ahead of us . . . They blew up the aircraft and we went and defended the airfields. Then they blew up the railways so we had the whole division guarding the railway and six months later they blew up all the bridges over the River Jordan so we guarded the bridges. It was an unending job.'

'The atrocities and casualties at times were barbaric,' recalled

Patrick Maloney. Two junior Intelligence Corps sergeants from 253 Security Squadron, Mervin Pace and Clifford Martin, were abducted and held prisoner in an airless underground hideout by terrorists. They were hanged in retaliation for Jewish hangings 'for membership of the criminal Nazi British Army of Occupation'. Two days later they were found still suspended by their necks in a eucalyptus grove near Nathanya. One of the booby-trapped bodies exploded as it was being cut down, severely wounding a British officer and showering everyone else with putrid flesh. The skill and ruthless ferocity of the Irgun, Stern and Haganah organisations meant the initiative was invariably held by the terrorists. 'The Jews had the free run of two-thirds of the country and ran no risk of interference,' recalled Sergeant Major Ron Kent. 'They could sit and watch the movement of sentries and strike when and where they liked.' Provocation was intense. Five unarmed paratroopers from the 5th Battalion were gunned down in tents by the Stern Gang, while securing a car park in Tel Aviv. As Kent explained, 'after an attack, the raiders could disappear amongst their own people in minutes.' Bitterly angry, a number of 6th Division paratroopers vented their fury on the inhabitants of the nearby settlement of Beer Tuvya, beating up Jews and damaging property. The ringleaders were disciplined by their units.

Major John Waddy described a more artful retribution following a Jewish lorry bomb attack against an Arab children's hospital which 'wasn't a pretty sight to see'. Another truck bomb attempt aimed at his company area went wrong when the 50-gallon drum packed with explosives tipped off the back of the lorry and rolled down to come to rest against a block of flats in the Jewish quarter. 'Jewish Haganah people came out from them and said, "We will take it away."' The paras disagreed, insisting they were not allowed to handle explosives because of the danger from booby-traps. Airborne sappers were sent in to disarm the device 'and they rubbed their hands', recalled Waddy, 'and brought along about another 100lbs of explosive and set it off'. There was a massive explosion and Waddy recalled, 'the front of these flats just dropped off and you could see inside every single room.'

Much of the material used by the terrorists was Second World War surplus, and many of the considerable skills employed had been passed on by the British. 'Jewish terrorists were trained by the

British,' Waddy claimed, 'thinking that the Germans were going to come through into Palestine.' They did not but, 'a lot of their weapons and ammunition, and the explosives they were issued with, they kept.' One consequence of this was in March 1946, 'they blew up 27 of our aircraft, whereupon the RAF disappeared back to Egypt and all parachute training stopped.' It was a highly professional job: 'The Halifaxes were blown up most expertly with only about a small amount of explosive which was placed against the wing route. So the aircraft looked almost immaculate, but with the wing route splintered, the whole aircraft was destroyed.'

Following the United Nations Partition Agreement in November 1947, the division was employed simply to keep Arab and Jew apart during the final days, until the Israelis proclaimed the State of Israel in March 1948. The British withdrew two months later and Egypt, Jordan, Syria, Lebanon and Iraq invaded the day the Mandate ended.

Little or no parachute training occurred during this Middle Eastern interlude and the 6th Airborne Division was disbanded on its return to England. Glider and air transport capability dwindled as successive British governments sought peace dividends rather than military capability in the face of near bankrupt post-war budgets. The one remaining 16th Independent Parachute Brigade was sent to Germany with its three sole parachute battalions in a non-airborne role. All Parachute Regiment officers who had been seconded to the Army Air Corps were sent back to their non-para parent units, thereby dispersing much of Britain's five years of accumulated wartime airborne expertise at one stroke. John Waddy described 'an influx of infantry officers who were inclined only to try and recreate their own regiments but in a maroon beret'.

The Parachute Regiment became an infantry regiment of the line, irrevocably placing distance between itself and any notion of an air corps. Senior British officers reverted to their previously insular view of 'funnies' and special forces. The commando role in the amphibious context was passed to the Royal Marines under the Royal Navy and the SAS, regarded as the army's commandos. Apparent failure at Arnhem and immense casualties for limited territorial gain during the Varsity Rhine crossing operation stultified the future development of British airborne forces. Waddy recalls a depressing period of decline lasting decades 'of the few remaining airborne warriors who caught the cautious habit of "We don't want another Arnhem, old boy".' Parachute assaults in the teeth of radar-directed anti-aircraft defences and in the age of the jet fighter just did not seem to be a rational act of war.

16th Parachute Brigade, because of its light equipment scales, was used as a light infantry fire-brigade that would invariably air-land rather than parachute. In 1951 it was flown back to the Middle East as a reinforcement during the Iranian crisis and used again in Egypt the following year. Six years after an entire division had dropped in a single lift at the Rhine, Britain's remaining brigade, short of transport aircraft, with scant parachute training facilities, could hardly drop a single battalion. In 1956 terrorism perpetuated by the Greek extremist EOKA organisation on Cyprus, seeking political union with Greece, resulted in yet another air-land by the 16th Parachute Brigade battalions to assist the island's crumbling security forces. It appeared the role of British Sky Men was being subverted by air-mobile light infantry. They were eminently suited to counter-insurgency ground sweeps, once deployed by aircraft.

Although they remained conscripts, Britain's parachute soldiers were still volunteers, subjected to the rigours of pre-parachute selection before being jump trained. As during the Second World War, the by-product of selection was to produce first-class aggressive infantry suited to an air-portable fire-brigade role, compared to the more static armour-heavy units garrisoning the British Army of the Rhine and elsewhere. Patrolling and cordon and search operations in Cyprus were conducted in difficult conditions. The Troodos mountain range produces snow in winter, despite the hot and dusty Mediterranean summer climate. 'To get into any sort of position from which one can observe successfully, we have to climb up to about 2,500 feet,' recalled Sergeant D.S. Scott with 2 PARA. 'The mountainsides are very sheer and covered six or eight inches deep in soft shale, which makes going very difficult and exhausting.' Scott was as much involved in an intelligence war, which was conducted alongside the police. They developed new tactics, peculiar to the situation, forming so-called Q-Patrols composed of police and soldiers dressed in civilian clothes, armed mostly with foreign automatic weapons. The aim was to pass themselves off as EOKA terrorists. Scott described how one such patrol killed one and wounded another of a gang of five in a Troodos village, 'whom they contacted after successfully bluffing several householders'.

Counter-insurgency sweeps in the Cypriot mountains alongside civilian police was a world apart from the high intensity operations the Parachute Regiment trained for. Scott was unimpressed by the English-imported inspector in charge of the police station he was required to work with, whom he regarded as 'a complete oaf'. He was in fact a village police sergeant from Derbyshire promoted to a two-star inspector under the Emergency Regulations. They were strange allies and Scott dismissed him with the typical disdain that highly trained soldiers reserve for lesser qualified colleagues. 'He is openly afraid of taking action against even minor offenders and keeps saying: "*We mustn't get their backs up, you know!*" Not long to do here, must get 'ome in one piece.' Scott recalled they were on stand-by as a Middle East Strategic Reserve. 'Egypt seems to be the favourite at the moment,' he recalled in a letter home, 'but no one really knows.'

'In early August 1956, we were in Cyprus and realised that something was going on,' recalled Corporal Grout with 3 PARA, 'but knew that we were not in a position to deal with a serious situation.' Airborne planning for an operation called Musketeer had begun with a small transport staff team from RAF Transport Command working with Headquarters 16th Independent Parachute Brigade in Aldershot. Angered by Gamal Abdel Nasser's nationalisation of the Suez Canal on 26 July 1956, Britain and France began to plan a joint operation to re-occupy the Canal Zone. Plans were made for a drop south of Alexandria, but attention subsequently switched to an assault centred on Port Said. Initial planning was based on dropping a light-scale brigade in two lifts but, as Corporal Grout had already deduced from the state of the brigade's equipment preparedness, they were not really configured for a high intensity conventional parachute assault. 'So we were sent back home to the UK for intensive training and to collect the necessary armament.'

As the events leading up to the 1956 Suez Crisis unfolded politically and diplomatically, the shoestring nature of Britain's parachute capability became apparent. Lieutenant Colonel Paul Crook was initially alerted in January for trouble in Jordan. They departed at short notice 'in the ropiest aeroplanes you could imagine'. Private Coles in B Company flew to Cyprus in an uncomfortable Second World War Shackleton. 'Not only was it cold,' he recalled, 'I think I counted all the rivets on that aeroplane.' 3 PARA were returned to conduct a battalion practice jump at Imber on Salisbury Plain in August, but nothing was clear. 'This period was a great strain on the men as they did not know what was happening,' recalled Corporal Grout. 'My demob was actually held back because of the Suez Crisis,' complained Lance Corporal Harry Wivell with the battalion. 'I was fully expecting to be home for my 21st birthday – the Egyptians have a lot to answer for!' The CO of 3 PARA recalled how on Monday 29 October his battalion was fully committed clearing terrorists in the Paphos Forest in Cyprus. Tension in Egypt had apparently cooled but he soon began to pick up indications that his battalion would be required to conduct a parachute assault. He was not formally told this was indeed the case until 1 November. They were to jump five days later, twenty-four hours ahead of the projected Anglo-French amphibious landings.

British air transport designs to replace the American C-47 Dakota were not particularly distinguished. The Vickers Valetta had more speed and range but paratroopers had to negotiate the main wing spar box, 18 inches high and 12 inches wide inside. This was no mean achievement weighted down with a heavy container and parachute ready to jump. The Handley Page Hastings with four engines was a two-door side loader like the Valetta. Both were more suited to air-land rather than parachute delivery. The French, due to jump near the British, had the rear-door cargo-carrying Noratlas, which could carry 35 paratroopers against the Hastings 30 and Valetta's 20, the latter only a minimal improvement on the previous Dakota. The proposed parachute assault was on a city, so space to drop was at a premium. El Gamil airfield just to the west of Port Said was chosen and would enable a rolling up of the coastal defences that would otherwise hinder the proposed sea landings. It was 1,600 yards long, but the troops would have to jump preceded by their heavy equipment platforms. Neither the Hastings nor Valetta aircraft could drop any of the current army vehicles or guns in any case. Moreover the Valetta's single-door exit meant there was barely space to drop sticks of 20 along the proposed runway length.

Britain's parachute capability 11 years after the previous high point at the Rhine was in a parlous state. Reservists had to be assimilated and refresher trained to bring the reduced Parachute Brigade Group up to full combat strength. Some 106mm anti-tank recoilless guns had to be purchased from the Americans and their crews trained on the new weapons and special containers introduced to drop them by air. Mounting would have to be from Cyprus because of the limited ranges of the aircraft, and the island had space for only a battalion's worth of aircraft. The French 2nd Colonial Parachute Regiment (2nd RPC) with their superior Noratlas aircraft possessed the easy familiarity of recent combat experience in Indo-China. Whereas the British conducted one large-scale annual exercise, the French jumped every month and were completely at ease with the rapidly approaching P-Hour. Unlike the British, they had been ready since August.

'Jeeps – we had to find them first,' recalled MT Sergeant Tukovich with 3 PARA. 'That was a bit of a problem, because there weren't many jeeps in Cyprus, so I spent a number of days meandering from one ordnance depot to another, collecting any old wreck which called itself a jeep and pinching spare parts.'

The aircraft could only drop Second World War vintage vehicles. Seven jeeps and four trailers and six 106mm anti-tank guns were to be suspended and dropped from spars, mounted 1945-style, on the Hastings over the airfield in the first lift. Equipments were checked as they arrived, creating some anxiety because much of it came later than scheduled, incomplete or unserviceable. By Friday 2 November all the aircraft and equipment was in place, a testament to focused airborne determination, improvisation and ingenuity. Eighteen Valettas and Hastings would drop the first wave of paratroopers. 'Dropping a jeep from under the fuselage, with a few men as well in the back and seven other Hastings in the personnel role enabled us to end up cramming everybody in with 668 people,' remembered 3 PARA's Air Adjutant Captain Geoffrey Howlett. 'Personal loads were incredibly heavy,' he recalled, 'signallers and the mortar baseplate people were carrying loads that were heavier than their own bodyweight.' Parachute reserves were left behind. They had only just been introduced and as they were going to jump low it made little difference; it was preferable to jump with the extra ammunition.

Attacking a defended airfield had been the Arnhem nightmare and a battle-losing distraction. There was little choice at El Gamil. An Egyptian company was sited on the airfield itself, another nearby in a cemetery to the east and another company beyond supported by two 37mm anti-aircraft guns and three Russian SU-100 self-propelled tank guns. These formed the coastal defence west of Port Said. Talaat Badrawi was one of the many civilian militia irregulars who had rushed to join up when the Suez Crisis unfolded. 'Most of us, the young people, decided we were going to defend the country,' he declared, but they were untrained. 'We didn't really know what we were going to do,' he admitted. Cases of Kalashnikov rifles still coated in grease were handed over and they were told, 'these are your rifles.' He was a member of the Cairo militia and nervous. 'Everybody's a parachutist and somebody had just come down from the sky,' he recalled after hearing a burst of militia test firing into the air. 'It was a very tense moment and we were scared.' But Cairo was not to be the target.

'On 4 November 1956 I was 21 years old, but there was no birthday party,' recalled Harry Wivell with 3 PARA, 'I was too busy packing equipment.' 'We were not too busy to attend one of the most moving open-air church services I have ever attended,' remembered Major Michael Walsh, commanding A Company. Conducted by Padre Horace McClellan from the tail-board of a three-ton lorry, 'the men of the battalion group, sun-bronzed and bare-headed, prayed for safe deliverance'. Paramount to all was the fact they were following in the footsteps of their epic predecessors, the men who had jumped in North Africa, Normandy, Arnhem and the Rhine. 'Now it was our turn,' reflected Walsh, 'to uphold and to honour our elders in the first airborne operation since 1945.' Forward Air-Controller Captain Bill Hancock with 3 PARA recalled how 'during the planning everyone was neurotic about Arnhem and the failure of communications'. As a consequence all radios were duplicated and rifle company men directed to jump with spares. There was nothing more to be done. As Michael Walsh reflected, the battalion group was confident, well led, fit and hard trained. 'Tomorrow it was going to be put to the test.'

Dust and smoke was still rising from shattered buildings and defence positions at 0715 on 5 November after the preliminary fighter-jet strafing and bombing at El Gamil when the British aircraft stream hove into sight. They bore down on the runway line flying east to west with the sun streaming directly in their eyes. The heavy drop fell free at the western extremity from aircraft, stepped up in pairs at 100-foot intervals in blocks of six, with each block separated by 15 seconds. 'Engines were feathered back and our speed dropped off,' Michael Walsh recalled, feeling very concerned because, 'looking down I could only see the sea, no land, nothing.' El Gamil airfield was a narrow strip 1,600 yards long and 500 yards wide between El Manzala Lake and the Mediterranean. Contrary cross winds would push men either over the sea or lake. With the heavy drop released first, any overshoot would result in paratroopers denied space on the restricted pax DZ and having to exit over the Egyptian-held sewage farm coming up. Companies were tactically loaded inside different aircraft so that they dropped as closely as possible to their nominated objectives. First out in all the aircraft was Walsh's A Company and he now faced a dilemma. 'Should I leave my aircraft to drop into the sea? Agony decision! Resolved by *Green On – Go!* And bang – out I went.' As he swung out into the slipstream he caught a momentary glimpse of 'the narrow DZ below and the control tower, yellow in the Mediterranean early light – all was well.'

Corporal Tony Lowe 'was weighed down with enough equipment and rations to double my own bodyweight', he recalled. He was 'Tubby' Butler, the 16th Brigade Commander's batman and bodyguard. Strapped to his equipment was a Bren LMG with six full magazines of ammunition and six 36 hand grenades. 'I felt rather like a pregnant duck!' he later admitted. Each man with equipment weighed over the 350lb peacetime limit of the X-type parachute used. The flight had been crowded and he was sweating profusely with the amount of equipment wrapped about his body. His descent was over very quickly. 'We'd flown in at 600 feet, the lowest we could go, and with my weight in equipment it only took around 20 to 30 seconds to hit the sandy desert floor with a hard bump.'

Egyptian defenders were aghast. In spite of the air attacks they still did not really believe the British would invade over an issue as slight as Suez Canal nationalisation. 'As soon as you saw the soldiers coming down with parachutes we started shooting at them,' recalled

Egyptian irregular Ahmed Helal. 'It was my first time,' he declared, 'I was happy to kill even one of them, I was happier than God can grant.' 'We went to the El Gamil airfield,' remembered another militia irregular Hag el Araby Fadl after being warned just before dawn that foreign troops would be landing. 'So when we saw them coming down in their parachutes, we started shooting.'

'Carrying, as we did, more than 100lbs of equipment in our weapons containers, there was a good deal of anxiety about getting out in time,' remembered Lieutenant Sandy Cavenagh, the 3 PARA medical officer jumping from a Valetta. They had to cross the main wing spar at knee height in 'a cramped and awkward little twin-engine transport plane'. Speed was vital, 'since we knew that machine guns covered both ends of the airfield which was just long enough to take a stick of 20 men.' As he pitched out he remembered the lovely colours, absent now from the many black and white photographs that show the event: 'Lavender sky, slate-blue sea, buff sand, airport control buildings exactly where they should be, an enormous black cloud of smoke streaming away from them, fed by a great tongue of flame.'

He noticed 'glow worms buzzing all over, and a lot of shooting'. His ironic reaction to this was, 'We must be giving them hell,' but it was all incoming fire. As he sensed the pull of his parachute opening, 'I felt a smack in the right eye, which then registered nothing but white fluff.' He had been struck by shrapnel. 'The blow was too hard to hurt,' he recalled, 'but I knew that whatever hit me must have gone in a long way and probably out the other side.' Dark puffs of smoke and crackling flashes were bursting about the Hastings aircraft now coming overhead.

'The slipstream hits you at about 120 mph,' recalled Harry Wivell, jumping from a Hastings, 'you have to be positive and force yourself out of the door, otherwise you'll be blown back into the aircraft.' Once outside 'the sense of relief is incredible', he recalled as the excessive weight of his kit bag was taken up by the parachute harness, dangling on the suspension line he released below. 'No time to lose; every second counts,' he realised. 'It is calculated we will only have half a minute in the air at the near suicidal jump height of 600 feet.' He had to quickly spot a place to land. Corporal Grout in the Assault Pioneer Platoon, jumping number 2, remembered, 'my aircraft was hit in the tail by flak and filled with dust a few minutes before jumping.' 'Keep out of my way,' his number 1 Sergeant Meadows shouted, 'you've got a hundredweight of explosives in your pack!'

B Company, landing near a pill box at the eastern end of the drop zone, experienced heavy casualties during the descent and shortly after landing. 'The very first thing I saw when I landed,' recalled Private Jonathan Bennetts, 'was I rolled over and landed right next to an individual who had half his face blown away.' It was a shock. 'His cheek was torn out and half his jaw was gone and he was screaming, 'what do I look like?' There was little Bennetts could do except say, 'relax, it's all right, you're going to be OK.'

Corporal Tony Lowe quickly orientated himself from the control tower billowing black smoke, burning from the preceding air strike. Using the cover provided by oil drums strategically placed around to hinder air landings, he set off. 'I remember seeing the sand spitting up around my feet from the bullets being fired at us from the Egyptian side,' he recalled.

Within ten minutes 85 per cent of the troops and heavy equipment loads were on the ground. Two men landed in the sea on the north side of the drop zone and another was killed as he descended into a minefield. Five aircraft flew a double run, still under fire, to get the remainder of their soldiers out. Nine aircraft were damaged but all made it back to Cyprus. Twelve men were wounded by machine gun and mortar fire. There were some lucky escapes. Geordie Landford fell over the wing spar in his Valetta, picked himself up but exited the aircraft too late. Fortunately he landed in shallow sea water. 'I went into the sea and they was all firing at me,' he recalled, 'and I was laying face down in the sea and breathing through my arse-hole!' Within 15 minutes air strikes were flying back over in support of the paratroopers and, 45 minutes after the drop, El Gamil airfield was secure. Major Mike Walsh recalled there were only two palm trees on the airfield and precariously swinging eight feet above ground from one of them, amid a storm of fire, was Private Pugsley from his company. One of Walsh's platoons 'going like hell, firing for all they were worth, swept past him,' heading for their immediate objectives. As they ran past they could plainly hear him damning his misfortune, looking up at his suspended 'chute and exclaiming, 'Cor – fuck me!'

Fifteen minutes after the El Gamil assault, Noratlas transports dropped the 2nd RCP on the French objective at Raswa. They cleared the aircraft in 10 to 15 seconds, achieving a half mile spread, well within the mile needed to clear a Hastings. The aircraft flew a tight formation of pairs stepped up at 100 foot intervals in boxes of six with 15-second intervals. This meant some dropped as low as 400 feet to achieve the crucial compact landing required on such a restricted drop zone. 'Although the jumping altitude had been reduced to 150 metres, 30 metres less than the normal minimum,' explained their Commander Colonel Château-Jobert, 'the stretch of water as seen from the air seemed much vaster than the land emerging from it, and the risk of drowning was rather alarming!' The Raswa DZ was only 150 yards across and bounded by the sea, roads, the Canal and lines of trees. The first objective was the two bridges near the waterworks crossing the interior basin waterway, a vital link on the road between Port Said and Suez. General Jean Marcellin Gilles, commanding the French airborne task force, directed operations from aerial Noratlas command post, another French initiative learned in Indo-China.

'On went the klaxon horn, a second of buffeting and blankness and then the gentle swaying accompanied by the sigh of relief,' recalled British Captain M.P. de Klee, a pathfinder, jumping with the French. Fire was heavy, he remembered, 'anti-aircraft shells were bursting above us and the Noratlas aircraft were weaving and jinking all over the sky to the north.' Looking about he saw 'Frenchmen drifting down and firing from their parachute harnesses'. Château-Jobert quickly appreciated, 'they had become the target for automatic weapons, which were trying to pick them off as they floated down.' Some of the leg valises suspended beneath the parachutists exploded in mid-air and mortar shells were erupting on the drop zone below. 'The DZ might well have been a battle scene from an American film,' thought de Klee, 'littered with parachutes and abandoned equipment, dead Egyptians and wounded Frenchmen, spurts of sand and earth with all the accompanying noise.' Fortunately the DZ was heavily pitted with holes and craters, enabling the landing paratroopers to take cover.

Pierre Leulliette recalled the rush as 17 paratroopers in his stick cleared their side of the aircraft in 15 seconds. 'From impulse, as if frantic at seeing the broad back of the man ahead suddenly drop away, each of us in turn goes through the door,' he recalled, 'his breath suddenly cut off.' During a brief free fall 'our eyes close, our legs fold – then the opening – the incredibly brutal wrench to the whole suffering body'. Dropping low, they were on the ground within 20 to 30 seconds. He found one of his sergeants dead, suspended from a palm tree, 'slowly dripping blood into the sand', shot on the way down. The bridges were strongly defended and one was blown during the rapid assault conducted in short sharp rushes until the opposite bank was secured. A second drop came in at 1517 to reinforce the first. After a series of intense fire fights the French had killed 203 Egyptians and taken 138 prisoners by the end of the first day, losing ten dead and 41 wounded in the process. They saw a second British lift of five aircraft arrive the same afternoon, dropping the last of 3 Para's men and equipment platforms.

C Company 3 PARA was meanwhile spearheading the battalion advance west to east from the airfield, attempting to roll up the coastal defences before the amphibious landings planned for the next day. Air strikes preceded the advance through the cemetery complex beyond the sewage farm, which bordered blocks of flats. Although the Egyptians fought hard in defence, they were less aggressive and competent in attack. They were psychologically and tactically caught off balance. 'How could a rifle fight against a war plane?' questioned Egyptian irregular Hag el Araby Fadl. 'We were hiding in the cemetery and a war plane came flying above us and dropping bombs.' The results were truly macabre. 'We saw graves blow up and corpses swirling around in the air.'

'If anyone has seen pictures of Dante's *Inferno* it would be a pretty good vision of the cemetery,' described Private Jonathan Bennetts with 3 PARA: 'Because when we got there, there were these disinterred corpses, enormous mausoleums with bits and pieces of them falling down and collapsing on themselves under fire. There were Egyptian soldiers running around all over the place . . . There'd be half a body here and half a body there. Coffins sticking up, quite a few dead Egyptian soldiers and quite a few live ones.'

It was hard, fast and very much like house to house fighting, claimed Bennetts, ironically adding 'grave to grave' with grenade and Stirling sub-machine gun. 'Paras don't take prisoners,' declared Sergent Bob

Read, caught up in the same fighting. 'Didn't then, you hadn't the men to guard them.' Ruthless determination to succeed and no support apart from air until the sea landings the next day, impelled a pitiless attitude toward resistance. 'You're out to survive,' confirmed Read, 'a few hundred against potentially thousands and something's going to get in the way, be a problem – get rid of the problem – you kill a lot of people.' Company commander Mike Walsh appreciated the intensity of the close-in fighting. 'All our soldiers knew it, if they took any prisoners, these were to be treated humanely.' But the Egyptians fought on. 'Your training is ultimately to kill,' explained Sergeant Read. They were in a desperate predicament. There could be no retreat. 'Your training becomes instinctive – you kill.'

Resistance in the cemetery was broken. 'When we realised that nearly three-quarters of us were killed,' recalled Hag el Arby Fadl, 'we pulled out – we ran away.' Jonathan Bennetts retrieved a post card from the pocket of an Egyptian soldier he had killed amid the debris: 'I wanted to see who it was. This was the first person I'd ever killed to my knowledge. I looked at that photograph a few times over the years and certainly reflected on how easy it is to take a life when you have a gun in your hand.'

These were conscripts reliving the harsh lessons of World War Two. Aided by air strikes, the cemetery was fought through, killing 30 Egyptians at no loss to themselves. The battalion consolidated their positions that night. At dawn the amphibious fleet was visible off the beaches of Port Said.

El Gamil was the last and only occasion the Parachute Regiment has conducted a parachute assault under fire since 1945. Suez in 1956 became an airborne watershed of sorts for the British, because their last parachute attack was to coincide with their first ever helicopter insertion. The sea landings were conducted alongside commando helicopter assaults in support.

Helicopters with their limited lift capability had only been used for limited troop ferrying and medical evacuation roles. There were serious doubts about their vulnerability to fire, which stymied their full tactical potential. After the final briefings, at 0400 on 6 November Royal Marines from 45 Commando were on stand-by on the flight decks of aircraft carriers HMS *Ocean* and *Theseus,* waiting for the call forward. Marine Ray Turley, watching the early morning sun break through, remembered it was 'so exciting, you couldn't believe it you know, it was the very thing you'd joined up for.' They were waiting to lift off. 'Here we were actually doing it – we couldn't believe our luck.' At their disposal were six Whirlwind helicopters, which could carry five Marines each and six Sycamores, able to lift three. All had been stripped of non-essentials and were ready for action to fly with the Joint Helicopter Unit. This had previously been designated experimental but the label was quietly dropped so as not to influence morale. Flying alongside were ten more Whirlwinds belonging to Number 845 Royal Navy Squadron. At 0600 they received the code word to proceed.

'Just as we were about to get into the helicopters,' recalled Second Lieutenant Nick Vaux, a cheerful naval commander announced over the ship's intercom: 'We've just received word that 45 Commando can expect heavy opposition ashore.' That was the last word the groups of threes and fives received as they boarded. Waves of helicopters began to take off. Like a parachute assault, the immediate transformation from inactivity to delivery into the centre of a fight was to be traumatic.

'We were flashing across the water, 50 feet above the sea,' recalled Marine Ray Turley, looking through salt-stained helicopter portholes: 'and then suddenly we're over the beach and I could see the shacks which are on fire, still burning, the beach huts, then we were down, down, down and suddenly we hit the deck in a cloud of dust.'

Bulbous clouds of black smoke were clearly visible curling up over the city. The Marines inside the helicopters were momentarily blinded by intermittent flashes of early morning sunlight streaming through portholes as the machines wheeled into the line of approach. Emerald blue sea provided a pleasing contrast to the more austere white-washed facades of multi-storey flats coming up near the shore. Dust and smoke momentarily obscured the rubble strewn buff-coloured waste-ground next to the statue of de Lesseps, the French Canal builder, the selected landing site. Each helicopter wave orbited over the objective, allowing individual machines to swoop in for a rapid touch down. Men disembarked under sniper fire, as one was hit he was immediately pulled back inside.

Turley recalled the pell-mell nature of the sudden bump down: 'We leapt out, not knowing where we were really,' a 'hot' landing site, still under fire: 'I don't remember if we were told we were going to be near the de Lesseps statue. We landed, hit the deck, bang – out through the doorway, which we'd been trained to do. Run out for 20 yards, fling yourself down, and come on aim into a firing position for all round defence.' The sound of receding helicopter blades beating the air was replaced by more sinister noises: 'There's bullets flying over and the sound of gunfire and you think to yourself – God we're here!'

Helicopter frames were found to be able to absorb more punishment than previously envisaged. One Whirlwind attempting to disembark a reconnaissance group in the Egyptian Stadium received 22 hits during the aborted landing attempt before taking off again. Another badly hit Whirlwind from 845 Squadron ditched amid a huge splash of rotating spray 40 yards from the *Theseus*, but the crew and wounded were saved. The helicopter group had landed 425 Marines and 23 tons of stores by 0830, vindicating the experimental conceptual work that had been directed by Royal Navy Vice Admiral Sir Guy Sayer.

The frantic motion and release of pent-up energy experienced by soldiers leaping into action from hovering helicopters under fire was not far removed from post-parachute landing euphoria. Soldiers moved aggressively into the assault hyped-up with adrenalin. The psychological low that follows the energy surge accentuated the threatening situation soldiers found themselves in, a veritable cold-shower immersion into battle. Turley, forced to take cover with others behind a wall, recalled, 'We were cowering down, really scared, the noise from the machine gun fire around us was just really terrific.' Vicious cracking noises denoted the missiles breaking the sound barrier as they sped past, accompanied by the thumping reports of the guns being fired. Cool heads are able to detect the likely range of the weapon engaging by calculating the interval between 'crack and thump'. Turley's thoughts were elsewhere and more related to immediate survival. 'All through my head I thought *that's it*,' and began to conjure up images of his parents: 'It may have been a one or two second instant and I thought, God! I'm not going to see them again. I'm only 19, never had sex, never been in love, never been with a woman. I felt so despondent for about three or four seconds – because I thought I was going to die – and I thought *It's so unfair!*'

The Egyptians fought back tenaciously in some areas and fled in others. Die-hards were a problem in the close-in street fighting that followed. 'The British didn't think the people in Port Said would fight in this way,' recalled Ahmed Helal, a recently recruited militia fighter. 'They thought the people would welcome them and overthrow Abdul Nasser, but it was the opposite, people fighting to the death.' 'People who did not know how to use guns just held sticks,' Hag el Araby Fadl fervently claimed, 'even women came out to fight with us.'

Differentiating between fighters and non-combatants in street fighting is difficult. 'We would reach the ground floor of a building and work our way up and clear it, clear each floor,' remembered Marine Corporal Colin Ireland, 'killing everybody who was in a room.' 'The die-hards were stuck in flats,' he recalled, so they used 106mm recoilless weapons to get them out. 'We saw this emplacement disappear in a cloud of smoke and dust and people screaming.' No time was lost because 'the routine then is to charge and kill anyone who is still alive'. They came across a boy, who was probably about 12 years old: 'I saw one sergeant take the weapon away, cuff him around the ear and tell him to bugger off. He could hardly carry the weapon, a kind of under-nourished little lad.'

Ireland reflected on the difficulty of handling the women and children that suddenly emerged amid the fighting. 'You don't want to kill civilians or children particularly,' he explained, 'it would make you hesitate slightly, unless he was firing at you, and then you wouldn't hesitate.'

'Of course in those days, I've got to admit it, without any hesitation, they were "wogs" to us in the Marines in 1956,' remembered Ray Turley, and 'gippos' to the paras. 'We freely used that expression,' he admitted, 'and we considered them less than mortals.' This was a continuation of the colloquial disregard the British soldier always had for his enemies: 'Fritz', 'Hun' and 'Jerry' for the Germans and 'Nips' for the Japanese. Like the French in Indo-China and Algeria, they had a racist attitude to Asians and Arabs. 'We had no qualms about shooting them,' Turley pointed out. 'We were carrying out the aims of the British Government. Take the Canal we would and the devil take the hindmost.' After being deployed in the Middle East with all the pre-conflict riots and confrontations around the Canal Zone it was a time to settle old scores: 'they were just trouble' in any case.

The international community did, however, 'take the hindmost'. Though militarily successful, the Suez invasion aroused such world-wide condemnation that Britain and France were compelled to agree to a cease-fire within 48 hours. They had advanced 23 miles down the Canal.

Lieutenant Sandy Cavenagh, treating the wounded from 3 PARA in a hastily requisitioned garage, was initially taken aback at the massive influx of casualties, way beyond his previous experience. 'Their wounds were appalling,' he recalled. 'There was a sucking chest wound, a large mortar splinter in the knee, a divided brachial artery'; despite his own wound he set to work. 'If we go on losing chaps at this rate we're in for real trouble,' he began to think. 'We'd taken 600 odd and if we could lose 20 in half an hour or so, I thought this was going to be a real party.' But it was all over in three days. Major Mike Walsh was pleased at their success. 'But what we couldn't understand was why our advance had been halted.' They had killed over 100 Egyptians and captured many prisoners and material at a cost of four killed and 32 wounded.

The paratroopers and Marines were being introduced to the new realities of post-1945 soldiering. Technology had provided superior fire-power and greater air mobility on the one hand, but improved communications created frustrating political checks and restraints on the other. The soldiers were more philosophical about this than the politicians, diplomats and senior officers. 'If we had carried on as we wanted to for a further five days,' recalled Corporal Grout with 3 PARA, 'there could have been 20 lives lost and half a battalion wounded!' 'I thought it was simply terrible,' declared Lieutenant Sandy Cavenagh: 'We'd gone off on this bloody expedition, which nobody could justify and these boys had been ruined and died for nothing. That doesn't seem right.'

Suez was the last time the British Parachute Regiment jumped to war in the twentieth century. For the rest of the period it was to be involved primarily with counter-insurgency operations and short-term conventional conflicts. As one old soldier told Lance Corporal Harry Wivell after the operation: 'At least at Suez you could see who the enemy was, no bullet in the back there.'

10

COLD WAR AIR MOBILITY

COLD WAR AND COUNTER-INSURGENCY

As British paratroopers were gathering at Cyprus for the Suez drop, two regiments of the Soviet 31st Guards Airborne Division were air-landing at Veszprem airport at the eastern end of Lake Balaton in Hungary. Another two regiments from the 7th Guards Airborne Division were also landing at Tekel in the suburbs of Budapest. The 108th Regiment alone flew in with 99 Illyushin IL-12D aircraft. Twenty-four hours before P-Hour at Suez, Marshal I.S. Konev launched Operation Whirlwind, to suppress the Hungarian Uprising of November 1956. Russian airborne (VDV *Vozdusthno-Desantnye Vojska*) troops bore the brunt of the heaviest street fighting in Budapest between 4–7 November. They were to receive 18 per cent of the decorations, despite being less than 6 per cent of the Soviet troop strength engaged, losing 97 dead and 265 wounded from the total of 720 Russian troops killed and 1,540 wounded. As many as 2,000 Hungarian fighters were killed and 19,000 wounded, the majority civilians. Operation Whirlwind changed the perception of the Soviet General Staff to its airborne arm, rebuilt by General Vasily Filipovich after 1945. Their efficient and rapid air deployment, proven reliability and combat effectiveness on the ground placed them at the forefront of the post-war Soviet Army.

It had not been until the Tushino Air Show in 1956 and Red Square parades the following year that western observers realised the Soviet Union had rebuilt and trained a large airborne army. At Tushino a complete assault force with light vehicles and guns was landed by helicopter, an event as ground-breaking as the 1936 Kiev parachute drop and manoeuvres. Clearly the Soviets were ahead of the west by introducing specialised air-portable self-propelled guns, heavy lift tail-loading aircraft and a variety of parachute dropping platforms, as well as training at least six divisions of parachute troops. Russia's technical shortcomings revealed during the Second World War had been compensated for by the tenacity and quality of her airborne troops. Confusion with transport aircraft availability was settled by the creation of the VTA Transport Command, and special airborne weapon systems were introduced to upgrade the fire-power of Soviet paratroopers.

'Here, one out of every two paratroopers is an outstanding man in military and political training,' boasted the commander of the Guards, Airborne Chernigov 'Red Banner' Division. Paratroopers were trained, he claimed, for 'conducting combat operations deep in the enemy rear, in isolation from their own forces'. They mastered their weapons and equipment, were subjected to psychological conditioning and able to fight superior enemy forces and were prepared 'not to lose self-control in the most complex and seemingly hopeless situation'. To do this they had to be 'hardy, cold-blooded and decisive'. Soviet paratroopers, the commander claimed, possess 'high political awareness and ideological conviction'. By 1968 they were wearing their own distinctive blue and white striped shirt, symbolising their elite status and the cornflower blue beret, paying homage to their Second World War traditions and exploits.

'Not every soldier can stand being rolled over by tanks,' explained General Kuz'menko and Soviet paratroopers were taught to endure just that. The aim was 'to convince him not to fear the armoured equipment, and teach him how to neutralise them with all the weapons available'. Tank 'roll-overs' and other risk-taking activities conducted across high trainasiums, parachute tower descents and leaping over blazing fire zones were all instituted to instil courage, daring and aggression in recruits and propagate their elite status. Guards Private N. Vizyuk 'demonstrated how to throw oneself under the tank between the tracks', his commander explained, while Guards Sergeant G. Chernyavsky was made to 'jump on a tank from trees and buildings' and demonstrate how to 'blind a tank with a cape or other available objects'. Many Komsomol party member youth activists were encouraged to join the paratroopers. Bad weather parachuting was practised to promote stress while concurrently honing parachute skills as well as promote bonding through shared hazards. Care was taken to mix veteran jumpers with novice conscripts to alleviate early parachuting fears. 'At the airfield, before loading parachutists into the aircraft, the Communist and Komsomol activists engaged in relaxed conservations, with a kind word and joke,' Kuz'menko benevolently explained. 'They often fly with the new men and are the first to hit the silk.' Soviet Sky Men regarded themselves as special and they were reserved for special tasks.

Around 2030 on the evening of Monday 20 August, in the midst of the 1968 Czechoslovakia reform crisis, an Antonov An-24 aircraft with Aeroflot civil airline markings landed at Ruzyne airport on the western outskirts of Prague. It taxied to the far end of the runway and remained parked in the gathering dusk. It was a Soviet Air Force air-control aircraft available on station should the control tower have to be knocked out. A second Aeroflot flight came in from Lvov in the Ukraine a few hours later. Civilian government officials and KGB agents dispersed around the airfield. The control tower was told to shut down the airport at midnight to all outgoing or incoming flights.

At 0337 two Antonov An-12 military transports flew in, escorted by MIG-21 fighter aircraft. As the ramps came down over 100 paratroopers from the 2nd Company 7th Guards Airborne Division trotted out of the back and quickly dispersed and sealed Ruzyne airport. The division operations group and the KGB special operations team swiftly seized the control tower. Soon the huge An-12 transport aircraft began landing one after the other at 30-second intervals, quickly manoeuvring to the runway sides. Troops and vehicles from the 7th Guards Airborne Division streamed off the ramps. By 0430, paratroopers hanging from the sides of ASU-85 and ASU-57 self-propelled assault guns and a small number of BRDM-2 armoured anti-tank vehicles were moving through the streets of Prague. Two 70-seater tourist buses and four cargo trucks were requisitioned to accompany them. Even as the inhabitants of Prague began to wake at daybreak on 21 August, paratrooper columns were converging on the presidential palace and party headquarters in the city centre.

Aleksandr Dubcek, the Czech First Secretary and leader of the Reform Movement, was surprised, alongside most of the Czech government during their weekly meeting. Czech government officials had learned of the impending invasion that had begun on the border by telephone, but assumed it would take 10 to 11 hours before the Soviet Warsaw Pact contingents would begin to drive into Prague from the Polish or German borders. By 0615 the entire first wave of the 7th Guards Airborne Division was down on the ground at Ruzyne airport. It was an impressive performance: the 108th Guards Parachute Regiment, complete with the anti-tank, air-defence, engineer and division communications battalions. Assault teams were immediately formed up by the division operations group commanding from the control tower and swiftly despatched into Prague. There was sporadic firing and vehicle and barricade burnings but the coup was virtually bloodless. Unlike the Hungarian experience of 1956, the sudden appearance of Soviet troops had prevented Czech civilians from seizing weapons from police stations or army barracks. Dubcek had attempted to telephone Leonid Brezhnev in the Kremlin as his government was lined up against the wall in his offices. The telephone was ripped from his hands by a young paratrooper officer. 'The Soviet Army has come to protect Socialism in Czechoslovakia!' he was informed.

NATO came to the sobering realisation the Soviets possessed perhaps seven airborne divisions, which at any moment in the Cold War nuclear stand-off in Central Europe, could appear in their vulnerable rear areas. With Soviet air mobility came the awful recognition in the west that such troops would be utilised even under nuclear war conditions. 'The parachute troops will be dropped into an area immediately after it has been taken under fire by tactical nuclear weapons,' explained Soviet Major General Rudakov, 'to occupy, hold, and if possible, expand the sector.' Exercises were regularly carried out to practise locating NATO nuclear missile-launching sites. Exercises took place in bad weather, at night and involved long marches crossing wind-felled trees, barriers and water obstacles. 'No matter how well and carefully the enemy's nuclear missiles were camouflaged and concealed from outside eyes,' Yarenko reported, 'and no matter how vigilantly the enemy defended them, the paratroopers were able to detect and "neutralise" these important installations, and then escape pursuit by a forced march.'

In 1970 two regiments from the 8,000-strong 76th Guards Chernigov Airborne Division dropped in 22 minutes while a third regiment air-landed during a simulated nuclear exchange exercise during Byelorussian military district manoeuvres. New An-22 heavy transport aircraft flew in bulky SA-4 air defence missiles and FROG-5 tactical nuclear delivery rocket systems. It was clear that both the modernisation of the VDV Airborne and the related VTA Transport Force in the 1970s signified that Soviet intervention – unlike that of their primarily seaborne potential adversary the United States – if it came, would be by air, preceding ground advances. NATO as a consequence, had to plan on stationing considerable forces in the interior of Europe as well as border security.

The British drop at Suez in 1956 had been conducted using World War Two vintage small arms, with aircraft container loads wing-mounted or slung beneath fuselages as they were in 1945. None of the aircraft were configured to drop modern army vehicles or artillery pieces. The Beverley box-shape transport, about to be introduced, was criticised already in the post-Suez after-action report as 'expensive and unsuitable' compared to the French Noratlas or US C-119. It entered service two years later and was the first tail-loader, but payload and range limitations meant it had to be based within a few 100 miles of its objective DZs. Cyprus was required to fly-in the 16th Parachute Brigade for the Jordan crisis in 1958, whereas the United States could fly its troops to the Lebanon the same year in one six-hour hop from Germany with the newly introduced C-130 Hercules aircraft. A conversation one 3 PARA soldier had with a Jordanian counterpart after the air-land summed up the state of Britain's parachute capability. 'You can't be the battalion that jumped at Port Said!' claimed the Jordanian. 'They were all wiped out by the Egyptians.' Perception, aided by Middle Eastern propaganda, appeared not so far removed from the truth. The British replaced its Beverley, Hastings and Argosy transports with the C-130 in the mid-1960s.

British paratroopers became a predominately air-land light infantry force during the 1960s and 70s. The only exception was a brief NATO parachute reinforcement contingency interlude, before the 16th Parachute Brigade was disbanded in 1977. Quite often British paratroopers flew to operations on chartered civilian or RAF converted airliners, an incongruous precursor to quite often intense low-level counter-insurgency operations. 'The first sight I had of Aden was from a VC-10 that I flew in from Gatwick airport,' explained Private Boot, with B Company 1 PARA in 1967. He transitioned through one flight from mundane European routine to exotic Middle Eastern surroundings. 'It was not what I expected; instead of tents and camel trains I could see well made roads, modern buildings and streams of cars. That made Aden look more like a suburb of London than a little terror-stricken state in the Middle East. I remember thinking that Aden surely couldn't be as violent as the newspapers made out, not with all the civilised buildings and machines I could see from the aircraft. Later, I learned I was very wrong.'

Boot's battalion formed part of the force deployed to cover the final British withdrawal from Southern Arabia and hand-over of the protectorate at Aden. He emerged from the aircraft like a tourist. 'By the time I had stepped on the tarmac,' he recalled, 'every piece of clothing I had on was sticking to my sweating body.'

'The Kalashnikov cracked again and again,' recalled Private Murray with 1 PARA, watching an Arab terrorist firing at them from a mosque 200 yards across a road. This was his first armed contact in 'Sheikhers', the notorious Sheikh Othman district, a renowned trouble-spot in Aden town. 'This was our first taste of action and judging by the way I felt I didn't want to see any more. When I started training for the Parachute Regiment at the Depot I had not bargained for anything like this. We had trained in the extreme cold of Salisbury Plain. Now we were in Aden in the extreme heat which, at times, grew almost unbearable, but I had joined the Army of my own volition, so, I'd virtually nothing to complain about, at least that's what I kept telling myself.'

Boot's experience replicated the French para experience in Algeria, 'of being really scared in a dirty narrow Arab street and seeing people who have one ambition; to kill a British soldier', he recalled. These men, like all airborne soldiers, had something of the pioneering spirit about them, they sought adventure and the exotic. 'Now it is all past,' he reflected later, 'a time in my life I will never forget.'

Two years before, the 2nd Battalion of the Parachute Regiment was flown to Singapore to complete a crash jungle-training course in

January 1965, in response to Indonesian threats to destabilise the young Malayan Federation on its Borneo border. This typified rapid 'Out of Area' air-portable fire-brigade interventions conducted by the 16th Parachute Brigade outside Europe during the Cold War. Between 1962–3 and 1965–6 parachute contingents flew into Bahrain to conduct trouble-shooting riot-control operations. The typical British parachute soldier was no longer a conscripted National Servicemen; they were now professional volunteers. They were flown to areas of tension to conduct helicopter-supported counter-insurgency sweeps, such as 3 PARA in the Radfan mountains north of Aden in 1964. The volunteers were attracted to soldiering in exotic locations.

The 2 PARA main body was not ready for operations in Borneo until the end of March 1965, after completing its basic jungle training. Companies were lifted in and then supported by helicopter. Intensive patrolling and establishing fortified jungle bases along the Indonesian border became the modus operandi to block infiltration. B Company, occupying a fortified base at Plaman Mapu, typically conducted ten-day jungle patrols, followed by 36 hours' rest. Conditions were humid and muddy with the onset of the monsoon rains. 'As the Company Sergeant Major I made sure the first we did when a patrol came back in was to give everyone a tot of rum,' recalled CSM John Williams: 'Then they had a shower, de-loused, got new gear, read their mail, had a couple of big hearty meals, because this was the first cooked food they would have had in the period, then a reasonably goodnight's sleep.'

The next day they were briefed and got ready for the next ten-day patrol, which would set off that night. 'The pressure was very much on,' Williams explained, 'it was killing.' Many of the soldiers were new volunteer recruits, whose training had been cut by three weeks so that they could be included on this operational tour.

At first light on 27 April as the new recruits were on their 36-hour change-over, the company base was assaulted in the pouring monsoon rain by an Indonesian battalion. Only 35 men were in camp because the rest were out on patrol. The attack got inside the perimeter, killing and wounding those on security. The normal practice was to sleep with boots, slacks and basic belt and ammo pouches on. This enabled a rapid stand-to which saved the position amid chaotic close-quarter jungle fighting. As John Williams described:

The situation was very confused but I shouted to the men around me that anything that came in front of them was enemy. There followed a savage close-quarter battle with these Indonesians. One shot when one was able to but in nine cases out of ten it was hand-to-hand stuff, actually one to one combat. It was very frightening but it became a survival experience, because one knew if one didn't manage to push them out of the position or kill them, then they would kill you and overrun the position.

Williams lost an eye as he doggedly manned a general purpose machine gun. Covered from head to foot in slippery mud, the still half-dressed paratroopers beat off repeated Indonesian attacks for two hours. Only 15 men were left standing, covered in mud and blood and patched with field dressings when it was over. It is likely that over 50 casualties were inflicted on the Indonesians who, fearing retribution from helicopter reinforcements, withdrew. Williams never forgot the subsequent helicopter evacuation with the other wounded. 'We've come through,' he declared with some relish: 'And the people who had done it were 18 and 19-year-old soldiers, not battle-hardened veterans but 18 and 19-year-old boys who nine months before had been long-haired hippies on the streets of our cities and towns.'

Cold War could often be hotly contested.

Counter-insurgency operations were often conducted in conditions below the level of violence in conventional conflict. Paratroopers were often at the forefront of these 'undeclared wars'. Their highly mobile, aggressive no-nonsense approach, combined with creative solutions to seemingly intractable tactical problems, made them peculiarly suited and eminently deployable. Nevertheless, they were often accused of operating at the harsher end of the spectrum of violence. During World War Two they were seen as shock troops and were employed in the same vein in world-wide counter-insurgency situations. In Indo-China the attitude of the French paras and Foreign Legionaries meant little distinction was made between non-combatant civilians and the Vietminh. Henry Ainley, a legionnaire, recalled, 'rape, beating, burning, torturing on entirely harmless peasants and villagers were of common occurrence in the course of punitive patrols and operations by French troops, throughout the length and breadth of Indo-China.' How was anyone in any case able to differentiate between civilians and Vietminh irregulars? 'Well, hell they are only *bounyouls* [natives],' Ainley was told and, 'who the devil cares, anyway?'

The Jews called the 6th Airborne Division the SS of the British Army, recalled Major John Waddy with 9 PARA, 'not because we were brutal in any way, but because we stuck to the rules of road blocks and who was arrested.' These were difficult circumstances, fending off boatloads of illegal immigrants who had survived the Holocaust in Europe, and 'anti-terrorist operations against very expert terrorists'. Paratrooper responses to atrocities were harsh and robust but generally exercised with disciplined restraint. Stone-throwing Jewish children likened red-bereted paratroopers to 'red poppies with black hearts'. Counter-EOKA operations in Cyprus likewise became a ruthless game of cat and mouse, whereby occasionally the requirements of the intelligence war transcended the legal safeguards laid down by the laws of armed conflict. Sergeant D.S. Scott's 2 PARA company captured Polycarpos, the intelligence officer working directly to Colonel Grivas, the EOKA leader. 'The gentleman spent two eventful hours in my company before being handed over to higher formation,' Scott admitted. 'He was in a somewhat reduced condition at that time . . . gentleness is not a characteristic of 2 PARA.' The outcome, as Scott explained, was 'unearthing many caches of arms, clothing, ammunition and food', causing 'havoc amid the Troodos mountain gangs'. The behaviour was not unprecedented and indeed featured in operations in Palestine eight years before. 'We just acted naturally,' explained Andrew Gibson-Watt, an officer during the Palestinian troubles. 'We did what we thought we had to do under the circumstances.' This was a new form of conflict and nobody could tell them what to do.

'I'm fed up with people always equating paratroopers and torture,' declared Lieutenant Robert Andre in Algeria, referring to detained insurgents. He claimed he rarely saw it and likely shared the view of Cesar Delbellow, another conscript parachutist, who pointed out, 'it's nonsense what people say, making martyrs of them all. Most of these people,' brought in for interrogation, 'were simply scared and they'd talk, not necessarily spontaneously, it might take a day or two.' Many paratroopers simply handed over prisoners to intelligence, suspecting what might result, and not going out of their way to view it. 'Some changed sides and became *Harkis*, others maybe got killed – I don't know – they weren't our concern any more,' Delbellow explained.

'Do I torture or let the bombs go off?' asked Robert Andre, voicing the inevitable dilemma of such operations. But, he pointed out, 'There's a difference between that and what went on in lonely outposts – that stemmed from fear, from sadism and not from trying to stop terrorist bombings.' They were in an unsustainable position. 'There's no such thing as a clean war,' he declared, 'war itself is a terrible thing.' France was prosecuting an undeclared and pitiless war in Algeria with widespread torture and intimidation inflicted by both sides. Conscript soldiers were under enormous psycholog- ical pressure and subjected to hideous atrocities themselves. 'You'd rather kill yourself than be taken prisoner,' declared paratrooper Gregoire Alonso who served in Algeria between 1957–9. 'The word was that paratroopers and legionnaires would get killed out of hand.' He saw no mutilated dead because he claimed, 'paratroopers did not leave their dead behind, we took them with us or went back for them.'

Counter-insurgency, unlike the conventional wars of the twen- tieth century, was conducted in smaller groups, fighting amid the civilian population, away from higher commanders. Personal moral choices had therefore to be made and then reconciled by soldiers. Pierre Leulliette was part of General Jacques Massu's 10th Parachute Division, which conducted a ruthless systematic strike-breaking campaign against the FLN in Algiers. Members were forced back to work at gunpoint. Their ringleader Ali la Pointe and his hard core remaining terrorists were blown to pieces during a French counter- insurgency operation. Algiers was totally subjugated and some 3,000 individuals died in suspicious circumstances. 'What am I to them, till proved otherwise,' declared Leulliette, regarding the local population, 'a bloody brute with hands as red as the scarlet beret I am noncha- lantly holding.' He described their distasteful role: 'For three months, our life will be ugly. We shall be doing the hard and thankless job of policemen. A few will enjoy it, others will be miserable, some won't be affected one way or the other, but the majority will miss the mountains where they were only asked to fight an enemy capable of self–defence. Here it will be all–round street corner ambushes, secret arrest, foul play, and murder.'

Systematic torture was shaming and not easily hidden from the media. Massu and his paratroopers argued that, while regrettable, torture was a necessary tool in the armoury against the FLN. The streets of Algiers were cleared, but open knowledge that the French state appeared to sanction torture and summary executions by its soldiers caused unease within the French Army and widespread condemnation in France and the wider world. The total commit-ment of the Paratrooper and Legion units to the *pied noir* concept of *Algérie français* resulted in an open bid to seize power and subvert the French government through a military putsch in Algiers in April 1961. The mutineers held Algiers for just five days. Simon Murray, serving with the 2nd REP at the time, recalled, 'De Gaulle has brought up tanks in France and threatened to shoot parachutists out of the air if a drop is made.' The coup fell apart and the 1st REP found to be at its core was disbanded in perpetuity. In July 1962 Algeria was given its independence.

From 1969 the British Army, including its parachute battalions, was much involved combating Republican and Loyalist terrorism and counter–insurgency operations in Northern Ireland. The tran-sition, following similar operations in Bahrain, Aden, Radfan and other areas of the Middle East and Cyprus, could not have been greater. This time the enemy spoke English and indeed sheltered among British citizens. Operations had to be conducted with sensi-tive restraint in conditions not far removed from the hot situations that had been confronted in the Middle and Far East. 'During the briefing the Intelligence Officer warned us all that all roads had been barricaded and that quite a number of gunmen would be active in "Free Belfast",' recalled a 1 PARA observer, commenting on intern-ment riots in January 1972:

How right he was: at every roundabout and road junction on the way in there were scenes of the most indescribable destruction, with overturned burnt-out lorries, buses, cars and even a fire engine. Everywhere the streets were littered with broken glass and the crushed remains of giant lamp standards felled across the road. As D Company approached the still burning barricade astride the Monagh Road leading into Turf Lodge, the first burst of automatic fire crackled above our heads – we hoped.

Fighting conducted on the streets of the United Kingdom was different from that of two years before in Aden. Paratroopers came up with new and creative tactical solutions to deal with similar problems. The ringleader of the riot could no longer be shot by an army sniper. The new solution was aggressive seizures and arrest by 'snatch-squads', lightly equipped pairs of fast-moving paratroopers, who would sprint forward armed with batons, protected by the third member of the squad with a rifle. During violent clashes in the Bogside area of Londonderry on 30 January 1972, 13 civilians were shot dead by paratroopers in 25 minutes. An ongoing inquiry into the loss of life is still reviewing the controversial and emotionally charged incident, but accurately or not, the perception emerged that the paratroopers were unnecessarily harsh and unsurprisingly ruthless in suppressing disorder. Seven years later 16 paratroopers were killed in two explosions at Warrenpoint in County Armagh, likewise viewed as an atrocity. It was a shattering setback, 'yet there has been no gloom,' remarked a 2 PARA witness of the tragedy. 'Deep sadness, yes, anger and frustration at our ability to hit back, yes; but no despondency.' 'So we go on,' was the determined response that encapsulated the aggressive fighting spirit of airborne soldiers world-wide, whatever the type and level of conflict being fought.

Northern Ireland helicopter operations began in the early 1970s and were sustained until the mid-1990s. Some military bases like Bessbrook on the Southern Irish border were virtually exclusively reinforced and supplied by helicopter. Covert operations, troop moves, observation and re-supply were all conducted by helicopter – the longest sustained campaign ever mounted by the British Army and key to countering insurgency. But until the mid-1960s the helicopter had never been seriously considered a viable option for transporting air-mobile troops across the conventional battlefield. The Vietnam experience was to change all that.

'SLICKS' AND 'SNAKES': AIR MOBILITY, VIETNAM

Following the French ejection from Indo-China after Dien Bien Phu, American assistance to the Republic of South Vietnam combating a Vietcong insurgency from the north expanded from a handful of military advisors in 1954 to 539, 400 troops by 1969. The support by the United States of the South against the Communist North developed into the largest and most intense of the proxy wars physically fought during the Cold War.

Manoeuvre over the jungle and tree-covered terrain of Vietnam was, as the French discovered to their cost, a perennial nightmare for command and control. 'Two things struck me,' declared US Marine second Lieutenant Philip Caputo on arrival in Vietnam. 'The first thing was the intense humid heat, it was really something, it was like Florida times three; then the sheer beauty of the country, it is an exceptionally beautiful country.' Early operations by the newly arrived 173rd Airborne Brigade in 1965, joining the 1st Brigade from the 101st Airborne Division, were conducted as heliborne countrywide 'fire-fighting' missions. These quickly became repetitive walks in the sun looking for an elusive enemy who melted away at will. 'You stumbled around out in the jungle until you ran into a bunch of guys from the other side, who were also stumbling around and you mixed it up and got into a fire-fight,' remembered Philip Caputo. 'You would go out there and there seemed to be these ghosts, shooting at you from the distant tree lines,' he recalled. 'That seemed to be the nature of the war.'

Former wartime 82nd Airborne Division Commander James Gavin had written a provocative article in *Harper's* Magazine in April 1954 entitled 'Cavalry, And I Don't Mean Horses!' He presented a visionary glimpse of high-powered helicopters freeing infantry from the tyranny of terrain, enabling warfare to be conducted within a three-dimensional spectrum at a dramatically increased pace. In 1962, Secretary of State Robert McNamara, impatient at unimaginative army development, directed the Howze Board, chaired by Lieutenant General Hamilton Howze commanding the XVIII Airborne Corps, to establish new tactics and doctrine.

The relevance of helicopter mobility to the developing situation in Vietnam was recognised and tests conducted just as new jet propulsion engines were transforming helicopter lift capability. The Bell Company of America produced the XH-40 Iroquois and later the UH-1B Huey, able to carry seven troops with a crew of two or three stretchers with an orderly and two sitting casualties; or 3,000lbs of freight out to 360 miles. Howze conducted 40 test exercises using 150 army helicopters, which included extensive live firing and, significantly, anti-guerrilla exercises. He recommended the establishment of Air Assault Divisions and Air Cavalry Brigades with an anti-tank capability. The 11th Air Division (Test) was redesignated the 1st Cavalry Division (Air Mobile) and in June 1965 was directed to move to Vietnam the following month.

Four helicopter workhorses were to be employed and these constantly evolved in capacity and design throughout the war. Observation helicopters were used to find the enemy, utility machines to carry air assault troops, recover wounded and replenish ammunition. Cargo helicopters would carry artillery support and set up fire bases and provide logistic lift, and attack helicopters would give direct fire support and escort the fleets on the move. Lieutenant Colonel Harold 'Hal' G. Moore, commanding the 1st Battalion 7th Cavalry in this new formation, was optimistic as his unit was moved to Vietnam: 'If this system could be made to work, the soldier's time would be spent fighting, not walking or waiting for a truck or wondering whether supplies would ever find him. Like the knight on a chessboard, we could now attack the flanks and rear of the enemy in a matter of minutes. The helicopter would add a 110 mile an hour fast forward capability to ground warfare.'

Major General Harry Kinnard's 1st Cavalry Division deployed to An Khe in the Central Highlands, through which it was anticipated North Vietnamese regulars were planning to infiltrate to attack in the South. He had more than 400 helicopters and 16,000 men with 1,600 vehicles. The new soldiers were not selected, they were light infantry assigned from existing divisions. Harold Moore found many Second World War and Korean veterans, including ex-airborne, in his battalion. They had come from the 2nd Infantry Division, assigned to the new 11th Air Assault Test and then came to him as the 1st

Battalion 7th Cavalry. The core strength of his battalion was the sergeants, many combat veterans, most of whom had served three to five years in the battalion. This cadre of experienced senior NCOs in the American Army was to steadily dissolve and die during ten years in Vietnam.

Morale and expectations at the start were high. 'We had the ability to get above the ground and not be hindered by terrain, trees, and mountains and everything else,' recalled Captain John Bahnsen, developing new helicopter tactics with his 'bandit platoon'. Until now the Vietcong and North Vietnamese regulars had dominated ground wherever they chose. The new air cavalry would contest this supremacy. 'You could move your soldiers very quickly by helicopter,' Bahnsen observed, 'it was revolutionary at the time.' It appeared that true air-mobility in the visionaries' purist sense was to emerge on the modern battlefield for the first time. It was a far cry from the stand-by French parachuting companies flying out from Saigon and Hanoi in the early 1950s.

The new air assault philosophy had its own peculiar language. Collectively helicopters were called choppers, birds, ships or helios by soldiers. Attack helicopters were labelled gunships generally and specific types such as the AH-1 Cobra attack helicopter were snakes or hogs, depending on armament. The ubiquitous utility helicopters carrying troops were affectionately termed slicks or school buses. Command and control machines were Charlie-Charlie or Chuck-Chuck and medical evacuation helicopters, often Huey slicks, were called dust-offs, after their medical call-sign. Crews were often two pilots, one the senior aircraft commander, with a crew chief in the back who doubled as door-gunner, with occasionally a fourth man as an extra gunner. Boeing CH-47 Chinook cargo helicopters flying in support were called forty-sevens or shit-hooks. To an outsider listening to the marshalling and complex radio jargon required to coordinate an air assault, the language would have seemed virtually unintelligible.

Lieutenant Colonel Hal Moore's first substantial air-mobile battle was launched on 14 November 1965 in the Ia Drang Valley, 37 miles from Pleiku City. His mission was simple in the extreme: he had to 'conduct an air assault and find and kill the enemy'. Reconnaissance was the precursor to any air-mobile assault and not easy. Colonel Moore flew a high-level observation flight before the insertion, more to identify potential landing sites (LS) rather than for intelligence of enemy troop concentrations, which was loose. OH-6 light scout helicopters normally reconnoitred these and the surrounding area. Experienced pilots became adept at identifying recently used jungle trails and the square angular outlines of bunkers from the air. Lieutenant Hugh Mills, piloting an OH-6, recalled paying 'strict attention to contrast, colour, glint, angles and movement'. Anything suspicious was marked with coloured smoke and attacked by a Cobra gunship, often pairing up as part of the mission.

'You actually *could* smell concentrations of the enemy from the air,' Mills recalled. 'I don't know if it was a lack of personal hygiene, their mostly fish diet, or a grim combination of the two. But you could catch a very distinctive odour when enough VC [Vietcong] were together in one place – a pungent odour, heavy and musk-like.' Ground reconnaissance was also conducted by Ranger 'Recondo' teams. 'They gave you coordinates, go here and see what you can find,' Gary Hillyer was told. They were hazardous missions he remembered because, 'I'm working in *their* backyard and it's not *my* backyard.' Fellow operative Cal Rollins agreed: 'We went ahead of everybody. You are extremely apprehensive initially, I know I was.'

The next stage was to mount the operation from the helicopter pick-up point. Soldiers would form up in seven-man sticks preparatory to boarding the lines of aircraft that would land in prearranged stick-order. Moore's first wave into Ia Drang Valley was carried by 16 slicks carrying the equivalent of a rifle company of 80 men. As he boarded Moore reflected, 'what I was really fearful of was if we made heavy contact before I had all my troops in.' His intelligence was sparse. 'I knew the enemy had been retreating into the Ia Drang River Valley.' They would be isolated on the ground for the first half hour.

Pre-flight briefings could be cursory. Moore's battalion had spent much time practising assault landings from helicopters and mastering the complexities of artillery, tactical air support, aerial rocket artillery and sorting out the all-important flow of helicopters in and out of the battle zone. 'Brief your men and let's get going,' was often the final word from company commanders to platoon commanders who, having done the drills so often, already knew in outline what was required. As the flights arrived to pick up the troops the down-draft flattened and ruffled thick grass and the stench of aviation fuel was in the air. Last minute orders were hardly comprehensible in any case as they were drowned out by the whine of engines and clatter of helicopter blades as they began to take off. Attention focused on finding a safe place inside the helicopter, heaving aboard rucksacks totally weighed down with as much ammunition as they could physically carry. Some sat on their helmets or extra flak jackets, despite being told not to in the interests of flight safety. Rifles were held muzzles down to avoid damage should there be any accidental discharges.

Heavily laden Huey slicks dipped their noses to pick up air speed and gain momentum as they flew out in a cacophony of reverberating sound. 'God, there was nothing like a combat assault when you went in with twenty, thirty, forty choppers,' recalled CH-47 Flight Engineer Jim Soular with the 1st Cavalry Division. 'I mean Hueys everywhere and gunships and CH-47s – just that energy! It was an adrenalin rush.' These were enduring memories to veterans. 'I loved it. I hate it now, but at the time, as a kid, I loved it,' insisted Soular. 'Every time those turbines started winding up, I just thought, *yeah!*'

There were no doors on the Slicks and the wind whipping through open troop compartments offered blessed relief from the oppressive jungle humidity. 'It was so beautiful out,' recalled Lieutenant Dennis Deal, flying into Ia Drang Valley with Moore's battalion. 'It was like a national park – really, really peaceful.' They were approaching the base of the 900 foot Chug Pong Mountain that overlooked the river valley, part of a 174 square mile massif straddling the border with Cambodia. Flight formations were commonly arrowhead, a diamond shape or a staggered column referred to as 'trail', dictated by the size of the landing sites coming up or any observed enemy in the vicinity. Flying at 1,500 to 1,000 feet was considered a safe approach, out of range of most small arms fire. Side-door guns would be test-fired shortly after departure, the 100 knot slipstream quickly dispersing cordite fumes. Nearer the landing sites soldiers would perk up, having been warned touch down was imminent as the sudden descent for the fly-in began. The last few miles were flown low-level, 'nap of the earth'.

'Until I had actually taken that helicopter fall from 1,500 feet to treetop level,' explained Lieutenant Hugh Mills, 'I had no idea how dramatic and violent, how exhilarating and terrifying that manoeuvre was.' Hueys abruptly plummeted into a near-vertical descent 'and your stomach felt as though it had just been pitched into the roof of your mouth'. High speed at treetop level below 100 feet made it extremely difficult for an enemy ground gunner to hit a helicopter that flashed past fast and low offering an exposure of only seconds. The double canopy of forests and rubber trees was virtually impossible to see through from above and below. 'The next thing you noticed was how close you were to the trees – how they suddenly were rushing by your feet at what seemed like hundreds of miles an hour,' Mills remembered. 'All I could see was a sea of green – a blurred rush of foliage beneath the ship's bubble that was totally indistinguishable.' The sensation often induced air-sickness, the antidote being to look at something in the open compartment that was not moving.

Vietcong and North Vietnamese (NVA) regulars were taught to aim by leading ahead of the aircraft based on their angle of approach and airspeed and then firing into engines and pilot's compartments. The reality, as Mills explained, was, 'the Vietnamese ground gunners had a habit of firing right at you without applying any lead.' They therefore had to fly fast. 'By moving across the ground at 60 to 70 knots, their rounds would often hit three or four feet behind the ship.' In the mid-1960s they had yet to learn. Battle-wise NVA regulars did not expose their positions as readily as the Vietcong irregulars, observed Mills: 'Waiting to shoot meant a better chance at knocking low, slow flying scout ships out of the sky.' The preferred tactic was multi-direction fire from .5 and 12.7mm anti-air ambushes. United States forces were to lose 2,066 helicopters from the 12,000 sent to Vietnam between 1961–71; a further 2,566 were lost in operational accidents, mishaps and the weather. The losses, however, should be viewed in the context of some 36 million sorties flown.

At 1017 hours with machines approaching at low-level, the landing sites erupted from being an oasis of peace to fire zones as multiple artillery strikes descended as if from nowhere. Lieutenant Colonel Hal Moore's first company fly-in was supported by two batteries of artillery fire shooting from a fire base set up by helicopters five miles away. The final minute of preparatory fire was 30 seconds of aerial rocket artillery, followed by another 30 seconds of helicopter gunship strafing. 'Gunship pilots were loud, cocky and boisterous,' recalled Chuck Carlock, flying with the 71st Assault Helicopter Company. 'I believe that the slick pilots really liked gunship pilots to act like that,' he explained, 'because, while sitting in a landing zone with tracer bullets flying everywhere, it was comforting to look up about 20 to 30 feet and see those boisterous loud-mouths blowing the hell out of Charlie [i.e. "Charlie Cong" – Vietcong].' Cockiness exuded confidence and hence a measure of security.

Slick pilots viewed the approaching landing site through cockpit windows that slanted from horizon to horizon as they flew in, closely hugging the terrain. Ragged black and grey smoke untidily denoted the perimeter, often with coloured smoke marking the centre. Wispy rocket trails could be made out streaking ahead of steeply diving gunships. 'Every LZ [landing zone] was an unknown,' recalled Crew Chief Joseph Fornelli, flying slicks, 'whether you were bringing troops in or taking them out.' As the first helicopter hovered to touch down the perennial question was, would it be a hot LZ?, because as Fornelli emphasised, 'It's a very spooky and scary thing to do.' 'We went in as fast as we could, trying to maintain an element of surprise,' recalled pilot Jack Swickard. 'We didn't want them to hear us coming, so if we went in low, they wouldn't hear us until the last minute.' Two white phosphorous rounds striking the landing site was generally the signal that artillery fire would cease, fired two minutes before the first machine landed, working on the 'big sky, little bullet' principle.

Lieutenant Colonel Moore's 1/7th Battalion was flying 16 slicks at a time, flanked by four groups of four gunships flying protection. They landed at 1037 hours in waves of eight, rotor pitches deepening the noise as they rapidly descended. High-pitched whines from the decelerating engines was accompanied by chattering machine gun fire as M-60 door gunners sprayed the surrounding undergrowth at the edge of the landing site with suppressive fire. Each helicopter needed 20 to 75 yards to land, whipping up dust, sand and debris from the rotor wash. This gravel and other hard flotsam took a toll on engines and rotor blades. If it was a hover delivery, soldiers would descend with legs over the side and step off the skids. Actual landing was preferable, reducing the injuries from jumping out with heavy equipments, but increased the risk of mines and rotor strikes from steep slopes cloaked by long elephant grass. Even if one man came under fire, the standard procedure was all out. Moore's men quickly debussed and fanned out from the helicopters, firing weapons into the surrounding foliage and then going to ground to cover the machines taking off. Flights could deposit their loads at intervals between 15 to 30 seconds. As the suppressive fire died away and the sound of the departing helicopters began, Moore realised his landing at LS X-Ray had not been contested. That brought some relief but did not allay tension.

Within minutes of landing, an unarmed North Vietnamese soldier was captured. 'He told us there were three battalions, that's over 1,500 enemy – North Vietnamese,' Moore recalled. 'They wanted very much to kill Americans but hadn't found any.' Twenty-nine-year-old company commander Tony Nadal recalled the interpreter asking where the enemy was and he pointed to the base of the mountain towering above them, barely 500 yards away. 'Well, that kinda made us all pucker up a little,' remembered Lieutenant Dennis Deal, looking on. Moore was understandably apprehensive when a sudden burst of heavy firing indicated his lead platoon was already engulfed in a serious contact. 'My worse fears were realised,' the inherent vulnerability of all airborne actions, 'we were in a heavy fire fight before all my troops were in.' His launch base was 14.3 miles away, a 13 minute 15 second average run. Only 80 men had landed in the first wave, but later lifts could carry more, 90 to 100 men as helicopters burned off more fuel. The immediate urgency was to fan out and cover the landing site from all directions, to safeguard reinforcements and re-supply.

An air assault was always a surprise for both sides. The intensity of fire around the embattled perimeter rose as subsequent waves were landed. The second wave at 1120 raised Moore's strength to 160 against an estimated 1,600 North Vietnamese beginning to mass around his perimeter. By 1445 he had all three companies down and heavily engaged but had already lost the use of the larger clearing on the landing site for helicopter landings. He was fighting an intense battle with piecemeal reinforcement against elements of the 66th and 33rd NVA Regiments at odds of about ten to one.

'When you landed,' recalled North Vietnamese Lieutenant Colonel Nguyen Huu An, fighting the sudden American intrusion at X-Ray, 'you landed right in the middle of three of our battalions of the 66th Regiment, our reserve force. It was the strongest we had.' The North Vietnamese found the mass employment of helicopters unsettling. Air cavalry could arrive in strength from any direction, with little or no warning. Ia Drang was the first conventional engagement against American troops. 'Many things were new to us,' recalled Lieutenant Colonel Dang Vu Hiep with the North Vietnamese command group. 'Sometimes we had to fight against airborne units with 400 helicopters,' he reflected. 'With all these choppers they seemed terribly strong. How could we manage it?' Ia Drang was to be a searing learning experience. 'Fighting the US wasn't easy,' he claimed, 'we had to rely on our creativity.' They discovered the best course of action was to string out American forces, luring them from their large bases. North Vietnamese General Chu Huy Man was very clear what he wished to derive from this particular engagement: his aim was 'not to liberate land, only to destroy troops'. Lieutenant Colonel Nguyen Huu An echoed the icy resolve of his general as the North Vietnamese regulars converged on the American 1/7th Battalion isolated at Ia Drang. 'We discovered that we couldn't destroy a battalion at one go, but had to do it one company at a time'.

Lieutenant Dennis Deal fought his men to within 100 yards of a platoon cut off beyond the LS perimeter. He found the noise from this intense fire fight he was engaged in, even as air support pounded the North Vietnamese attacks around X-Ray, completely beyond any previous experience: 'Now here was a jet engine screeching and falling apart, shot to hell, and we did not hear it. That's how loud the battlefield was. And there was a napalm strike 300 metres to our rear and we didn't hear that either. It was terrifying. I was terrified to the point of insanity.'

His mission to rescue the platoon transitioned from a break-in assault to his own unit fighting for its very survival. 'I'm telling you without exaggeration that at any given second there were a thousand bullets coursing through that small area looking for a target – a thousand bullets a second.' One of his first losses was his platoon sergeant Wilbur Curry and likely his most valuable man. He knelt down and took his head in his arms and 'focused on him as hard as I knew how because I never wanted to forget what this wonderful man looked like'. Fifteen of his men were killed and wounded within minutes. The platoon was literally disintegrating before his eyes. He recalled trying to rescue a single simulated casualty during a Ranger training exercise that had reduced the 24 men earmarked to carry him to 'almost hallucinogenic exhaustion'. Now he realised he had only sufficient men left for four to carry each casualty, which soon reduced to three. 'OK, we'll go with three,' he told himself, but when he was reduced to only two effectives per casualty, 'I knew I had to get out of there otherwise, I was going to have to leave people behind, which is not an option.' The rescuers now needed saving themselves.

Flying into a hot or contested LS like X-Ray was the nightmare scenario for air-mobile soldiers in Vietnam. Pilot Larry Liss recalled having to extract a cut-off South Vietnamese (ARVN) unit under intense fire. 'The second time around you know how bad it is; then you know the possibility of a continuous existence,' he recalled. The logic of shrinking odds was inexorable. 'It doesn't take a genius to figure out that the perimeter had passed the shrink and ultimately there would be no perimeter; and ultimately little or no odds.' 'It's really scary to be in a helicopter and coming down into that stuff,' confessed Marine 2nd Lieutenant Philip Caputo. 'You don't know if the chopper's going to get blown out of the sky or what.' Aircraft noise inside the fuselage added to the unreality of the experience because what was happening outside tended not to register. 'It was noisy as hell because we tore out all the sound-proofing,' recalled CH-47 Flight Engineer Jim Soular, 'so you could see where the bullets went through and what lines were hit.' Bullet strikes caused electrical shorts that set wires burning and as Lieutenant Chuck Carlock described: 'When numerous hits came through the floor of the helicopter, the heat of the bullets, mixed with the heat of the aluminium shrapnel [from the floor] and some hydraulic fluid on the aluminium shrapnel gave off a burning smell. This burning smell alarmed me.'

Crews developed an instinctive sense of just how much punishment their machines were enduring or could take. 'I could tell if things weren't working right just by feeling the hull of the ship or listening to the pitch of the rotors and transmissions,' Jim Soular claimed. Twenty-two-year-old pilot John B. Morgan recalled the sense of detachment that might result working above the noise of decelerating engine whine and beating rotor blades during a landing approach under fire: 'We could hear the machine guns and rockets launching second-hand through our head-sets as the gunship drivers chattered over the air-to-air VHF. Impacting rockets and our own door guns added to the roar of battle.'

A distinctive new sound was added to the din, 'the sound of bullets passing through the aluminium aircraft skin'. They struck the centre of the LS still descending at about 15 knots. The chopper rolled and the rotor blades came apart and scythed through the rear of the machine. 'I remember watching the LZ and the tree line do a beautiful slow roll to the sound of crumpling metal, and I remember wishing that this would come to an end.'

It was worse for those sitting at the front, because they could see what they must endure. 'The hair on the back of your neck stands up,' described Captain John Bahnsen, flying search and destroy missions. 'You get some chills down your spine when you realise what's going on, especially when they shoot back at you.' Vertical seat adjustments could be lowered as slicks came in to land and 'you hear the thunk-thunk-thunk in the back of the helicopter and you know they're trying to kill ya.' 'Eye-ball defilade, we called it,' recalled Lieutenant Hugh Mills, when the seat was dropped down inside the armoured plate: 'Then, when enemy rounds cracked through your aircraft, only your legs, part of your arms, and the top of your head were outside the armour plate. The front of your body was protected by the chicken plate, and the .45 holster tucked neatly between your legs, protected your masculinity.'

'You could see the artillery and air-strikes going in,' recalled Delta Company Commander Captain Ray Lefebvre, flying in the lead heli-copter during a reinforcement run into X-Ray LS in the Ia Drang Valley. 'You watch this battle and listen to all this shit going on, on the radio.' He was very apprehensive because the transition from forward flight to hover was a highly vulnerable moment. 'The pilot Bruce Crandall turned around, shook his head and made this face like,

"Man, what are we getting into?"' They had to actually fight their way through pith-helmeted North Vietnamese khaki-clad troops as they jumped off the helicopters. There was banging on the back of armoured seats from incoming rounds as pilots sought to take off. Plexi-glass chin bubbles were bursting with bullet impacts, while instrument panels spluttered with smoke and sparks. Crews did not hear incoming fire for the most part until the damage was registering in front of their eyes, or they could feel the impacts from strikes. Both pilots held onto the control stick should one be hit. They could not risk engaging surrounding muzzle flashes around them because they rarely knew the precise location of their own troops.

Squad leader Sergeant John Setelin recalled his crew chief shouted, 'We are going into a hot LZ and hover, get your men out fast and head to the right!' He could see men below in khaki and thought, 'We must be really desperate if we're bringing in guys back from R and R without giving them time to change into their fatigue uniforms.' He only realised they were enemy when he saw they were pointing rifles at them. 'When we jumped out, people were firing down on us – the Gooks were up in the trees!' Incoming fire was indescribably intense. 'Picture a fish that you've just brought on the deck of a boat, flopping and flipping,' described platoon commander Dennis Deal, 'that was me on the ground trying to avoid these bullets.' Bracketed by machine gun fire, 'twigs were kicking up, grass, dirt, everything. I mean I was dead.' The North Vietnamese were 'hugging' LS X-Ray to get inside the lethal ring of fire-support and crush the life out of the isolated battalion.

The transitional leap forward in the effectiveness of US air-mobility was its ability to provide the sort of direct fire support the early visionaries of airborne warfare could only dream about. North Vietnamese soldiers, able to cope with limited and poorly directed French air support in the 1950s, had to radically reappraise their tactics to deal with the Americans. Artillery fire-support was lifted in by CH-54 Tarhe 'Flying Cranes' or the CH-47 Chinook. Fire-support bases were located on hilltops. Initial clearance might be done by dropping special 'Daisy Cutter' blast bombs primed to explode just above ground level to topple trees. Advance engineers would then be landed to clear undergrowth with chain-saws, axes and more explosives. Command bunkers were dug in by bull-dozers and trenches and emplacements constructed to take delivery of helicopter-lifted 105mm medium howitzers. Two batteries were shooting in support of LS X-Ray in the Ia Drang Valley.

Despite reinforcement by an additional company, Lieutenant Colonel Moore's original insertion of 450 men was down to a total of 8 officers and 260 men by dawn of the second day. Charlie Company alone of the 1/7th lost 42 men killed in a dawn attack and was rendered virtually ineffective as a rifle company. Moore was outnumbered at least three to one by North Vietnamese regulars and 'It was clear to me,' he recalled, 'that they were very well trained, well armed and they were not afraid to die.' Successive human-wave assaults that threatened to engulf his position led to a desperate Broken Arrow code radio call, which went to all aircraft in range that an American unit was in danger of being overrun on the ground. 'I pulled the chain on everything I could lay my hands on, fighter bomber aircraft, gunships, I had two batteries of artillery – I really poured it on,' Moore recalled. 'Had it not been for that massive fire support we were going down.'

Artillery crews at LZ Falcon supporting X-Ray went without sleep for three days and nights. Captain Robert Barker commanding C battery 1st Battalion 21st Artillery remembered both batteries firing more than 4,000 rounds of high explosive shells on the first day alone. 'On the first afternoon both batteries fired for effect [directly on target] for five straight hours.' This is normally the rate of fire fired for minutes to break up an identified attack concentration, in short a climax, not prolonged fire. One Huey slick pilot, Captain Paul Winkel, briefly touched down at Falcon that afternoon and was amazed to see: 'Stacks of shell casings, one at least ten feet high, and exhausted gun crews. They had fired for effect for three straight hours by then, without even pausing to level the bubbles. One tube was burned out, two had busted hydraulics. That's some shooting!'

Sheets of napalm fire sluiced through the ranks of fanatically brave North Vietnamese soldiers, immediately transforming them into fire-blackened, frantically dancing scarecrows. Convinced one last push would carry the day, they persisted, only to be beaten back by well directed mortar and machine gun fire, the lynch-pin of the defence.

A-1E Sky Raider pilot Captain Bruce Wallace recalled 50 sorties were flown that afternoon, flying precise bombing runs. He watched the Huey gunships at work. Each carried 48 rockets and refuelled every third trip, re-supplied by CH-47s flying in load after load of ammunition. 'To watch four or eight of them at a time manoeuvering up and down and laterally and even backwards boggles a fighter pilot's mind. Those guys swarm a target like bees over honey. I had to hand it to these Huey guys. They really got down there in the trees with the troops.'

Weapons delivery was much influenced by the changes in the aircraft's three-dimensional aspects, involving cross winds, change of wind direction and speeds at different altitudes. Estimating the range and hitting a moving target while flying different angles of attack required skill and dexterity. It was also dangerous work. Gunship pilot Chuck Carlock remembers that eight pilots were shot down, four wounded and one captured during a six-month tour with his Warbird platoon between 1967–8. Pilot Jack Swickard believed: 'The helicopter pilot in Vietnam was twice as likely to be killed in combat as an ordinary soldier.' About one in eighteen never made it back home.

Moore could fight his isolated battle, anticipating like all airborne troops, that he would be surrounded from the start, but secure in the knowledge he could count on direct air support. 'No matter how bad things got for the Americans fighting for their lives on the X-Ray perimeter, we could look out into the scrub brush in every direction, into that seething inferno of exploding artillery shells, 2.75 inch rockets, napalm canisters, 250 and 500lb bombs and 20mm cannon fire and thank God and our lucky stars that we didn't have to walk through *that* to get to work.'

Medical evacuation of the wounded was coincidental with ammunition re-supply. 'They removed the dead and the wounded from my bird,' recalled Major Bruce Crandall, flying casualties back to Plei Me from X-Ray, 'and this act is engraved in my mind deeper than any other experienced in my two tours in Vietnam.' A huge black enlisted man clad only in GI shorts and boots with 'hands bigger than dinner plates' reached inside his helicopter and picked up one of the white soldiers. 'He had tears streaming down his face and he tenderly cradled that dead soldier to his chest as he walked slowly from the aircraft to the medical station.' His grief was simply for a fallen comrade. 'I never knew if the man he picked up was his buddy or not – I suspect not.' 'Maimed and bloody wrecks of humanity were wedged in all over the slick,' recalled Lieutenant Chuck Carlock with the 71st Assault Helicopter Company. A young, delirious and badly wounded black soldier gripped his arm in flight, causing some panic until he was gently patted on the shoulder and calmed down by one of the walking wounded. 'Sometimes, the look in his eyes and his garbled plea haunt my memory,' Carlock confessed. 'I am thankful that I had made it my policy not to look back while we transported these fellows.' The dead went too; better not to view what in other circumstances might be him. 'The memories of the few I did actually see will stay with me forever.' Buckets of water were sluiced through the Huey troop compartments before the ships took off again.

Helicopter extractions under fire to retrieve troops in hopeless tactical situations could be especially traumatic, and this was often the case with Special Forces missions. Jim Soular, the flight engineer of a CH-47, remembers having to extract one platoon of about 30 troops near Kontum through a hole cut in the jungle canopy by explosives in 1967. 'The jungle was just fierce up there, incredibly dense and menacing.' They had to descend into a dark tunnel artificially created within the canopy and 'there was just barely enough room'. They could hardly see five feet ahead as the soldiers 'started to materialise out of the jungle; they had been out so long their fatigues were rotting off.' One man disconcertingly climbed aboard with four or five human scalps hanging from his belt. 'These were bad-looking dudes,' he recalled, 'but I could tell they were just young guys like us.'

'You saw people taking rounds on the ground,' recalled Jim Dopp, a medic crewing a Huey, one of two tasked to extract 100 cut-off South Vietnamese ARVN soldiers under fire in May 1967. 'There were people that were trying to move toward the helicopter that didn't make it.' Enemy forces were no more than 25 yards away, lurking in the undergrowth and firing as they loaded casualties. So desperate was the situation that pilot Harry Liss got out to assist to speed up the process. 'I just said to myself, I'm going to get shot in the back,' he recalled, 'then I'm going to be a paraplegic – all this stuff is going through my head.' The pilots could not understand why they had not been picked off in the cockpit. 'We were just amazed,' declared Tom Bacca, flying the same rescue mission, 'they were shooting people getting on the aircraft, but they weren't shooting us, and we were just waiting – any second.' Five perilous missions were flown under fire, hacking aside the jungle undergrowth with their chopper blades, to gain entry to the narrow track where the troops were forming to extract. 'At one point the soldiers who had been climbing aboard,' remembered pilot Jack Swickard, 'if they came across a body I saw them throw it off the side. We didn't put any of the dead on board, that was room for the living.'

Twenty-two men were perched on the last Huey slick that made it out, with a terrified Vietnamese soldier hanging onto the landing gear skid. 'I reached out and held these guys, I was holding them,' declared Harry Liss, 'and you could see in their eyes that they were elated they got out and scared to death that they would fall off.' Inevitably not all made it during the pell–mell of a hot extraction. The overloaded Huey had to skim forward along the ground to get more air under the revolving blades, like a conventional fixed-wing lift-off, all within the confines of a narrow jungle track. With damaged rotor blades beating aside the jungle canopy and low on fuel, flight engineer Al Croteau peered down: 'In one of those circular pits there was this one South Vietnamese soldier, holding the ground. I said to myself, "Oh my God, we've left someone behind." To this day all I can see is this one individual standing his ground, protecting our lives and we're leaving him there. Never forgotten that.'

Croteau was haunted by this image for 40 years until a chance reunion with one of the pilots, Henry Liss, enabled him to bury his ghost. Liss insisted nobody had been left alive.

Lieutenant Colonel Moore's 1st Battalion 7th Cavalry at Ia Drang was not finally relieved until the morning of the third day when the 2nd Battalion 5th Cavalry, approaching overland, caused the North Vietnamese to at last break off the fight. Moore had managed to relieve his cut-off platoon the previous day. They were traumatised by their experience, surrounded by mounds of North Vietnamese dead, having held their own for 30 hours. 'None of the people who were in the lost platoon were standing, not a one of 'em,' observed

Lieutenant Dennis Deal: 'They were laying down and looking at us like we had totally taken leave of our senses. They were still in a state of shock. They didn't want to get up. Even the men who *could* stand up were so traumatised by what had happened to them they preferred to lay down and be as safe as possible.'

Only seven were left standing. The 29-strong platoon had lost nine dead and 13 wounded, all in the first 90 minutes of combat. The survivors were gently led back into the battalion perimeter. Recondo Ranger Cal Rollins gave one indication of a fraction of their experience. 'I'll be honest with you,' he confided, 'the rush, all that adrenalin gets-a-pumping' during the fire fight. 'It sometimes takes you a whole day to come down off that adrenalin high you had. When it's over, it's, Oh shit! How in the hell did you survive!' The 2nd Platoon Bravo Company had endured this emotional roller-coaster for one and a half days.

Air-mobile casualties, like the airborne missions of World War Two, were high enough to question whether the ends justified the enormous human and material expenditure. Lieutenant Moore's battalion lost 79 killed and 121 wounded, killing a confirmed 634 enemy and perhaps as many as 1,000. 'One of the North Vietnamese bodies had literally had his buttocks shot off and his insides were leaking out a large hole – a very ugly sight,' observed Dennis Deal. As badly wounded as he was, Deal noticed he had booby-trapped himself with a grenade. 'I thought, man, if we're up against this, it's gonna be a long-ass year.' On the following day the 2/7th Cavalry moving from Ia Drang to Albany LS to extract by helicopter was caught in a major linear ambush. During the afternoon and evening 151 American soldiers were killed and 121 wounded, despite killing 403 Vietnamese. Operations continued in the area until 27 November. Major General Kinnard's 1st Cavalry Division (Air-mobile) had killed an estimated 1,519 NVA, wounding 1,178 but the cost to the division had been 304 dead and 524 wounded. This represented one man in 15 of its fighting elements.

The new tactics were confusing to the North Vietnamese; their innate jungle mobility advantage had been compromised by an enemy capability that could come at them anywhere, at any time, from every direction. They could not really cover this new 'vertical flank'. Helicopters could air-assault light infantry, bring in ammunition and take out casualties while providing virtually inexhaustible direct fire support. Practical difficulties remained: locating usable landing sites and accurately coordinating artillery and air support while engaged in close-proximity jungle fighting. Technology could not circumvent the human factor. Helicopter-landed troops tended to shy, moving beyond easy striking distance of landing sites because of re-supply considerations with their light scales and the need to evacuate wounded. There were those that argued armoured cars or mechanised ground units were less vulnerable, better protected and projected greater firepower.

American air-mobile veterans were reluctant to rationally question achievements because, as Dennis Deal explained, 'I hold in such reverence my comrades in arms who were killed and maimed.' He did feel that 'national resolve' was lacking, as well as higher direction in this war: 'The generals who were running this show tried to cover up the fact that we all felt we'd been beaten. We vowed never to forget the people who denigrated this battle by calling our casualties light to moderate. That enraged us. Westmoreland [the Supreme US Commander in Vietnam at that time] would have sacrificed you in a minute.'

Success in war is all about human perception. Sergeant Fred J. Kluge in the 1/5th Cavalry recalled a sergeant from the decimated 2/7th Cavalry caught in the Albany ambush discussing the outcome. 'You know, we won that battle,' he said. 'How do you reckon that?' was the indignant response. 'I know because I counted the dead,' the 2/7th sergeant insisted, 'and there were 102 American bodies and 104 Gooks.'

11

BY AIRLINER TO WAR

OUT OF AREA: AFRICA

On 3 July 1976 four Hercules transport planes flew low over the Red Sea, their silhouettes just distinguishable in the opaque light given off by the setting sun reflecting on the water below. Lieutenant Colonel Joshua Shani of the Israeli Defence Force contemplated the difficulties that lay ahead. They flew low to avoid Saudi and other radar, 'so nobody would see us'. An eight-hour flight of 3,000 miles to Entebbe Airport, Uganda, stretched before them. At the end of it, Shani, flying the lead aircraft, knew he would have to land on a darkened runway 'which is not an easy exercise'.

Sitting in the back of the four Israeli C-130 transports were 30 Special Forces and 200 parachute infantry. 'We took off but we still didn't know if the mission would go ahead,' recalled Sergeant Amnon Peled, 'the government hadn't reached a decision.' Not until the aircraft turned west and headed into the African continent over Ethiopia did the message come though to the force commander, Brigadier General Dan Shomran. All it said was '*Authorised – good luck.*' Shani, the lead pilot, was less worried about death than failure. 'I was 30 years old, and somebody put this responsibility on my shoulder and I wasn't ready for it,' he remembered. As the foremost aircraft in a Tactical Air Land Operation (TALO), everything hinged on his faultless technical performance.

Seven days before, Air France Flight 139 with 12 crew and 246 passengers had been hijacked and flown to Entebbe. Non-Jewish hostages were released, leaving the crew and 105 Israeli passengers confined in an old terminal building at Entebbe secured by at least six terrorists and

306

Ugandan soldiers belonging to President Idi Amin's dictatorial regime. Two German Baader-Meinhoff terrorists had separated Jew from non-Jews. 'Germans! They're doing the same thing,' reflected Joshua Shani, determined not to see a bizarre repeat of the Holocaust 'selections'. 'It made me very angry and ready to kick arse,' he recalled.

A number of raid options were considered, including an approach through Lake Victoria. But as Special Forces Major Muki Betser pointed out, 'the crocodiles in Lake Victoria immediately ruled out the possibility of parachuting into the water.' He added, 'we can cope with many things, but battling with crocodiles was not one of them.' One of the raiders, Sergeant Amir Ofer, pondered, 'we have a very long unsettled account with the Germans.' He locked his jaw in a determined manner at the thought that 'Germans would aid someone hijacking Israeli citizens'. Whatever the risk, they were on their way.

A TALO has always been a risky enterprise, reliant on achieving absolute surprise. Shani would lead four aircraft landing at seven-minute intervals and they would soon stack up on the main runway. Paratroopers would drop off the rear ramp of the first aircraft to place lighted beacons to guide follow-on aircraft. The lead aircraft was crucial, packed with 86 troops, including the command group, a black Mercedes for deception and two Land Rovers. 'Our unit was supposed to storm the building, kill the terrorists and secure the building itself until all the additional forces had landed,' recalled Sergeant Amir Ofer. Major Muki Betser pointed out, 'When a Ugandan soldier sees a black Mercedes approach he stands to atten-tion and salutes.' By a combination of bluff and subterfuge, they would get as close as possible to the old terminal building. 'They would never fire on a vehicle like that,' he explained, 'and by the time they had realised what was going on our forces would have stormed into the terminal.'

The interminable flight was a navigational and logistic feat in itself. There was plenty of time to dwell on the likely outcome. 'You know there is a time when you are flying and flying and flying and you suddenly look at your watch and understand there is no way back any more,' recalled Sergeant Amir Ofer, 'because there is not enough fuel, and we understood – that's it!' Low-level flight turbulence took its toll. Stormy weather and lightning flashes forced the pilots to divert north, close to the Sudanese border. On the final approach to Lake Victoria they encountered a solid mass of storm cloud from ground level to 13,000 metres. There was no recourse but to plough through. 'This was the worst flight I ever had,' admitted Ofer, 'the turbulence! I became extremely sick and threw up maybe ten times – the floor was covered.'

Lieutenant Colonel Shani slipped into Entebbe airport behind a cargo flight towards midnight. The runway lights were still on. 'We landed,' he recalled, 'I don't know why, I just knew no one had spotted us. I knew it – total quiet, nothing moving.' He taxied gently to the end of the runway, feathering his engines to reduce the noise, and turned right toward the terminal building. Ofer cocked his weapon 'the moment the wheels hit the ground'. One of his friends remarked when he held his AK-47 at the ready that 'you shouldn't load your gun within the plane'. 'I told him to shut up,' recalled Ofer, 'this is real war, no rules any more!' They all peered out of the back as the ramp came down and some of the paratroopers dropped off with beacon lights as they went along. 'There was nothing,' Ofer observed, 'a standard airstrip, like all the other places in the world.' The vehicle engines were quietly running.

'I gave the green light to the Mercedes,' remembered Shani, and this and the two Land Rovers festooned with troops gently eased down the ramp onto the tarmac. 'I saw them driving quietly the one kilometre to the terminal.' Another C-130 was already gliding down onto the main runway. Captain Isaac Bakka with the Ugandan Air Force, standing nearby, recalled, 'I hear planes landing and then I hear boot-thumping.' But he did not feel compelled to react. Some of the Ugandan infantrymen deployed around him began to speak to each other in Swahili. He picked up 'maybe the Children of God are coming' and explained, 'That was the joke, the soldiers termed Israeli soldiers "Children of God", like in the Bible.' One of sentries raised his weapon at the approach of the official black Mercedes smoothly coasting toward them in the dark. 'Advance,' he called out, to identify the occupants.

Two low-level *phuts* from silenced weapons sounded and the wounded sentry collapsed. His companion ran off. 'Someone from the Land Rover and Mercedes opened fire at the same time without using silencers,' recalled Muki Betser and 'the element of surprise was lost'. Sergeant Ofer jumped off the rear of the last Land Rover. 'I looked to the left and right, there was darkness.' He could not see his commander, and sped off towards the terminal. 'I wasn't entirely sure what was going on in his head,' recalled Sergeant Amnon Peled. 'I started to run after him.' The raid was now live.

'Someone was in the terminal shooting outside,' Ofer saw as the glass came cascading down. 'He was shooting at me, the bullets,' he gesticulated right and left of his head, 'one was here, one was there, but I was so focused I didn't hear the shots at all, I just saw him shooting.' Training and instinct took over. 'I shot something like three or four shots and all of them hit him: *tac-tac-tac*.' He leaped through the terminal door 'and shot him again to make certain he would not recover'. On entering he was exposed to the two German terrorists, who aimed at his back from barely two metres, but were rapidly cut down by Peled following him up. 'I shot them both once or twice and then kicked their weapons away from them,' Peled remembered. Ofer realised the close call he had experienced. 'What a piece of luck!' he reflected. There was no compassion for the dead Germans. 'Really, I'm not proud I killed someone, but in this situation – I think they deserved it.'

The hostages were caught in the middle of a brief fire fight. 'I remember hearing a noise which to me resembled a box of glass bottles dropping,' recalled 13-year-old Benny Davidson. 'All hell broke loose,' he recalled as his mother shielded his body. He felt 'frightened as hell'. Sara, his mother, saw 'in a second there was such a shooting going around, we couldn't think where it was coming from'. Her son prayed beneath her, while 'all this shooting was around, all these noises, smells and smoke all over'. A loud-hailer announced: 'We are the IDF, stay down, do not get up!' One 18-year-old Israeli disregarded the advice and leaped to his feet, bubbly effusive with his thanks but was promptly shot down. Sara Davidson emotionally recalled: 'There was a minute of quiet. They stopped the shooting somehow and somebody said in Hebrew: "Listen, there are Israeli guys here," and I remember seeing an Israeli soldier with a big gun, standing there, looking at us and saying, "Listen, guys – we've come to take you home."'

The Entebbe rescue raid was a classic TALO. All four Hercules transports were on the ground within eight to ten minutes and resistance was rapidly extinguished by the soldiers and vehicles that poured off still-moving ramps. Three Israeli civilians and the commander of the air-landed force, Lieutenant Colonel Jonathan 'Yori' Netanyahu, were killed in the short fire fight. More than 20 Ugandan soldiers were killed alongside all the hijackers. One hostage left behind in hospital was murdered after the raid. Within an hour the Hercules aircraft were taking off. Idi Amin's MIG-17 Air Force was shot into ruins prior to takeoff to prevent pursuit. Even as the aircraft flew low into their homecoming at Lod airport on the morning of 4 July, tired aircrew could see Israeli civilians excitedly waving below. The welcome was rapturous. Airspace across the vast expanses of the African continent was considered a lot less lethal than that of Cold War Europe. Tactical air-land alongside parachute insertion has remained a practical option.

The complete spectrum of rescue options was only available to a limited number of democratic nations in 1978 when a force of 4,000 rebel fighters crossed the border from bases in Angola and captured Kolwezi in Zaire, formerly the Belgian Congo. Some 3,000 Europeans in situ effectively became hostages. On 14 May Zaire's President Mobutu appealed to the French and Belgian governments for military assistance. These governments in turn sought airlift support from other nations.

The unexpected requests illuminated the parlous state of British airborne forces, whose 16th Parachute Brigade had been disbanded as a cost-cutting measure in 1977. It confirmed paratrooper veteran John Frost's previous assertion that: 'The endemic trouble with British airborne forces was that the army never believed in them.' Despite achieving an enviable UKJATFOR [Joint Airborne Task Force] NATO reinforcement capability, British planners regarded going by air to battle as transport, as distinct from a fighting capability. Heavy troop commitments dedicated to counter-insurgency in Northern Ireland and a total focus on the likely armoured confrontation that would occur in the event of conflict with the Soviet Warsaw Pact, precluded any priorities for airborne forces. Philosophical confusion was to continue even with the resurrection in 1983 of the 5th Airborne

Brigade post the Falklands War, with experimental helicopter air-mobile formations until a combined 16th Air Assault Brigade was formed in 1999.

France, meanwhile, had maintained its traditional 'fire-brigade' stand-by parachute contingency force, continued after Indo-China and Algeria and beyond. A Belgian parachute-commando brigade which, like the French, had evolved from Second World War SAS contingents, had already intervened at Stanleyville in the Congo in a similar situation in November 1964. It too was placed on alert. The crisis developing in Shaba Province, Zaire, required just such a fire-brigade intervention at Kolwezi. Democratic governments tend not to react quickly to diplomatic and political crises. The Kolwezi experience, however, was to vindicate the advantages of a shared strategic airlift and the maintenance of quick-reaction intervention forces with high readiness troop training and well maintained ready-to-use equipment. Colonel Erulin, the 2nd REP commander stood by for Kolwezi, succinctly described the requirement for such no-notice emergency deployments: 'You come as you are.'

On 17 May 1978 soldiers from the 2nd REP began to converge on their headquarters at Calvi in Corsica, when their readiness to move was reduced to six hours. After hasty packing, the issue of weapons, rations and ammunition and an outline orientation of the likely task, the inevitable soldier complaint, 'Hurry to wait', applied. This changed at 0300 the following morning when the regiment departed on a four-hour mountainous truck journey to Solenzara Air Force Base. Five civil Air France jumbo jets flew the force non-stop for ten hours from Corsica to Kinshasa in Zaire, the only sleep time many soldiers would muster for five days. They flew from a springtime cool Mediterranean Europe to the humidity of late summer in Central Africa, arriving at 2300 on 18 May. The regiment's second echelon of 100 vehicles lifted by USAF cargo flights was 24 hours behind.

There was little respite on arrival. Colonel Erulin was told a Katangese radio intercept revealed the rebels had been ordered to sabotage mining installations and kill and abduct as many hostages as possible and withdraw to their Angolan bases. This was the only information available. Drunken guerrillas were running amok in the town, shooting, killing, maiming and raping. The 2nd REP had to jump in as soon as possible, but their parachutes and vehicles had still to arrive. T-10 parachutes were borrowed from the Zairian Army, which meant the para legionnaires had to improvise a fit for their own leg parachute containers to unaccustomed harnesses. There were only four Zaire Air Force C-130s available and three French C-160 Transalls, one of which was earmarked to act as a flying command post (CP).

Erulin was constrained by this aircraft capacity to jump two waves. He decided to drop the first wave at the northern edge of the Old Town at Kolwezi, where it was thought the main part of the population and hostages was accommodated and confined. Companies were given specific areas to clear and to block rebel withdrawal routes. The aim was to promote such insecurity through aggressive attacks on landing that the rebels would run for their lives before thinking of executing or abducting the hostages.

'We originally had 66 jumpers, but on take-off one C-160 blew a tyre and the troops were told to un-ass and get on the other planes,' recalled American legionnaire Sergeant Paul Fanshaw. 'In the transition we picked up 14 extra men.' Take-off was delayed until 1100 by early morning fog. Paratroopers by this time had been on the go without sleep for 48 hours. 'We were packed in like sardines' on lift-off, Fanshaw remembered, and 'the heat was suffocating and we fought sleep.' It was a four and a half hour flight.

Erulin took his command post with three infantry companies on the first wave. The remainder of his headquarters, scouts, mortar platoon and fourth rifle company would arrive on the second insertion. 'Taking off my helmet and leaning back, I closed my eyes and tried not to think of my predicament,' recalled Fanshaw, looking around at paratroopers packed in virtually on top of each other with 80 to 85 troops levered into space designed for 64. In addition they carried four days of combat supplies and six to eight door-bundles, which were stacked near the doors, ready to be thrown out. 'The ride was pure torture,' Fanshaw recalled and they had to jump 'chutes 'with which they were not familiar' and 'were expected to descend on an enemy force that outnumbered us five or six to one'. It was the classic airborne trade-off of surprise versus force generation and 'everyone looked anxious'.

Three hours following the French lift-off the first of the Belgian para-commando aircraft started to straggle into Kamina. Some 1,170 men were spread over eight Sabena Civil 707s, two Boeing 727s and eight military C-130s. The latter required 22 hours to cover the 11,700 kilometres, the long delays caused by the inability of staging airfields to refuel more than one aircraft at a time. Both these and the arrival times of USAF aircraft flying both the French and Belgian follow-on vehicles and heavy support were correspondingly delayed.

At 1540 the stillness of a hot and humid afternoon in Kolwezi Old Town was broken by a distant murmuring that intensified to an approaching roar. Seven heavily laden transports made a low-level pass just to the north of the Old Town. 'Looking out of the window, I saw nothing but bush for miles; then some houses came into view,' recalled Fanshaw. His plane made a steep bank to line up on the drop zone, knocking over two dozen paratroopers in his stick. They shuffled about to regain balance and some equilibrium as the jumpmaster pushed and shoved the weapons containers to the open doors as the red light flashed on. 'Green light,' remembered Fanshaw, 'jumpers tumbled out of the doors,' and with the crush easing as para-troopers exited, 'for a few seconds I could breathe.' At virtual stalling speed, 'The plane dipped and quaked and, while butterflies kicked in my stomach, I pushed out Legionnaire Misse, who could hardly walk because of the weight of his machine gun and the other gear,' recalled Fanshaw. Paratroopers trickled out of the aircraft, a sinister and shocking sight for the completely surprised rebels below: 'We fell out of the door simultaneously: feet, sky, earth, sky, shock. The big American 'chute popped open! All around me billowed green 'chutes; under me a large cluster of houses stood . . . I ploughed in 400 metres from the Impala Hotel.'

Two passes occurred after the first orientation swoop, to get all the paratroopers out on the restricted drop zone. Instead of landing a few yards north of the Old Town, legionnaires pursued by inac-curate ground fire were crashing into houses and trees; some even landed on the railway station. Despite this, there were only four frac-tures and two sprains on the drop. The majority unexpectedly landed in tall elephant grass, six feet high, which complicated rallying and finding containers but cloaked them from rebel sight and fire. Within

15 minutes Erulin's companies were ruthlessly clearing their allotted sectors. Four rebel machine guns were quickly overrun and a hesitant incursion by Panhard armoured cars swiftly knocked out by 89mm rocket launchers or deterred by punishing fire.

'There were some horrific sights there,' recalled Sergeant Jonathan Harris who arrived on the second lift. 'Bodies – mostly Europeans – piled up one upon the other, quite disgusting to see, lying out in the streets and at the end of drives.' Fifty hostages were soon located amid signs of looting and violence, with the putrefying stench of corpses pervading the town. Colonel Erulin had quickly consolidated his grip on the Old Town by sunset and decided to wave off the second lift when it arrived at dusk to avoid adding to the confusion in the dark. Aggressive night raids and ambushes kept the rebels off balance until the second wave arrived at dawn and the Belgian para-commandos air-landed at the airport, which was finally secured after three days fighting by Zairian paratroopers. The Zairian force remained on the airfield while the Belgians secured safe passages for evacuees within the town. The 2nd REP continued to dislodge and mop up rebel forces. By 21 May French legionnaires conducting night patrols and ambushes were enduring their fifth night without sleep.

Thirty-two whites and one black were found murdered in a single room and Jonathan Harris recalled 'the horrible smell of death all over the place'. Overall it was discovered that 190 Europeans and 200 black civilians had perished but, as Harris commented, the men 'didn't stop to commiserate', they continued to mop up resistance. About 500 to 600 rebels were killed in and around a village complex called Metal-Shaba on the northern outskirts of Kolwezi. 'I don't think many of the ordinary legionnaires thought of letting them escape,' admitted Sergeant Harris. The legionnaires were in little mood for mercy: 'After seeing what had happened there was more than a bit of retribution or revenge on behalf of the hostages.' Harris saw what he assessed to be about 300 to 350 bodies lying about after the successful action. They took a lot of prisoners, 'youngsters mostly, who didn't know what was going on – some of them out of their brains with alcohol'. Prisoners were handed over to the arbitrary justice of the Zairian Army and few survived.

The Belgians flew out 500 evacuees on the first day on 20 May and a further 1,927 in 24 hours. The 2nd REP lost five men killed in action and 25 wounded, inflicting over 250 deaths on the rapidly dispersing Simba rebels, capturing over 1,000 modern weapons and destroying two armoured cars. A combination of civilian and USAF strategic airlift made this operation possible. The US 82nd Airborne Division was to demonstrate its rapid deployment capabilities both in Grenada in October 1983 and again at Panama alongside Ranger and other air-landed units in December 1989.

'COME LIKE THE WIND, GO LIKE THE LIGHTNING': CASSINGA, ANGOLA 4 MAY 1978

Deep airborne raids were traditionally costly missions because much of the force was often killed or captured evading the enemy. This was the case with the first British parachute raid against the Tragino Aqueduct in Italy in 1941, as also on numerous occasions during the French war against the Vietminh in Indo-China in the 1950s. Improved helicopter lift and range can create manoeuvring space in previously static parachute-secured airheads. Close terrain needed for cover to survive, such as in the jungle, has often precluded the possibility of operating substantial parachute drop zones alongside smaller helicopter landing sites. The American air-mobile experience in Vietnam demonstrated the potential of the helicopter as a battle-field carrier, but helicopter operating ranges for planning purposes are measured up to 100 miles, whereas parachute transport aircraft normally plan for missions over 500 miles distant.

Punitive parachute raids at battalion strength sufficient to over-whelm a substantial objective normally require relief by mobile ground forces or extraction on foot, an exceedingly risky option in depth. One available option to create air mobility for landed para-troopers within a deep airhead is to site Forward Operating Bases (FOBs) or Helicopter Administrative Areas (HAAs) in between the two extremes of range. Helicopters can then tactically deploy paras about the airhead, to block enemy approaches or extract them in extremis. Helicopter extractions staged across FOBs where helicop-ters can refuel can enable heavy parachute raids deep into enemy territory. Fifteen days before the onset of the Kolwezi operation the South African Defence Force (SADF) demonstrated just such a combination, a deep punitive raid against Marxist guerrillas at Cassinga in Angola. Parachute transports carried a surprise airborne assault in tandem with an equally unexpected deep helicopter extraction. 'Come like the wind, go like the lightning,' enjoined Chinese philosopher Chang-yu in 1000 AD. He was referring to light cavalry raids, but could well have been describing an airborne aspiration expressed nearly 1,000 years before the practical reality.

At two minutes past eight on the morning of 4 May 1978, Comrade P. Nanyemba, a SWAPO [South West African People's Organisation] fighter, watched the morning muster parade forming up in the open space in the middle of the small former mining town of Cassinga in Angola. Cassinga was a collection of about 30 well spread permanent buildings with wide roads in between, generous gardens and numerous trees alongside the Culanga River, 155 miles north of the then South African border. Surrounded by scattered bush and scrub interspersed with sparse trees, nobody saw the four rapidly approaching SADF Canberra bombers in double pair formation streaking north to south along the line of the main road through town. One thousand two hundred football-size Alpha bombs filled with explosive and small ball-bearings bounced among the crowds forming up for early morning assembly and detonated ten metres above the ground. So fast were the jets that the crackling of multiple explosions preceded the roar of the over-flying aircraft. 'The first bomb was thrown right in the parading group, killing some comrades right at the spot,' recalled Nanyemba, 'including prominent cadres like comrade Houduwa, Mbarangandja and Naikohole, the camp commander.' It is thought there were 4,000 people in the camp at the time.

Four low-flying Buccaneers, flying the same stealthy axis, followed immediately behind the Canberras and lobbed 32 1,000lb bombs into the hamlet. Ruusa Naango-Shaanika, a 16-year-old young woman, was forming up with her group next to the hospital. 'We saw four planes coming this side,' she recalled, 'I never thought there was something like that.' As she ran into the hospital, 'I heard all over things burst burst!' Initially there was paralysis. 'I was just standing still, not knowing what to do,' remembered Maggy Amutenya, 'people started to run and I did not know why.' As explosions erupted around the hospital confusion set in. 'When I saw the planes coming my way I lay down waiting for anything to happen.' Two Mirage jets dived in behind the Buccaneers and started strafing the recruit camp with 30mm high-explosive fragmentation shells.

'Airplanes! Airplanes!' was the call that startled fighter Mwaanga Paulus Ngodji as he walked toward the parade ground. Everyone started running. 'Suddenly the dust flew up under a shower of bullets and many fell while the refugees started running in all directions,' recalled another witness. Screams of terror were almost drowned out by the ragged screech of Mirage jets pulling out of their dives. 'You hear the roar only just after they have passed,' he claimed. The lead Buccaneer circled Cassinga after the air strike and reported considerable damage had been done. Multiple columns of smoke and dust were hanging in the air above the north–south road as if a gigantic whip had been cracked across the hamlet from the air. He observed flames, dust and bodies through gaps in the smoke. Masses of people were fleeing in all directions as if from a violently disturbed termite nest. Paratrooper Company Sergeant Major Robbie Roberts was later to describe the parade ground as 'looking like a scrap yard for body parts'.

Within four minutes it was over. At 0806 hours three C-130 transport aircraft suddenly swung into view in 'V' formation, flying the same attack axis at 600 feet. Two others wheeled in from east to west and another transport banked in moving west to east. This mixed force of four Hercules and two C-160 Transalls were clearly tying an invisible string that would effectively box in the town. After the shock of the air strikes the force commander Colonel Jan Breytenbach was 'convinced, and rightly so, that the mass drop of paratroopers all around the SWAPO base would seriously unnerve the occupants'. They had 'come like the wind', as the Chinese philosopher Chang-yu had advocated. Their appearance was indeed intimidating, as Breytenbach observed: 'A mass drop is always an impressive sight to behold, but six lumbering C-130s and C-160s disgorging unending streams of paratroopers, all bent on a killing mission and on their way down to come to grips with the enemy, had to be a frightening sight for those poor sods gazing up into the sky.'

The SWAPO commander Dimo Amaambo fled during the confusion on the ground. The constant in airborne operations is to prepare to encounter the unexpected. Many of the 370 paratroopers spilling from the aircraft soon appreciated, gazing apprehensively at the meandering line of the Culanga River growing ever wider beneath them, they were not going to land in the right place.

These paratroopers about to jump into a highly intense confrontation were not the norm, measured against earlier historic airborne assaults. They were a composite force taken from three parachute battalions in the newly formed 44th SADF Parachute Brigade and were in the main 'citizen soldiers'. They were part-time servicemen like Britain's Territorial Army. Mixed within were two platoons of recently trained regular conscript soldiers, some with only a few months' service. Many of their physical and military proficiency skills had just been refreshed because they had been selected during a series of 'call-out' exercises, which had included specially tailored pre-operational live firing training schemes. Some of the soldiers had never worked together before.

The airborne assault on Cassinga, code-named Reindeer, 155 miles deep into Angola, was part of a coordinated assault on Chetequera by a ground force 15 miles over the border and a counter-insurgency helicopter sweep through a series of smaller bases ten to 12 miles further east of Chetequera. Cassinga was the main target, thought to hold between hundreds and a thousand SWAPO fighters as well as being a feeder and logistic hub for cross-border guerrilla raiding into South Africa. It was a calculated risk because the unusual depth of the airborne incursion would require a helicopter extraction to get the force out. Cuban-piloted MIG-21s might well impede this, as also an Angolan Army (FAPLA) armoured force based at Techamutete, which was only nine to ten miles from Cassinga. Being so far north of the border meant that shock and speed had to be the essence of this surprise search-and-destroy penetration. Only two hours on the ground were envisaged to kill terrorists, destroy key material and remove intelligence and prisoners once the town had been cordoned off by the parachute assault. Nineteen helicopters, a mix of French-built Super-Frelon and Puma, were made available for this task. Shock was achieved through the complex air movements producing a crushing air bombardment followed almost simultaneously by a surprise parachute assault. Speed, however, began to be unravelled by the inaccuracy of the drop.

While the air attacks were going in, the lumbering transports orbited in a circle a few miles short of the objective. The constant banking of the aircraft impeded equipment fitting inside, further adding to the strenuous effort required to stand up with 50 to 55kg of equipment clipped onto the parachute harness. Each man carried two days' dry rations, battle pouches with ten 20-round magazines and two M-26 fragmentation grenades and three one-litre water bottles. Spread among them all were 20 anti-tank mines, white phosphorous and smoke grenades, plastic explosives and ten anti-tank rockets for each of the 12 RPG-7 rocket launchers taken along as well as machine gun belts, mortar rounds, radios and medical kits. Each paratrooper was straining even to stand up, hanging onto the static-line cable and trying to maintain balance in gyrating and banking aircraft. They were carrying the equivalent of two standard airline holiday suitcase allowances in weight attached to their bodies.

'My thoughts were mostly occupied with trying to ease the pinching and discomfort of my kit,' recalled Forward Air Controller Captain Frans Botes, carrying two radios. Paratrooper Mike McWilliams carried a full company medical kit with drips. Once everyone had stood up and hooked up, the dragging effect of parachute, reserve and bulky loads 'produced a bunch of Quasimodos', he recalled. Empty seats to the side were utilised to rest loads and gain some relief to legs and shoulders. Queasiness fuelled by adrenalin pumping at the thought of the approaching drop and the heat and discomfort from the swaying aircraft and bumpy low-level ride produced nausea and some sickness. Everyone jostled for space within the claustrophobic confines of the bucking aircraft to achieve the control and equilibrium needed at the door for the jump. 'Many of us were farting away almost uncontrollably,' recalled Colonel Jan Breytenbach, 'the bane of a paratrooper's life.'

Suddenly the banking ceased as they straightened up for the final approach. Air dispatchers raised an exaggerated single finger indicating 'One minute to go', which led to another increase in palpitating heart-beats. Open doors drowned all sound apart from the pulsating slipstream roar but did at least sluice fresh air through the aircraft interiors. 'All I could and also had to do,' recalled Breytenbach, 'was look back at the paratroopers in my stick with a false grin of fake encouragement plastered all over my face.'

'Prop tips skimmed the treetops,' recalled Mike McWilliams. 'It was early morning over Angola and we were coming in under their radar and washing lines to surprise them at reveille.' At the command 'Stand in the door' they were still skimming foliage at treetop height. Suddenly the aircraft lifted steeply to 500 feet and G-forces caused many heavily laden paratroopers to sink down on their knees. Almost immediately the green light came on. Platoon commander Hans Human saw the dust clouds and a burning Cassinga slipping past the rear, catching glimpses through the starboard exit door. 'We were jumping late,' he realised. McWilliams remembered the weight of his equipment seemingly doubled as G-forces pressed down on him during the rapid pop-up ascent to jump height. *Go!* was called up ahead and the scrambling, ponderous, ungainly shuffle-run to the door began. 'We lurched left, then right, then became momentarily weightless as the aircraft hit an air pocket.' He stumbled out with an appalling exit, 'a copy-book pike with one and a half twists.' McWilliams could see: 'Little lazy flecks of tracer suddenly appeared and became green and red neon beach balls speeding by. One went through both sides of my canopy, leaving two heat-sealed holes as big as my fist. The sound from below then hit me. It was a bone-shaking, eccentric string of slurred-together explosions.'

Follow-on aircraft dispatchers saw the approach of smoke and dust from Cassinga abruptly whip by. Asked what he could see by the chief pilot, Jan Delport, Major Grundlingh shouted back, 'lots of flak.' 'What do you mean?' asked the perturbed pilot, whose view of Cassinga passing directly beneath was mercifully obscured. 'It looks like a gigantic Christmas tree coming up at us,' he was told.

'You can walk for weeks in Angola and not come across a stream,' claimed McWilliams and, 'now, directly below me, was not a stream but an economy-size river.' Paratroopers had jumped into a strong gusting wind of over 13 knots and this, combined with a three-second delayed exit for most, blew the bulk of the force away from their designated drop zones. Their heavy loads meant certain death if they floated into the water. One heavily laden mortar platoon soldier splashed in unwitnessed and was never seen again, as also many mortar bomb containers. Paratroopers pulled down and half collapsed canopies in desperate attempts to lose height as quickly as possible. 'I saw some little puffs of white smoke,' recalled paratrooper Anthony Modena, distracted by flak. 'It looked like white cotton wool following the plane I had just left.' He was exasperated. 'Hey, the Canberras should have bombed here! How can anyone still be shooting that stuff?' Once he became aware of his surroundings, he realised he was on the wrong side of the Culanga River.

'Alarm bells started to ring,' recalled Colonel Jan Breytenbach, looking down. 'I was facing Cassinga but more than half of it seemed to be too far to my left.' They were in the wrong place. It became obvious to Breytenbach that the original plan to box in the hamlet and then assault west to east was becoming unhinged. He needed to regroup and wait for those on the wrong side of the river to recross and then switch his attack axis from south to north. All this was to take one and a half hours after the shock of the immediate assault, before his men could begin the nasty close-in task of clearing the town of its SWAPO fighters. Meanwhile, the paratroopers had to regroup. Up to one-third of the force was on the wrong side of a very deep river and the advantage of surprise was trickling away.

Resistance to the fragmented parachute landings was disorganised and ineffective. McWilliams recalled one paratrooper suspended ten feet above ground from a tree having to endure a SWAPO guerrilla emptying an entire AK-47 magazine at him as he helplessly swung to and fro. The paratrooper managed to disentangle his R3 7.62mm rifle from his equipment in the midst of this hail of fire and cock the weapon. 'The SWAPO, noticing things had equalised, threw up his hand to surrender', but the completely unscathed paratrooper shot him. He then pulled his reserve rip-cord, disentangled himself from his harness and slid down the rigging lines. Abandoned by their leader, most guerrillas were seeking to flee the airborne box, which was leaking like a sieve, before it closed. Engagements were fleeting. SWAPO guerrillas trying to escape ran into the steadily advancing paratroopers still forming up in groups, also desperate not to be overrun.

The guerrillas were more courageous than they were competent.

AA gunners had missed the opportunity to lead and fire ahead into the slow-moving transports, but their size at low level belied their 120 knot speed and the flak invariably burst behind. Guerrillas then fired too high at the descending paratroopers, who were difficult to hit while oscillating and were at an indeterminate range in any case. Private Fenton engaged a group of guerrillas that hid behind vehicles. 'The enemy may have thought by hiding behind the trucks they had adequate cover.' They simply aimed at the legs and as they fell they were shot dead. Fenton came across a young unarmed woman, eyes bulging in terror, whom he spared. 'What would I benefit by shooting her?' he rationalised, rapidly moving on among settlement huts. Behind he heard the double-tap gunfire of another paratrooper shooting her, assuming the outline of her body was a terrorist lying in ambush. 'By now there were many bodies lying around and anybody who so much as moved or jumped up was shot immediately,' he recalled. Sergeant Manderson observed one paratrooper from his platoon coming across five enemy, feigning death, all lying in a neat row. 'This was too obvious so he sprayed them all with his R3 rifle.'

There is controversy about the numbers of civilian refugees caught up in the fighting for Cassinga. Women and children were certainly trapped inside the cordon, which was steadily tightened and finally wiped out by the advancing paratroopers. They doubtless included a mix of abducted civilians, 'comfort women' for the fighters, and the inevitable gathering of families, traders, logistic and other non-combatants who would have been formed part of the innate structure of any substantial terrorist base, safely situated deep within Angola. These innocents were caught up in the horror of pitiless close-quarter fighting. Fenton realised to his dismay that large numbers of children, averaging between four to ten years old, were following his squad's grim progress. 'Whenever they walked the children would follow,' he noticed. 'When they stopped or went down for cover the children followed suit.' They were copying their every move. Because they posed no threat they were left alone. Playing their bizarre game undoubtedly saved their lives.

The paratroopers had swiftly to make up lost time to secure their objective before the arrival of the enemy's armoured reinforcements. SWAPO resistance centred on a bunker and trench zigzag system around a 14.5mm AA gun and lighter 12.7mm AA guns, lavishly protected by sandbags, forming an effective strongpoint. 'Acrid smoke from burnt and burning thatch filled one's nostrils,' recalled Jan Breytenbach as the fearsome close-quarter fighting developed. He recalled: 'African battlefields had a special tang, a sort of sickly smell that defies any attempts at describing it but burning thatch, or grass, seems to be an important contributor to the sickening aroma. The smell of human excrement, however, always forms the major portion of the end "aromatic" product. Add to that the sharp tang of cordite and one can, perhaps, get an idea of what some reporter would probably describe as the deadly smell of battle.'

The fierce fighting creating this unsettling stench was equally disturbing. Trenches were cleared by grenade and bullet by para-troopers working in twos and threes. They fought to clear the 'zig', killing all within before turning the corner to throw grenades and spray automatic fire within the 'zag' as they methodically suppressed the trench configuration. Fenton saw many women and children killed cowering inside the trenches. 'Some of them had lain flat on their stomachs with their arms wrapped around their heads, seeking whatever cover there might be, hoping to escape the terror of the situation.' This was to little avail because 'many had the backs of their heads blown away by R1 bullets'. Captain Tommie Lamprecht found himself fighting female combatants dressed in uniform. A woman's body was blown out onto the parapet of the trench system, the front of her green fatigues bloodily shredded by the explosion suggesting she had attempted to block others from the blast. 'When you shoot someone with the R1 rifle it is incredible to see the power of the bullet,' recalled Fenton describing the impact of 7.62mm rounds. 'It's like a truck driving at 120km per hour hitting a guy!' he claimed. 'The force of the bullet pulls the body around like you can't believe.' Once the AA complex was overwhelmed resistance collapsed. Carefully placed mortar fire managed to smash the 14.5mm gun being employed in the ground role. Fenton saw the three-man crew had been flung to all corners of the emplacement by the sheer force of the 60mm mortar bomb blast. 'One body seemed to be almost twice its normal length, as if someone had stretched it out, with huge chunks of flesh missing.'

The first call for helicopters was put out at 12 noon, three hours late. A helicopter medevac lifted the casualties and some soldiers with five machines. It had been anticipated the force would be on the ground for only two hours, yet six hours later they were still fighting. The anti-tank platoon had meanwhile been despatched to the south of Cassinga, where they laid a tank ambush along the road coming from Techamutete. The anti-tankers were disgruntled, declaring they were 'pissed-off' and felt like dodos missing the action, all too clear from the sound of thumping grenades and receding fire-fights as the paratroopers constricted the cordon around the town. Mines were laid in a shallow 'W' shape across the sandy road. Much cursed because of their weight during the drop, 'I tell you what,' declared Sergeant Jay, 'at the end of the day those landmines saved our arses!' Digging them in had been nerve-wracking. 'It is incredible how long it feels digging a small hole while so exposed on an open enemy road!' confided Second Lieutenant Law. Hours of uneventful and tense waiting were suddenly rudely interrupted by roaring tank engines and squealing tracks. The first appearance was by wheeled armoured personnel carriers that broke cover when least expected.

A joint Cuban and FAPLA column of five T34/85 tanks with 30 BTR-152s and some BMDs had spread either side of the mined road and were entering Cassinga in a loose attack formation. The lead vehicle was festooned with about 40 Cubans and guerrillas, hanging from the vehicle brandishing AK-47 rifles over their heads, totally relishing their liberation role. Multiple RPG strikes lanced into the vehicle fired from paratroopers sited at the road's edge. 'They were only about 10 metres away,' Law recalled, 'and he shot and shot like a machine with no feeling.' Minds sharpened by the adrenalin of springing the ambush translated into an intense focus to eliminate as many of the dismounting enemy as they could. Soldiers were cut down by fire from both sides as they tried to jump or clamber down vehi-cles. 'It was a turkey-shoot!' Law declared. Five BTR-152 armoured personnel carriers and one of the tanks were shot into flames by a combination of rocket and mine strikes. With the armoured column momentarily checked the anti-tank platoon sought to disengage and run back to the helicopter extraction site.

What followed was a nightmare scenario. As the helicopter lift started, FAPLA and Cuban armoured vehicles arrived in sight of the LS. An emergency extraction site was hastily established further east and this had to frequently edge further away as more and more enemy armoured vehicles appeared to their south. South African Mirage and Buccaneer aircraft howled down in the nick of time and began to wreak fiery mayhem among the stalled armoured vehicles. The column was checked but time was a commodity the paratroopers no longer had. 'Move into the bush – an enemy convoy has been sighted!' Fenton heard at the landing site. 'To me this was the end!' he admitted. 'By now you could hear the convoy approaching, especially the tanks.' They saw aircraft overhead and appreciated there had been an alarming upsurge of fighting to the south, around the road leading in from Tetchamutete. The squeal of distant tank tracks alongside the gruff roar of revving tank engines was as alarming as it was menacing. 'It is a frightening sound to hear a tank approaching and you are armed with only a rifle,' Fenton remembered.

The beating sound of approaching helicopters was soon distinguishable above the noise of gunfire, explosions and the crack of tank guns. The helicopters had been scrambled from their base area on an *extract now* order 13 miles away in the bush to the east of Cassinga. The ragged take-off sorted itself into a reasonably cohesive formation during the hasty low-level flight. Their appearance was greeted as the proverbial 7th Cavalry rescue from hordes of swiftly approaching enemy. Platoon commander Lieutenant Willie Jooste recalled 'a gaggle of the most beautiful helicopters swooped in, their chalk numbers in bright, white masking tape on their noses'. There was no time, however, to line up for an orderly extraction. 'The Frelons literally crash-landed among the paratroopers.' Jooste's chalk number *AG*, a Puma, 'arrived like an angel from heaven'. The cluster of 15 Pumas and four Super-Frelons put down and it was virtually every man for himself as paratroopers scrambled aboard the nearest helicopter. Prisoners and captured material were abandoned.

Different helicopter types could only lift certain numbers of men, further complicating the operation and adding to the frenetic activity as crew chiefs would only take 12, 14 or 16 soldiers. Boarding was conducted in an atmosphere of tension verging on panic. One pilot, 'Monster' Wilkins, was taken aback at how close the Cubans actually were. 'We saw spurts of dust as the bullets "walked" a path between the choppers,' he noticed. The approaching tanks could not depress their guns sufficiently to hit the helicopters because of the ground configuration and these tracer-lit shells following a crack, curved languidly over the machines, adding to the unreality of the scene. 'Miraculously no one was hit,' Wilkins observed. Peter Booth, another pilot, saw 'Parabats storming aboard, so fast we could not get order', their legs dangling over the tail-gate ramp. 'We were briefed to lift out 11 Parabats but there must have been 30-plus when I looked back.' His co-pilot and crew chief began to throw men out the back until 'gradually the rotor rpm began to start climbing in response to the reduction in all-up weight'.

Anti-tank platoon soldiers were shooting to their rear and moving backwards toward the waiting helicopters. The unceremonious dumping of 'extraneous' paratroopers added to the anxious strain bearing down on them all. Fitness was an issue for some of the over-weight citizen soldiers. General Constand Viljoen, observing from one of the machines, a disciplinarian and fitness fanatic, was quietly disdainful. 'One man was so exhausted when he was running to get to a helicopter that he collapsed right next to it and had to be picked up by his comrades and dragged into the aircraft.' Discipline was beginning to creak as the last helicopters lifted off under Cuban tank fire. Lieutenant Willie Jooste, looking back at the departing LS, still under fire saw 'a lone paratrooper was standing on the LZ languidly waving his arms at us as if to saying a casual goodbye'. It was a sight he never forgot.

The lone paratrooper was probably Sergeant Manderson, the 'hitch-hiker of Cassinga', who had been ordered to deplane from an overloaded helicopter that took the last of his troops. 'Here we are, 250 kilometres inside enemy territory with a tank column approaching,' he recalled. 'My guys are safely on board and I am safely on board – I can't see any reason to get off!' He philosophically accepted the risk to his men was too great and stepped off when directed by the loadmaster. Loading a fresh magazine on his folding stock R3, he reflected, 'Well, here comes the escape and evasion plan everybody has been talking about.' Jooste was watching as his helicopter gained height. 'My heart bled for this individual as there was nothing I could do for him. We had a full complement on board.' As Manderson was about to run for the bushes to his right a Puma helicopter piloted by John Church swooped in and landed just behind him. He immediately sprinted for it and dived straight into the fuselage hovering a few feet off the ground. A tank round sailed over the helicopter as it lifted off through a curtain of small arms fire. Manderson hitch-hiked the last ride out.

The South African paratroopers had 'come like the wind' at 0800 hours that morning, but the 'lightning' extraction was not within two but ten hours, finally flying out at 1900 that night. The Cassinga raid was both a controversial and remarkable airborne action. 'No one smiled or spoke and the tension was still high in the chopper as everyone sat looking at each other,' recalled Fenton during the flight back. They were uncertain whether they were heading home or to another rendezvous. Suddenly they were over the border. 'As we crossed the "cut-line" the chopper pulled up and the flight engineer took off his earphones and, with raised arms and clenched fists, shouted, "*Yeah!!!*"' They were safe.

12

AFGHANISTAN

BLUE BERETS

Intervention in Czechoslovakia in 1968 appeared to suggest that the blue-bereted Soviet paratroopers would be the future Soviet imperial vanguard. Events in Afghanistan eleven years later confirmed this view as Soviet paratroopers formed part of the spearhead for the Soviet occupation of Afghanistan in December 1979, paving the way for the arrival of the 40th Army on New Year's Day 1980. As Spetznaz Special Forces stormed the Taj-Bek Presidential Palace in Darul-Aman, paratroopers from the 103rd Guards Airborne Division began securing key road junctions in Kabul. Amin, the President, was killed and his chosen replacement Babrak Karmal was escorted into Kabul by the 345th Guards Airborne Regiment the day after the official start of the Soviet intervention. This represented the zenith of Soviet airborne forces and its army. It was to be reduced to a shadow of its former prestigious self after ten years of Afghan attrition.

'Well, you know, at that time, we were all unaware of the problems we were to face in Afghanistan,' recalled the regiment's later commander, Valeri Aleksandrovich Vostrotin. 'We considered it as a walk in the park type of mission and everybody wanted to go.' There were echoes of the heady days of support to the Republican cause during the 1930s Spanish Civil War. A young major heading the division's political department commented to Vostrotin, 'Valeri, some time we will be proud of you as we are of the Spanish heroes today.' They were at the aerodrome loading for departure in December 1979 and 'I remembered the phrase and we flew away with it in our minds,' Vostrotin recalled.

Like Spain, blood was expended in Afghanistan to maintain an idealistic charade. Babrak Karmal's belated invitation to Soviet entry was preceded in the radio address by the traditional Islamic benediction, immediately viewed popularly as a farce and an insult to the faithful. A *jihad* or holy war was declared against the Russian *infidels* and their puppet government. The Soviet Union became a backer in yet another internal civil war.

'The first impression when we got to Afghanistan, having flown in, was of an exotic country,' declared paratrooper Iskander Islamgalievich Galiev, serving with the 345th Regiment. The country was 'in the sub-tropics, unbearable daytime heat, very cold at night, beautiful girls – although you can't really make out much with the veil on, just a silhouette.' Afghanistan was a land of incongruous contradictions. 'The contrast between the natural beauty and the danger ingrains itself so deep inside you that the feeling doesn't ever leave you,' recalled Private Ruslan Yurievich Bezborodov with the same regiment.

The average Russian paratrooper believed they were freeing the country from a feudal system. Modern reconstruction was not, however, what the austere Islamic fundamentalists wanted. 'It was all done from the heart,' maintained Galiev, 'but we were unaware that we were breaking the habits and traditions of that proud freedom-loving nation.' Only slowly did it dawn on the idealistic young paratrooper conscripts how wrong and unwelcome they actually were. 'We entered mosques with weapons and in flak jackets,' he admitted. 'Now I understand why they hated us, why they shot at us.'

The paratroopers and spetznaz were far more adaptable to operating in local conditions than the road-bound conscripts belonging to the 40th Army Tank and Motor-Rifle Divisions. Guerrilla warfare caught them totally unprepared. In March 1980 a motor-rifle company operating in Paktia Province was cut off by a series of Mujahideen ambushes. They fought their battle from within their armoured vehicles, reluctant to dismount. The guerrillas waited until their ammunition was expended, moved down to the roadside in darkness and wiped them out. During the first year of the occupation 484 soldiers were killed. Newly arrived Sergeant Igor Ivanovich Kosenkov remembered that as soon as he landed in Kabul to join the 345th Airborne Regiment 'straight away the instructions came', and they were not encouraging. 'You see there, 500 metres away?' he was told. 'Cross that and you'll get a bullet in your brain.' And so it continued: 'Walk there and you could get kidnapped, a bullet in your brain.' It was endless: 'Go there . . . a bullet in your brain.' They swiftly learned to listen to veteran advice. 'We were just like kids from a kindergarten,' he confessed, 'we tried to copy them in every possible way.'

The rugged terrain precluded the use of the parachute in combat and the initial heavy vehicle road-bound tactics proved fruitless. The only force-multiplyer able to unhinge the Mujahideen was the helicopter and its faltering initial use produced more frustration than tactical success. Parachute insertion had been the primary modus operandi in Cold War Central Europe and it took nearly two years to successfully integrate helicopter tactics. By the summer of 1981 the Soviet helicopter fleet had expanded five times beyond that of entry to include four regiments and several independent squadrons. The backbone of helicopter lift was the Mi-8, which made up 60 per cent of the 300 helicopters in-theatre; there were also Mi-6 Hook heavy lift machines and Mi-2 light utility helicopters. The 'Hunch-back' or Mi-24 Hind provided fire-support and was soon nicknamed the 'devil's chariot' by the Mujahideen. As in many world-wide operational theatres, the paratroopers were seen as the cutting edge in terms of quality light infantry, better able to close with the elusive guerrillas on the ground.

Valeri Vostrotin had personally selected his soldiers before going to Afghanistan. The 345th Regiment had been at only 60 per cent strength when it was unexpectedly called forward for special operations. 'Intuitively I didn't choose the most disciplined ones,' he explained when directed to take his pick from the division, rather he looked at 'those best prepared on a personal level'. He swept up the best gun-layers, mechanics, drivers and machine-gunners he could find because their problem-solving skills would be superior: 'Even if he's a soldier who's been in a military prison, he'll always be more combat reliable – more daring.' Selection created an elite form of bonding. 'We were really convinced that we were the bravest and the strongest and the mightiest,' declared Sergeant Igor Kosenkov. They were constantly at loggerheads with neighbouring tank and motor-rifle units. 'There were even punch-ups and the 345th Regiment would always beat them,' he claimed.

A training regiment was established at Fergana in Uzbekistan to specially prepare young Soviet paratrooper conscripts for their two-year duty tours in Afghanistan. It was needed. Generally road-bound and occasionally heliborne, Soviet forces were far less mobile, once dismounted, than the hardy Afghan mountain people. 'I had about 50kg of ammunition,' remembered Private Dimitri Roaldovich Baranovsky on dismounting his BRDM armoured carrier with the 345th Regiment, 'My own weight was a little over 60kg.' It was his first operation and he was totally dismayed: 'I didn't know if I could take a step. Then I took that first step, thinking my legs wouldn't carry me any further, and I would lose face in front of my comrades, that all my load would be distributed among them. They would carry it, swearing at me. So I stepped like a pack-animal. Under different conditions, I wouldn't have been able to walk. It was so hard to walk, that I was relieved to hear the first shots on my first mission.'

'My experience of the first fight was very shocking, I didn't know where to shoot,' admitted Private Yurievich Bezborodov with the same regiment. 'Everything I was taught in Fergana Training School had evaporated somewhere' and naked fear took over. 'At last I was just pulled up and shown the direction to shoot in.'

The war was to last ten years, starting with consolidating the invasion and then country-wide sweeps to destroy the Mujahideen. Attrition resulted and ushered in a period of 'Afghanistisation' designed to equip Afghan soldiers to fight their own civil war. Failure to meaningfully achieve this left withdrawal as the only realistic option. Throughout this period nobody understood the war back home. With only six out of the 70 divisions that confronted NATO in Afghanistan at the height of the Cold War, it was regarded as a side-show. The summer campaigns of 1985 saw the largest employment of air-mobile helicopter sweeps yet. Seven thousand Spetznaz, VDV Airborne, and other troops were airlifted by helicopter to relieve Afghan forces besieged in the Kunar Valley. Later that year three paratrooper and three Afghan battalions were flown to relieve another hard pressed garrison around Khost. More than 12,000 troops were airlifted in an operation that significantly caught the Mujahideen temporarily off balance.

Balance was restored with the advent of western-supplied Stinger anti-aircraft missiles provided for the Mujahideen in 1986, this stymied air-mobile operations and produced a form of stalemate. Whereas 60 missile attacks in 1984 cost ten aircraft, two years later 600 launches downed 100. 'For nine years the dragons have ruled the sky,' announced one Afghan resistance leader, 'now the dragon is dead.' Deaths peaked in 1984 at 2,345, from the total of 13,136 soldiers perishing between 1979 and 1989. Tactical focus switched to the interdiction of supplies coming from across the Pakistani border. Some of the bloodiest paratrooper battles were fought along this border to crush the rebel strongholds that facilitated these movements.

In January 1988 the 9th Company of the 345th Airborne Regiment was cut off by a force of Mujahideen and Pakistani troops, dressed in local garb, from across the border. They were holding a mountainside defensive position blocking the approaches to suspected arms caches in Srana. A bitter fight took place for Point 32.34, a nondescript mountain hillock. 'The fight itself broke out in the daytime,' recalled Staff Sergeant Andre Nikolaevich Kuznetsov. 'No one expected it to last so long and that so many people would be killed.' It was to prove among the most intense of the small-unit engagements that characterised the struggle in Afghanistan. Kuznetsov had joined the airborne because he had been a civilian sport parachutist. 'I wasn't keen to go to Afghanistan,' he claimed, being one of just two soldiers selected from his training intake to join the 9th Company at Bagram. They were grossly outnumbered in a stand–off defensive battle:

It started at about six o'clock. There were at least 300 to 500 mercenaries walking upright – full height – one attack after another coming in waves. We repulsed them all. They took breath and struck again. Our people got killed one after another. In that fight the machine-gunners kept them back and as a result they all died: Heksandrov, Tsvetkov and Melinkov. We ran out of grenades, we were running out of bullets too. We tried to collect whatever was left scattered all over that hill.

Paratroopers often called the Pakistani irregulars 'Black Tulips' because of their black turbans. Later they were told they had been assaulted by the 'Black Storks', well trained mercenaries, dressed in black clothes and well equipped with flak jackets. 'They were advancing fearlessly,' Kuznetsov described, 'walking upright, puffing on joints shouting *Moscow – Give In!* We would shout back something like *Up Siberia! Up Moscow!*'

This was no fanatic assault but a considered and deliberate attack. The lead wave was supported by the second, who brought up more ammunition and heaved the dead away. 'For the 19-year-olds it was of course frightening and confusing,' the sergeant explained. 'Everything was jumbled up: the dead and the wounded.' The fight continued throughout the night and into dawn. 'Many different thoughts and emotions went through my mind,' Kuznetsov explained. 'When an attack is coming in waves, you stop thinking about anything but your comrades, who were just calling out to you from the sides and have not fallen silent.' During lulls they pulled back the dead and wounded from the forward rocky sangaars, out of the line of fire. 'It was just unbearable,' he reflected nodding to himself, 'that's why you went back to the front line to fight.' As the hours fretfully passed they fought themselves into a semi-comatose state. 'At the end I felt completely exhausted,' he declared, 'and didn't even notice how it had finished; lying there almost asleep, half dreaming.' So engrossed were they in the detail of the action that, 'I wasn't thinking about death at all.'

Close combat is especially traumatic. 'I hadn't ever thought that I'd have to shoot, not just at targets, but shoot live targets – not really people – but live targets,' rationalised Staff Sergeant Vladimir Vitalievich Shchigolev. He determined, 'It's either us or them', and he didn't like to think of them as people. But 'they were worthy rivals.' The paratroopers fighting these intense engagements 'were ordinary simple guys', he explained. When Shchigolev described combat, he deliberately distanced himself from the action: 'And now you see someone fall down and he never stands up again. If someone stands up, it's partially, so to speak, missing an arm or a leg. But it's war, real war, real carnage. The main thing is that we endured that war, didn't fall down or lose face.'

Ninth Company was decimated. A helicopter courageously came in and evacuated the wounded amid the fighting. 'They die here in their arms; they carry everything in their arms,' laments a popular Russian paratrooper song describing a helicopter rescue. 'They swear on the ground, he may be rescued', knowing not all taken aboard will survive.

Vostrotin, the regimental commander, managed to cobble together a scratch relief force composed of headquarters personnel, regimental scouts and even staff officers. The position was held with this tenuous reinforcement. Artillery fire was brought down directly upon their own positions. 'We crouched down among those rocks to hide from our own shells,' recalled Staff Sergeant Kuznetsov. 'Only when morning came did they retreat,' he remembered, 'knowing that they would not be able to take that height.'

One year later the Soviet airborne troops successfully covered the skilful Russian withdrawal along the Kabul–Salang road. The last units crossed the Amu Darya Bridge linking Afghanistan with the Soviet Union on 15 February 1989. Vostrotin's 345th Regiment kept open portions of the main highway. VDV paratroopers were to receive 15 of the 28 Hero of the Soviet Union awards made to Soviet ground troops throughout the war. The last formed unit to cross the Amu Darya Bridge was a VDV airborne company.

Civil war followed and during the 1990s, Afghanistan became a failed state ruled by warlords. The Taliban emerged as a dominant force by the middle of the decade, and seized Kabul in 1996. By the end of the millennium they had created the Islamic Emirate of Afghanistan, which controlled 95 per cent of the country. After the 9/11 New York terrorist attack in 2001 the United States invaded Afghanistan to remove the Taliban, who had sponsored Al-Qaeda training camps, the organisation responsible for the atrocity. An interim Afghan Authority was set up and democratic elections held in 2004. Surviving Taliban elements had fled to the south of the country, where they remained a potent insurgent force.

RED BERETS

The British Parachute Regiment experience has not differed markedly from that of the Soviets who preceded it. In January 2002 the 2nd Battalion the Parachute Regiment deployed to Kabul as part of NATO's international peacekeeping force (ISAF). Following elections, ISAF announced its intention in 2005 to expand its security presence to the west and later south of Afghanistan. Helmand Province in the south was a recognised centre of Taliban resistance and the 16th Air Assault Brigade conducted operational tours there alongside other units in 2006 and 2008.

British paratroopers have fought across the same terrain as the Russians in the same weather against a very similar foe. Combat loads were equally heavy in punishing combat conditions. Warrant Officer A.M. Lynch, serving with 3 PARA, described how: 'Soldiers were required to carry an inordinate amount of equipment, in excess of 60 to 70 kgs, in up to 50°C heat, across undulating terrain at altitude, for prolonged periods, whilst responding to continuous and often relentless attacks of small arms fire, RPGs, rockets, mortars, improvised explosive devices and so on, *the real deal.*'

Even assault ladders were carried to scale compound walls. All this activity was conducted in temperatures varying from minus 20°C in winter to a soaring 50°C by May. Corporal Matthew 'Des' Desmond with 2 PARA in 2008 recalled his desert boots melting while he was forced to 'lug' 90lb packs while wearing body armour. One sniper recorded a ground temperature of 70°C during a shoot.

Helmand had been a wealthy agricultural area during the Soviet invasion, whose irrigation system had collapsed during the prolonged fighting. Reactivated to grow opium, conditions had not altered since the Russian occupation. As Lieutenant Colonel Stuart Tootal described: 'This was close country with patches of orchards, irrigation ditches, high compound walls so you couldn't see more than 50 metres, and there were Taliban popping up all over the place.' One pathfinder soldier explained: 'It's so hard to target a fleeting enemy just from one RPG round and off he goes', instantly swallowed up by the 'busy' terrain. 'They got into pre-planned points, we hardly ever see them.' Soldiers of 2 PARA described chasing Taliban insurgents through shoulder-high cornfields, shooting men from punching range and pulling bodies of comrades through streams with banks ablaze from rocket-propelled grenades. 'You see the fire and he's gone again,' described the pathfinder soldier, 'the odd rocket, and then he's moved on.'

Dealing with austere xenophobic Islamic locals in order to gain intelligence was as daunting as it had been for the Russian before, a consequence of the same cultural divide. Afghans are friendly and hospitable, but livelihoods riven by conflict and loss engender a bleak response to western soldiers whose arrival can only portend more trouble inside Taliban-dominated communities. Determined village elders harbour nervous resentment at this intrusion in their daily lives, particularly as the Taliban insurgents are a more tangible influence than the rarely viewed Afghan government presence. Perception is influenced by a faith that Allah controls everything and that every-thing happens – including a Taliban presence – according to his will. Upholding fierce family and community pride is paramount. 'Up here, the majority of the people working in these villages are Taliban,' surmised pathfinder Corporal Ben Garwood on operations in 2008. 'But they're only Taliban when they pick up their weapons, when they don't do that they're back to being Civpop [civilians].' He was brutally frank in his appraisal of the trust and opinion of the locals. 'People tell you what you want to hear, and then when your back's turned, they have a bite.'

Fighting the Taliban is like Darth Vader taking on a primeval foe, a case of technology versus naked human skill and guile. One 3 PARA officer described the Taliban as 'a hard wily character who is skilled in the use of ground'. Shortage of resources has reduced some of the technical edge and obliged the British to resort to the same aggression and fighting skill as that projected by the Taliban fighters. The Soviets had over 300 helicopters in the country at the beginning of the 1980s. Parachute Battalion Commander Stuart Tootal remem-bered there were just seven CH-47 Chinooks able to lift 40-plus troops each for his 1, 200-strong battle group in 2006, 'where it was highly risky to move by road'. Two years later there were only eight Chinooks for four battle groups. This meant playing God for commanders like Tootal because 'the lack of helicopters meant I had to make some very hard decisions'. His biggest fear was to lose one of these precious helicopters in action, 'a question of when, not if'. He described a typical dilemma: 'One of my men was left for nearly seven hours with his throat ripped out, but the doctor was telling me I had that long. I had no choice – I was balancing 16 lives against one life.'

These conditions were not new for the British. The requirement for helicopters and other special-to-role equipments for counter-insurgency has been the situation for under-resourced British battalions for five decades, from Malaya through Northern Ireland and the Falklands to Iraq and Afghanistan.

Technology does not, in any case, provide all the tactical answers. 'What we're doing,' explained pathfinder Corporal Ben Garwood in 2008 'is, we're fighting a conventional war against guerrilla warfare, and they're just finding the gaps we're giving them.' Pairs of RAF Harrier jets carrying enhanced Paveway laser and satellite guided bombs and rocket pods can still miss. Detecting sources of enemy fire, even when direction is supplied, is as frustratingly difficult from the air across undulating rugged terrain as on the ground. 'The Royal Air Force have been utterly, utterly useless,' complained company commander Major Jamie Loden with 3 PARA, seeking urgent fire support in 2006: 'A female Harrier pilot couldn't identify the target and fired two phosphorous rockets that just missed our own compound so that we thought we were receiving rocket-propelled grenades and then mis-strafed our perimeter, missing the enemy by 200 metres.'

Human beings direct technology. Men like Jamie Loden fighting amid bloody irrigation ditches or from isolated compounds are unforgiving when their men are denied support for whatever reason, in extremis. Apache attack helicopters 'have been excellent bringing fire as little as 25 metres from friendly personnel', Loden observed, whereas, 'others have been unable to identify targets even though people are receiving incoming on the ground.' The view from 1,500 feet up is entirely different dimensionally and in human awareness terms. 'As ever, they are fairly egotistical people,' Loden complained, 'and are heard to dismiss contacts in the JOC [Joint Operation Centre] as insignificant on the basis that there are no casualties on the ground.' Whatever the technical problems and human responses parachute veterans of the 2006 and 2008 deployments were emphatic: 'the bottom line is that there are not enough of them.'

Technology could not ease or mask the horror that accompanied the need to physically close with the Taliban in the fierce often hand to hand fighting that characterised operations in Helmand Province.

In some forward operating bases there was an average of two hours' sleep in every four. At Sangin in 2006 one company had a tour of 35 days, 31 of which were in contact with the enemy, a combat extreme not seen since the Korean War. Paratrooper Nathan Pierce with B Company 3 PARA recalled, 'Our company commander gave us a bit of a talk to boost our confidence', an ongoing requirement. 'He told us, "Maximum speed and aggression lads, this is why you joined the Army. It's not gonna get any more real than this."' Major Jamie Loden recalled concerns with two soldiers after a series of particularly heavy fights in August 2006. 'There is a fine line between giving them time to accept what has happened and adjust, and gripping them hard and forcing them to focus,' he judged.

The psychological pressures of combat leave scant time for sentiment at losses. Emotion is controlled but also shared as part of the bonding that inevitably holds young soldiers together in battle. 'There has been plenty of tears, which as you know is all rather humbling,' Loden e-mailed a friend from the front. 'I have followed the same line as far as keeping them together and injecting humour where possible.' Soldiers sustained each other. 'Overall I'd sum up my time in Afghanistan as: tough at times, hard at times, sad at times and very good at times,' recalled Lance Corporal Danny Kelly with 3 PARA. He spent his 21st birthday in 2006 fighting through the prevailing average of three or four contacts they were having each day. 'We're paratroopers,' he declared, 'and we are always gonna work to the max.'

'Before you go into an open area you get into a bit of a twitch,' admitted one pathfinder. Ambush was the Taliban antidote to counter-insurgency sweeps. 'Looking round, thinking where's it going to come from, when it's going to happen.' With all senses heightened and the team covering all directions, 'You're expecting it, and when it does come it's almost like a relief.' Like the Russians before them, British paratroopers respected 'Terry Taliban'. 'They're light on their feet, they can move around,' explained pathfinder Corporal Ben Garwood, 'they're just fantastic.' 'The amount of fire-power was phenomenal,' recalled Sergeant Phil Stout, caught in an ambush, 'they must have had their finger on the trigger the whole time.' The essence of a good ambush is accurate weight of fire.

Ensnared by an ambush set up by four Taliban groups, Corporal Matthew Desmond with 2 PARA described how: 'The weight of fire was incredible, their weapons were rocking and rolling without stopping. In 13 years in the army that was the best initiated ambush I've come across.'

Two section mates, Privates Jeff Doherty and James Bateman, were instantly killed. Another went down, shot in the leg; the machine-gunner was struck in the face by a bullet that miraculously skimmed his chin. His friends wiped the blood from his face and he got to work. In 18 minutes the paratroopers fired back 9,000 machine gun and automatic rifle rounds and called in 179 mortar rounds. 'Time stops during such moments,' recalled Desmond and the fight 'is like a waltz, quick, quick, slow, slow'. They beat them off through sheer and controlled aggression. Desmond shot one gunman from only two metres away with his pistol. He was emotionless. 'You'd feel more anguish shooting a bunny rabbit,' he ruefully admitted later. 'We never relied on air cover, we always fought them head on,' remembered Captain Josh Jones as the 2 Para campaign continued. Despite losing five men in one week the paratroopers refused to be cowed, gaining a certain measure of psychological ascendancy according to Taliban mobile telephone intercepts. The isolated 2 PARA Company outpost called Gibraltar was also nicknamed 'The Mouth of Hell' by the Taliban. 'Every time we saw them we would smash them,' claimed Desmond. 'They would choose the ground and we would beat them – every time.'

As with the earlier Soviet confrontation, the British and Taliban learned painfully from each other. Taliban bravado and their reckless courage initially took the British by surprise. Unusually in counter-insurgency, the enemy was seeking them out also. The 2006 experience reflected this. 'You just had to keep cool and make sure every shot counted,' recalled one 3 PARA soldier, unnerved to see the enemy actually running at him with grim determination. 'The more they came, the more we dropped – it was intense and nothing prepares you for it.' The Taliban adapted. Private Shaun Robb with B Company pointed out: 'The Taliban up to this time had been a sloppy shot. In the past they tended to hold their rifles up and just shoot them over the top of walls or around corners without looking. But this time they were taking a bit more time. Although still not accurate, they were attempting to take aim as if they had been preparing for this operation and had been training.'

By the second tour in 2008 the Taliban were both confrontational and more stealthy. Suicide bombs now began to feature, something not experienced by the Soviets. There is no guaranteed defence against suicide attack, illogical to western soldiers and crudely effective as a consequence. 2 PARA lost five soldiers in one explosion. The more common ambush was that set off by or consisting only of an Improvised Explosive Device or IED, lethal and less risk to the insurgents. The IED impacts upon the pace of ground operations, where tactical advantage comes with speed and immediate reactions. 'It's always in your head,' acknowledged Sergeant Phil Stout, describing the stultifying effect the hidden charges had. 'Am I going to lie on something or kneel on something and get blown up?'

Sergeant Scottie Paterson described how he was caught out aboard his Jackal armoured pathfinder vehicle: 'I was coming out of the Wadi and then *bang*, then just this ringing in my ears.' The next few moments were subconscious 'just go with it' memories before coming to on the ground. 'What the fuck was that?' he asked himself, feeling dazed and shaking, like 'just after a bad parachute landing or something . . . I got up on my elbows and I was just looking up at this dust cloud everywhere. I tried to stand up and my legs were just dragging behind me. I thought "Oh – legs are broken, I think." Then the lads banged the morphine into me.' He was immediately evacuated to England, requiring extensive and painful treatment to his badly injured legs.

As with the Russians before them, dead and injured comrades returned to the UK virtually unnoted beyond regimental circles during the early tours. Battalion commander Stuart Tootal was horrified visiting his battle casualties during leave to find there were no military wards with military staff and patients. 'Instead they were mixed with all sorts of civilian patients, young paras next to 80-year-old geriatric women.' One of his sergeant majors, shot through the arm, was assisting a civilian patient next to him, unable to control his bowels. 'It got so bad my Warrant Officer would get out of bed and clean it with his bare hands.' Tootal found a form of institutionalised if benign neglect; machines broken down, an amputee left unattended in agony. His sergeant major's response to being asked how he was came back with disturbing directness: 'Pretty shit, sir.' Tootal returned to theatre with some haunting images on his mind. 'It filled me with foreboding every time we flew on a helicopter, thinking if one of my guys gets hit they're going to go back to that.' It was left to the British public, generous as ever, to respond to reports more akin to William Russell's nineteenth-century Crimean despatches than e-mailed paratrooper experiences from the twenty-first.

At the end of an operational tour or fiercely fought engagement paratroopers gather together to bond and drink. Following Northern Ireland tours, the Falklands, Kosovo, Sierra Leone, Iraq and, more recently, Afghanistan the companies and sometimes platoons of the British Parachute Regiment engage in a 'smoker' in their favourite pub at Aldershot and now Colchester. They toast the dead and the wounded. Memories of lively, humorous and professionally respected soldiers are affectionately bantered among comrades before returning to their families. They are not part of the shared experience and would not understand in the same way.

Fallschirmjäger after Crete and les Paras after Indo-China and Algeria gathered in similarly respectful groups. They celebrate a life rather than mourn the dead. A haunting Russian folk song sung by Russian paratroopers about Afghanistan encapsulates the mood of these group bonding occasions.

> Those who do not believe, let them not believe,
> Whoever was there, will understand.
> A man in a ground sheet was given a helicopter lift.
> Twenty years is so little, a guy in a ground sheet.
> Exactly what was left, would be put in a zinc coffin,
> And would be rolled up, the blood on their hands,
> They don't know at the other end,
> They wait for him to come back alive.
> Fill out the addresses and fly them back to the Soviet Union . . .

The song celebrates the feelings of many paratroopers fighting intense operational tours in exotic locations far from home:

And somewhere there's a last flight taken by oneself,
Where the sun shines hot, where there's still war.
Those who don't believe, let them,
Those who've been there know everything.

Like the dead Soviet airborne, British paratroopers were at first delivered home anonymously. Bringing the dead home was a break in the practice established by imperial tradition, when British soldiers were buried where they fell. Commonwealth War Graves were established for them and immaculately kept. Hardened fundamentalist Muslim opinion has made this practice less appropriate more recently. The British public characteristically picked up the initiative, taking their fallen soldiers to their hearts. Without being asked, the citizens of a small Wiltshire country town cut through seeming bureaucratic indifference and independently instituted a simple poignant ceremony to mark the return of British war dead from Iraq and Afghanistan. The doleful ring of the church bell at Wootten Bassett as its dignified inhabitants line the streets and toss flower stems onto Union-Jack draped coffins movingly encapsulates the nation's collective grief.

Thirty-three soldiers were killed during the 2008 16th Air Assault Brigade Afghan tour. Paratroopers gathered in their favourite drinking haunts on return to celebrate the lives of their fallen comrades, exactly as their contemporaries had done decades before, after Arnhem.

POSTSCRIPT

'What manner of men are these who wear the red beret?' asked Field Marshall Bernard Montgomery rhetorically in 1947. 'They are in fact men apart – every man an emperor,' he declared. There is general acceptance that airborne soldiers are indeed special. A number of characteristics, tangible and intangible, set Sky Men apart from other soldiers. Modern British paratroopers regard non-parachute soldiers colloquially as 'crap-hats' because they wear a mixture of coloured berets rather than the maroon 'red beret'. 'If you pass through P Company you get your red beret,' explained Corporal John Geddes who fought with 2 PARA in the Falklands, declaring: 'And that is a moment I'll savour for the rest of my life. I held it in my hands as though it were made of gold and encrusted with diamonds. To me it was the dog's bollocks and I couldn't wait to put it on.'

American paratroopers regard non-parachute infantry as simply 'legs', because they do not go by air to battle. Russian paratroopers agreed doctrinally they were 'more equal than others', an exception to normal socialist egalitarian values. German Fallschirmjäger saw themselves as 'the chosen fighting men of the Wehrmacht'. This exclusivity lies at the core of the 'airborne spirit'. French parachute regiments not only dressed differently in distinctive tiger-stripe camouflage fatigues from the start, like many other airborne forces, they emphasised their functional difference. They were an elite 'fire-brigade' that France called upon in her hour of need. Most French parachute regiments were part of the Colonial Army or Foreign Legion; few were Metropolitan French Army. American regiments have retained their '500' numeral distinction within regimental designations, even though one of its two airborne divisions, the 101st, is air-mobile.

Iconic battle honours, like Arnhem for the British, represent the spirit of the formation concerned. Officers were killed during the Falklands battles of 1982 exhorting their troops to attack and 'remember Arnhem'. Dien Bien Phu, another epic defeat, is commemorated each year by French paratroopers. The Pyrrhic victory at Crete represents the qualities the German Fallschirmjäger wish to see endure, while for the American airborne Normandy and the Battle of the Bulge personifies the qualities inherent in fighting alone against impossible odds.

Battle honours are not only unique to airborne units in promoting or personifying an indistinguishable spirit. Other characteristics are identifiable within the Paratrooper 'Ten Commandments' promoted by the Fallschirmjäger of World War Two and the American 'Parachutist's Creed' that emerged in written form during the 1950s. Both extol elitism. 'You shall be the German Warrior incarnate' proclaimed the final German Commandment, whereas the Americans 'belong to the finest fighting unit in the Army'.

It was always anticipated paratroopers would have to fight alone and often unsupported. American paratroopers were expected to display a 'higher degree of initiative than that required of other troops'. Likewise, German Fallschirmjäger had to 'grasp the full intention of any operation, so that if your leader is killed you can fulfil it yourself'. Acceptance of high casualties was implicit in all of this. 'Surrender is not in my creed' even 'though I be the lone survivor' the Americans' creed pronounced. Germans were told simply, 'You will do or die'. Common to both creeds was the belief they were shock troops and that they were likely to die leading the way.

Volunteering for a tough selection process and the act of parachuting, a tangible display of courage and daring, produced a range of rigorous physical and psychological demands as near to actual combat as can be devised by any military training. It was this immediate physical and psychological readiness that differentiated parachute and commando soldiers from other line infantry during the Falklands War of 1982.

As the helicopter became increasingly more powerful and sufficiently robust for primarily counter-insurgency operations, a belief arose in many armies that helicopters were the equivalent of 'flying trucks'. As with glider infantry, less individual proficiency was required to achieve the same or similar impact on the battlefield. Landing within piloted aircraft does not require the physical and emotional resolve needed to jump with a parachute. For this reason many nations have retained parachute forces even though technical alternatives are available. 'To be fair,' stated one British airborne veteran commenting on why a paratrooper company was directed to assist the SAS Operation Barras rescue mission in 2000, 'you cannot have an organisation which carries out an additional level of selection and one that specialises in light airborne and heliborne operations and then pretend it is the same as the line infantry.' Helicopters are broadly useful at ranges up to 100 miles, parachutists out beyond 500 miles.

The whole point of individual preparation still remains in the amount of combat power such forces can generate on landing. British paratroopers jumping through customised bomb bay holes in the floors of converted bombers required more individual parachute ground training than those jumping the open doors of a C-47 Dakota. Likewise the skills required for paras are greater than for the heliborne. Fighting power on the ground has traditionally been more pronounced from those who have undergone parachute selection and training than light infantry adapted for helicopter insertion. Paratroopers are selected for their psychological staying power and courage and determination to withstand the rigours of a low-level jump, probably in darkness. They are imbued with a raider mentality, enabling them to operate alone, with minimal supervision when surrounded by the enemy, which is often the case when they are parachuted to battle. A unique blend of tactical flexibility enables them to fight conventionally, then, if tactically required, disperse into small groups, maybe to reform again elsewhere.

The close bonding that results from parachute selection allows all volunteers, whatever their country, race or creed, to identify easily with other paratroopers. British paratrooper Corporal John Geddes explained the bonding that sustained his unit in the Falklands: 'To me it's quite clear that we were a brotherhood and what bound us together in a solid fraternity was our initiation into the regiment. It's a horrible test of guts, stamina and determination called P Company and it's the only membership card there is to the airborne club.'

This ability to identify closely with comrades in battle is the essence of small unit combat durability, which means that, if properly led, such men can produce those defining impacts in conflict that enable battles to be won.

These are the characteristics that have traditionally set Sky Men apart from other soldiers. They are extremely robust, physically and mentally, which reinforces a general air of confidence and well-being. All appreciate they are part of an elite, who seek to excel in an unconventional way of fighting, by air to battle, soldiers with a buccaneering mentality, able instantly to switch on controlled aggression, which produces tenacity in both attack and defence. Free-thinking is enmeshed within a 'will do – can do' attitude, as comfortable working alone or with a major size formation.

These are the Sky Men.

ACKNOWLEDGMENTS

A considerable amount of fresh archive material emerged with the move of the Airborne Assault Museum Archive to Duxford in Cambridgeshire in 2008. The part digitisation of the new archive enabled an electronic retrieval of many previously unseen papers that had been gathering dust in filing cabinets at the Aldershot Museum. I am greatly indebted to Alan Brown, the then Assistant Curator, for bringing many interesting items to my attention for inclusion within the new 'Paradata' website covering the history of the Parachute Regiment and airborne forces, of which I was the editor. A lot of this uncovered material included fascinating human stories charting the development of the airborne soldier and was largely unseen.

I am particularly indebted to Colonel John Waddy for his helpful advice, supplemented by numerous articles and material covering his career from the beginning of airborne forces and by his own specialist knowledge. There was further excellent support from Sir John Keegan, Lieutenant Colonel (retd) Christopher Walch and Andrew Orgill, the Chief Librarian at the Royal Military Academy at Sandhurst. I am indebted to Cathy Pugh and the staff of the Second World War Experience Centre at Leeds for a number of vivid interview accounts. The staff at the newly opened Airborne Assault Museum at Duxford are as helpful as their predecessors at Aldershot and should capitalise on the amazing archive material and airborne library they have at their disposal.

I had excellent support from a large number of airborne soldiers past and present and these are acknowledged in the notes to sources. I hope I have accurately reflected the private thoughts of my interviewees and the experiences and emotions they so generously shared. I wish to thank in particular Tony Hibbert, my uncle William Kershaw, 'Kit' Carson and Harry Chatfield. I received expert technical guidance and assistance from Emily Sands in conducting a number of interviews and Bob Hilton, who very generously placed some of his own interviewed material at my disposal.

Every effort has been made to trace the source and copyright of quotations and photographs in the text and these are acknowledged where appropriate. My thanks to those publishers who have permitted quotations and extracts from their books; sources are annotated in the notes and the bibliography at the end of the book. My apologies are offered in advance to those with whom, for any reason, I was unable to establish contact.

My thanks again to my agent Charlie Viney and editor Rupert Lancaster for their astute advice and encouragement. Finally, as ever, my love and gratitude to my wife Lynn for putting up with the long gestation period required to acquire the material and actually finish this book.

R K

PICTURE ACKNOWLEDGMENTS

Author's collection: 4 above, 5 below, 7 above, 14 above. From S. Badsey, *D-Day*, CLB, 1993: 9 below. From J.P. Bernier, *Dien Bien Phu*, Michel Lafon, 2003: 12 below. From E.R. Bonds, *The Vietnam War*, Salamander, 1979: 14 below. From M.W. Bowman, *Remembering D-Day*, Harper Collins, 2004. Corbis: 11 below. From D. Francois, *The 507th Parachute Regiment*, Heimdal, 2000: 4 below, 5 above, 8 below. From W.Geriche, *Soldaten Fallen von Himmel*, Berlin 1940: 1 below right, 2, 3. Illustrated London News: 6 above. Imperial War Museum: 10 above (BU 1163), 10 below (CL 1168), 11 above (EA 59364A). From J.P. Pallud, *L'Operation Merkur*, Heimdal, 1987: 6 below. Pegasus Magazine, Winter 2008: 1 above, 16 below. From A. von Roon, *Bildchronik der Fallschirmtruppe 1935–45*, Podzun Pallas, 1985: 8 above. TopFoto/The Granger Collection: 1 below left. United States Army Heritage and Education Center: 7 below. From *War in Peace*, Orbis, 1983 vol 1: 16 above, *ibid* vol 2: 12 above, *ibid* vol 3: 13, *ibid* vol 8: 15.

Every reasonable effort has been made to contact the copyright holders, but if there are any errors or omissions, Hodder & Stoughton will be pleased to insert the appropriate acknowledgment in any subsequent printing of this publication.

Appendix I

THE FALLSCHIRMJÄGER
TEN COMMANDMENTS

1. You are the chosen ones of the German Army. You will seek combat and train yourselves to endure any manner of test. To you, the battle shall be fulfilment.
2. Cultivate true comradeship, for by the aid of your comrades you will conquer or die.
3. Beware of talking. Be not corruptible. Men act while women chatter. Chatter may bring you to the grave.
4. Be calm and prudent, strong and resolute. Valour and enthusiasm of an offensive spirit will cause you to prevail in the attack.
5. The most precious thing in the presence of the foe is ammunition. He who shoots uselessly, merely to comfort himself, is a man of straw who merits not the title of Parachutist.
6. Never surrender; to you death or victory must be a point of honour.
7. You can triumph only if your weapons are good. See to it that you submit yourself to this law – first my weapon and then myself.
8. You must grasp the full purpose of every enterprise, so that if your leader is killed you can fulfil it.
9. Against an open foe, fight with chivalry, but to a guerrilla, extend no quarter.
10. Keep your eyes wide open. Tune yourself to the topmost pitch. Be nimble as a greyhound, as tough as leather, as hard as Krupp steel and so you shall be the German warrior incarnate.

Appendix II

THE AMERICAN PARACHUTIST'S CREED

I volunteered as a Parachutist, fully realizing the hazards of my chosen service – and by my thoughts and by my actions will always uphold the prestige, honor and high esprit-de-corps of the only volunteer branch of the Army.

I realize that a Parachutist is not merely a soldier who arrives by parachute to fight, but is an elite shock trooper and that his country expects him to march farther and faster, to fight harder, to be more self-reliant and to soldier better than any other soldier. Parachutists of all allied armies belong to this great brotherhood.

I shall never fail my fellow comrades by shirking any duty or training, but will always keep myself mentally and physically fit and shoulder my full share of the task, whatever it may be.

I shall always accord my superiors fullest loyalty and I will always bear in mind the sacred trust I have in the lives of the men I will lead into battle.

I shall show other soldiers by my military courtesy to my superior officers and non-commissioned officers, by my neatness of dress, by my care of my weapons and equipment that I am a picked and well trained soldier.

I shall endeavor always by my soldierly appearance, military bearing and behavior, to reflect the high standards of training and morale of parachute troops.

I shall respect the abilities of my enemies; I will fight fairly and with all my might. Surrender is not in my creed.

I shall display a higher degree of initiative than is required of other troops and will fight on to my objective and mission, though I be the lone survivor.

I shall prove my ability as a fighting man against the enemy on the field of battle, not by quarreling with my comrades in arms or by bragging about my deeds, thus needlessly arousing jealousy and resentment against parachute troops.

I shall always realize that battles are won by an army fighting as a team, that I fight and blaze the path into battle for others to follow and to carry the battle on.

I belong to the finest fighting unit in the Army. By my appearance, actions, and battlefield deeds alone, I speak for my fighting ability. I will strive to uphold the honor and prestige of my outfit, making my country proud of me and of the unit.

NOTES ON SOURCES

PROLOGUE

p. 4 'They thought if', Bangura, interview, *SAS Jungle Rescue*, Prod/Dir M Catling, Darlow Smithson Production 2009.

p. 5 'When I had drunk', 'Turkish', interview, ibid.

p. 6 'We were dealing', Mathews, interview, ibid. Sheard, interview, *Soldier* Magazine, Oct 2000.

p. 6 'I did not expect', Sheard, interview, ibid. Para veteran, quoted *Operation Barras*, W. Fowler, p. 115.

p. 6 'You are excited', Mathews, interview, *SAS Jungle Rescue*. Cradden, interview, Soldier Oct 2000.

p. 7 'Mayhem reigned', Blood and Kamara, Fowler p. 141. Turkish and Kallay, interviews, *SAS Jungle Rescue*.

p. 8 'The Lynx helicopters', Kamara, Fowler, p. 139. Mathews, interview, ibid. Sheard *Soldier* interview.

p. 8 'It was almost chaos', Mathews and Sheard ibid.

p. 9 'These kids have grown', Burke, quoted *Modern Warfare*, R. Connaughton, p. 286.

p. 11 'How did you find', British trainer, quoted *Operation Barras*, R. Connaughton, *Small Wars and Insurgencies*, Vol 12, No. 2, Summer 2001, p. 119.

1 THE LOCUST WARRIORS

From guardian angel to instrument of war.

p. 13 'Five hundred years later', Nicholas and O'Malley quotes and account based on *Guardian* newspaper article 9 Jul 2000 and report by R.H. Williams Invisible Heroes.com2003.

p. 14 'Five thousand balloons', Franklin quoted *Out of the Sky*, M.Hickey, p. 9.

p. 16 'a sudden crackling', Struck, quoted *Soldaten Fallen vom Himmel*, W.Gericke, pp.33–5.

p. 16 'required no small amount', Wilkinson and observer, quoted *The Big Umbrella*, J. Lucas, pp. 56–7.

p. 17 'An estimated 800 to 900', Figure from *Bale Out!*, I.B. Wright, p. 11.

p. 17 'I truly wished him', Rickenbacker, quoted *Paratrooper!*, GM Devlin, p. 21.

p. 18 'With little required', Wedgwood Benn, *On the Sidelines*, Hodder and Stoughton 1924, quoted P. Hearn, pp. 97–8.

p. 18 'Tandura survived the experience', Evrard and Kossel, quoted from *Achtung Fallschirmjäger*, A. von Hove, pp. 11 and 14.

p. 18 'We should arm', Mitchell, quoted *Paratrooper!*, GM Devlin p. 22.

From stunt men to locust warriors

p. 20   'climbed over the cockpit', Smith, quoted P. Hearn and Devlin pp. 24 and 27.

p. 20   'Nah don't fergit', Corlett, *Flight Magazine* article, AAM archive.

p. 21   'no training whatsoever!', Harry Ward, interview 16 Aug 1988, AAM Archive.

p. 21   'There were only two ways', Ward and Corlett ibid.

p. 22   'Gleb Kotelnikov', Kotelnikov, based on article *Airborne Troops of the Soviet Army*, I. Lisov and *Parachuting Sport*, AM Lukin. (See Bib).

p. 22   'On 16 July 1934', Evdokimov, *Prelude to Glory*, M. Newnham, p.125.

p. 23   'anyone desiring to do so', Notes on a conversation with Lt Gen Browning 26 Jul 1944, AAM Archive.

p. 23   'it fosters and strengthens', Research, *The Effect of Acting Parachuting on the Human Organism*, quoted from *Airborne Assault Training, Vozdushno-desantnaya podgotovka*, Lt Gen II Lisov, Moscow 1977, AAM Archive.

p. 23   'Jumps from an aeroplane', Pamphlet, quoted M. Newnham, p.128.

p. 23   'permitted them to be', Lisov, *Airborne Assault Training*, p. 20.

p. 24   'As was always the case', Starinov, *Over the Abyss*, pp. 45 and 47; Medical research, M. Newnham, chart p. 126.

p. 24   'Even an organisation', Experimentation, *Desantniki Vozdushnye desanty*, II Lisov, *Russian Airborne History*, Moskva Voenizdat 1968, pp.14–16, AAM archive.

p. 25   'Wild acceleration', Starinov, *Over the Abyss*, p. 46.

p. 26   'The foreign observers', Figures and detail, Lisov, p. 24 and 26–7; and *A History of Soviet Airborne Forces*, D. Glantz, p.17.

p. 26   'The French immediately', Loiseau and Monti, quoted *Inside the Blue Berets*, S. Zaloga, p.14; Dastikh, quoted Lisov, p. 27; Voroshilov, quoted M. Newnham, pp. 127–8.

p. 27   'The endemic trouble', Frost, *Nearly There*, Leo Cooper 1991, p. 70.

2 NEW SKY MEN: FALLSCHIRMJÄGER

Special men for a special task

p. 28   'In November 1935', Demonstration background, *Deutsche Fallshirmjäger 1939–45*, F Kurowski, Zeit Geschichte, 1990, p.13. Baumer, interview quoted *Green Devils–Red Devils*, E. Blandford, pp. 14–15.

p. 29   'In October 1935', German press 4 Oct 1935, quoted *A History of Soviet Airborne Forces*, D. Glantz, p. 19.

p. 30   'We relied on', Baumer, Blandford, p. 16.

p. 30   'Recruitment came in waves', Stastical data from *Chronik 1940, Statistische Zahlen*, p. 212 and *The 1st Fallschirmjager Division in WW II*, B Christiansen, p. 19.

p. 30   'Men, are you willing', Shulz and Merreys, Christiansen, pp. 78–9 and 23. Weise, interview Blandford, p. 20.

p. 31   'Fallschirmjäger!', Von Hove, *Achtung Fallschirmjäger!* p. 22. Karl D., interview, full name withheld, *Der Adler* Luftwaffe pictorial magazine, Heft 16 1942, p. 98. Career highlights, Christiansen, p. 19.

p. 31   'at once struck me', Seibert, interview, Blandford, p. 19. Pöppel, *Heaven and Hell*, p. 9.

p. 32   'In the Hitler Youth', Köppen and Damaske, interviews, *Hitler's Children*, G Knopp and P Hartl, ZDF German TV, 2000.

p. 32 'We were harassed', Gaerte, Chritiansen, p. 22.

p. 32 'unbelievably hard', Pöppel, *Heaven and Hell*, pp. 10 and 17. Merreys, Christansen, p. 26.

p. 33 'First came the ground', Pollman, Christiansen, p. 26. Pöppel, p. 12. Pickert and Seibert, interviews, Blandford. p. 25 and 23.

p. 34 'Twelve soldiers sat', Pickert, Baumer and Seibert, Blandford, pp. 16, 26 and 24. Pöppel, p. 12.

p. 35 'shock of opening', Fink, *Der Komet auf Kreta*, pp. 35–6.

p. 36 '. . . jumping off a low roof', Von Roon, *Die Bildchronik der Fallschirmtruppe 1939–1945*, pp.12-13. Von Hove, *Achtung Fallschirmjäger!*, p. 337.

p. 36 'Wonderful – I'm out', Pöppel, p.12. Seibert and Pickert, Blandford, p. 24. Merreys, Christiansen, pp. 26–7.

Vertical envelopment or circus stunting?

p. 37 'I am sure you will', Milch and Moreau, *Junkers Ju 52*, HJ Nowarra, p. 43.

p. 38 'By 15 September', Detail ibid p. 43 and *Achtung Fallschirmjäger!*, A von Hove, p. 26–7

p. 39 'In those days', Paul, quoted *Die Geschichte des Fallschirmjäger Regiment 2*, W Kamman, p. 11.

p. 39 'Vertical envelopment', Trettner, interview 1991, *Fort Eben Emael*, W Mauder and S Sessner, German TV doc AV-Medienproduktion.

p. 40 'For the planned', Bassenge, interrogation report, CSDIC(UK) 24 Sep 45, Para 33, AAM archive. Para strength, von Roon, p. 29.

p. 41 'Some hundred Ju's', Pöppel, p. 11.

p. 41 'through sympathetic farmers', Intelligence background, von Roon, p. 28.

p. 42 'this completely insignificant', Bassenge, interrogation report ibid.

p. 42 'I had no girlfriend', Pickert, Blandford, p. 26.

p. 42 'These developments', W Buckingham, *Paras*, Tempus 2005, pp. 43–4.

p. 43 'I left at 1,000 feet', Interview, 16 Aug 1988, AAM archive.

p. 44 *Picture Post*, 11 Feb 1939, p. 28.

p. 44 Italians, *Airborne Warfare*, B Gregory and J Batchelor, Phoebus 1979, p. 54. Americans, *Paratrooper!* , GM Devlin, pp.34–7.

p. 45 'Vertical envelopment', Von Roon, *Achtung Fallschirmjäger!*, pp. 40–1. Göring, confidence to US fighter ace EV Rickenbacker, quoted *The Fall of Eben Emael*, Mrazek, p. 39. Speech, interview J Steinhoff, *Voices From the Third Reich*, Steinhoff, Pechel and Showalter, Grafton Books 1991, p. 36.

p. 45 'Strongly impressed', Räbel, *Green Devils*, Jean-Yves Nasse, Histoire and Collections 1997, pp. 6–7.

p. 46 *Der Adler*, Heft 15, 1939, p. 78. Frettlohr, interview, P Liddle, SWWEC, Jun 1999.

p. 47 'This seemed to me', Cartland, *The First Towed Glider*, *The Eagle* (AAC) magazine, Vol 6, No 5, Apr 90.

p. 47 'This question naturally', Interview, 1991, *Fort Eben Emael*, W Mauder and S Sessner, German TV doc AV-Medienproduktion.

p. 48 'nobody gives a damn', Jeschonnek, quoted Mrazek, p. 42.

p. 48 'It happened very quickly', Pöppel, pp. 19–20 and 21. Von Roon, p. 33.

p. 49 'we should know', Holland, quoted *Early Days at Ringway*, M. Lindsay, article Pegasus magazine Vol 1, No 1, Apr 46 and private letter 24 Jul 76 AAM Archive.

3 THEORY INTO PRACTICE: THE LOW COUNTRIES, MAY 1940

Scandinavian prelude, 9 April 1940

p. 50 'They wanted to know', Gericke, *Der Deutsche Fallschirmjäger* magazine, No 4, 1953, p. 5.

p. 51 'knees trembling', Gericke, *Soldaten Fallen vom Himmel*, p. 95.

p. 51 'We have already', Krupp, Christiansen, *The 1st Fallschirmjager Division in WWII*, p. 50.

p. 51 'escorted by Messerschmitt', Walther and Wagner, Christiansen, p. 51.

p. 53 'very experimental', Pickert, interview, Blandford, p. 57.

p. 54 'drip-landing', Brauchitsch, *Achtung Fallschirmjäger!*, Von Hove, pp. 44–5.

Aerial break-in: the low countries, 10 May 1940

p. 56 'Gefreiter Wilhelm Alefs', Alefs, *The Fall of Eben Emael*, Mrazek, p. 62. Witzig and Lange, interviews, *Eben Emael*, Film W Mauder and S Sessner 1991. (Henceforth EE Film).

p. 56 'Hauptmann Karl Lothar Schulz', Schulz, *Sieg uber Frankreich*, p. 37. Kamman, *Die Geschischte des Fallschirmjager Regiments 2 1939–45*, p. 22.

p. 57 'Wilhelm Alefs recalled', Alefs and Witzig, Mrazek, pp. 63 and 66.

p. 58 'Every pilot was allotted', Pfitzner, interview, EE Film. Hitler, quoted *Fort Eben Emael*, T Saunders, p. 76.

p. 58 'I could hear a single', Alefs, Mrazek, p. 68.

p. 59 'One by one', Baumbach, *The Race for the Rhine Bridges*, A McKee, pp. 32–3.

p. 59 'As we picked up', Alefs, Mrazek, ibid. Wenzel, interview EE Film.

p. 61 'It was dawn', Engelmann, quoted T Saunders pp. 91–2, Distelmeier, interview EE Film.

p. 61 'A few observation posts', Lecluse, quoted article *Plötzlich Kamen Grosse Graue, Stumme Vögel* from *Der Zweite Weltkrieg*, Band 1, John Jahr Verlag 1975, pp. 278–9.

p. 62 'It was somewhat strange', Langer, interview EE Film and Mrazek p. 88.

p. 62 'I have to say', Interview, *Fort Eben Emael*, Film by W.D. Mauder and S. Sessner, AV-Medien Produktion 1991.

The envelopment of 'Fortress Holland'.

p. 64 'We had thought', Schulz, *Sieg über Frankreich*, pp. 37–8.

p. 65 'Air raid alarm red!', Dutch officer and Baumbach, McKee, pp. 33–4.

p. 66 'As if by magic', Dutch officer, McKee p. 36.

p. 67 Shooting at parachutes data from *Der Komet auf Kreta*, F Fink, pp. 45–6. Schulz, pp. 38–9.

p. 68 'During this last maneouvre', Lead pilot, quoted from *Die Deutsche Fallschirmjager 1939–45*, F Kurowski, p.103.

p. 70 'shocking', Pilot reports, *Chronik der IV/KG z.b.1.*, Kurowski, p. 104.

p. 70 'they were magnificent', Mommaas, quoted *Blitzkrieg in the West. Then and Now*. JP Pallud, After the Battle, 1991, p. 116.

p. 72 'The howl of aero-engines', Von Choltitz, quoted McKee p. 38.

p. 72 'In stark contrast ', Bruns, quoted McKee p. 41–2.

p. 72 'The situation', Figures, JP Pallud, p. 123.

p. 73   'We find his body', Pöppel, *Heaven and Hell*, pp. 34–5.

p. 74   'There's great jubilation', ibid p. 35.

p. 75   'The new warfare ', Casualties, *Achtung Fallschirmjäger!*, von Hove, p. 82.

p. 75   'There are no longer', Pöppel, p. 35.

4 WE NEED A CORPS OF PARACHUTE TROOPS

Playing 'catch-up'

p. 76   'The Paris newspaper', *Le Figaro* report, Christiansen p. 99. *Herald Tribune* report from *Notes on Parachute Troops, No 2 Commando*, 12.11.40. AAM Archive. (Henceforward referred to as *No 2 Cdo Notes.*) *Svenska Dagbladet*, Christiansen, p. 99.

p. 77   'we ought to have', Memo, WSC to Ismay, 22.6.40.

p. 77   'start parachute troops', Lindsay, Letter 24.7.76, AAM Archive.

p. 78   'There are very real', M Newnham, *Prelude to Glory*, p. 7.

p. 78   'the usual cold stares', Strange, *The History of No 1 PTS Ringway 1940–45*, PW Jevons, Ms held by AAM Archive.

p. 79   'The First Sergeant', Soldier's comments, quoted *Paratrooper!*, GM Devlin, p. 49.

p. 79   'Japan began training', Japanese para, *Japanese Parachute Troops*, Ed DB McLean, Normont Tech Pub 1973, p. 1.

p. 80   '5 deaths and 12 cases', Japanese intelligence extracts, *No 2 Cdo Notes*.

p. 80   'We were a motley crowd', Lawley, *An Account of the Experiences of an Early Parachutist*, AAM Archive. Elvin, Letter 31 Aug 1987 and Cook, Letter 30 Jul 1987, quoted from *The Men of the Maroon Beret 1940–45 a Social History*, T Deane, BA Dissertation 1988. (Henceforward *Deane Dissertation*).

p. 81   'Some time in June', Smith, *The Formation of the Parachute Regiment from No 2 Cdo and 11 SAS Regiment*, private Ms 2007, AAM Archive. Chinnery, Letter to Canopy Club Secretary, 12 Sep 1998, AAM Archive. Hibbert, interview with author, 18 Dec 2007. Timothy, *Tim's Tale*, H Grenville, private pub 2008, p. 4, AAM Archive.

p. 81   'eight little blobs', Hibbert, interview ibid. Hancock, *A Citizen's Journal*, private pub, pp. 1–2, AAM Archive.

p. 82   'In the early days', Smith, private pub, p. 43. Curtis, *Churchill's Volunteer*, p. 47.

p. 82   'At Ringway', Deane-Drummond, *Return Ticket*, p. 14.

p. 82   'Some conditions were', Curtis, pp. 54 and 63.

p. 83   'How to land?', Smith ibid.

p. 83   'You had to crawl', Ward, interview, 16 Aug 1988. Dawes, *History of No 1 PTS*, PW Jevons, pp. 4–5.

p. 84   'Unfortunately we usually', Lindsay, *Early days at Ringway, Pegasus* magazine, Vol I, No 1, Apr 1946.

p. 84   'When the red light', Smith, pp. 42–3.

p. 86   'Lieutenant John Kilkenny', Kilkenny, interview 5 Dec 1989, AAM Archive. Devlin, *Paratrooper!* , p. 55.

p. 86   'Like the British', Parachute test drop, Devlin, p. 60.

First blood

p. 88   'We arrived at the Drome', Likely 27 Aug 40. Lawley.

p. 88   'Corporal Ernie Chinnery', Chinnery, letter 12 Sep 1998, AAM archive, Lawley P.1 ibid. Kilkenny, interview 5 Dec 1989, AAM archive.

p. 89   'Of this number', Newnham , *Prelude to Glory*, p.21. Lindsay, letter 24 Jul 1976, AAM Archive.

p. 90   'To drop 600 or 700', Note, DCOS Office Note. Secret B(4)3 dated 23 Aug 1940, AAM Archive.

p. 90   'I am strongly', Note to PM, 27 Jul 1940, AAM Archive.

p. 90   'Some of these adventures', Garlic story, Curtis pp. 49–50 and Newnham p. 37. Hibbert, interview, 18 Dec 2007.

p. 91   'The success of the past', Minutes of Air ministry Meeting headed by VCIGS, 1530 5 Sep 1940, AAM Archive.

p. 91   'Ignorance about gliders', Gliders, *We Want a Glider*, article Pegasus magazine, Vol 1, No 1, Apr 1946. p. 49.

p. 92   'It was the gliders', Ward, interview, 16 Aug 1988. Maufe, *Memories of RAF Ringway 1940–42*, Manchester Airport Archive, copy held by AAM Archive.

p. 92   'The first prototype', Test flights, *We Want a Glider*, *Pegasus* Art ibid.

p. 93   'I got three', Ward, interview, ibid.

p. 93   'To keep position', Fender, quoted article *How it Began*, Reg Leach, Eagle Journal, Vol 6, No 5, Apr 1990, p. 7.

p. 94   'It was worse', Observer, *We want a Glider*, *Pegasus* Art, p. 50.

p. 94   'Normally, one reduces power', Johnson, Leach article, p. 8 and referring to accident 19 Dec 1941.

p. 96   'Sergeant Arthur Lawley', Lawley, personal account, p. 2. Deane-Drummond, *Return Ticket*, p. 17.

p. 98   '*Whoomf!*', Lawley, p. 4. Deane-Drummond, pp. 25–7 and 31.

p. 100   'All that we could', Maufe, Memories of RAF Ringway 1940–42, p. 2. Ward, interview, 16 Aug 1988.

p. 100   'Let me have this day', Letter PM to Ismay, 28 Apr 1941 cabinet 120/262, quoted *Paras*, W Buckingham, p. 139

5 CRETE: A STRATEGIC GOAL

Prelude: the first airborne corps in history

p. 102   'Company Commander', Von Roon and Sturm, quoted article *Fallschirmjager Einsatz bei Korinth 1941. Deutscher Fallschimjäger* magazine. No.3, Mai–Jun 84, pp. 6–8.

p. 103   'What was that?', Von der Heydte, *Daedalus Returned. Crete* 1941, pp. 30–31.

p. 104   'To parachute down', Reinhardt, *Trilogy*, private publication, p. 10.

p. 104   'Advance parties', Von der Heydte, *Planned Airborne Operations*, Interrogation Report conducted 23 Dec 1944, Secret CSDIC (UK) SIR 1438, 31 Jan 1945, AAM Archive.

p. 105   'the existence of a German', Reinhardt, *Trilogy*, p. 10.

p. 105   'Media publicity . . .', Schmelling, Adler, Heft 4, 1941, p. 33. Propaganda statements quoted from article *Nur ganze Kerle sind dabei. Adler* magazine, Heft 16, 1942, p. 98.

p. 106   'idealists', Von der Heydte, *Daedalus Returned*, pp. 25–6.

p. 107 'The parachutist on the other hand', ibid pp. 22–3.

p. 107 'Although the National Socialist', Fink, Der Komet auf Kreta, pp. 55–7. Reinhardt, Trilogy, p. 11.

p. 108 'Communists and Socialists', Reinhardt, pp. 16 and 23. Hüttl, Spitz and Ball, Christiansen, The 1ˢᵗ Fallschirmjäger Division in WWII, p. 23.

p. 108 'I liked the adventurers', Von der Heydte, Daedalus Returned, pp. 25–6. Pöppel, Heaven and Hell, pp. 45–6. Austermann, Christiansen, p. 23.

p. 109 'Student presented his plan', Logistic detail, Air Supply Problems of the Crete Campaign, Interrogation report Maj Gen Conrad Seibt, APWIV 97/1945 dated 1 Sep 1945. AAM Archive.

p. 111 'These reinforcements', Von der Heydte, p. 43.

p. 111 'German intelligence was inaccurate', Student's intelligence appreciation personally given during 16 Para Bde battlefield tour of Crete 12 Feb 1970, AAM Archive.

p. 112 'Compresses into the space', Bräuer, quoted The Sky People, P. Hearn, p. 103.

p. 112 'psychologists may ponder', Von der Heydte, p. 66. Meindl and figures, General Meidl und seine Fallschirmjäger, M Winterstein and H Jacobs, p. 19.

'Touch and Go': The Fallschirmjäger experience on Crete

p. 113 'The 28ᵗʰ Maori Battalion', Dyer, Dittmer quoted, Te Mura o tea hi – The Story of the Maori Battalion, W. Gardiner, pp. 59 and 61. Marriott, oral account, Battlefield Tour of Crete, 44 Para Bde, 4–8 Aug 1966, AAM Archive. Thomas, interview, Touch and Go – The Battle for Crete May 1941, T. Steel and J Isaacs, NZ Broadcasting Corp TV documentary. (Henceforward Touch and Go).

p. 115 'On 19 May', Pöppel, Heaven and Hell, p. 54. Strauch, article Dieser Sieg war Keiner, Diary account from Deutsche Fallschirmjäger magazine, No 2, Mar/Apr 1981. Reinhardt, Trilogy, p. 31.

p. 115 'The air-land soldiers', Mountain soldier, Gebirgsjager Auf Kreta, S Dobiasch, pp. 32 and 41. Fink, Der Komet Auf Kreta, pp. 94–8 and 101–3.

p. 117 'We started to move', Von der Heydte, Daedalus Returned pp. 52–3 and interview Touch and Go.

p. 118 'A glider has cut loose', Fink, p. 104.

p. 118 'In the early hours', Donald and Irving, interviews, Touch and Go.

p. 119 'Only a few minutes', Fink, pp. 104–11.

p. 119 'The first we had', Kippenberger, Infantry Brigadier, OUP 1949, p. 52.

p. 119 'infernal din of firing', Seiler, interview, quoted Green Devils-Red Devils, E Blandford, pp. 76–7.

p. 120 'a pathetic looking German', Ashworth, Crete 1941. Eyewitnessed. Hadjipateras and Fafalios. Greek publication. Farren, interview, Touch and Go.

p. 121 'I was quite confident', Von Schutz, interview, Touch and Go. Von der Heydte, pp. 57–8.

p. 122 'I saw them crawling', Ashworth, Eyewitnessed, p.84. Queerie and Gordon, interviews, Touch and Go.

p. 122 'A machine gun burst', Könitz, article Wir holen ihn heraus! Deutsche Fallschirmjager (DF) magazine, No 3, Mai/Jun 1982. Wenzel, article DF, No 5 Sep/Okt 1983.

p. 123 'We just kept firing', Wakahuru, interview, Touch and Go.

p. 123 'I know I cursed', Pickert, Green Devils-Red Devils, E Blandford, p. 79.

p. 123 'I think I'll never forget', Thomas, interview, Touch and Go.

p. 124   'Only the II and IV', German signals traffic Gruppe West, Radio log: *Funkverkehr des Regimentsstabes während des Einsatzes Kreta vom 20.5.41.*, taken from *Kreta 1941*, H Mühleisen, Verlag Rombach Freiberg 1968, p. 97.

p. 124   'I could see no soldiers', Von der Heydte, pp. 62 and 97.

'A victory that wasn't a victory': the second wave and air-land experience

p. 126   'The parachute insertion', Pöppel, *Heaven and Hell*, p. 54. Reinhardt, *Trilogy*, pp. 32–4. Strauch, Diary article. Eiben, *Erlebnisbericht eines Sanitatsoffiziers.*, *DF*, No 5, 1991.

p. 127   'At 16.00 hours', Marriott, oral account, 44 Bde battlefield tour 1966, AAM Archive.

p. 128   'Even before reaching', Eiben, *Elebnis Bericht*, ibid. Strauch, diary article.

p. 128   'We were regaled', Marriott, ibid. Lind, *Flowers of Rethymnon*, Kangeroo Press Pty Ktd, 1991, pp. 19–20.

p. 129   'we have few hopes', Strauch, diary, 24 May.

p. 129   'If only we could', Thomas, interview, *Touch and Go*.

p. 130   'The spotter planes', Irving, interview, ibid.

p. 130   'On the second night', Naval engagement, article *Die Tragodie auf See*, *DF*, No 2, Mar/Apr 1982.

p. 130   'When finally are they', Jäger, *Gebirgsjäger Auf Kreta*, S Dobiasch, pp.34 and 36–7. Leutnant, ibid, p. 54. Neher, article *Gebirgsjager Landen Auf Kreta* taken from *Von Serbien bis Kreta*, p. 144.

p. 131   'a huge reddish dust', Leutnant, Dobiasch, p. 55. Fink, *Der Komet auf Kreta*, pp. 324–7.

p. 132   'Now he grits his teeth', Neher, *Serbien bis Kreta*, p. 146.

p. 133   'War! And we stand', Gefreiter Regiment 85, Dobiasch, p. 60. Fink, pp. 332 and 334.

p. 133   'by May 23rd', Chappel, *HQ. 14 Inf Bde Report 14 I B/Ops/I* Dated 4 Jun 1941, para 7, AAM archive. Marriott, oral account.

p. 134   'For many paratroopers', Wenzel, article *DF*, No 5, Sep/Oct 1983. Von der Heydte, p. 71. Eiben, *Erlebnisbericht*, *DF*, No 5, 1991. Rzeha, quoted *Fallschirmjager in Crete*, JY Nasse, Histoire and Collctions 2002, p. 78.

p. 135   'In no time', Thomas, interview, *Touch and Go*. Von der Heydte, *Daedalus Retuned*, p. 181.

p. 135   'The faces of some', Von der Heydte, ibid p. 130 and interview *Touch and Go*.

p. 136   'We didn't believe it', Gordon, interview, *Touch and Go*.

p. 136   'When the word came', Aircraft losses, *Flugzeug Foto-Archive Band 3 Kreta*, H Birkholz, Flugzeug Pub GmbH, p. 4

p. 136   'Our comrades lay there', Reinhardt, *Trilogy*, pp. 38–9. Pöppel, *Heaven and Hell*, p. 66. Strauch, diary account. Casualty figures from *Unternehmen Merkur. Die Schlacht um Kreta vom 20 Mai bis zum 1 Juni 1941*, F Berberich, Freiburg, pp. 109–10.

6 ALLIED SKY MEN

Allied expansion

p. 138   'How we at Ringway', Newnham, *Prelude to Glory*, p. 36.

p. 138   'This is a sad story', Churchill, letter PM to Ismay, 27 May 41, AAM archive. Frost, *Nearly There*, p. 71.

p. 139   'From the first', Browning, *Converstion 'Boy' Browning Notes*, 26 Jul 1944. AAM archive.

p. 139 'Did you volunteer?', Hancock, *Citizen's Journal*, private ms, pp. 5, 7 and 9, AAM Archive. Kershaw, author interview, 27 May 09. Sims, *Arnhem Spearhead*, pp. 4–5. Frost, *Nearly There*, p. 71.

p. 140 'What an eye-opener', Morgan, research notes by brother, Aug 2001, AAM archive. Hancock, p. 11.

p. 141 'We were stuck', Waddy, author interview, 9 Aug 07 and *Pegasus* magazine article *151 Parachute Battalion*, Oct 1951. Reid, quoted *Without Tradition. 2 PARA 1941–5*, R Peatling, p. 22. Kershaw, author interview, 27 May 09.

p. 141 'Later second wave', Burkinshaw, Price and Wood, quoted *Para Memories. 12th Yorkshire Parachute Battalion*, E Barley and Y. Fohlen, pp. 5–6 and 8.

p. 142 'The attack on Pearl harbour', Gabel, *The Making of a Paratrooper*, p. 4. Lipton, interview, *We Stand Alone Together*. W Richter and M Cowen, TV documentary HBO, 2001. (Henceforward *HBO Doc.*)

p. 142 'Like the British', Hashey, Winters and Malarkey, interviews, *HBO Doc.*

p. 143 'These men had lived', Guarnere and Maynard, interviews, ibid. Ollam, interview *82nd Airborne Trooper from Sicily to the Siegfried Line*, S Anderson and L Eschle, *Military History* Magazine, Jun 2003, p. 51.

p. 143 'The hard knocks', Gabel, *The Making of a Paratrooper*, pp. 37, 38, 44 and 55. Pass rate and march 506th PIR, *Band of Brothers*, S Ambrose, pp. 18 and 29. Wynn, interview, *HBO Doc.*

p. 143 'For a few seconds', Gabel, pp. 101 and 131.

p. 145 'Parachuting is really', Lunn, *Parachuting and Skiing, Pegasus* magazine, Vol 1, No 3, Oct 46. Kilkenny, interview, 5 Dec 89, AAM archive.

p. 145 'Parachuting should be "debunked"', Newnham, p. 55. Kilkenny, ibid.

p. 146 'didn't pop [their] chute', Starinov, *Over the Abyss*, p. 50.

p. 147 'On 20 September 1937', Selbach and Heidrich , quoted from *Achtung Fallschirmjäger!* A. von Hove, pp. 23–4. Zimmermann rescue, report by friend Otto Laun, *Der Deutscher Fallshirmjager* magazine, 2/83 and Mar/Apr 3/83.

p. 148 'The type of aircraft', Strohl, Hashey, Garcia and Guth, interviews, *HBO Doc.*

p. 149 'dry lipped, white knuckled', Abbot, *Memories of RAF Ringway*, Letter, AAM Archive.

p. 149 'Jumping through the hole', Ward, interview, 16 Aug 88. Turnbull, interview 4 Jan 90. Kilkenny, interview, 5 Dec 89, all AAM Archive. Timothy, interview, H Grenville, *Tim's Tale*, private pub 2008, AAM Archive.

p. 149 'The apparatus consisted', Waddy , author interview, 9 Aug 07 and article *Pegasus Journal* Oct 1951.

p. 150 'I took an army bod', Ward, interview, 16 Aug 88, AAM Archive.

p. 151 Parachute refusals, Letter Newnham to Browning, PTS/S 1/Air 10 Dec 42, AAM Archive. Boffin incident, Ward, *There I was at 500 Feet: Anecdotes from the First 50 Years of No 1 Parachute Training School*, P Hearn, AAM Archive. *6 AB Div Inquiry into Parachute Refusals*, 15 Jan 44, *Gale Papers* and letter *Training of Paratroops in Whitley Aircraft at PTS Ringway*, Sqn Ldr BJO Winfield 31 May 43, AAM Archive.

p. 151 'The fear that applied', Dyckmeester, letter to Manchester Airport Archive, Apeldoorn 30 Sep 88, AAM Archive. Female agent incidents, Val Valentine, *There I was at 500 Feet*. Kilkenny, interview, Ibid. Throwing out agents, Newnham, p. 145.

p. 152 'British paratroopers wore', Frost, Nearly There, P. 76. Kershaw, author interview, 27 May 09. Waddy, author interview, 9 Aug 07.

p. 153 'Once you got in', Stokes, interview, *HBO doc.* Gordon, *Band of Brothers*, S. Ambrose, p. 20. Ollam, interview, *Military History* Magazine, S. Anderson and L. Eschle, Jun 03, p. 52.

Raiders to airborne battalions

p. 154 'The oil refineries', Japanese parachute operations, *Japanese Parachute Troops*, Ed DB McLean, Normont Tech Pub 1973, pp. 23–9. Report, *Japanese Parachutists at Koepang*, Wg Comd Blyth, Ringway Notes, AAM Archive. Notes, *Japanese Parachute Troops* and *Japanese Airborne Operations*, AAM Archive.

p. 155 'What absolute nonsense', Newnham, *Prelude to Glory*, p. 36.

p. 155 'I find it hard', Cox, Appendix II to post raid report : BITING Personal accounts, stamped 29 Sep 43. Frost, *A Drop Too Many*, p. 47 and *Pilots Operations (Log) Record Book 51 Sqn 27 Feb 42*. Soldier, Film *The Bruneval Raid*, SKC C.1462 Crown Copyright 1982.

p. 156 'was a small blob', Jones, interview, SKC Film.

p. 157 'we did not pay', Cox, *BITING Personal Accounts*. Soldiers, veteran accounts, SKC Film.

p. 157 'The whole thing', Soldier veteran account, SKC Film. Frost, *BITING Personal Accounts*.

p. 158 'Intermittent firing', Cox and veteran accounts ibid. Frost, ibid and *Nearly There*, p. 73 and *A Drop Too Many* p. 54.

p. 159 'Just over two weeks', Frost, a Drop Too Many, p. 54. Soldier veteran account, SKC Film. Humphries, *BITING Personal Accounts*.

p. 159 'You have put airborne', Browning, quoted *Nearly There*, p. 73. Press, Capt F Cook unpub naval account of raid, AAM Archive. German report, Cabinet Office German Doc, TSD/FDS/X.378/51. Student, interrogation report *German Airborne Troops and Operations*, War Office Int Review Nov 1945, AAM Archive.

p. 160 'a fit, tough, combative', Hancock, *Citizen's Journal*, p. 2. Humphries, quoted *BITING Personal accounts*. Hill, SWWEC interview by P. Liddle, Feb 01.

p. 160 'On the day before', US para N Africa, Devlin, Paratrooper! , pp. 159–60

p. 162 'I was given 32', Hill, SWWEC interview, P. Liddle, Feb 01.

p. 163 'I had to undertake', Frost, *Nearly There*, p. 75.

p. 163 'A first class example', Hancock, *Citizen's Journal*, pp.85–92 and 94–5. Timothy, *Tim's Tale*, p. 22.

p. 164 'The assault on Oudna', Hancock, pp. 108–9, 118 and 111. Frost, *Nearly There*, p. 75.

p. 166 'The coldest I have ever', Menzies, *Diary North Africa*, 6 Jan 43, AAM Archive. Curtis, *Churchill's Volunteer*, pp. 110, 108 and 120. Morgan, Notes by brother when with C Coy 2nd Para, Aug 01.

p. 167 'Geoff Ellis not dead', Menzies, diary 14 May and 15 Mar 43, AAM Archive. Curtis, p. 102. Hancock, *Citizen's Journal*, p. 2.

p.167 'We couldn't take men', Timothy, H Grenville, Tim's Tale, pp. 31–2.

7 THE BLUNT INSTRUMENT: SICILY TO D-DAY

Forging the airborne instrument: the mediterranean

p. 169 Malta, *Planned Airborne Operations*, Interrogation Report Obstl von der Heydte, CSDIC (UK), 31 Jan 45. AAM Archive.

p. 169 Soviet figures and statistics from *Unfulfilled Promise: The Soviet Airborne Forces 1928–45*, L. Thompson, International Graphics Corp 1983, pp. 25–6 and *Inside the Blue Berets*, SJ Zaloga, pp. 28 and 30.

p. 171   'We used to make', Prout, article in the *Eagle*, Vol 10, No 3, Dec 2002.

p. 171   'Gliding was dangerous', Shackleton, SWWEC interview, P. Liddle, Jul 02, Prout, SWWWEC interview, D.Talbot, 27 Jan 04. Kingdon, SWWEC interview, P.Liddle, Sep 00.

p. 173   'There was a myriad', Accidents, *Glider Training Accidents*, D.Hall, *The Eagle*, Vol 17, No 4, Apr 93. Lansdell, article *The Eagle*, Vol 10, No 1, Apr 02, p. 4.

p. 174   'this was all experimental', Shackleton, interview,Liddle, Jul 02.

p. 174   'The first American glider', Fink, *Der Komet Auf Kreta*, p. 53.

p. 174   Glider songs and posters, *Paratrooper!* , Devlin, pp. 119 and 661.

p. 175   'British glider infantry', Ist Para Bde witness, *Parachutist!* , by Pegasus, Jerrolds London 1943, pp. 70–1. Hancock, *A Citizen's Journal*, p. 58.

p. 175   'parachutists' wings were more highly', Devlin, *Reminiscences of a Rifleman in Normandy France 1944*, private pub presented to AAM Archive 5 Jun 92, pp. 27–8.

p. 176   'In March 1943', Chatterton, *The Gliders*, A. Lloyd, p. 26–7. Frost, *Nearly There*, p. 78–9.

p. 177   'First of all', Prout, SWEEC interview, ibid.

p. 178   'All I'd been shown', Miller, quoted *The Gliders*, p. 38. Hardy, interview, *The War Years*, Purnell, p. 146.

p. 179   'They flew east', Mills, Miller and Chatterton, quoted The Gliders, pp. 39–40

p. 180   'We were winding', Baker, *A Day in the life of a Glider Pilot*, Pegasus magazine Vol XLII, No 2, Aug 87, p. 131.

p. 180   'which I did not', Lansdell, article *The Eagle*, Vol 10, No 1, Apr 02.

p. 181   'Actually, it's amazing', Tillet, *The Soldier's Story d Day and the Battle of Normandy*, Brasseys 2001, p.12

p. 181   Glider casualties, article *The Drowning of over 300 British Troops*, The Eagle, Vol 8, No 8, Dec 97.

p. 181   'He's dropped us!', Swan, 18 Pl C Coy 1st Bn Border Regt interview by R Milton, AAM Archive undated.

p. 182   'As we struck', Lansdell, Eagle, Ibid. Hardy, *The War Years*, Purnell, p. 146.

p. 182   'suddenly a darker mass', Baker, *Pegasus* article, p. 131. Moore, *The War Years*, p. 147.

p. 183   'Grimly determined', Casualty figures, Lloyd, p. 51. Frost, *A Drop Too Many*, p. 176.

p. 183   'As the Dakotas', Gavin, *On to Berlin*, pp. 19–20.

p. 183   'Gavin's 266 C-47s', Misdrop stats, *Paratrooper!* , Devlin, p. 229. Ollam, interview, S. Anderson and L. Eschle, *Military History*, Jun 03, p. 53.

p. 185   'Having failed to halt', Tucker's drop, *Paratrooper!* , Devlin, pp. 239–41. Gavin, *On to Berlin*, p. 42.

p. 186   'Two nights later', Morgan, Notes by his brother, Aug 01, AAM Archive. Pearson, *The Sky People*, P. Hearn, p. 116. Frost, *A Drop Too Many*, pp. 172, 177 and 179. Curtis, *Churchill's Volunteer*, p. 143.

p. 187   'Approbation was heaped', Quinn, SWWEC interview, P. Liddle, Nov 01. Frost, p. 187. Mockeridge, article *Sicily and Our Allies*, Pegasus, Vol XLIII, No 2, Aug 88, pp. 159–162.

p. 188   'No aircraft', Waddy, author interview, 9 Aug 07.

p. 189   'The Krauts are kicking', Soldier, quoted *Paratrooper!* , Devlin, p. 301.

p. 190   'It was a nightmare', Glider Pilot, quoted Lloyd, p. 51. Hackett, quoted *The Parachute Regiment – An Irregular View*, Pegasus, Vol XLII, No 1, Apr 87, p. 128. Eisenhower, quoted Lloyd, p. 246. Frost, *A Drop Too Many*, p. 185.

Crossing the English Channel

p. 191 'to navigate various', Howard, *D-Day Then and Now*, Vol 1 , Ed. WG Ramsey, *After The Battle* pub 1995, *Account by S/Sgt Roy Howard Glider Pilot Regiment 1944*, pp. 224 –5.

p. 192 'They looked so young', Summersby, *Account by Kay Summersby* 1976, ibid, p. 293

p. 193 'You're going to be', Winters, interview, *HBO Doc.*, 2001.

p. 193 'Remember, the country', Hill, Personal address given at the Royal Hospital Chelsea, 12 May 94, AAM Archive.

p. 193 'On the night', Figures, *Never Surrender*, RJ Kershaw, Hodder and Stoughton 2009, p. 298 and *D-Day Then and Now*, p. 233 and *US Airborne Forces*, B Gregory p. 72.

p. 193 'The first few planes', Edwards, *Normandy Diary*, Tue 6th Jun, AAM Archive.

Sweeny, A personal account of the 5th and 6th June, AAM Archive

p. 194 'The American stream', Dispersal figures, *D-Day Then and Now*, pp. 266 and 299.

p. 195 'one shell hit', Pond, quoted *D-Day and the Battle for Normandy*, M.Windrow, p. 32. Samman, ibid, p. 27.

p. 195 'Overall results', Percentage figures, *D-Day: Piercing the Atlantic Wall*, RJ Kershaw, pp. 74 and 278.

p. 195 'As the time', Alex, Windrow, p. 22. O'Connor, *To France Without a Passport*, unpub ms, p.46 AAM Archive. Guarnere, interview, *HBO Doc.*

p. 196 'Stand up', Evans, quoted Windrow, p. 23.

p. 197 'my thoughts were', O'Connor, *To France Without a Passport*, pp. 50–52.

p. 197 'Paratroopers and glider men', Chatfield, author interview, 22 Sep 07. Martin, interview, *HBO Doc.*

p. 198 'wasn't bad either', Stokes, interview, HBO Doc. Burgett, quoted *US Airborne Forces*, B Gregory, p. 74. Ste Mère Eglise, *D-Day Then and Now*, pp. 269–70.

p. 199 'Not every man', Capon, unpub *ms 3rd September 1939,* chapt *Merville*, AAM Archive, pp. 25–6. Hill, address *Camberly British Staff College Talk 7 Jun 68*, AAM Archive.

p. 200 'the night was now', Barrett, *Tom His War*, unpub ms, AAM Archive, p. 3.

p. 200 'I saw at least', Gavin, interview ITN Jun 84, quoted *D-Day Piercing the Atlantic Wall*, RJ Kershaw, p. 75.

p. 201 'I was heading', Hill, personal account, AAM Archive. Beckingham, personal account. *Normandy- Ardennes- Rhine Crossing*, AAM Archive, p. 1.

p. 201 'It became very tricky', Edwards, Diary 6 Jun 44, AAM Archive.

p. 201 'We were supposed', Read, SWWEC interview, B.Atkinson undated.

p. 202 'Most of the paratroopers', Lesniewski, Winters and Lipton, interviews, *HBO Doc.*

p. 203 'These airborne landings', German reports, *Gefechtsbericht 716 Div, Gefechtsbericht über die Kämpfe im Abschnitt der 716 Inf Div am 6.6. 1944*, Kershaw, *D-Day*, pp. 91–4.

p. 205 'My God', Tottle, personal letter, AAM Archive.

p. 205 'Landed! 20 miles', Browne, letter *Behind Enemy Lines in Normandy June–19 Aug 44*, Maj BR Browne, likely 9 Para, AAM Archive.

p. 205 'six days adrift', Lycett, *Six Days Adrift in Normandy Jun 44*, ref L/206.02.09, AAM archive.

p. 205 'The important thing', Barrett, *Tom His War*, pp. 4 and 8–10. German after-action report, *Gefechtsbericht III/858 Gren Regt über die Zeit von 10–12. 6. 44*, author's collection.

p. 206 'Atrocities begat worse', Taylor, *Band of Brothers*, S Ambrose, p. 65. Lefebvfre and Cartledge, Windrow, p. 26. Fitzgerald , ibid, p. 28. Rosie, ibid, p. 24.

p. 207 'I was just amazed', Read, SWWEC interview, B. Atkinson. Capon, *3rd September 1939* ms, p. 28, AAM Archive. Lycett, personal account AAM Archive. Barrett, *Tom His War*, p. 12.

p. 208 'I never thought', Guarnere, interview, *HBO doc*. E Coy cas, *Band of Brothers*, S Ambrose, p. 105. Div cas, *Paratrooper!* , Devlin, pp. 414 and 416.

p. 208 'You just didn't see', Read, SWEEC interview. Capon ms pp. 26–7.

p. 209 'There had been many', Beckingham, personal account, AAM Archive. 6th AB cas extracted from 6th AB post-combat report, Appendix Q-1, AAM Archive.

8 PARACHUTISTS' SWAN-SONG

Arnhem and the airborne spirit

p. 211 'We suddenly discerned', Volz, *It Never Snows in September*, RJ Kershaw, p. 62.

p. 211 'Two massive aircraft', Student, *Arnheim Letzter Deutsche Erfolg, Deutsche Fallschirmjager*, No 9, 1964. Aircraft figures, article *Arnhem: The RAF Operation*, CM Hobson, Librarian RAF Staff College.

p. 213 'All you could see', Burriss, interview, *The Lost Evidence: Operation Market-Garden*, T Downing and S Baker, Flashback TV 2006, (henceforth *Lost Evidence*.) Baker, article *Arnhem Story*, *The Eagle*, Vol 9, No 10, Dec 01. Hibbert, author interview, 18 Dec 07. 'The Allies were', Mitchell, SWWEC interview, tape 1533. Guarnere and Winters, interviews HBO Doc. Webster and 101st Report, Band of Brothers, S Ambrose, p. 123.

p. 214 'I can remember', Burriss, interview, *Lost Evidence*.

p. 214 'If Hitler could', Smith, SWWEC interview, P Liddle, Nov 02.

p. 215 'You couldn't take', Clark, interview, *Lost Evidence*.

p. 216 'Open space or not', Tucker, quoted *Nijmegen*, T Saunders, Leo Cooper 2001, p. 39.

p. 216 'Platoon commander', Flavell, author interview 1989. Frost, *A Drop Too Many*, pp. 209 and 211. Hibbert, author interview, 18 Dec 07.

p.218 'In the dark', Killick, SWEEC interview, P Liddle, Oct 01.

p.218 'A further characteristic', Frost, *A Drop Too Many*, p. 203. Killick, SWWEC interview.

p.218 'Major John Waddy', Waddy, author interview, 9 Aug 07. Frost ibid, Carr, personal account *17 Sep 44*, AAM Archive.

p. 219 'When the streams', John Waddy private account, passed to author.

p. 221 'Come on, Monty', Waddy, author interview.

p. 221 'just fleeting', Shackleton, SWWEC interview, P. Liddle Jul 02.

p. 222 'Someone shouted out', Blackmore, interview, *Lost Evidence*. Cain was awarded the Victoria Cross. Long and Ashworth, *Victoria Cross*, J. Clark pres, R. Pearson and A. Wilman, BBC Midlands TV.

p. 223 'The 2nd para', Hibbert, author interview, 18 Dec 07. Youngman, interview, *Lost Evidence*. Flavell, author interview, 1989. Killick, SWWEC interview, P. Liddle Oct 01.

p. 224 'At 1500 on', Burriss, interview, *Lost Evidence*. German artillery, *It Never Snows in September*, RJ Kershaw, p. 197. Pitt and Holabird, quoted *Nijmegen*, T.Saunders, pp. 152–3.

p. 225 'The adrenalin was flowing', Vandeleur and Browning, quoted Saunders, p. 155. Downs, *BBC War Report*, Ariel Books 1946, transcript of broadcast 24 Sep 44, p. 193. Buriss, interview, *Lost Evidence*.

p. 226 'The surprise assault', Buriss/Carrington incident, Saunders, p. 185.

p. 226 Morgan notes researched by his brother in 2001, passed to author by John Waddy, AAM Archive.

p. 227 'You know as well', Lonsdale, quoted *Arnhem*, Maj Gen RE Urquhart, Pan 1972, p. 106.

p. 227 'Things went from bad', Baker, quoted *Arnhem Story*, *The Eagle*, Vol 9, No 10, Dec 01. Shackleton, SWWEC, interview. Peters, interview, *Lost Evidence*.

p. 228 'Arnhem became', Paras with knives incident quoted *It Never Snows in September*, RJ Kershaw, p. 296.

p. 228 'Soviet Russia', Voroshilov, quoted *Prelude to Glory*, M. Newnham, p. 127. Von der Heydte, *Daedalus Returned. Crete 1941*, p. 66. Pervitine, *Notes on Parachute Troops No 2 Commando*, 12 Nov 40, AAM Archive, sheet 7.

p. 229 'Personal bonding forms', Waddy, personal correspondence with author, 2 and 12 Aug 07. Willcock, quoted *Without Tradition 2 Para 1941–5*, R. Peatling, p. 20. Downing, *First Para Padre 1942 – Gunners and Paras*. Private ms, AAM archive, p. 27. Sims, *Arnhem Spearhead*, J. Sims, IWM pub 1978, p. 1.

p. 230 'Parachute jumping produced', Medical opinion, *History of No 1 PTS Ringway 1940–45*, PW Jevons, ms, AAM Archive, P. 8. Hastings, article *Picture Post* magazine, Vol 22, No 12, 18 Mar 44.

p. 230 'Volunteer selection', Hill, Talk given at Staff College Camberly, 7 Jun 68, AAM Archive. Timothy, *Tim's Tale*, private ms, H.Grenville, p. 12. Bernhard, Hilary George Saint- Saunders research notes, AAM Archive. Read, SWWEC interview, B. Atkinson.

p. 231 'If people had', Waddy, author correspondence, 12 Aug 07.

p. 231 'The shared paratrooper', Kershaw, author interview, 27 May 09. Simcox, Jefferson and Andrews, quoted *The Men of the Maroon Beret 1940–45*, T Deane, BA Dissertation 1988, pp. 55 and 65. Flying Trapeze song, ibid, p. 54.

p. 231 'Edward "Babe" Heffron', Powers, Heffron and Winters, interviews, *HBO Doc.*

Across the Rhine

p. 232 'shuffled all over', Capa, *Images of War*, Grossman 1964, p. 137.

p. 233 Strength statistics quoted from *Op Varsity Battlefield Tour* presentation 29 Feb 84, AAM Archive and *Paratrooper!* , Devlin, p. 615.

p. 233 'We were told', Devlin, *Battle for the Rhine Crossings*, personal account, AAM Archive, p. 2. Arnhem aircraft losses, article *Arnhem:The RAF Operation*, CM Hobson.

p. 234 'Soldiers were understandably', Clark, Letter Feb 1998, AAM Archive. Krell, quoted *Yank:The Army Weekly*, S. Kluger, Arms and Armour 1991, p. 235.

p. 234 'We removed our', Devlin, personal account, pp. 2–3. Sweeney, Op Varsity account, *The Eagle*, Vol 17, no 9, Dec 94. Shackleton, SWWEC interview, P. Liddle, Jul 02. Boucher-Giles, article *Memories of the Rhine Mar 24 1945*, *The Eagle*, Vol 3, No 1, 1955.

p. 235 'There was last-minute', Capa, *Images of War*, p. 137. Devlin, personal account. Crookenden, quoted *Airborne at War*, Ian Allan 1978, p. 96. Krell, *Yank*, p. 235.

p. 236 'Flight Lieutenant B. S.', Evenden, notes, AAM Archive. Richards, Flt Lt, *Op Varsity* personal account, AAM Archive, p. 4. Capa, p.137.

p. 237 'I saw Chalk 68', Goodacre, quoted *There I was at Five Hundred Feet*, P. Hearn 1990, p. 23. Wensdorf and Hammerfahr, report *Stars and Stripes* newspaper, 26 Mar 45. Capa, p. 138.

p. 238 'Just before my feet', Glaister, *Images of War*, Marshall Cavendish, pp. 196–7.

p. 238   'By the time', Richards, personal account, AAM Archive. Clark, letter Feb 98, ibid.

p. 239   'German gunners turned', Hagenberg, letter 12 Jul 95, (English improved), AAM Archive. Crookenden, *Airborne at War*, p. 102. German gunner, quoted *The Gliders*, A. Lloyd, p. 181. Glaister, *Images of War*, p. 197.

p. 240   'and frightened us', Sweeny, *Eagle* article. Lough, article by R. Dawson, *Hemel Hempstead Evening Post and Echo*, 1983, AAM Archive. Brocks, *Images of War*, p. 195.

p. 241   Glider crash figures, Napier Crookenden, p. 133. Clark, *Stars and Stripes*, 27 Mar 45.

p. 241   'They say that', Devlin, pp. 4 and 8. Richards, personal account.

p. 242   'We lost many', Capa, Images of War, p. 138.

p. 243   Loss statistics compiled from Napier Crookeneden statistics, pp. 143–4 and *Op Varsity Battlefield Tour* 29 Feb 84, AAM Archive.

p. 243   'There's no future', Capa quoted *Life Magazine*, from *What Price Glory?* , W. Mitchell, AAM Archive, p.1.

9 THREADBARE PARACHUTING

'Les Paras'

p. 244   US Joint airborne Troops Board quote, Out of the sky, M. Hickey, p.187. Accidents, *Glider Training Accidents*, D.Hall, *The Eagle*, Vol 17, No 4, Apr 93.

p. 245   Geography, *Street Without Joy*, B. Fall, Pall Mall 1963, p. 15.

p. 246   'The average number', Visiting British officer, *French Airborne Troops in Indo-China*, RAF officer Transport Support Wing visit to Saigon 26–28 Sep 1950, School of Land/Air Warfare Report 28 Sep 50, AAM Archive.

p. 248   'We hastened to assist', Aparvary, *Voices of the Foreign Legion*, AD Gilbert, p. 207.

p. 248   'Fourteen major airborne', Casualties, *French Paratroops II*, N. Arena, article Armies and Weapons, undated, AAM Archive. Bodard, Gilbert, p. 210.

p. 248   'Action rates', 2nd BEP, *The Last Valley*, M. Windrow, Cassell 2006, p. 195.

p. 250   'By the end of March', Grauwin, *Doctor at Dien Bien Phu*, pp. 18, 99 and 205, 206. Pilots and volunteer paras, *Street Without Joy*, pp. 259–60 and 320–1.

p. 251   'they have a part', Grauwin, ibid, pp. 211 and 221.

p. 252   'The French suffered', Figures, *The Vietnam Experience: Passing the Torch*, Boston Pub 1981, p. 77.

p. 253   'Many of the paratroopers', Alonso and Andre, interviews, *The Undeclared War. Algeria 1954–62*, B. Travernier and P. Rotman, Le Studio Canal et GMT Productions. (Henceforth Undeclared War).

p. 254   'which did terrific', Alonso, interview, ibid. Ysquierdo, *Voices of the Foreign Legion*, AD Gilbert, p. 228

p. 255   'Fighting, when it did', Leullette, *The War in Algeria*, pp. 176–7 and Gilbert p. 226. Andre, interview, *The Undeclared War*.

p. 256   'Like all officers', Sergent, Gilbert, p. 228. Alonso, interview, *The Undeclared War*.

Shoestring operations: the British

p. 257   Casualties, quoted *Cordon and Search*, RD Wilson, Gale and Polden Ltd 1949, Appendix J, p. 228. Williams, *Pegasus* Journal, Summer 05, p. 65. Kent, *First In! Parachute Pathfinder Company*, Batsford 1979, p. 154.

p. 258   'A lot of it', Waddy, author interview, 9 Aug 07.

p. 258 'The atrocities and casualties', Maloney, p. 39. Kent, pp. 156–7.

p. 259 'wasn't a pretty sight', Waddy, author interview.

p. 260 'an influx of infantry', Waddy, article *The Parachute Regiment – an Irregular View, Pegasus Journal*, Vol XLII, No 1, Apr 87, p. 130.

p. 261 Note the British parachute delineation of 2 Para or 3 Para etc denoting the 2nd or 3rd *Parachute Battalion* changed with the demise of the Army air Corps and the formation of the Parachute Regiment as line infantry. The new shortened 2 PARA or 3 PARA etc denotes the 2nd or 3rd *Battalion of the Parachute Regiment*.

p. 262 'whom they contacted', Scott, compiled from letters written in 1955–6 by Sgt and later C/Sgt Scott to Maj Corbould, his previous company commander at the Depot Airborne Forces at Aldershot. AAM Archive.

p. 262 'In early August', Grout, BBC interview, *Suez Soldiers 1956*, ms AAM archive.

p. 262 'As the events', Crook, and Coles, interviews, *El Gamil 40 Years On*, Video of Suez Presentation Depot PARA Aldershot 1996, AAM Archive. Wivell, *In Action at Suez 1956, Medal News*, Jan/Jul 1998, p. 17.

p. 264 'Jeeps . . .', Tukovich and Howlett, interviews, *El Gamil 40 Years On*.

p. 265 'Most of us', Badrawi, interview, *The Other Side of Suez*, D. Gallagher and W. Cobbon, BBC Scotland 2009.

p. 265 'On 4 November', Wivell personal account, Walsh, interview, *El Gamil 40 Years On*. Hancock, letter to ABFM Curator 31 Oct 96, AAM Archive.

p. 266 'Engines were feathered', Walsh, interview, ibid. Lowe, *Suez 1956 Op Musketeer. Cpl Lowe's Story*, AAM Archive.

p. 266 'Egyptian defenders', Helal and Fadl, interviews, *Suez A Very British Crisis*, (Henceforth *BBC Suez*) P. Molloy, BBC 2006.

p. 267 'Carrying as we did', Cavenagh, interview *BBC Suez* and interview *Soldier* Magazine 28 Oct 96. Bennetts, interview, *BBC Suez* . Wivell, personal account. Grout, BBC interview 1956. Lowe, personal account. Landford and Walsh, *El Gamil 40 Years On*.

p. 269 'Fifteen minutes after', De Klee, *A Jump with the French*, MP de Klee Scots Guards, article *Household Brigade Magazine*, 1956. Château-Jobert, confidential report *Op Amlicar*, 2nd RPC, 19 Nov 56, AAM Archive. Leulliette, *The War in Algeria*, pp. 201–4.

p. 270 'C Company 3 PARA', Fadl, Bennetts, Read and Walsh, interviews, *BBC Suez*.

p. 271 'Helicopters with their', Turley, interview, *BBC Suez*. Helicopter facts and figures, *Suez. The Forgotten Invasion*, R.Jackson, Airlife 1996, pp. 104–5.

p. 273 'The frantic motion', Turley, Helal and Fadl , interviews, *BBC Suez*.

p. 274 'Differentiating between fighters', Ireland and Turley, interviews, ibid.

p. 275 'Lieutenant Sandy', Cavenagh, interview, *BBC Suez*. Grout, interview, *Suez Soldiers 1956*, AAM Archive. Wivell, account, *Medal News* 1998.

10 COLD WAR AIR MOBILITY

Cold war and counter-insurgency

p. 276 Figures, *Inside the Blue Berets*, SJ Zaloga, pp. 137–141.

p. 277 'Here, on out of', Maj Gen L Kuz'menko, *The Psychological Conditioning of a Paratrooper*, Moscow, *Kommunist Vooruzhennykh Sil*, No 1, Jan 1973, pp. 38–43.

p. 277 'Not every soldier', Kuz'menko, ibid, pp. 47–9 and 52–3.

p. 278 'Around 2030', Paratrooper officer, and Czech Crisis, quoted *The Blue Berets*, pp. 160–3.

p. 279   'The parachute troops', Kuz'menko, p. 46.

p. 280   'You can't be', 3 PARA soldier, quoted *Suez- Operation Musketeer*, G. Ferguson, ms submitted to ABFM 13 Nov 85, AAM Archive, p. 15.

p.280   'British paratroopers', Boot and Murray, personal accounts, compiled from an A and B Company 1 PARA 'Newspaper' produced by the soldiers in Aden 1967, AAM Archive.

p. 282   'The 2 PARA', Williams, compiled from post combat reports and Williams comments from: *The Men of the Red Beret*, M. Arthur, Hutchinson 1990, pp. 346–50 and *The Savage Wars of Peace*, C. Allan, Futura 1990, pp. 117–119.

p. 283   'rape, beating, burning', Ainley, *Voices of the French Foreign Legion*, AD Gilbert, p. 216

p. 284   'The Jews called', Waddy, author interview, 9 Aug 07. 'Red Poppies', G. Williams account, *Pegasus*, Summer 05, p. 65. Scott, letters to Courbold 1955–6, AAM Archive. Gibson-Watt, interview, *The Jewish War*, W. Treharne Jones, BBC 2004.

p. 284   'I'm fed up', Andre, Delbellow and Alonso, interviews, doc film *The Undeclared War*. Leulliette, *The War in Algeria*, p. 231.

p. 286   'De Gaulle has', Murray, *Voices of the French Foreign Legion*, Gilbert, p. 235.

p. 286   'During the briefing', 1 PARA observer, *Pegasus* Magazine, Jan 1972. 2 PARA witness, *Pegasus* Magazine, Oct 1979.

'Slicks' and 'snakes': air-mobility, Vietnam

p. 288   'Two things struck me', Caputo, interview, *Code Broken Arrow:Vietnam Battle Stories*, TV production J Towers, Nat Geo 2008. (Henceforth *Broken Arrow*).

p. 289   'If this system', Moore, *We Were Soldiers Once . . .and Young*, p. 25.

p. 290   'We had the ability', Bahnsen, interview, *Broken Arrow*.

p. 291   'strict attention to contrast', Mills, *Low Level Hell*, Bantum 1992, pp. 49 and 74. Hillyer and Rollins, interviews, *Broken Arrow*.

p. 292   'God, there was nothing', Soular, interview, *Vietnam. The Definitive Oral History Told from All Sides*, CG Appy, p. 157.

p. 292   'It was so beautiful', Deal, interview, Appy, p. 130. Mills, *Low Level Hell*, p. 45.

p. 293   'Vietcong and North Vietnamese', Mills, p. 116. Helicopter losses quoted, *Vietnam. Airmobile Warfare Tactics*, GL Rottman, Osprey 2007, p. 11.

p. 294   'Gunship pilots', Carlock, *Firebirds*, Bantum 1997, p. 13.

p. 294   'Slick pilots viewed', Fornelli, interview, *Broken Arrow*. Swickard, interview, *Helicopter Warfare. Vietnam*, R. Max, Windfall Films 2008.

p. 295   'Within minutes of landing', Moore and Nadal, interviews *Broken Arrow*. Deal, interview, Appy p. 131.

p. 296   'Many things were new', Hiep and Man quoted, *We Were Soldiers . . .*, H Moore, pp. 57 and 59. An quoted, Appy p. 10.

p. 296   'Now here was', Deal, interview, Appy, pp. 131–2.

p. 297   'Flying into a hot', Liss, interview, *Helicopter Warfare. Vietnam*. Soular, Appy, p. 157. Carlock, *Firebirds*, p. 128. Morgan, *Nam. The Vietnam Experience*, Ed T. Page, J. Pimlott, Orbis 1988, p. 34.

p. 298   'You could see', Lefebvre, quoted *We Were Soldiers . . .*, p. 108. Setelin, ibid, p. 148. Deal, interview, Appy, p. 133.

p. 300   'it was clear to me', Moore, interview, *Broken Arrow*.

p. 300   'Artillery crews at', Barker and Winkel and Moore, *We Were Soldiers . . .*, pp. 122–3. Wallace, ibid, p. 121. Warlock, *Firebird*, p. 291. Swickard, interview, *Helicopter War. Vietnam*.

p. 301   'Medical evacuation', Crandall, *We Were Soldiers . . .*, p. 126. Carlock, *Firebirds,* pp. 232 and 234.

p. 302   'The jungle was', Soular, Appy, p. 154.

p. 302   'You saw people', Dopp,Liss, Baca, Swickard, Croteau, interviews, *Helicopter Warfare. Vietnam.*

p. 303   'None of the people', Deal, Appy, p. 134.

p. 304   'I'll be honest', Rollins, interview, *Broken Arrow.*

p. 304   'Air-mobile casualties', Deal, interview, Appy, p. 135. Casualty figures, *Vietnam. The Decisive Battles,* J. Pimlott, Guild 1990, p. 59.

p. 305   'I hold in such', Deal, interview, Appy, p. 135. Two Sergeants, *We Were Soldiers . . .*, p. 350.

11 BY AIRLINER TO WAR

Out of area: Africa

p. 306   Shani, Betser and Ofer, interviews, *Age of Terror, Terror International* BBC Series, J. Thynne 2009. (Henceforth *Age of Terror*).

p. 308   'I hear planes', Bakka and Peled, interviews, ibid.

p. 309   'The hostages were', Benny and Sara Davidson, interviews, ibid. Additional material from *Strike From the Sky. Israeli Airborne Troops,* Ed. A. Brown, Villard Books, pp. 72–82.

p. 310   'the endemic trouble', Frost, *Nearly There,* p. 70.

p. 311   'You come as you are.', Erulin, Comd 2nd REP, quoted *Kolwezi* article, J Hatte, *Infantry* (US) Magazine, Vol 69, No 6, Nov/Dec 79.

p. 312   'We originally had', Fanshaw, *Voices of the Foreign Legion,* AD Gilbert, p. 239.

p. 314   'There were some horrific', Harris, ibid, pp. 242–3.

p. 314   'The Belgians flew', Casualty figures, J Hatte, *Kolwezi* article, p. 29 and article *Kolwezi,* JG Depoorter, Military Review, Vol LIX, No 9, Sep 79, p. 34.

'Come like the wind, go like the lightning': Cassinga, Angola, 4th May 1978

p. 316   'The first bomb', Nanyemba, SWAPO Report Cassinga Raid. *Testimony by Comrade P Nanyemba, Luanda, 9 May 78.* Quoted from *'Parabats',* M Paul, p. 246.

p. 316   'Four low-flying', Naango-Shaanika and Amutenya quoted, *The Cassinga Raid,* EGM Alexander, MA Thesis University of SA Jul 03, p. 123.

p. 317   'Airplanes! Airplanes!', Ngodji and eye-witness, Alexander, Ibid, p. 124. Roberts quoted, *Eagle Strike,* J Breytenbach, p. 286.

p. 317   'convinced, and rightly', Breytenbach, p. 159.

p. 319   'My thoughts were', Botes, ibid, p. 329. McWilliams, ibid, p. 247. Breytenbach, ibid, pp. 242 and 237.

p. 320   'You can walk', McWilliams, Human and Grundlingh, ibid, pp. 247–8 and 249. Breytenbach, p. 245.

p. 321   'The guerrillas were', Fenton, *Parabat,* pp. 52–3. Manderson, ibid, p. 43.

p. 322   'Whenever they walked', Fenton, ibid, p. 53.

p. 322   'The paratroopers had',Breytenbach, p.321. Lamprecht, Alexander, p.137. Fenton, *Parabat,* pp. 55–6,

p. 324   'The first call', Jay, *Parabat,* p. 26. Law, ibid, pp. 33 and 35.

p. 324   'What followed was', Fenton, ibid, p. 57. Jooste, Breytenbach, p. 345.

NOTES ON SOURCES

p. 325   'Different helicopter types', Wilkins, Breytenbach, p. 342. Booth, ibid, p. 352.

p. 326   'Anti-tank platoon', Viljoen, Alexander, p. 148. Jooste, Breytenbach, p. 354.

p. 326   'The lone paratrooper', Manderson, *Parabat*, p. 48. Jooste, Breytenbach, pp. 354–5.

p. 327   'No one smiled', Fenton, *Parabat*, p. 58.

12 AFGHANISTAN

Blue berets

p. 328   'Well you know', Vostrotin, interview, *Twenty Years Later*, doc film directed by V Pasichnik 2005

p. 329   'The first impression', Galiev and Bezborodov, 9th Company 345th Regt, interviews, ibid.

p. 329   'The paratroopers and spetznaz', Casualty figures and ambush, *Inside The Blue Berets*, S Zaloga, p. 242. Kosenkov, interview, *Twenty Years Later*.

p. 330   'The rugged terrain', Figures, Zaloga, pp. 247–8.

p. 330   'Valeri Vostrotin had', Vostrotin and Kosenkov, interviews, *Twenty Years Later*.

p. 331   'A training regiment', Baranovsky and Bezborodov, interviews, ibid.

p. 331   'Balance was restored', Figures and casualties, Zaloga, pp. 256–7.

p. 332   'In January 1988', Kuznetsov and Shchigolev, interviews *Twenty Years Later*. Paratrooper song 'Those who do not believe . . .', ibid.

p. 334   'One year later', Medals, Zaloga, p. 263.

Red berets

p. 335   'Soldiers were required', Lynch, *The Real Deal*, personal account 2008, AAM archive.

p. 335   'Even assault ladders', Desmond, *Sunday Observer* article, M. Townsend, 26 Oct 08

p. 335   'Helmand had been', Tootal, *Sunday Times* article, C Lamb, 20 Jul 08. 2 PARA soldiers, Townsend article. Pathfinder soldier, *Pathfinders –Into the Heart of Afghanistan*, S Ramsay, B Sky B TV report 2009. (Henceforth *Pathfinders*.)

p. 336   'Up here, the majority', Garwood, interview, *Pathfinders*.

p. 336   'Fighting the Taliban', 3 PARA officer, *Cordon and search. Op Mutay 4 Jun 06*. A Coy 3 PARA. AAM Archive. Tootal, *Sunday Times* Lamb article 20 Jul 08.

p. 337   'Human beings direct', Loden, *E-Mails from Helmand*, J Loden OC A Coy 3 PARA 2006, AAM Archive.

p. 338   'Technology does not', Pierce, *The Battle for Helmand*, D Reynolds, p. 95. Loden, e-mails. Kelly, Reynolds, p. 101.

p. 339   'Time stops during', Desmond, article *Sunday Observer*, M Townsend, 26 Oct 08. Stout, article *Sunday Times*, C Lamb 5 Oct 08.

p. 339   'You just had to', 3 PARA soldier and Robb, Reynolds, pp. 41 and 101.

p. 340   'By the second tour', Stout, C Lamb article 5 Oct 08. Paterson, interview, B sky B *Pathfinders*.

p. 341   Song, 'Those who do not believe . . .' *9th Company 20 Years Later*, Dir V. Pasichnik 2005.

Postscript

p. 343   'If you pass through', Geddes, *Spearhead Assault*, Arrow Books 2007, p. 45.

p. 345   'you cannot have', W. Fowler, *Operation Barras*, p. 118.

p. 245   'To me it's quite', Geddes, p. 42.

BIBLIOGRAPHY

GENERAL PUBLISHED SOURCES

Arthur, M., *The Men of the Red Beret*, Hutchinson 1990.

Ambrose, S.E., *Band of Brothers*, Simon & Schuster 1997.

Blandford, E.L., *Green Devils-Red Devils*, Leo Cooper 1993.

Christensen, B., *The 1ˢᵗ Fallschirmjäger Division in World War II*, Schiffer Pub Ltd 2007.

Brown, A., Ed. *Strike From the Sky: Israeli Airborne Troops*, Villard Books 1986.

Crookenden, N., *Airborne at War*, Ian Allen 1978.

Connaughton, R., *A Brief History of Modern Warfare*, Robinson, 2008.

Devlin, G.M., *Paratrooper!* Saint – Martin's Press, NY 1979.

Edwards, R., *German Airborne Troops 1936–45*, Purnell 1974.

Fall, B., *Street Without Joy*, Pall Mall 1963.

Gardiner, W., *Te Mura o te Ahi – The Story of the Maori Battalion*, Reed Books 1995.

Glantz, D.M., *A History of Soviet Airborne Forces*, Frank Cass, 1994.

Gregory, B., *US Airborne Forces*, Brian Trodd 1990.

Gregory, B. and Batchelor, J., *Airborne Warfare*, Phoebus 1979.

Hadjipateras, C.N. and Fafalios, M.S., *Crete 1941-Eyewitnessed*, Efstathiadis Group 1989.

Hawkins, D., Ed. *BBC War Report*, Ariel Books 1946.

Hearn, P., *The Sky People*, Airlife 1997.

Heydte, F., Baron von der, *Daedalus Returned: Crete 1941*, Hutchinson 1958.

Hickey, M., *Out of the Sky*, Mills & Boon 1979.

Hove, A. von, *Achtung Fallschirmjäger!* Druffel-Verlag 1954.

Jackson, R., *Suez-The Forgotten Invasion*, Airlife 1996.

Kammann, W., *Die Geschichte des Fallschirmjäger-Regiment 2 1939 bis 1945*, private pub 1987.

Kershaw, R.J., *D-Day. Piercing the Atlantic Wall*, Ian Allan, 1994.
  – *It Never Snows in September*, Crowood Press, 1990.
  – *Never Surrender*, Hodder & Stoughton 2009

Kluger, S., *Yank. The Army Weekly*, Arms and Armour 1991.

Lisov, II., *Russian Airborne History*, Moscow, 1968.
  – *Airborne Troops of the Soviet Army*, Novesti Pub, Moscow, 1974.

Lucas, J., *The Big Umbrella*, Elm Tree Books 1973.

Lukin, A.M., *Parachuting Sport*, National Pub House of the Defence Industry, Moscow, 1952.

McLean, D.B., *Japanese Parachute Troops*, Normont Tech Pub 1973.

McKee, A., *The Race for the Rhine Bridges*, Stein & Day 1971.

Millar, G., *The Bruneval Raid*, Cassell 1974.

Mrazek, J.E., *The Fall of Eben Emael*, Robert Hale 1970.

Moshkovsky, V., *Parachute Jumping and Gliding*, Foreign Languages Pub House, Moscow 1939.

Mühleisen, H., *Kreta 1941*, Verlag Rombach Freiberg 1968.

Nasse, J.-Y., *Green Devils!* Histories and Collections 1997.

Neher, K., *Von Serbien bis Kreta*, Aspioti-Elka AG Athen 1942.

Nowarra, H.J., *Junkers Ju-52*, Haynes 1987.

Oberkommando Der Wehrmacht, *Sieg Über Frankreich*, Wilhelm Andermann 1940.

Pallud, J.P., *Blitzkrieg in the West: Then and Now*. After the Battle 1991.

Pimlott, J., *Vietnam-The Decisive Battles*, Guild 1990.

Ramsay, W.G., Ed *D-Day: Then and Now*, Vol 1, After The Battle 1995.

Reynolds, D., *The Battle for Helmand*, DRA Publishing 2007.

Rottman, G.L., *Vietnam Airmobile Warfare Tactics*, Osprey 2007.

Roon, A. von, *Die Bildchronik der Fallschirmtruppe 1935–45*, Podzun–Pallas 1985.

Steinhoff, J., Pechel and Showalter, *Voices From the Third Reich*, Grafton Books 1991.

Saunders, T., *Fort Eben Emael*, Pen and Sword 2005.
  – *Market-Garden – Nijmegen*, Leo Cooper 2001.

Weeks, J., *The Airborne Soldier*, Blandford 1982.

Wilson, R.D., *Cordon and Search*, Gale & Polden 1949.

Windrow, M., *The Soldier's Story: D-day and the battle for Normandy*, Brassey's 2001
  – *The Last Valley*, Da Capo 2004

Wright, I.B., *Bale Out! A History of the Parachute*, GMS Enterprises 1991.

Zaloga, S.J., *Inside the Blue Berets*, Presidio 1995.

PERIODICALS

Anderson, S. and Eschle, L., '82nd Trooper from Sicily to the Siegfried Line', *Military History* Magazine Jun 2003.

Baker, 'Bunny Baker's Arnhem Story', *The Eagle*, Vol 19, No.10, Dec 2001.

Boucher-Giles, A.F., 'Memories of the Rhine', *The Eagle*, Vol 3, No.1, 1955.

Buckingham, W., 'Paras', *Tempus* 2005.

Cartland, B., 'The First Towed Transport Glider', *The Eagle*, Vol 6, No 5, Apr 1990.

Cavenagh, S., 'Suez Interview', *Soldier* Magazine 28 Oct 1996.

Connaughton, R., 'Operation Barras', *Small Wars and Insurgencies*, Vol 12, No. 2, Summer 2001.

Deporter, H.J.G., 'Kolwezi', *Military Review*, Vol LIX, No.9, Sep 1979.

Eiben, Dr., 'Unternehmen Merkur. Erlebnis bericht eines Sanitätsoffiziers', *Deutsche Fallschirmjäger* No.5, 1991.

Essex-Lopresti, 'The Hazards of Parachuting', *British Journal of Surgery*, No.133, Vol XXXIV, Jul 1946.

Hall, D., 'Glider Training Accidents', *The Eagle*, Vol 7, no. 4. Apr 1993.

Hastings, M., 'Paratroops', *Picture Post*, Vol 22, No.12, 18 Mar 1944.

Hatte, J., 'Kolwezi: an Airborne Assault', *Infantry* Magazine, Vol 69, No.6, Nov/Dec 1979.

Könitz, 'Wir holen ihn heraus!' *Deutsche Fallschirmjäger* No.3, May/Jun 1982.

Kuz'menko, L., 'Psychological Aspects of Paratrooper Training', Moscow Kommunist Vooruzhennykh Sil, No. 1, Jan 1973.

Klee, M.P. de, 'A Jump With the French', *Household Brigade Magazine* 1956.

Leach, R., 'How it all Began', *The Eagle*, Vol 6, No 5, Apr 1990.

Lindsay, M., 'Early Days at Ringway', *Pegasus*, Vol 1, No.1, Apr 1946.

Lloyd, A., *The Gliders*, Arrow Books 1989.

Ludwig, F., 'Spektakulare Luftrettung', *Deutsche Fallschirmjäger*, No.2, Mar/Apr 1983.

Lunn, P., 'Parachuting and Skiing', *Pegasus*, Vol 1, No.3, Oct 1946.

Mockeridge, J., 'Sicily and our Allies', *Pegasus*, Vol XLII, No.2, Aug 1988.

Newspaper, *Stars and Stripes*, 26 and 27 Mar 1945.

Pegasus, 'We Want a Glider', *Pegasus* Vol 1, No.1, 1946.

Prout, J., 'Portrait of a Pilot', *The Eagle*, Vol 10, No.3, Dec 2002.

Roon, A. von, 'Fallschirmeinsatz bei Korinth 1941', *Deutsche Fallschirmjäger*, No.3, May/Jun 1984.

BIBLIOGRAPHY

Rudakov, Maj. Gen., '30 Years of Soviet Airborne Forces', *Wehrkunde* Dec 1960 and *Military Review* Jun 1961.

Simms, A., 'Special Report', Interviews Op Barras, *Soldier* Magazine, Oct 2000.

Strauch, A., 'Dieser Sieg war Keiner', *Deutsche Fallschirmjäger*, No.2, Mar/Apr 1981.

Student, K., 'Arnheim Letzter Deutsche Erfolg', *Deutsche Fallschirmjager*, No 9, 1964.

Suez, *Report on the Air Aspects of the Airborne Operation at Gamil Airfield Port Said*, Secret report 1956, AAM Archive.

Sweeny, H.J., 'Op Varsity', *The Eagle*, Vol 7, No.9, Dec 1994.

Trettner, Gen., 'Unternehmen Merkur', *Deutsche Fallschirmjäger* No 2, 1991.

Waddy, J., '151/156 Para Battalion', *Pegasus* Oct 1951.

– 'The Parachute Regiment – An Irregular View', *Pegasus*, Vol XLII, No.1, Apr 1987.

Wenzel, H., 'Auszug aus meinum Tagebuch von damals', *Deutsche Fallschirmjäger*, No.5, Sep/Oct 1983.

Wivell, H., 'In action at Suez, 1956', *Medal News* Jun/Jul 1998.

Various from *Der Adler* the German wartime Luftwaffe Magazine:

– 'Wir brauchen harte Männer' Heft 15, 1939.

– 'Max Schmelling in Reih und Glied' Heft 4, 1941.

– 'Nur ganze Kerle sind dabei' Heft 16, 1942.

PUBLISHED MEMOIRS AND PERSONAL ACCOUNTS

Appy, C.G., *Vietnam*, Ebury Press 2008.

Barley, E. and Fohlen, Y., *Para Memories*, Parapress Ltd 1996.

Breytenbach, J., *Eagle Strike*, Manie Grove Pub 2008.

Carlock, C., *Firebirds*, Bantam 1997.

Capa, R., *Images of War*, Grossman 1964.

Curtis, R., *Churchill's Volunteer*, Avon Books 1994.

Deane-Drummond, A., *Return Ticket*, Collins 1953.

Dobiasch, S., *Gebirgsjäger auf Kreta*, Wilhelm Limpert 1942.

Fall, B.B., *Street Without Joy*, Pall Mall Press 1963.

Fink, F., *Der Komet auf Kreta*, Gelka-Druck und Verlags GmbH. Undated.

Franks, A.H., *Red Devils*, W.H. Allen, 1944.

Frost, J., *Nearly There*, Leo Cooper 1991.

– *A Drop Too Many*, Sphere 1983.

Gabel, K., *The Making of a Paratrooper*, University of Kansas 1990.

Gavin, J.M., *On to Berlin*, Bantam 1979.

Gericke, W., *Soldaten Fallen vom Himmel*, Schützen Verlag Berlin 1940.

Gilbert, A.D., *Voices of the Foreign Legion*, Mainstream 2009.

Grauwin, P., *Doctor at Dien Bien Phu*, Hutchinson 1955.

Grenville, H., *Tim's Tale*, private pub 2008.

Kent, *First In! Parachute Pathfinder Company*, Batsford 1979.

Kippenberger, H., *Infantry Brigadier*, Oxford University Press 1949.

Leulliette, P., *The War in Algeria*, Bantam 1987.

Mills, H.L., *Low Level Hell*, Dell 1992.

Moore, H.G. and Galloway, L., *We Were Soldiers Once . . . And Young*, Corgi 2002.

Newnham, M., *Prelude to Glory*, Sampson Low 1948.

Pegasus, *Parachutist*, Jarrolds 1943.

Page, T. and Pimlott, J. Ed, *Nam. The Vietnam Experience 1965–75*, Orbis 1988.

Paul, M., *Parabat*, My Books 2008.

Pöppel, M., *Heaven and Hell*, Spellmount 1988.

Reinhardt, E., *Trilogy*, Private pub Fallingbostel 1984.

Sims, J., *Arnhem Spearhead*, IWM 1978.

Starinov, I.G., *Over the Abyss*, Ballantine, 1995.

Urquhart, R.E., *Arnhem*, Pan 1972

FILM AND TV

Age of Terror – Terror International, Thynne, J., BBC 2008.

The Bruneval Raid, SKC C.1462, Crown Copyright 1982.

9TH Company 20 Years Later, Pasichnik, V., Contender Films, 2007.

El Gamil 40 Years On, Video of Suez Presentation at Depot PARA Aldershot 1956.

Fort Eben Emael, Mauder, W.D. and Sessner, S., AV-Medien Produktion Germany, 1991.

Helicopter Warfare – Vietnam, Max, R., Windfall Films 2008.

Hitler's Children, Knopp, G. and Hartl, ZDF German TV 2000.

The Jewish War, Treharne-Jones, W., BBC 2004.

The Lost Evidence – Operation Market Garden, Downing, T., Flashback Television 2006.

BIBLIOGRAPHY

The Other Side of Suez, Gallager, D. and Cobban, W., BBC Scotland 2009.

Pathfinders – Into the Heart of Afghanistan, Ramsay, S., B Sky B Prod 2009.

SAS Jungle Rescue, Catling, M., Darlow Smithson Productions, 2009.

Suez – A Very British Crisis, Molloy, P., BBC 2006.

Touch and Go – The Battle for Crete 1941, Steel, T. and Issacs, J., NZ Broadcasting Corporation.

We Stand Alone Together – The Men of Easy Company, Cowen, M., HBO 2001.

The Undeclared War. Algeria 1954–62, Travernier, B. and Rotman, P., Le Studio Canal et GMT Productions.

Victoria Cross, Dir Pearson, R., BBC Midlands Pres on Robert Cain, V.C.

Vietnam Battle Stories – Code Broken Arrow, Towers, J., National Geographic 2008.

UNPUBLISHED ACCOUNTS AND MEMOIRS

AAM Archive denotes the Airborne Assault Museum Archive located at Duxford Cambridgeshire.

Abbott, G., RAF Fitter at Ringway, letter *Memories of RAF Ringway*, AAM Archive.

Alexander, E.G.M., *The Cassinga Raid*, MA Thesis University of South Africa Jul 2003.

Barrett, T., Airborne Sapper, *Tom – His War*, private manuscript AAM Archive.

Bassenge and Student, Secret report CSDIC(UK) on Lt Gen Student and Maj Gen Bassenge, dated 24 Sep 1945. AAM Archive.

Beckingham, A.L., Parachute Regiment Padre, *Normandy-Ardennes-Rhine Crossing* personal account, AAM Archive.

Browne, B., 9th Para, letter *Behind Enemy Lines in Normandy June-19 August 1944*, AAM Archive.

Browning, F., *Conversation 'Boy' Browning Notes 26 Jul 1944*, dated 29 Jul 1944, AAM Archive.

Carr, S., Lt 10 Para, personal account *17 Sep 44*, AAM Archive

Capon, S., 9th Para, *3rd September 1939*, private manuscript, AAM Archive.

Château-Jobert, Report on *Op Amlicar*, 2nd RPC 19 Nov 1956.

Chinnery, E., Cpl No 2 Commando and 11 SAS,

  – Letter to Canopy Club 12 Sep 1998, AAM Archive.

  – *Reminiscences of the Early Days*, private account 1984, AAM Archive.

Churchill, W., AAM Archive:
- RAF reluctance to support, Air Staff Note 23 Aug 1940.
- Minutes of Air Ministry meeting 7 Sep 1940.

Crete, H.Q. 14 Bde Report 14, IB/Ops/1 dated 4 Jun 41. AAM Archive.

Deanne, T., *The Men of the Maroon Beret 1940–45*, BA Thesis, Laurentian University 1988, AAM Archive.

Devlin Paddy:
- *The Battle for the Rhine-Crossings Germany 23/24 Mar 1945*, private manuscript, AAM Archive.
- *Reminiscences of a Rifleman in Normandy France 1944*, private pub presented to AAM Archive 5 Jun 92,

Downing, J., *First Para Padre 1942 – Gunners and Paras*, private pub, AAM Archive.

Dyckmeester, F. Th, experiences of a Dutch agent at Ringway, Apeldoorn letter, 30 Sep 1988, AAM Archive.

Edwards, D., *Normandy Diary*, manuscript AAM Archive.

'French Airborne Troops in Indo-China' School of Land/Air Warfare DS Report, 28 Sep 1950, AAM Archive.

Gale Papers:
- 6th Airborne Division Inquiry into Parachute Refusals, dated 15 Jan 1944.
- Letter parachute training refusals 17 Feb 1944.
- Letter summary of Whitley training aircraft problems 31 May 1943.

Hagenberg, H., letter and account relating to Rhine crossing, 12 Jul 1995, AAM Archive.

Hancock, W.J.G., Forward Air Controller 3 PARA Suez 1956, letter 31 Oct 1996, AAM Archive.

Heydte, F. von der, *Planned Airborne Operations*, interrogation report conducted 23 Dec 1944, secret CSDIC(UK)SIR 1438 dated 31 Jan 1945.

Hill, J., Brigadier 3rd Para Bde, Copy of talk covering the training and briefings delivered to 6th Airborne Division prior to Op Overlord, Camberley Staff College Battlefield Tour 8–14 Jun 1968, AAM Archive.

Hancock, E., *A Citizen's Journal*, private publication 1995, AAM Archive.

Hearn, P., Ed manuscript *There I was at Five Hundred Feet . . . Anecdotes from the first 50 years of No.1 PTS*, 1990, AAM archive.

Jevons, P.W., manuscript *The History of No 1 Parachute Training School Ringway 1940–45*, AAM Archive.

Lawly, A., CSM No 2 Commando, 11 SAS and Parachute Regiment, *An Account of the Experiences of an early Parachutist*, AAM Archive.

BIBLIOGRAPHY

Lindsay, M., Captain Parachute Regiment, letter describing early parachuting at Ringway, 24 Jul 1976, AAM Archive.

Loden, J., OC A Coy 3 PARA, *E-Mails from Helmand*, 2006, AAM Archive Lowe a, Cpl 3 PARA, personal account Suez 1956, AAM Archive.

Lycett, T., 7th Para, *Six Days Adrift in Normandy*, private account, AAM Archive.

Lynch, A.M., WO1, *The Real Deal*, Op Herrick 4, personal account, AAM Archive.

Marriott, J.H., Adjt 1 R Leics Regt, personal account of Crete, AAM Archive.

Maufe, M., Flt Lt RAFVR, Memories of Ringway 1940–42, private account 1988, AAM Archive.

Menzies, A.C.V., Padre 3rd Para, *Diary North Africa*, AAM Archive.

Morgan, G., Pte 2nd Para notes on Arnhem, AAM Archive.

Notes, Notes on Parachute Troops, No 2 Commando dated 12 Nov 1940, AAM Archive.

O'Conner, G., 13th Para, *To France Without a Passport*, private manuscript, AAM Archive.

Operation *Biting* official report, Appendix II *Personal Accounts*, dated 29 Sep 1943, AAM Archive.

Operation *Musketeer*, official 3 PARA Report 1956.

Pearson, A., CO 8 Para, talk given to Normandy Staff College tour in 1960, AAM Archive.

Richards, D., Flt Lt RAFVR, Rhine crossing account, AAM Archive.

Saunders, H. Saint-George, Research notes for *The Red Beret*, AAM Archive.

Scott, D.S., Sgt 2 PARA, letters from Cyprus 1955–6, AAM Archive.

Seibt, C., Maj Gen, Air Supply Problems of the Crete Campaign, Interrogation of Conrad Seibt A-4 Fliegerkorps XI, Air P/W Interrogation Unit USAF in Europe APO 696 dated 1 Sep 1945, AAM Archive.

Smith, I., *Formation of the Parachute Regiment from No 2 Commando and 11 SAS Regiment*, private pub 2007, AAM Archive.

'Suez Soldiers 1956', transcript of BBC interview Cpl Grout 3 PARA, AAM Archive.

Tottle, D., medic attached to 9th Para, personal freehand letter of experiences, AAM Archive.

Waddy, J., Colonel Parachute Regiment:
– Private correspondence with author 2 Aug and 12 Aug 2007.

INTERVIEWS

SWWEC denotes the Second World War Experience Centre at Leeds

Carson, K., Flt Sgt 512 Sqn RAF Flight Engineer, D-Day and Arnhem, author interview 22 Sep 2007.

Chatfield, H., Flt Lt 512 Sqn RAF, glider tug pilot D-Day and Arnhem, author interview 22 Sep 2007.

Deane-Drummond, A., Maj Gen, Tragino and Arnhem, E. Sands Paradata interview, Jul 2007.

Hibbert, A., Major Parachute Regiment, No 2 Commando to Arnhem, author interview 18 Dec 2007.

Killick, J., Capt 84 Para Field Security Squadron at Arnhem, SWWEC interview, P. Liddle, Oct 2001.

Kershaw, W., L/Cpl 4th Para, author interview 27 May 2009.

Kilkenny, J., Flt Lt PJI at Ringway, interview 5 Dec 1989, AAM Archive.

Mitchell, M., Stirling Pilot 190 Sqn RAF, SWEEC interview tape 1533.

Prout, J., Glider Pilot Regiment, SWWEC interview D. Talbot, 27 Jan 2004.

Read, H., Airborne Signals, SWWEC interview B. Atkinson.

Shackleton, A., Glider Pilot Regiment SWWEC interview P. Liddle, Jul 2002.

Turnbull, G., Sgt PTI Ringway, interview 4 Jan 1990, AAM Archive.

Swan, J., Pte, 18 Platoon C Company, 1st Bn Border Regiment, interview R. Milton, AAM Archive.

Waddy, J., Colonel Parachute Regiment, early days to Palestine 1948, author interview 9 Aug 2007.

Ward, H., the Yorkshire 'Birdman' and early paratrooper and instructor at Ringway, interview 1988, AAM Archive.

INDEX

INDEX

INDEX

INDEX

INDEX

INDEX

INDEX

INDEX